新航道
NEW CHANNEL

MW01716929

胡敏 主编
胡敏 马凤祥 编著

NEW SAT

新SAT词汇精选

世界知识出版社

图书在版编目（CIP）数据

新 SAT 词汇精选 / 胡敏主编；胡敏，马凤祥编著 .—北京：世界知识出版社，2016.4

ISBN 978-7-5012-5203-9

Ⅰ.①新… Ⅱ.①胡… ②马… Ⅲ.①英语－词汇－高等学校－入学考试－美国－自学参考资料 Ⅳ.① H313

中国版本图书馆 CIP 数据核字（2016）第 077421 号

策划编辑 马 蕾
责任编辑 龚玲琳 余 岚
责任出版 赵 玥 靳 婧
责任校对 马莉娜

书　　名 新 SAT 词汇精选
Xin SAT Cihui Jingxuan

主　　编 胡 敏
编　　著 胡 敏 马凤祥

出版发行 世界知识出版社
地址邮编 北京市东城区干面胡同 51 号（100010）
网　　址 www.ishizhi.cn
电　　话 010-65265923（发行） 010-85119023（邮购）
经　　销 新华书店
印　　刷 北京合众伟业印刷有限公司
开本印张 889×1194 毫米 1/16 19 印张
字　　数 350 千字
版次印次 2016 年 4 月第 1 版 2016 年 4 月第 1 次印刷
标准书号 ISBN 978-7-5012-5203-9
定　　价 59.00 元

前言 Preface

在万众期待的目光下，新 SAT 考试终于在 2016 年 3 月于北美揭开了神秘的面纱。面对 ACT 考试的竞争，新 SAT 放下身段，以更加务实的态度重新定义了美国大学的入学标准。在这个标准之下，新 SAT 综合考查了学生在人文、社会科学、自然科学各个方面的修养，全面融合了基础的数学常识，并把写作提高到一个新的高度。针对新 SAT 的这些特点，我们在编写这本《新 SAT 词汇精选》时，充分考虑了这些变化，并力求把新考试的要求与词汇学习的特点结合起来，为读者创造一种全新的学习体验。

一、词汇选择贴近官方范本

由于官方目前公布的考题范本数量较少，我们没有仅仅从官方题库中挑选词汇。从长远来看，出题者并非仅要求学生能够阅读选中的寥寥几篇文章，而是暗示要有能力阅读这一类的文章或书籍，所以我们把范本中的文章作了反向延伸——我们对考题来源的整本书籍进行了词汇的整理和统计，挑选出兼顾难度和实用性的词汇。因此，读者将会看到，本书涵盖了《论美国的民主》、《联邦党人文集》及《傲慢与偏见》等著作中的精选词汇，当然也涵盖了官方指南和 3 月考试中出现的重要词汇。根据 COCA（The Corpus of Contemporary American English）的词频显示，这些词汇明显脱离了老 SAT “高冷难看”的特点。为了与托福考试顺利衔接，我们也保留了一些同时出现在托福考试中的较难词汇。我们将这些词汇分为 20 个单元共 1600 个词条，连同词条下的扩展词汇（派生词或同根词）共约 3500 词左右。

二、涵盖政治与文化类词汇

新 SAT 官方指南明确提出要考查学生对重要政治文献的理解能力。由于涉及美国建国的相关文献产生时间较早，文献中使用的个别词汇虽然现已少用，但明显具有当时的时代烙印，仍然属于学生需要掌握的词汇。因此，在本书中还保留了如 thereupon、anon、hitherto 这样的词汇。这些词汇类似于中文的“之乎者也”，是理解历史文献不可缺少的。另外，在本书的附录中还增加了关于美国历史与政治类的常用词汇。

三、词义标注突出一词多义

本书中的少量词汇可能与托福词汇有所重叠，但作为新 SAT 词汇，本书更强调这些词汇的一词多义。例如词条 liberal，通常在托福中作为“自由的”之义，但在新 SAT 中，它可能作为“通识（教育）的”之义。所以恳请读者在阅读每个词条时，仔细浏览书中标注的各个义项。同时，在练习及阅读过程中，遇到释义尴尬的语境时，要主动查阅权威词典。（这里推荐权威的《韦氏大学词典》，它的词汇释义涵盖了较全面的美式英语中的意思，同时兼顾了一些略显旧式的用法，这些用法对于阅读历史文献帮助很大。）

四、原味例句贴近生活

如何让一本词汇书更有趣、更容易被翻阅？本书的例句大量引用了当代美国新闻报道、文学作品及科学报告中的内容。在这里，读者将遇到关于美国总统大选候选人特朗普、最高法院大法官遴选的新闻中的句子，也会遇到《冰与火之歌》（regent 词条）、《哈利·波特》（upright 词条）等流行小说中的表达，以及《科学美国人》（foliage 词条）、《世界是平的》（chancellor 词条）这样的杂志或商业类著作中的说法，甚至还有涉及《唐顿庄园》（saga 词条）、《疯狂动物城》（conceit 词条）及《超人大战蝙蝠侠》（weary 词条）等流行影视剧的内容。此外，还有关于引力波（infinitesimal 词条）、孔夫子与磕头（sage 词条）、彩礼（feudal 词条）、春节（deity 词条）等话题的例句。这些例句一方面很容易引发读者的共鸣，意会单词的使用；另一方面也表明，新 SAT 考试中的词汇是活的词汇，不是只有“孔乙己”式陈腐学究才懂的生僻怪词。

五、图文并茂学有所乐

为了加深对词汇的理解，本书配备了约 200 幅美国新闻类漫画（书中所收漫画版权归原图作者所有，如有问题，请致电 010-84921043）。这些漫画大多一目了然，既体现了词汇表达的本义，又反映了美国人民社会生活中的种种现象，显示出美国人民的智慧。希望这些漫画能够让读者在枯燥的词汇学习中获得一丝轻松和快乐。

六、美式发音听读并进

新 SAT 词汇当然不是仅仅躺在阅读长文中的，它也是鲜活的、有声音的表达单位。事实上，本书中的部分词汇也曾经出现在流行美剧中。更重要的是，将来学生们出国后在大学课堂讨论中也会遇到这些词汇（包括数学词汇），所以单词发音的重要性不言而喻。在记忆单词的过程中，发音不仅有助于记忆词义，也有助于区别形近词，甚至有助于拼写。因此，我们为本书配备了标准的美音 MP3 音频文件，包含所收所有词条及其例句。读者可到相应的读者服务群免费下载。

关于本书的用法：

释义部分：同一词性下的不同义项用数字明确标出；不同的词性下，单词若有不同的变形，也分别在相应部分明确给出。

【记】多数记忆法是依据单词的词根词缀，少部分使用了谐音法。读者可根据自己的需要灵活参考。

【例】所有例句全部与词性及义项一一对应，方便读者领会理解。

【辨】形近词辨析。

【扩】主词条的派生词或同根词、同源词，多数也是考试范本中的高频词汇。

本书在编写过程中参考了大量国内外相关的词典、书籍和网站，无法一一注明，在此谨表示感谢！虽然已经过编、译、审、校，多次修改，力求审慎，但恐仍有疏漏之处，恳请读者予以赐正。

编者

2016 年 4 月 5 日

目录 Contents

01 高频词汇

02 常频词汇

03 附录

01

GAO PIN CI HUI

LIST 1 —— LIST 9

高频词汇

List 1

render
[ˈrendər]

v. 1. 使成为…，使得；2. 给予，提供

记 与 rent（租金）有关 → 提供

例 1. The news rendered her speechless. 这个消息使她很无语。

2. They rendered assistance to the disaster victims. 他们向受灾者提供了援助。

扩 rendering *n.* 表演；翻译作品

同 make; provide

sovereign
[ˈsɑːvrən]

adj. 1.（国家或地区）有自治权的；2. 至高无上的；*n.* 君主，元首

记 sove (=super-) + reign (=rule) → 居上统治

例 1. The Russian Federation declared itself to be a sovereign republic. 俄罗斯联邦宣布自己为主权独立的共和国。

2. The government's sovereign duty is to protect the rights of its citizens. 政府的首要职责是保护公民的权利。

3. In March 1889, she became the first British sovereign to set foot on Spanish soil. 1889 年 3 月，她成为第一位踏上西班牙领土的英国君主。

扩 sovereignty *n.* 主权

prevail
[prɪˈveɪl]

v. 1. 盛行，流行；2. 战胜

记 pre- (=before) + vail (=valor 力量) → 有力量的

例 1. We were horrified at the conditions prevailing in local prisons. 我们对当地监狱的普遍现状大为惊骇。

2. Justice will prevail over tyranny. 正义终将战胜专制。

扩 prevalent *adj.* 流行的，普遍存在的

prevalence *n.* 流行，盛行

propensity
[prəˈpensəti]

n. 习性

记 pro + pens (=pend 悬挂) + ity → 向前倾 → 习性

例 He showed a propensity for violence. 他表现出暴力倾向。

tyranny
[ˈtɪrəni]

n. 1. 专制；2. 专制统治

例 1. I'm the sole victim of mother's tyranny. 我是唯一受母亲严加管制的人。

2. The king sought an absolute tyranny over the colonies. 国王试图对这些殖民地进行专制统治。

扩 tyrant *n.* 专制者，专制君主

tyrannical *adj.* 专制的

tyrannize *v.* 专横地对待

propriety
[prə'praɪəti]

n. 适当，合乎礼仪或习俗
记 可以看作 proper 的名词
例 She doubted the propriety of letting him buy her presents. 她犹豫让他给自己买礼物是否合适。
辨 property *n.* 财产；属性
扩 impropriety *n.* 不当行为

monarchy
['mɑːnərki]

n. 1. 君主国（对应共和国）；2. 君主制
记 mon(o) (=single) + arch (=rule) + y → 一个人的统治 → 君主制
例 1. There are several constitutional monarchies in Europe. 欧洲有不少君主制国家。
2. Is monarchy relevant in the modern world or should it be abolished? 君主制在现代社会是否过时或应当废除？
扩 monarch *n.* 君主
monarchical *adj.* 君主的

inclined
[ɪn'klaɪnd]

adj. 1.（只作表语）愿意的；2. 倾向于…
记 incline（斜坡）+ d → 愿意（与 decline 相反）
例 1. No one seemed inclined to help. 没有人愿意伸出援手。
2. He was inclined to agree with them. 他倾向于同意他们的观点。
扩 disinclined *adj.* 不情愿的
disinclination *n.* 不乐意

induce
[ɪn'duːs]

v. 1. 劝说，引诱；2. 引起，导致
记 in + duce (=lead) → 使进入
例 1. More than 4,000 teachers were induced to take early retirement. 有4000多名教师被说服提前退休。
2. Doctors said surgery could induce a heart attack. 医生们说手术有可能引起心脏病发作。
扩 inducement *n.* 引诱，刺激

resolve
[rɪ'zɑːlv, -'zɔːlv]

v. 1. 解决；2. 做出抉择；3. 变成，分解成；*n.* 决心
例 1. The couple resolved their differences and made an effort to get along. 夫妻俩解决了他们的分歧，努力和平相处。
2. He resolved not to tell her the truth. 他决定向她隐瞒真相。
3. The discussion eventually resolved itself into two main issues. 这一争议最终变成两个主要的问题。
4. His comments were intended to weaken her resolve, but they only served to strengthen it. 他的意见本欲动摇她的决心，但只能让她更加坚定而已。

temper
['tempər]

n. 1. 脾气；2. 民族性格，氛围；*v.* 节制，抑制
记 与 temperature（温度）同源 → 使金属加热锻打 →（使不太硬）节制；暴脾气

例 1. I found it hard to keep my temper with so many things going wrong. 面对诸多不如意，我觉得自己快要发脾气了。
2. Her novels capture the temper of the times. 她的小说充分体现了那个时代的氛围。
3. My enthusiasm for the venture was somewhat tempered by my knowledge of the work that would be involved. 相关知识的贫乏压抑了我对这项事业的热情。

formidable
['fɔːrmɪdəbl, fər'mɪdəbl]

adj. 1. 令人望而生畏的；2. 数量惊人的
例 1. The two players together make a formidable combination. 两名球员的组合令人生畏。
2. He has mastered a formidable amount of material. 他掌握了海量的材料。

resolution
[ˌrezə'luːʃn]

n. 1. 解决方案，决议案；2. 决心；3. 决定
记 源于 resolve（解决；决心）→解决方案；决定
例 1. We found a resolution to the dispute. 我们找到了解决这个争议的方案。
2. The reforms owe a great deal to the resolution of one man. 这些改革离不开一个人的决心。
3. She made a resolution to visit her relatives more often. 她决定多去看看她的亲戚们。

扩 resolute *adj.* 坚决的
irresolution *n.* 犹豫不决

supposition
[ˌsʌpə'zɪʃn]

n. 设想，假定
记 suppose（猜测）的名词
例 The report has been rejected by the authorities, who said much of it was based on supposition or inaccuracy. 当局驳回了该报告，称其许多内容纯属臆测或存在偏差错误。

requisite
['rekwɪzɪt]

adj. 必要的，必备的；*n.* 必需品，必要条件
记 与 required 同源
例 1. The requisite number of countries have now ratified the convention. 批准协定的国家数量目前合乎法定要求。
2. A college degree has become a requisite for entry into most professions. 多数职业现在都要求有大学学位。

subordinate
[sə'bɔːrdɪnət]

adj. 1. 次要的；2. 下级的；*v.* 使从属，让位于
例 1. In this business everything is subordinate to making a profit. 在这个行业里，一切都应让位于盈利。
2. In many societies women are subordinate to men. 在很多社会中，女性附属于男性。
3. Her personal life has been subordinated to her career. 她的私人生活已经让位于职业生涯。

扩 insubordination *n.* 不顺从，反抗

sanction
['sæŋkʃn]

v. 1. 惩罚；2. 正式批准或同意；3. 国际制裁

记 与 Saint 同根 → 宗教法令 → 批准；惩罚

例 1. Only the medical council can apply a sanction against a doctor. 只有医疗委员会才有权惩处医生。

2. The country acted without the sanction of the other nations. 该国未经他国批准就擅自行事。

3. Sanctions against the country have been lifted. 针对该国的制裁已经取消。

perpetual
[pər'petʃuəl]

adj. 1. 持久的，终生的；2. 频繁出现的

例 1. They lived in perpetual fear of being discovered. 他们一直害怕被人发现。

2. Lack of government funding has been a perpetual problem for the organization. 该组织经常面临缺乏政府资助的困境。

recourse
['riːkɔːrs]

n. 解决途径，手段

记 可能与 resource（资源）同源

例 It enabled its members to settle their differences without recourse to war. 这样，其成员就可以不必诉诸战争来解决分歧。

provincial
[prə'vɪnʃl]

adj. 1. 外省的，地方的；2.（贬）土里土气的，保守的

记 名词 province 与法国普罗旺斯（Provence）同源，当地原为罗马帝国行省

例 1. The majority of young professionals in the capital have moved there from provincial towns. 首都多数从业者都来自外省。

2. In spite of his education and travels, he has remained very provincial. 尽管他受过良好的教育，见多识广，但他仍然很保守。

singular
['sɪŋgjələr]

adj. 1. 明显的，超凡的；2. 奇怪的，异常的

例 1. Her father noticed her singular talent for music. 父亲注意到了女儿身上出色的音乐天赋。

2. He had a singular appearance. 他的样子很奇怪。

扩 singularity *n.* 古怪

lofty
['lɔːfti, 'lɑː-]

adj. 1. 高尚的，崇高的；2. 高处的

记 loft 原指阁楼，现常指带跃层的小公寓

例 1. It was a bank that started out with grand ideas and lofty ideals. 这是一家创办伊始抱有雄心壮志的银行。

2. The town hall's lofty tower dates from the fourteenth century. 市政厅的高塔建于 14 世纪。

inherent
[ɪn'hɪrənt]

adj. 内在的，本质的
例 She believes that goodness is inherent in all people. 她相信所有人都本性善良。
扩 inherently *adv.* 内在地

intellect
['ɪntəlekt]

n. 1. 智慧，领悟力；2. 英才
例 1. We were required to read a book every week in order to develop our intellects. 我们当时按要求每周读一本书以培养智力。
2. She was one of the most formidable intellects of her time. 她曾是那个时代最令人敬畏的才女。
扩 intellectual *adj.* 智力的；*n.* 知识分子

servitude
['sɜːrvətuːd]

n. 奴役
例 In the past, the majority of women were consigned to a lifetime of servitude and poverty. 过去多数妇女一辈子生活贫困，遭受奴役。

restraint
[rɪ'streɪnt]

n. 1. 限制；2. 自我克制
例 1. The government has imposed restraints on imports. 政府对进口实施了限制。
2. The government has acted with restraint in dealing with this crisis. 政府在应对这项危机时表现十分克制。

uniformity
[ˌjuːnɪ'fɔːməti]

n. 统一，规律性
例 There is little uniformity among the states in voting procedures. 各州的选举程序大相径庭。
扩 uniform *adj.* 统一的；*n.* 制服

mire
['maɪər]

n. 泥潭；*v.* 陷入泥潭
例 1. My name had been dragged through the mire. 我的名声受到了玷污。
2. Now Brazil is mired in its worst economic slump since the 1930s. 目前巴西已经陷入了自19世纪30年代以来最严重的经济危机之中。

politic
['pɑːlətɪk]

adj. 明智的，策略的
例 It would not be politic for you to pursue the matter further. 你这样继续追究这件事是不明智的。
扩 the body politic 全体国民，人民
politics *n.* 手腕，权术
impolitic *adj.* 不明智的

levy
['levi]

v. 征（税、人等）；*n.* 征收额
例 1. A new tax was levied on consumers of luxury goods. 政府向消费者新征奢侈品税。
2. The government imposed a levy on gasoline. 政府对汽油征税。

prompt
[prɑːmpt]

v. 1. 敦促，促使；2. 导致，造成；*adj.* 立即的，无拖延的；*n.* 提示词

例 1. Curiosity prompted her to ask a few questions. 她在好奇心的驱使之下问了几个问题。
2. The evidence prompted a criminal investigation. 这项证据引起了一项刑事调查。
3. The victims need prompt medical assistance. 受害人需要马上进行急救。
4. The actor was given a prompt by someone offstage. 有人在台下给演员提示台词。

扩 promptitude *n.* 迅速，无拖延
promptly *adv.* 迅速地；及时地

indifferent
[ɪn'dɪfrənt]

adj. 1. 漠不关心的，无兴趣的；2. 平庸的，不好不坏的

例 1. She was amazed that people could be so indifferent about the trial. 大家对这次审判居然如此漠不关心，这让她很意外。
2. She was tired and gave a rather indifferent performance. 她太累了，表演得乏善可陈。

扩 indifferently *adv.* 漠不关心地，冷淡地

solitude
['sɑːlətuːd]

n. 1.（自愿的）独居，独处；2. 荒芜之处

记 sol (=sole) + itude（名词后缀）→ 一个人的状态 → 独处

例 1. He enjoyed his moments of solitude before the pressures of the day began. 他喜欢在白天的压力到来之前享受独处的时光。
2. This double emigration crosses the Atlantic Ocean, and it advances over the solitudes of the New World. 双向迁移越过大西洋，推进到新世界的荒芜之处。

ratify
['rætɪfaɪ]

v. 签署或批准

记 形近词 rate（评级，评定）→ ratify（批准）

例 A number of countries have refused to ratify the treaty. 好几个国家拒绝批准这一条约。

扩 ratification *n.* 批准，认可

statute
['stætʃuːt]

n. 成文法，正式法令

记 源于 sta- (=stand)“建立”之意

例 The state legislature passed the statute by an overwhelming margin. 州立法机构以多数优势通过了这项法令。

usurp
[juː'zɜːrp]

v. 篡夺，越权侵占

例 Some people have accused city council members of trying to usurp the mayor's power. 有人指控市议会成员妄图篡夺市长的权力。

扩 usurpation *n.* 篡夺
usurper *n.* 篡夺者

resent
[rɪ'zent]

v. 怨恨，愤慨

例 The children resented the new woman in their father's life. 孩子们怨恨父亲生活中新出现的这个女人。

扩 resentment *n.* 怨恨，愤慨
resentful *adj.* 怨恨的

sect
[sekt]

n. （极端的）小教派，小党派

例 When he was fifteen, he ran away from home and joined a religious sect. 他十五岁时离家出走，加入了一个宗教小派别。

扩 sectarian *adj.* 教派的

pretext
['priːtekst]

n. 托辞，借口

例 The leaders used a minor clash at the border as a pretext for war. 决策者们借口边境上的小冲突而挑起了战争。

hostility
[hɑː'stɪləti]

n. 1. 敌意；2. 敌对行为，打斗

例 1. The townspeople showed open hostility to outsiders. 小镇上的人毫不掩饰对外地人的敌意。
2. Both sides are calling for a cessation of hostilities. 双方都呼吁中止敌对行动。

petty
['peti]

adj. 1.（定语）琐碎的，不重要的；2. 次要的，轻度的；3. 小题大做的，心胸狭窄的

例 1. Let's not waste time arguing over petty details. 我们别浪费时间纠结于琐碎的小事了。
2. Wilson was not a man who dealt with petty officials. 威尔逊不是个与小官小吏打交道的人。
3. It was a bit petty to make me apologize to everyone. 让我跟大家道歉真有点小心眼。

transient
['trænʃnt]

adj. 1. 短暂的，稍纵即逝的；2. 短期逗留的

记 trans- (=across) + ient → 迅速转变的

例 1. In most cases, pain is transient. 大多数情况下，疼痛是短暂的。
2. Most of the farm workers are transient workers. 多数农场工人都是短工。

precedent
['presɪdənt]

n. 1. 前例，先例；2. 模范，榜样

例 1. There is no precedent for a disaster of this scale. 之前从未发生过如此大规模的灾难。
2. The English and the Americans have retained the law of precedents. 英美人都保留了前辈人的法律。

扩 precedence *n.* 优先（权）
unprecedented *adj.* 史无前例的

impair
[ɪm'per]

v. 削弱，损害
例 His memory was so impaired by age that he often forgot where he was. 他的记忆力因年龄而损害，以至于常常忘了自己在哪里。
扩 impaired *adj.* 衰弱的，减退的

vigor
['vɪgər]

n. 精力，毅力
例 She defended her beliefs with great vigor. 她坚决维护自己的信仰。
扩 vigorous *adj.* 精力充沛的，强劲的

prerogative
[prɪ'rɑːgətɪv]

n. 特权
记 pre + rog (=ask) + ative → 提前要求
例 Education was once only the prerogative of the wealthy. 教育曾是有钱人才有的特权。

reproach
[rɪ'proʊtʃ]

n. 1. 责备，批评；2. 羞辱，不雅；*v.* 批评，责备
例 1. His actions were beyond reproach. 他的行为无可指责。
2. His conduct has brought shame and reproach to his family. 他的行为给家人带来了羞耻和难堪。
3. She reproached her daughter for her selfishness. 她批评女儿的自私行为。
辨 reapproach *v.* 再接触
扩 irreproachable *adj.* 无可指责的

insurrection
[ˌɪnsə'rekʃn]

n. 叛乱，造反
例 He led an armed insurrection against the elected government. 他领兵反抗民选政府。

kindle
['kɪndl]

v. 1. 激起，唤起；2. 点燃，使燃烧；3. 照亮
记 亚马逊公司出品的电子书设备 Kindle，意为“知识唤起兴趣”
例 1. A trip to the museum when she was a child kindled her interest in art. 她童年时去过一次博物馆，那点燃了她对艺术的兴趣。
2. We watched as the fire slowly kindled. 我们看着火焰慢慢点燃。
3. I thought Sylvie was going to smile, her dim eyes almost kindled. 我当时认为西尔维娅就要笑了，她的眼睛里闪着亮光。

partiality
[ˌpɑːrʃi'æləti]

n. 1. 偏见；2. 偏爱
例 1. Judges must not show partiality during the competition. 裁判在竞赛过程中不能有偏见。
2. I don't understand his partiality to modern art. 我不明白他怎么会喜欢现代艺术。
扩 impartiality *n.* 公正无私

impartial *adj.* 不偏不倚的，公正的

salutary ['sæljəteri]

adj. 1. 苦口良药般的，有益的；2. 有益健康的

记 salute（致敬，问候健康）+ ary → 有益健康的

例 1. The accident was a salutary reminder of the dangers of climbing. 这一事故有益的一面是提醒了我们攀登活动是有许多危险的。

2. This salutary weather would have a positive effect upon the children. 这种有益健康的天气将会对孩子们有好处。

扩 salute *v.* 敬礼，致敬

obviate ['ɑːbvieɪt]

v. 使多余，使不必要

例 The new medical treatment obviates the need for surgery. 这种新的治疗方式使得手术变得多余了。

subsistence [səb'sɪstəns]

n. 1. 维持生计，存活；2. 维持，存在

例 1. Hundreds of millions of people are moving up from subsistence to affluence before our eyes. 我们可以看到，数以亿计的人正从温饱走向富足。

2. Their very subsistence depends on his remaining in power. 他们的存在依赖于他的掌权。

warrant ['wɔːrənt, 'wɑː-]

v. 1. 使正当合理；2. 授权，批准；3. 保证，使确信；*n.* 1. 逮捕令，搜查令；2. 缘由，根据

例 1. Further investigation is clearly warranted. 很明显需要进一步调查。

2. The law warrants this procedure. 法律授权这样做。

3. The seller warrants that the car has no defects. 推销员保证这辆车没有丝毫缺陷。

4. The police had a warrant for his arrest. 警方持有对他的搜捕令。

5. There was no warrant for such behavior. 这种行为毫无根据。

扩 unwarrantable *adj.* 毫无根据的，无理由的

incompatible [ˌɪnkəm'pætəbl]

adj. 1. 冲突的，不相称的；2. 不兼容的，不支持的

例 1. The hours of the job are incompatible with family life. 工作时间安排与家庭生活相冲突。

2. New computer software is often incompatible with older computers. 新的电脑软件常会与旧式电脑不兼容。

foster ['fɔːstər, 'fɑː-]

v. 1. 促进，鼓励；2. 养育，收养

记 与 food 有关

例 1. The organization's aim is to foster better relations within the community. 该组织的使命就是培育良好的社区关系。

2. They have fostered over 60 children during the past ten years. 他们在过去十年间收养了 60 多个孩子。

List 1

precarious
[prɪ'kerəriəs]

adj. 1. 不稳定的，有危险的；2. 依情况而定的

记 源于 prayer（祈祷）→ 祈求他人的 → 取决于其他因素的，不稳定的

例 1. He was unable to get down from his precarious position on the rocks. 他无法从岩石危险的位置上下来。

2. His kingdom was still precarious; the Danes far from subdued. 他的王国仍未稳固；因丹麦人尚未臣服。

扩 precariously *adv.* 靠不住地，不稳定地

integrity
[ɪn'tegrəti]

n. 1. 廉正，诚实；2. 完整

记 integr (=integer) + ity → 使完整

例 1. He has a reputation for integrity in his business dealings. 他在商业经营中一直诚实守信。

2. They are trying to preserve the cultural integrity of the community. 他们努力要保护当地的文化完整性。

pecuniary
[pɪ'kjuːniəri]

adj. 金钱（方面）的

记 与 peculiar（个人的，特定的）同根 → 私人的（财产）→ 与钱有关的

例 She denies obtaining a pecuniary advantage by deception. 她否认通过欺骗手段获得经济利益。

pernicious
[pər'nɪʃəs]

adj. 恶性的，有害的

例 She thinks television has a pernicious influence on our children. 她觉得电视对我们孩子影响很坏。

judicious
[dʒu'dɪʃəs]

adj. 明智的，审慎的

记 judi (=judge 判断) + cious →（判断）明智的

例 The President authorizes the judicious use of military force to protect our citizens. 总统授权可以审慎地动用军队保护我们的公民。

扩 judicial *adj.* 司法的，法官的，审判的

judiciary *n.* 司法部，司法系统

judiciously *adv.* 明智地

magnitude
['mæɡnɪtuːd]

n. 1. 大量，大规模；2.（重要）程度，级别；3.（恒星的）亮度，（地震的）烈度

例 1. We hadn't grasped the magnitude of the task we were facing. 我们并未意识到这项任务的艰巨性。

2. The country's small army would be crushed in a war of such magnitude. 该国的微弱军力将在这种大规模的战争中被摧毁。

3. The San Francisco earthquake of 1906 had a magnitude of 8.3. 1906 年旧金山地震的震级为 8.3 级。

扩 magnify *v.* 放大，扩大，夸张

reconcile
['rekənsaɪl]

v. 1. 使屈服，使接纳；2. 使前后一致；3. 使调和，缓解

例 1. He eventually became reconciled to his position in life. 他最终接受了自己在生活中的位置。

2. I'm afraid her story cannot be reconciled with the proven facts. 恐怕她的说法与证据不符。
3. His attempt to reconcile his friends was unsuccessful. 他试图调和朋友们的矛盾，但失败了。

impel [ɪm'pel]

v. (impelled, impelled)（来自道德、感情等的）驱使

记 im (=on) + pel (=push) → 向前推 → 驱使

例 Even though I was angry, something impelled me to smile. 虽然我很生气，但某种东西仍迫使我微笑。

privation [praɪ'veɪʃn]

n. 贫困，困苦

记 源于 deprive（剥夺），而与 private（个人的）无关

例 The country has suffered through long periods of economic privation. 该国遭受了长期的经济贫困。

passive ['pæsɪv]

adj. 1. 单向的，易受影响的；2. 被动接受的，不参与的

例 1. Watching television is a relatively passive activity. 看电视是个相对易受影响的过程。
2. His passive acceptance of the decision surprised us. 他被迫接受决定让我们都很吃惊。

扩 passivity *n.* 被动，消极

tumult ['tuːmʌlt]

n. 1. 喧闹，叫嚷；2. 内心的剧烈起伏；3. 骚乱，动荡

例 1. We had to shout to be heard over the tumult. 在一阵喧闹中，我们必须得喊叫才能让人听到。
2. She had to bury the tumult of her feelings under the restraint of society. 在社会的束缚之下，她不得不压抑心中的起伏。
3. Most of the tumults that arose in the comitia at Rome were due to ignorance or neglect of this rule. 古罗马议事会的多数骚乱都是源于对这种规则的无知或忽视。

扩 tumultuous *adj.* 骚乱的，狂暴的

tenure ['tenjər]

n. 1. 使用权；2. 终身职位，终身教（授）职；3. 任职期间

记 ten- (=hold); 与 tenets（佃户）同源 → 使用权 → 终身职位

例 1. The defendant did not have tenure on the land. 被告无权使用土地。
2. After seven years I was finally granted tenure. 七年之后我终于获得了终身教职。
3. He was in the middle of his tenure as Oxford Professor of Poetry and at the height of his fame. 当时，他在牛津担任诗歌教授的聘期刚到一半，声誉正隆。

List 1

solicit
[sə'lɪsɪt]

v. 请求

例 Special interest groups are soliciting Congress for funds. 特殊利益集团正向国会请求资助。

扩 solicitude *n.* 牵挂，关怀
solicitous *adj.* 关怀的，操心的
unsolicited *adj.* 自发的，未经要求的

renounce
[rɪ'naʊns]

v. 1. 公开放弃，公开拒绝；2. 拒不遵守，拒不承认

记 re (=against) + nounce (=announce) → 宣布放弃

例 1. We will not deal with them until they renounce terrorism. 除非他们公开放弃恐怖主义，否则我们不会与他们打交道。
2. Many of his former supporters have renounced him. 他之前的很多支持者都抛弃了他。

扩 renunciation *n.* 声明摒弃；禁欲

prodigious
[prə'dɪdʒəs]

adj. 1. 不可思议的，天才的；2. 巨大的，庞大的

例 1. She was a prodigious musician. 她曾是个天才的音乐家。
2. DVDs can store prodigious amounts of information. DVD 可以储存海量的信息。

扩 prodigy *n.* 天才，神童
prodigal *adj.* 浪费的，挥霍的

theoretical
[ˌθiːə'retɪkl]

adj. 1. 理论方面的，抽象的；2. 假设的

例 1. The first year provides students with a sound theoretical basis for later study. 第一年为学生以后的学习奠定坚实的理论基础。
2. It's a theoretical possibility. 这在理论上是可能的。

扩 theoretically *adv.* 就理论而言，假设地

surmount
[sər'maʊnt]

v. 1. 战胜，克服；2. 处于…顶端

例 1. She was well aware of the difficulties that had to be surmounted. 她很清楚必须克服哪些困难。
2. The island is surmounted by a huge black castle. 岛的最高处耸立着一座巨大的黑色城堡。

palpable
['pælpəbl]

adj. 易于察觉的，明显的

记 palp (=pat 拍打) + able → 摸得到的，明显的

例 There was a palpable excitement in the air as the town prepared for the festival. 节日前的小镇明显洋溢着欢乐的气氛。

扩 impalpable *adj.* 感觉不到的，难以理解的

repel
[rɪ'pel]

v. (repelled, repelled) 1. 驱逐，赶走；2. 排斥，拒绝

例 1. Using water cannons and tear gas, police repelled protesters outside the embassy. 警方用水枪和催泪瓦斯驱逐使馆外的抗议者。
2. Far from desiring to conform his habits to ours, the Native

American loves his savage life and repels every advance to civilization. 印第安人一点也不想屈从自己的习俗来顺从我们，他热爱自己野蛮的生活方式，排斥任何文明的东西。
扩 repellent *adj.* 使人反感的，令人厌恶的

impediment
[ɪmˈpedɪmənt]

n. 1. 阻碍，障碍；2. 口吃，结巴
记 im (=in) + ped (=foot) + i + ment → 束缚住脚 → 阻碍
例 1. The level of inflation is a serious impediment to economic recovery. 通货膨胀是影响经济复苏的严重障碍。
2. John's slight speech impediment made it difficult for his mother to understand him. 约翰有轻微的言语障碍，母亲很难理解他的话。

prudent
[ˈpruːdnt]

adj. 谨慎的，精明的
记 与 provident（未雨绸缪的）同源同义 ← pro (=before) + vid(e) (=vis-, see) + ent (*adj.*)
例 It might be more prudent to get a second opinion before going ahead. 行动之前再征求一下意见也许更为慎重。
扩 prudence *n.* 审慎
imprudent *adj.* 不明智的，不谨慎的

indignation
[ˌɪndɪgˈneɪʃn]

n. 义愤，愤怒
记 in (=not) + dign (=respect) + ation (*n.*) → 认为…与自己不相称 → 愤怒
例 Some benefits apply only to men, much to the indignation of working women. 让职业女性大为不平的是，有些福利只提供给男性。
扩 indignant *adj.* 愤慨的

worldly
[ˈwɜːrldli]

adj. 1. 世俗的，入世的；2. 老成持重的，世故的
记 world (*n.*) + ly = worldly (*adj.*)（通常名词与 -ly 结合构成形容词）
例 1. They were ambitious for worldly power and possessions. 他们渴望世俗权力和财富。
2. At 15, he was more worldly than his older cousins who lived in the country. 他 15 岁时就比他那些居住在乡村的表兄们更懂得人情世故了。
扩 unworldly *adj.* 天真的；精神的，脱俗的

predecessor
[ˈpredəsesər]

n. 1. 前任；2. 前代（产品、工具等）
记 pre (=before) + decess (=decease, die) + or → 之前离开者 → 前任
例 1. The company's new president has changed many of the policies that were introduced by his predecessor. 公司的新总裁改变了许多前任者制定的政策。
2. Today's computers are much faster than their predecessors were. 今天的电脑比前代产品快许多。

List 2

relinquish
[rɪˈlɪŋkwɪʃ]

v. 1. 被迫放弃；2. 松开

记 re (=back) + linqu (=leave) + ish → 留下，不带走 → 放弃

例 1. They had relinquished all hope that she was alive. 他们对她是否还活着失去了希望。

2. I relinquished her hand and stood up. 我松开她的手，站了起来。

manifest
[ˈmænɪfest]

v. 清楚表明；*adj.* 易于理解的，能认出的；*n.* 载货清单，乘客名单

例 1. Their religious beliefs are manifested in every aspect of their lives. 他们生活的方方面面都体现着他们的信仰。

2. The truth was manifest to everyone but me. 除了我，别人都觉得真相显而易见。

3. Passenger boats are frequently overloaded beyond their manifests in Indonesia. 印尼的客船通常会超过准载人数。

扩 manifesto *n.* 宣言

manifestation *n.* 显示，表明

servile
[ˈsɜːrvl, -vaɪl]

adj. 1. 奴性的，恭顺的；2. 下贱的，卑微的

记 serv (=slave) + ile →（像奴隶一样）恭顺的

例 1. As a waiter you want to be pleasant to people without appearing totally servile. 当侍应生既要令人愉悦，又要不卑不亢。

2. Up until that point, African-American actresses had typically been cast in servile roles, playing housekeepers or maids. 直到在那之前，美国非裔女演员通常扮演下等角色，比如管家或女佣之类的。

incessant
[ɪnˈsesnt]

adj. 不间断的

记 in (=not) + cess (=cease) + ant → 不间断的

例 The neighbors were bothered by the dog's incessant barking. 狗一直叫，让邻居们很苦恼。

scanty
[ˈskænti]

adj. 1. 欠缺的，不足的；2.（衣着）暴露的

例 1. We have only received scanty information so far. 我们目前收到的消息尚不充分。

2. The cheerleaders wore scanty outfits. 啦啦队长们穿得非常暴露。

posterity
[pɑːˈsterəti]

n. 1. 某个祖先的后裔；2. 后代

记 post (=after) + erity → 后来的 → 后代，后裔

例 1. Their posterity would in a few generations become Dutch, and

so lose their interest in the English nation. 他们（清教徒）的后裔将在几代之后变成荷兰人，从而变得对英格兰漠不关心。
2. Posterity will remember her as a woman of courage and integrity. 后来人将铭记她的勇气和正直。

unanimous
[ju'nænɪməs]

adj. 上下一心的，意见一致的
记 un(i) (=one) + animous (=mind) → 想法一致的
例 Local people are unanimous in their opposition to the proposed new road. 当地居民一致反对拟建的新公路。
扩 unanimity *n.* 意见一致，认同
unaminously *adv.* 一致地

refrain
[rɪ'freɪn]

v.（自我）节制，克制
记 re (=back) + frain (=bridle) → 把（马笼头）拉回来 → 克制
例 They appealed to the protesters to refrain from violence. 他们呼吁示威者避免使用暴力。

redress
[rɪ'dres]

v. 纠正，伸张（正义）；*n.* 1. 纠正方式；2. 赔偿
记 re (=again) + dress (=direct) → 恢复笔直的状态 → 纠正
例 1. It is time to redress the injustices of the past. 是时候纠正历史上的冤屈了。
2. When an individual or a party is wronged in the United States, to whom can he apply for redress? 在美国，当有人或有党派受到不公时，他能向谁寻求解决呢？
3. Their lawyer has said that they intend to seek redress through the courts. 律师称他们有意通过法庭寻求赔偿。

ingenious
[ɪn'dʒiːniəs]

adj. 1.（物）巧妙的，独特的；2.（人）心灵手巧的；机敏的
记 in + gen (=produce) + inous →（产生于内在的）能力 → 精巧的，机敏的
例 1. They have worked out an ingenious way of saving energy. 他们找到了一种节约能源的巧妙方法。
2. She's very ingenious when it comes to finding excuses. 她很善于找借口。
扩 ingeniously *adv.* 巧妙地

tender
['tendər]

adj. 1. 温柔的；2. 敏感的；3. 年幼的，嫩的；4. 疼痛的
例 1. What he needs now is a lot of tender loving care. 他现在需要的是充分的关心和爱护。
2. He has a tender ego. 他的自尊心十分敏感。
3. She shouldn't be having to deal with problems like this at such a tender age. 她小小年纪涉世未深，实在无须处理这样的问题。
4. Ward vowed he would play a week from Sunday despite a tender ankle. 沃德发誓他周日起要打球一周，尽管他的脚踝还在疼。
扩 tenderness *n.* 友好，和善
tenderly *adv.* 温和地；体贴地

mutable
['mju:təbl]

adj. 可变的，会变的

记 mut(e) (=change) + able → 可变的

例 Our condition in this world is mutable and uncertain, alterable by a thousand accidents. 我们在这个世界上的状况是变动不定的，有数以千计的事情可以产生变化。

扩 immutable *adj.* 永恒不变的
mutability *n.* 变化

formality
[fɔːr'mæləti]

n. 1. 正式手续；2. 例行公事；3. 遵守礼节

'...Look...I...mean...well, it's not really necessary... well, not every time...especially the toilet'

例 1. Let's skip the formalities and get down to business. 让我们省去繁文缛节，开始讨论实质问题吧。
2. He already knows he has the job so the interview is a mere formality. 他已知道得到了这个工作，所以面试仅仅是走走过场。
3. She greeted him with stiff formality. 她拘谨地按礼节向他致意。

扩 informality *n.* 随意，不正式

impunity
[ɪm'pjuːnəti]

n. 免于惩罚（或伤害 / 损失）

记 im (=not) + pun (=penal) + ity → 不受惩罚

例 They broke the law with complete impunity. 他们明目张胆地践踏法律。

mercenary
['mɜːrsəneri]

n. 雇佣兵；*adj.* 只为金钱的，只图利益的

记 merce (=money) + nary → 与钱有关的

例 1. If somebody wants soldiers to go in and fight they should hire mercenaries, not take UN soldiers. 如果有人想让士兵去打仗，他们应该找雇佣兵，而不是动用联合国的部队。
2. Fans of the Davis Cup complain that today's players are mercenaries who put self-interest over patriotism. 戴维斯杯的球迷们发牢骚说，现在的球员都是冲着钱去的，他们自私而不爱国。

partisan
['pɑːrtəzn]

n.（尤指盲目的）追随者，党徒，信徒

例 Much of the gridlock in Washington stems from checks and balances that have come to be used as partisan weapons. 各党派利用制约与平衡作武器，造成了华盛顿（美国国会）的大多数政治僵局。

superficial
[ˌsuːpər'fɪʃl]

adj. 1. 表皮的；2. 浅薄的，肤浅的，蜻蜓点水般的

例 1. The storm only caused superficial damage to the building. 风暴对建筑物的损害仅限于外部。
2. I have only a superficial knowledge of the subject. 我对这门学科略知一二。

perpetuate
[pər'petʃueɪt]

v. 使持久，使永久

记 per (=through) + pet (=seek) + uate → 持续追求 → 使持久

例 Fears about an epidemic are being perpetuated by the media. 媒体上持续弥漫着对流行病的恐惧。

扩 perpetual *adj.* 永久的

peruse
[pə'ruːz]

v. （悠闲或详细地）阅读
记 per (=completely) + use → 完全阅读 → 慢慢翻阅
例 A copy of the report is available for you to peruse at your leisure. 现有一份报告，供你闲暇时细读。
扩 perusal *n.* 仔细阅读

partition
[pɑːr'tɪʃn]

n. 1. 一部分；2. 分割，瓜分；3. 隔离墙；*v.* 1. 分割；2. 分裂（国家）
例 1. The partition doesn't allow the front passenger seat to slide back.（座舱）这一区域无法让前排乘客调低座椅。
2. India and Pakistan have fought two wars over Kashmir since independence and partition in 1947. 自 1947 年印巴分治以来，两国已就克什米尔问题发生过两次战争了。（见插图）

3. The bank teller sat behind a glass partition. 银行出纳员坐在玻璃隔板里面。
4. The room is partitioned into three sections. 这间屋子被隔为三小间。
5. After the war, Korea was partitioned into North and South Korea. 战后朝鲜被分割成南北两个国家。
扩 repartition *n.* 二次分割

recipient
[rɪ'sɪpiənt]

n. 接受者，领受人
记 reci (=receive) + pient → 接受的人
例 Google has removed an April Fool's Gmail button, which sent a comical animation to recipients, after reports of people getting into trouble at work. 谷歌公司去掉了愚人节的电子邮件按钮（玩笑按钮），这个按钮去给收件人发送一个动画；有人说这个按钮让他们在工作中陷入了麻烦。

opulence
['ɑːpjələns]

n. 豪奢，财富
记 opu (=operate, work) + lence → 大量制造 → 财富
例 This season's style is all about the Edwardian opulence of *Downton Abbey*.《唐顿庄园》这一季的风格属于那种爱德华时代的奢华。
扩 opulent *adj.* 豪华的，阔气的

repugnant
[rɪ'pʌgnənt]

adj. 使人反感的
记 re (=back) + pugn (=fight) + ant → 排斥的，不被接受的 → 使人反感的
例 The party's policies reflect a gross narrow-mindedness that almost everyone but conservative whites find repugnant. 该党的政策反映了一种严重的心胸狭隘，只有保守派白人才不觉得反感。
扩 repugnance *n.* 反感

franchise
['fræntʃaɪz]

n. 1. 选举权；2. 特许经营权；*v.* 授予特许权
记 franch (=frank, free) + ise → 使自由 → 给予选举权
例 1. The U.S. did not extend the franchise to women until the early 20th

century. 美国直到20世纪早期才给予妇女选举权。
2. She was granted an exclusive franchise in the city's west end. 她获得了该城西部的独家经营权。
3. Catering has been franchised (out) to a private company. 餐饮事务已外包给一家私人公司。

扩 disfranchise *v.* 剥夺（某人）选举权
affranchise *v.* 给予（某人）自由
enfranchise *v.* 给予（某人）选举权

reciprocal
[rɪˈsɪprəkl]

adj. 1. 互相的，双方的；2. 共同的；*n.* [数学] 倒数
记 reci (=back) + pro (=forward) + cal → 来回往复 → 相反的；相互的
例 1. But now she is discovering, painfully, that the feeling isn't reciprocal. 但她现在却痛苦地发现，这种感情只是一厢情愿。
2. We realized that we have reciprocal interest in this fight, and hopefully time will confirm that. 我们意识到在这场比赛中，我们的利益是一致的。希望时间能够证明这一切。
扩 reciprocally *adv.* 互相地
reciprocality *n.* 互相依赖，互相影响

withhold
[wɪðˈhoʊld, wɪθˈ-]

v. (withheld, withheld) 1. 拒绝，阻止；2. 拒绝给予，隐瞒
记 with (=back) + hold → hold back（不给）
例 1. FBI officials have withheld further comment on the shooting until a formal investigation concludes. 联邦调查局官员拒绝就枪击案置评，直到官方调查结论出炉。
2. She was accused of withholding information from the police. 她被指控对警方知情不报。
扩 withholding *n.* 拒绝给予

lament
[ləˈment]

v. 1. 大声哀悼；2. 对…极其失望、遗憾；*n.* 挽歌，哀诗
例 1. Social media in Vietnam has been flooded with posts lamenting her death. 越南的社交媒体上铺天盖地都是对她的哀悼。
2. Teachers and parents have long lamented that too much classroom time is spent "teaching to the test." 老师和家长们早就在哀叹用课堂时间来"应付考试"。
3. She, being the nearest woman relative, raised a formal lament for the dead of the family. 作为最亲的女亲属，她为亡故的家人唱起了挽歌。
扩 lamentable *adj.* 值得悲叹的

sinister
[ˈsɪnɪstər]

adj. 1. 邪恶的；2. 不吉利的；3. 伴随灾难的
例 1. There was something cold and sinister about him. 他给人一种冷酷阴险的感觉。
2. There's a sinister feeling about this old abandoned house. 这所遗弃的老房子有种不祥的感觉。
3. There is another, more sinister, possibility. 还有另一种更糟糕的可能。

vex
[veks]

v. 使烦恼，使忧虑

例 Teacher shortages have vexed a multitude of states this year. 今年教师短缺的问题困扰着好几个州。

扩 vexing *adj.* 令人烦恼的
vexation *n.* 烦恼，烦心事

remnant
['remnənt]

n. 1. 残余部分；2. 剩余人口

记 remn (=remain) + ant → 剩下来的

例 1. The woods are remnants of a huge forest which once covered the whole area. 这片树林只是剩下的一部份，原来这一带是一大片森林。
2. We should have a support for the remnants of the Syrian Free Army, and create safe zones. 我们应该支持叙利亚自由军的残余力量，并创造出一些安全区。

verge
[vɜːrdʒ]

n. 边缘；*v.* 接近

例 1. This week, one mother came to him about a teenage son on the verge of getting kicked out of school. 本周有一位母亲来找他，这位母亲的儿子面临被学校开除的境地。
2. Some of his suggestions verged on the outrageous. 他的一些建议都快到了荒唐的地步。

rally
['ræli]

n. 1. 公众集会；2.（汽车）拉力赛；*v.* 1. 召集，集会；2. 振作

记 谐音“拉力”→ 拉力赛，往返拉锯（击球）；拉人开会

例 1. They chanted his name until he addressed the crowd at a rally in Buffalo days after the loss. 失败几天后在布法罗的一次集会上，他们喊着他的名字，然后他向人群发表演说。
2. A group of several hundred drivers rallied Monday at an Uber office in Queens to complain about the fare reduction. 几百名司机周一在（纽约）奎因区的优步办公楼外集会，抗议减少补贴。
3. As the deadline approached, it was clear that we needed to rally the troops. 临近截止日期之时，很明显我们需要给部队打气加油。

扩 rallying point 号召力

inalienable
[ɪn'eɪliənəbl]

adj. 不可剥夺的，不能交出的

记 in (=not) + alien (=other) + able → 不能给别人的

例 He said the republic now had an inalienable right to self-determination. 他说共和国现在拥有不可剥夺的自决权。

trivial
['trɪviəl]

adj. 1. 普通的；2. 不重要的

记 tri (=three) + via (=road) + l → 三岔口 → 随处可见的 → 普通的；不重要的

例 1. This trivial incident is an everyday occurrence in Latin America. 这种普通的事情在拉美司空见惯。
2. Everything that came from a woman's experience was considered trivial. 在过去，女性经验中的任何感受对人们来说都是无足轻重的。

扩 trifle *n.* 稍微，一点儿；琐事

irksome
['ɜːrksəm]

adj. 令人厌烦的

例 This division of power in the Constitution has been really irksome over the last 250 years or so. 在过去的约250年中，宪法中这种权力的分配一直很让人厌烦。

扩 irk *v.* 惹人厌烦

tedious
['tiːdiəs]

adj. 冗长乏味的

例 We had to listen to the tedious details of his operation. 我们不得不听他唠叨他那次行动繁琐的细节。

扩 tedium *n.* 冗长

forbearance
[fɔːr'berəns]

n. 1. 宽容，仁慈；2. 耐心

记 for + bear + ance → 忍受，宽容

例 1. The mortgage company had acted with forbearance, only taking them to court as a last resort. 抵押公司表现得很仁慈，只在迫不得已时才诉诸法庭。

2. All the Greenpeace people behaved with impressive forbearance and dignity. 所有绿色和平组织人士表现出了超乎寻常的克制和大度。

辨 forebear *n.* 祖先

扩 forbearing *adj.* 宽容的

rigor
['rɪgər]

n. 1. 严厉；2. 严酷，严寒；3. 谨慎，严谨

记 与 rigid（坚固的；坚硬的；严格的）同源

例 1. They underwent the rigors of military training. 他们接受了严格的军事训练。

2. Winter fluid is designed for the rigors of winter weather and won't freeze on your windshield. 冬季玻璃水是专门针对冬天的严寒设计的，不会冻结在挡风玻璃上。

3. Adjusting to the academic rigors of college can be challenging for any student. 对所有学生来说，要适应大学的严谨都是一种挑战。

扩 rigorous *adj.* 谨慎的；严格的
rigorously *adv.* 谨慎地；严格地

laborious
[lə'bɔːriəs]

adj. 辛苦的，费时费力的

例 It's as laborious for the user to write as it is for followers to read. 不但读者读起来费力，使用者写起来也很费力。

insinuate
[ɪn'sɪnjueɪt]

v. 1. 旁敲侧击，暗示；2. 钻营，混入

记 in + sinu (=wind) + ate → 拐弯抹角地说、做

例 1. Secretary of State John Kerry said he should seek out a job as a stand-up comedian, insinuating his speeches are laughable. 国务卿约翰·克里说他应该找份说相声的工作，这是在暗示他的演说很可笑。

2. He solemnly insinuated himself among the men bearing the coffin. 他一脸严肃地混进了抬着棺材的人群。

扩 insinuating *adj.* 暗示的

intimacy
['ɪntɪməsi]

n. 1. 亲近，亲密；2. 亲密举动

例 1. Gradually, our attachment grew stronger until it passed beyond camaraderie into intimacy. 我们之间的彼此依恋慢慢变得越来越强烈，直到它超越了友情，变成了亲密的关系。
2. It is in our power to confine our friendships and intimacies to men of virtue. 把我们的友情和亲密举动留给高尚的男性，这是我们的权力。

tribute
['trɪbjuːt]

n. 1. 颂辞，悼念；2. 体现，显示；3. 贡金，献金

记 与 contribute（捐助，捐献）同源

例 1. Tributes poured in as news of his death was revealed on Sunday. 当星期天他的死讯传来时，人们的悼念络绎不绝。
2. It is a tribute to how France was able to bring a fractious world together. 这体现了法国有能力把动荡的世界团结起来。
3. The country was forced to pay tribute. 该国被迫缴纳贡金。

扩 tributary *adj.* 支流的；进贡的

mitigate
['mɪtɪɡeɪt]

v. 缓和，减轻

记 miti (=mild) + gate (=act) → 使变温和

例 The United States must work to mitigate this commercial espionage threat as well. 美国还必须努力减少这种商业间谍威胁。

扩 unmitigated *adj.* 完全的，十足的

insurmountable
[ˌɪnsər'maʊntəbl]

adj. 无法克服的，不可逾越的

记 in (=not) + sur (=over) + mount (=go up) + able → 不能超越的

例 Mr. Cruz held an insurmountable lead with 28 percent of the vote, with 99 percent of precincts reporting. 来自 99% 的选区报告显示，克鲁兹以 28% 的得票率取得了不可超越的领先战绩。

扩 surmount *v.* 克服，解决；置于顶端

vestige
['vestɪdʒ]

n. 1. 遗迹，残留部分；2. 丝毫，一点儿

例 1. The wall is revered as a vestige of Judaism's two ancient temples. 这堵墙被尊为犹太教两座神庙的遗迹。
2. The segregation that was a vestige of slavery caused many to leave. 作为奴隶制残余的隔离制度导致了许多人离开。

扩 vestigial *adj.* 残留的，退化的

harass
[hə'ræs, 'hærəs]

v. 1. 骚扰，侵扰；2. 不断攻击（敌人）

记 与 harry（折磨；不断骚扰）同源同义

例 1. Activists say police and authorities often misuse the law to harass homosexuals. 活动家们说警方和当局经常滥用法律去骚扰同性恋者。
2. The militias began harassing local Sunnis in Diyala, where the extremists also had carried out attacks. 国民卫队开始不断攻击迪亚拉当地的逊尼派，而那里的极端分子也进行了袭击。

扩 harassment *n.* 骚扰

impeach
[ɪm'piːtʃ]

v. 1. 控告，弹劾；2. 怀疑；*n.* 弹劾，控告

记 im (=into) + peach (=ped-, foot) → 束缚住脚，阻止 → 弹劾

例 1. She now faces either being impeached, or leading a lame-duck government for the next two years. 她现在面临的处境是要么被弹劾，要么在接下来的两年里领导一个跛脚鸭政府。

2. According to a motion filed by the defense, this new evidence might impeach the credibility of the complaining witness. 根据被告提出的动议，这项新证据可能质疑控方证人的可信度。

扩 impeachment *n.* 弹劾

forsake
[fər'seɪk]

v. (forsook, forsaken) 1.（不负责任地）遗弃；2. 离开（喜爱的事物）

记 for (=completely) + sake (=deny) → 完全否定 → 遗弃

例 1. If the federal government is forsaking the obligation to protect our citizens, we need to act. 如果联邦政府放弃保护公民的义务，那我们就需要有所行动。

2. The chill in the air is no reason to forsake the wines we enjoy all summer. 空气中的寒冷并不能让我们放弃整个夏天所享受的美酒。

lavish
['lævɪʃ]

adj. 1. 耗资巨大的，大量的；2. 慷慨的，大方的；*v.* 过分给予，滥施

记 lav(e) (=wash) + ish →（像水一样）大量的，花钱如流水

例 1. Melbourne and Sydney have welcomed 2016 with lavish firework displays. 墨尔本和悉尼均以盛大的烟花表演迎接 2016 年的到来。

2. He was lavish with praise when deserved, but was a severe critic of sloppiness and laziness. 他在应当表扬时绝不吝啬言辞，但批评马虎和懒惰也毫不留情。

3. Lavishing him with attention, even if our intent is to condemn or deride, is only falling into the trap he has set for us. 如果给予他过分的关注，即使是为了谴责或者嘲笑他，那也只不过是落入他为我们设置的圈套里。

扩 lavishly *adv.* 慷慨地；豪华地
lavishness *n.* 慷慨；华丽

meditation
[ˌmedɪ'teɪʃn]

n. 1. 冥想，沉思；2. 沉思录

记 med (=measure) + itation → 测量 → 衡量，思忖

例 1. Those in the meditation group had much less pain during the biopsy than those in the music group, the study found. 研究发现在进行活检时，进行冥想的受访者比接受音乐疗法的人疼痛更少。

2. She gave an extended meditation on religion in her public life. 她就宗教在她公职生涯中的影响进行了长篇论述。

辨 mediate *v.* 调停

扩 meditate *v.* 冥想，沉思
meditator *n.* 冥想者

predicament
[prɪ'dɪkəmənt]

n. 困境，窘境

例 Noble's fundamental predicament is that it is too indebted, and doesn't sustainably generate cash. 诺贝尔基金会的根本困境就在于，它现在欠债巨大，而且没有什么持续的现金收入。

humility
[hjuː'mɪləti]

n. 谦逊，谦虚

记 hum (=low) + ility → 放低姿态 → 谦逊

例 I accept this award with deep humility and gratitude. 接受这个奖项我诚惶诚恐，万分感激。

repeal
[rɪ'piːl]

v. 废除，撤销

记 re (=back) + peal (=call) → 叫回来 → 废除

例 An online petition calling for a repeal of the ban has garnered more than 1,500 signatures. 一项旨在取消禁令的网络请愿已经获得了 1500 多人签名。

扩 repealable *adj.* 可撤销的

intricate
['ɪntrɪkət]

adj. 错综复杂的

记 in + tric (=trick) + ate → 掉入圈套而错乱 → 错综复杂的

例 I underwent an ultrasound and had a dye injection so doctors could see intricate details of the blood vessels deep inside my eye. 我做了一次超声波检查，并接受了染色注射，这样医生就能看到我眼睛里复杂的血管了。

扩 intricately *adv.* 复杂地，精细地

misdemeanor
[ˌmɪsdɪ'miːnər]

n. 轻罪，不当行为

记 mis (=wrong) + de (=completely) + meanor (=direct) → 错误地引导 → 不当行为

例 Before this conviction, my dad had never been charged with even a misdemeanor. 在此次定罪之前，我父亲从未被指控过有丝毫不当行为。

lucrative
['luːkrətɪv]

adj. 获利多的

记 lucr(e) (=money) + ative → 产生钱的 → 有利可图的

例 Agriculture, mining and banking, three of the country's most lucrative industries, are dominated by whites. 该国最有利可图的三个行业——农业、矿业和银行业——全部为白人所把持。

扩 lucrativeness *n.* 有利可图

同 profitable

tacit
['tæsɪt]

adj. 心照不宣的，默许的

例 That, Putin and some Crimeans believe, reflects Ukraine's tacit approval for the activists' actions. 在普京和克里姆林宫官员看来，这反映了乌克兰对积极分子活动的默许。

扩 tacitly *adv.* 默许地

waive
[weɪv]

v. 1. 放弃（权利、要求等）; 2. 扔掉

记 可能跟 wave（波浪，来回反复）同源 → 放回去 → 放弃

例 1. He waived his right to appeal against the verdict. 他放弃了对判决进行申诉的权利。
2. We have decided to waive the tuition fees in your case. 我们已经决定对你免收学费。

homage
[ˈhɑːmɪdʒ]

n. 1. 效忠礼，宣誓仪式; 2. 尊敬，敬意

记 hom (=human, lord) + age → 给领主的（敬意）→ 尊敬，敬意

例 1. At his coronation he received the homage of kings from Wales, Northumbria and Scotland. 在他的加冕典礼上，威尔士、诺森布里亚和苏格兰的国王们向他宣誓效忠。
2. I consider the best homage an artist can make to his culture is a critical work. 在我看来，艺术家尊重自己文化最集中的体现就是创作批判性的作品。

incumbent
[ɪnˈkʌmbənt]

adj. 1. 有责任的，义不容辞的; 2. 在任的; *n.* 在任者，当权者

记 in (=on) + cumb (=lie down) + ent → 躺在上面的，占据的 → 在任的；在任者

例 1. So it's really incumbent upon the court to go into each of these cases with an open mind and listen to the facts. 因此法庭有义务以开放的姿态调查这些案件，并调查事实。
2. Incumbent President Ma Ying-jeou has pushed closer economic links with mainland China to boost the island's economy. 现任领导人马英九力促与大陆保持密切的经济联系以发展岛内经济。
3. He was soundly defeated by Democratic incumbent Joseph. 他被民主党现任者约瑟夫彻底击败了。

fortify
[ˈfɔːrtɪfaɪ]

v. 1. 加强; 2. 使强硬; 3. 筑城防御

例 1. He fortified himself against the cold with a hot drink. 他喝了一杯热饮御寒。
2. The news merely fortified their determination. 这消息仅仅增强了他们的决心。
3. They fortified the area against attack. 他们筑城以防袭击。

扩 fortitude *n.* 勇气，胆量
fortification *n.* 碉堡；加强

renown
[rɪˈnaʊn]

n. 名声，声望

记 re (=again, repeat) + nown (=name) → 重复名字，名字流传 → 名望

例 "Made in Germany" is a mark of global renown. "德国制造"已经成了一个荣誉的标志。

扩 renowned *adj.* 著名的

onerous
[ˈɑːnərəs, ˈoʊnərəs]

adj. 1. 繁重的，艰巨的；2. 义务超过权利的，不合理的

记 oner (=burden) + ous → 有负担的，繁重的

例 1. But the most vulnerable countries are already finding it onerous to fix the damage wreaked by climate change. 但是，最易受影响的国家早就发现要应付气候变化带来的问题十分困难。

2. They come with onerous restrictions and no promise of an education.（这些奖学金）附带不合理的限制条件，却没提供什么教育机会。

vehement
[ˈviːəmənt]

adj.（感情）强烈的，愤怒的

记 可能与 vehicle 同源 → 负载过重的 → 强烈的

例 Thompson leaped out of his seat in vehement protest. 托马逊从座位上跳起来强烈抗议。

扩 vehemence *n.* 愤怒

vehemently *adv.* 强烈地，愤怒地

shun
[ʃʌn]

v. (shunned, shunned; shunning)（故意或习惯性）避开

记 与 shut（关闭）形近 → 避开

例 After his divorce he found himself being shunned by many of his former friends. 他离婚后发现很多以前的朋友都躲着他。

harbor
[ˈhɑːrbər]

n. 1. 港湾；2. 避难所；*v.* 1. 庇护，保护；2. 心怀，珍藏

例 1. After reports of the crash, divers converged on an area about two miles outside a harbor entrance. 收到坠机报告后，潜水员聚集在港湾入口外两英里的地方。

2. Gold, another asset perceived as a harbor in times of turmoil, rose 1.6%. 黄金这种在动荡时期被视为避难所的资产上涨了 1.6%。

3. Islamic State was threatening to kill anyone who harbored a government fighter. "伊斯兰国"（极端组织）威胁杀死所有庇护政府军的人。

4. A target of bullying, Natalie cut her arms and harbored suicidal thoughts. 受人欺凌的娜塔丽割臂自残，并且一心想要自杀。

momentous
[moʊˈmentəs]

adj. 重要的，关键的

记 moment + ous → 关于某个时刻的 → 关键的

例 In the coming months, Britain will make a momentous decision: whether to stay in the European Union or leave and go it alone. 在接下来的几个月里，英国将做出一个重要的决定：留在欧盟内部还是脱离欧盟。

扩 momentously *adv.* 重要地

momentary *adj.* 短暂的，片刻的

precept
[ˈpriːsept]

n. 规则，规范

记 pre (=before) + cept (=taking) → 提前持有的 → 规则

例 But as complicated as that book was, it nonetheless observed some

basic precepts of storytelling. 但是，尽管这本书很复杂，它却遵循了讲故事的一些基本规范。
辨 percept *n.* 感觉，感受；印象

grandeur
[ˈɡrændʒər, -djər]

n. 宏伟，壮丽
记 grand (=great) + eur → 宏大
例 Saturn displays its full grandeur in this image from NASA's Cassini probe. 在这张由美国宇航局的卡西尼探测器发回的图像上，土星的雄伟一览无余。

predilection
[ˌpriːdɪˈlekʃn]

n. 偏爱
记 pre (=before) + dilect (=select) + ion → 偏爱
例 The human predilection to choose numbers that are familiar to us doesn't seem likely to go away. 人们偏爱选择那些他们熟悉的数字，这种倾向似乎无法克服。

futile
[ˈfjuːtl]

adj. 徒劳的，无用的
记 名词 futility 比反义词 utility 只多一个字母 f
例 Not only is this undertaking futile, but it's stressing us out. 这种行为不仅是徒劳的，它还给我们巨大的压力。
扩 futility *n.* 徒劳

scrutinize
[ˈskruːtənaɪz]

v. 仔细检查
记 形似 scrub（用力擦洗）→ 仔细检查
例 Ms. Mayer will be facing a lot of doubters and critics, so what she says will be especially scrutinized and dissected. 梅耶夫人将面临许多质疑者与批评者，所以她说的话将受到仔细检查和剖析。
扩 scrutiny *n.* 仔细检查

illicit
[ɪˈlɪsɪt]

adj. 非法的，违法的
记 il (=not) + licit (=licence) → 没有执照的，非法的
例 Singapore said it would not tolerate being used as a refuge for illicit funds. 新加坡声称它不会容忍本地成为非法基金的藏身之地。
扩 illicitly *adv.* 非法地
illicitness *n.* 非法

nominal
[ˈnɑːmɪnl]

adj. 1. 有名无实的；2. 象征性的，小的；3. 如愿的，符合计划的
记 nom (=name) + inal → 名字的，名义上的
例 1. Waldman speculates that Republicans might "give him nominal support, but not much more." 沃德曼认为共和党人可能会"给他（Trump）名义上的支持，但也仅限于此"。
2. Despite nominal job growth, wage growth and labor-force participation rates continue to disappoint. 尽管工作机会略有增长，但工资涨幅和劳动力增幅仍不尽人意。
3. All systems are nominal—everything is going well so far. 各个部门

都按部就班，一切都很顺利。

扩 nominally *adv.* 名义上地

obnoxious
[əbˈnɑːkʃəs]

adj. 极讨厌的，难闻的

记 ob (=to) + nox (=hurt) + ious → 带来伤害的 → 令人讨厌的

例 How do you strike a balance of not coming across as obnoxious or arrogant while boasting of your accomplishments? 你怎样做到既能夸耀自己的成就又免得招人厌烦、让人觉得傲慢?

扩 obnoxiously *adv.* 可憎地

sedition
[sɪˈdɪʃn]

n. 煽动叛乱

记 sed (=sect, apart) + ition → 分离，分裂 → 煽动不和

例 He led the congressional campaign to pass four laws in 1798 known as *the Alien & Sedition Acts*. 他领导的国会通过了1798年的四部法律，即《外侨和煽动叛乱法》。

扩 seditious *adj.* 煽动叛乱的

residue
[ˈrezɪduː]

n. 1. 残渣；2.（清偿债务后的）剩余遗产

记 resid (=reside, live) + ue → 留下来的 → 残渣；遗产

例 1. Not all produce is grown equally; some fruits and vegetables are more likely to have pesticide residues. 并不是所有的农产品都经过同样处理，有些水果和蔬菜更可能有农药残留。
2. The residue of the estate reverts to you through your mother, and I am nominally your guardian and the executor. 剩余的财产将由你母亲归还给你，而我将是你名义上的监护人和执行者。

扩 residual *adj.* 剩余的
residuary *adj.* 剩余遗产的；剩余的

turmoil
[ˈtɜːrmɔɪl]

n. 动乱，焦虑

记 tur (=turb, stir) + moil (=mill) → 搅动的筛子 → 动乱

例 The yen has been a traditional safe haven for investors in times of turmoil. 在经济动荡之际，对投资者而言，日元一直是一个传统的避险货币。

orator
[ˈɔːrətər, ˈɑː-]

n. 1. 雄辩家；2. 演说者

记 orat (=speak) + or → 说话的人 → 演说者

例 1. More actor than orator, Bill Clinton was not the most eloquent debater. 比尔·克林顿并不是最佳辩论者，比起雄辩家，他更像是个演员。
2. He is, by his own account, not a tribune but a technocrat, not an orator but a doer. 按照他自己的说法，他是技术专家而非护民官，是行动者而非夸夸其谈者。

remedial [rɪ'miːdiəl]

adj. 1. 旨在解决问题的，纠正的；2. 补习的，辅导的

记 rededi (=heal) + al → 能纠正的

例 1. Remedial action must be taken now. 现在必须进行补救。

2. Thirty percent of the new students need remedial courses in math. 有 30% 的学生需要上数学补习班。

扩 remedy *n.* 补偿，改进措施；治疗；解决办法

List 3

insatiable
[ɪn'seɪʃəbl]

adj. 不知足的，贪婪的

记 in (=not) + sati (=satisfy) + able → 不能满足的

例 People are hungry for political alternatives that will serve their interests for a change instead of the insatiable greed of Wall Street. 人们正渴望出现政治新人为他们的利益服务，而不是华尔街那些贪婪的人。

stigmatize
['stɪgmətaɪz]

v. 侮蔑，羞辱

记 stigma (=stain) + tize → 使有污点 → 羞辱

例 The gay community is still stigmatized in Africa, Eastern Europe and elsewhere, he said. 他说，同性恋群体在非洲、东欧和其他地方仍然受到侮辱。

扩 stigma *n.* 耻辱，羞耻

ordinance
['ɔːrdɪnəns]

n. 条例，指示

记 ord (=order) + inance → 命令，秩序

例 The update to the city's animal control ordinances also requires permits for certain reptiles and amphibians. 该市修订后的动物控制法令还要求饲养某些爬行动物和两栖动物也要有执照。

perturb
[pər'tɜːrb]

v. 使焦虑不安

记 per (=through) + turb (=disturb) → 扰乱，使烦恼

例 The prospect of machines stealing our jobs has perturbed and enraged humans for at least 200 years. 机器人偷走人类工作的这种可能性已经困扰人类至少 200 年了。

扩 perturbation *n.* 忧虑，不安

methodical
[mə'θɑːdɪkl]

adj. 有条理的

例 Mr. Nelson is a voracious and methodical reader who alternates between new books and classics he's never read. 纳尔逊先生是位渴求且有条理的读者，他交替阅读新书和未涉猎过的经典书籍。

扩 methodically *adv.* 井井有条地

implicit
[ɪm'plɪsɪt]

adj. 1. 含蓄的；2. 潜在的；3. 毫无疑问的，完全的

记 im (=in) + pli (=fold) + cit → 折叠在里面的 → 含蓄的

例 1. It is the implicit agreement between a state and its people about how a country should be governed. 州及其公民对如何治理国家心照不宣。

2. The ability to listen is implicit in the teacher's role. 教师的角色包括了懂得倾听。

3. She had the implicit trust of her staff. 她得到了全体职员的绝对信任。
扩 implicitly *adv.* 含蓄地

remonstrate
[rɪ'mɑːnstreɪt]

v. 抗议，抱怨
记 与 demonstrate（示威）同根 → 抗议
例 Dominican birth certificate in hand, I remonstrated with the officer. 我拿着多米尼加的出生证，向这位警官抗议。
扩 remonstrance *n.* 抗议，抱怨

relish
['relɪʃ]

v. 渴望，获得乐趣；*n.* 享受，乐趣
记 与 release（放松，享受）同源 → 享受，乐趣
例 1. He relished debating his critics at law schools and in public appearances, although he sometimes displayed a thin skin. 他喜欢在法学院和公开场合跟他的对手辩论，虽然他有时也很害羞。
2. She savored the moment with obvious relish. 她显然津津有味地回味着那一刻。

obligatory
[ə'blɪgətɔːri]

adj. 1.（法律等）强制的，必须的；2. 习惯性的，赶时髦的
例 1. Upper-class Englishmen used to send their sons on a grand tour of Europe as an obligatory part of their education. 上层英国人过去常常送儿子去欧洲长途旅行，作为对他们义务教育的一部分。
2. The standing ovation that followed felt real and heartfelt, not obligatory as many of these expressions of approval do. 随后的起立鼓掌是真心实意的，不像这种反应通常那样是习惯性的。

stifle
['staɪfl]

v. 1. 压制，扼杀；2. 使窒息
记 与 stuff（塞满）同源 → 使窒息 → 扼杀
例 1. The pharmaceutical industry has said that "arbitrary" prices set by the government would impede research and stifle innovation. 制药行业称政府制定的"随意"的价格可能妨碍研究，抑制创新。
2. I turn and see Ma put her hands over her mouth to stifle a scream. 我转身看到妈妈把手放在嘴边捂住叫声。

marshal
['mɑːrʃl]

n. 1. 司令；2. 法庭执行官；3. 警察局长或消防局长；*v.* 结集，安排
例 1. Prince Charles wore his field marshal uniform at the parade. 查尔斯王子穿着陆军司令制服走在队伍中。

2. A federal marshal was killed during the conflict, which came after an 11-day standoff. 经过 11 天的僵持之后，一名联邦法庭执行官在冲突中被杀。
3. A spokeswoman for the state fire marshal's office says the fire doesn't appear to be suspicious. 州消防局局长办公室的女发言人说火灾并无可疑之处。
4. Opponents marshaled evidence to prove this was untrue. 反对派搜集证据试图证明这是假的。

venerable
['venərəbl]

adj. 1. 值得尊敬的；2. 古老而令人尊敬的

记 vener (=Venus, love) + able → 与爱神有关的 → 尊敬

例 1. Energy production and distribution companies are desperate to find new talent. Not even the venerable Hoover Dam is exempt. 能源生产和输送公司迫切需要招募人才，连令人尊敬的胡佛水坝公司也不例外。

2. Many theater companies in the Washington area boast strong ties to the venerable dramatic traditions of Ireland. 华盛顿地区的许多剧院都自夸与爱尔兰古老的戏剧传统有所渊源。

扩 veneration *n.* 尊敬

quell
[kwel]

v. 1. 镇压，平息；2. 缓和，减轻

记 源于 kill（杀死，止痛）

例 1. Gaddafi was killed in 2011 after he violently quelled a popular uprising. 在卡扎菲暴力镇压了一次民众暴动后，他于 2011 年被杀。

2. But the White House efforts have done little to quell the anxiety back home. 但是白宫的努力几乎未能消除国内的焦虑情绪。

resigned
[rɪ'zaɪnd]

adj. 顺从的

记 resign 有两个意思：辞职；无奈地接受

例 He was resigned to the fact that an expensive vacation would have to wait. 他不得不接受这样的事实：昂贵的度假只能一拖再拖了。

扩 resignedly *adv.* 无可奈何地

obstinate
['ɑːbstɪnət]

adj. 1. 顽固的，倔强的；2. 棘手的，难处理的

记 ob (=by) + stin (=stand) + ate → 站在旁边 → 顽固的

例 1. The more the parent pushes, the more obstinate the youngling becomes. 父母逼得越厉害，年轻子女就越顽固。

2. This soap will remove the most obstinate stains. 这种肥皂能去除顽固的污渍。

扩 obstinacy *n.* 顽固
obstinately *adv.* 顽固地

sever
['sevər]

v. 1. 割断，切下；2. 分离，断交

记 se (=apart) + ver → 分开

例 1. In theory, the United States could sever fibre-optic cables and destroy satellite dishes. 理论上，美国政府可以割断光缆，破坏卫星接收器。

2. We severed ties with her years ago, and none of us feels like we're missing out. 我们已经与她断绝来往多年了，谁都没有感觉到互相怀念。

辨 server *n.* 服务器

同 separate

inordinate
[ɪn'ɔːrdɪnət]

adj. 过分的，超出预料的

例 Darwin famously said that God must have had an inordinate fondness for beetles, since there are more species of beetles than any other lifeform. 达尔文曾有句名言，说上帝肯定对甲壳虫过分偏爱，因为它的

物类最多。
扩 inordinately *adv.* 过分地
同 excessive

reminiscence
[ˌremɪˈnɪsns]

n. 1. 回想往事；2. 回忆录；3. 联想
记 re (=again) + minisc (=remember) + ence → 再次回忆
例 1. I am not sure he deserved such a generous reminiscence from his son. 我不认为他值得儿子如此想念。
2. His thoughts flooded with reminiscences of his own family and he began writing them down. 他的脑海里充满了对自己家人的回忆，于是他把这些回忆写了下来。
3. At that stage, this will give you a reminiscence of the meal, which is very pleasant. 在那个阶段，这会让你联想到饭菜，这一点令人愉悦。

infraction
[ɪnˈfrækʃn]

n. 违法，犯规
例 Minor infractions can cost $150 or more, while larger offenses mandate a court appearance. 轻微违法可能被罚至少 150 美元，而更严重的犯法就得上法庭了。
同 infringement

sublime
[səˈblaɪm]

adj. 1. 崇高的，壮丽的；2. 极端的
例 1. He composed some of the most sublime symphonies in existence. 他创作了一些非常壮丽的交响乐。
2. He battled on, in the sublime conviction that he was in the right. 他继续战斗，坚信他站在正确的一方。

treatise
[ˈtriːtɪz]

n. 专题论文
记 treat (=deal with) + ise → 处理，应对 → 论文
例 Descartes carried this mechanical view of the world into what he hoped would be a great treatise on physiology. 笛卡尔把这种机械的世界观写进了他认为的优秀生理学论文中。

indiscriminate
[ˌɪndɪˈskrɪmɪnət]

adj. 1. 随意的，恣意的；2. 不加判断的，不加选择的
记 in (=not) + discrimin (=discern) + ate → 不进行区别 → 随意的
例 1. He accused Russia of "carpet bombing" and carrying out "indiscriminate bombing" of civilian areas. 他指责俄罗斯"地毯式轰炸"，以及对平民区"恣意轰炸"。
2. She's always been indiscriminate in her choice of friends. 她一向择友不慎。
扩 indiscriminately *adv.* 不加区分地；随意地

indeterminate
[ˌɪndɪˈtɜːrmɪnət]

adj. 模糊的，结果不明的
记 in (=not) + determin (=decide) + ate → 不确定的
例 1. Out of 12,200 offenders serving life or indeterminate sentences,

only 57 people have been sentenced for their whole life. 在 12200 名判处无期或不定期徒刑的罪犯中，只有 57% 的人被判处无期徒刑。
2. The result from one Ebola patient tested 10 months after disease onset was indeterminate. 一名埃博拉患者在发病 10 个月后的测试结果不明。
辨 determinable *adj.* 可确定的，可查明的
扩 indeterminately *adv.* 不确定地

frivolous
[ˈfrɪvələs]

adj. 1. 不当的，愚蠢的；2. 无聊的，不重要的
例 1. Even if they are frivolous, I want to read the complaints and learn what we can improve. 即使这些投诉很不当，我还是愿意看看有什么可以改进的。
2. Curbing your spending on frivolous or unnecessary purchases leaves more money available to free up your budget. 限制自己不去购买不必要的物品，这能让你省下很多钱，让自己手头宽松一点。
扩 frivolously *adv.* 愚蠢地；无聊地
frivolousness *n.* 无聊，不重要

solemn
[ˈsɑːləm]

adj. 1. 冷峻的，表情严肃的；2. 郑重的；3. 庄严的，隆重的
例 1. At the end of the speeches she grew solemn and serious. 在演讲结束时她变得冷峻而严肃。
2. The U.S. and other members of the U.N. made a solemn vow. 美国和其他联合国成员作出了郑重承诺。
3. After bringing in the coffin, the eight pallbearers gave it a slow, solemn salute as family members and other mourners filed in. 灵柩抬进来以后，家属和吊唁者依次进入，八名护柩者缓慢而庄重地行礼。
扩 solemnity *n.* 庄严；（重大）仪式，礼仪
solemnly *adv.* 严肃地，庄严地

flagrant
[ˈfleɪgrənt]

adj. 骇人听闻的，公然的
记 flag (=flash) + rant → 闪耀的，公开的 → 公然的
例 Hillary Clinton's flagrant disregard of national security for personal convenience makes one a bit insecure about such a person leading the nation. 希拉里·克林顿为了个人便利，公然蔑视国家安全，这使得人们担心这样的人领导一个国家。

visionary
[ˈvɪʒəneri]

adj. 1. 幻觉的，虚幻的；2. 有远见的；*n.* 有远见的人
例 1. The game takes place in the year 2124 in NeoMars, a modern, visionary city on Mars. 游戏发生在 2124 年的新火星上，这是一个现代化的、虚幻的火星城市。

2. Their success owes a lot to his visionary leadership. 他们的成功很大一部分应归功于他的有远见的领导。
3. He was one of Silicon Valley's most brilliant leaders—a visionary who mentored many of today's leaders in technology. 他曾是硅谷最聪

明的领袖之一，作为有远见的人，他曾培养了今天科技界的许多领袖。

quorum
[ˈkwɔːrəm]

n. 法定人数

记 quo (=who) + rum → 人物 → 法定人数

例 We need five people to make a quorum. 我们需要5个人才能满足法定人数。

impute
[ɪmˈpjuːt]

v. 1. 把…归咎于；2. 把…归罪于

记 im (=in) + put (=put) + e → 放在里面 → 把…归咎于

例 1. They're trying to impute selfish motives to my actions. 他们企图认为我的行为是出于自私。
2. He insists that he is not responsible for all the crimes that have been imputed to him. 他坚持说他不应为受到的罪责指控负责。

indisputable
[ˌɪndɪˈspjuːtəbl]

adj. 无可置疑的

记 in (=not) + disput + able → 不容争辩的

例 It is indisputable that the crime rate has been rising. 毫无疑问，犯罪率一直在上升。

扩 indisputably *adv.* 不容置疑地

grate
[ɡreɪt]

v. 1. 磨碎；2. 发出刺耳的声音；3. 使人烦躁，使人烦恼

记 磨碎 → 摩擦 → 摩擦声使人烦躁

例 1. The recipe calls for half a cup of grated cheese. 这个食谱要求用半杯碎的奶酪。
2. The rusty hinges grated as the gate swung back. 大门荡了回去，生锈的铰链发出吱嘎吱嘎的刺耳声。
3. It grated with him when people implied he wasn't really British. 当有人暗示他不是地道的英国人时，他很是恼火。

扩 grating *adj.* 刺耳的

puerile
[ˈpjʊrəl]

adj. 孩子气的，不成熟的

记 puer (=child) + ile → 孩子（气）的

例 Concert organizers branded the group's actions as puerile. 音乐会的组织者指称该乐队的行为愚蠢幼稚。

idiom
[ˈɪdiəm]

n. 1. 习语，成语；2. 方言，语言风格；3.（艺术）风格

例 1. Proverbs and idioms may become worn with overuse. 谚语和习语会由于使用过多而变得俗套。
2. And nothing was so irritating as the confident way he used archaic idioms. 没什么比他使用过时的方言时那种自负的神态更气人的了。
3. It was an old building in the local idiom. 那是一座具有当地风格的古建筑。

imperious
[ɪmˈpɪriəs]

adj. 傲慢的，专横的

记 imper (=empire) + ious → 像帝国一样的 → 命令的，专横的

例 She put out an imperious hand to stop him. 她专横地伸手去阻止他。

扩 imperiously *adv.* 专横地

invigorate
[ɪnˈvɪɡəreɪt]

v. 1. 使精神焕发；2. 刺激

记 in (=enter) + vigor (=energy) + ate → 使注入精力 → 刺激

例 1. They invigorated and motivated their teams, and stayed positive and focused. 他们给自己的队伍打气，让他们保持积极向上，集中精力。
2. Yet low commodity prices and a crippling battle against Ebola have dented his popularity and invigorated the opposition. 然而物价低迷以及对抗埃博拉病毒的不利使他的民意锐减，刺激了反对派。

扩 invigorating *adj.* 令人精神振作的

submissive
[səbˈmɪsɪv]

adj. 顺从的

例 He expected his daughters to be meek and submissive. 他期望女儿都温顺听话。

扩 submissively *adv.* 顺从地

slacken
[ˈslækən]

v. 放慢，减缓，萧条

记 slacks (=lax, loose) + en → 放松

例 We've been really busy, but things are starting to slacken off now. 近来我们的确很忙，不过现在情况开始有所缓解了。

sanctuary
[ˈsæŋktʃueri]

n. 1. 圣殿；2. 保护区，避难所

记 sanct (=saint) + uary (=place) → 神圣的地方 → 圣殿，保护区

例 1. The sanctuary contains the altar of sacrifice. 圣殿里有献祭用的圣坛。
2. The refugees sought sanctuary when they crossed the border. 难民们穿越边境寻求避难所。

impede
[ɪmˈpiːd]

v. 阻碍，阻止

记 im (=in) + pede (=foot) → 束缚住脚 → 阻碍

例 Work on the building was impeded by severe weather. 楼房的施工因天气恶劣而停了下来。

扩 impediment *n.* 妨碍，阻碍

frigid
[ˈfrɪdʒɪd]

adj. 1. 寒冷的；2. 冷淡的

记 frid (=cold) + id → 冷的

例 1. The frigid gusts of wind stung their faces. 冷风刺痛了他们的脸。
2. There was a frigid atmosphere in the room. 房间里一片冷淡的气氛。

扩 frigidity *n.* 寒冷

intervene
[ˌɪntərˈviːn]

v. 1. 介入；2. 阻碍，干扰；3. 介于…之间

例 1. The President intervened personally in the crisis. 总统亲自出面处理这场危机。

2. They were planning to get married and then the war intervened. 他们正准备结婚，不巧却因爆发战事而受阻。
3. Only six months intervened between their marriage and divorce. 他们从结婚到离婚中间只有 6 个月。
扩 intervention *n.* 介入；干扰

pious
['paɪəs]
adj. 1. 虔诚的，宗教的；2. 虚情假意的，伪善的
记 可能源于 pure（纯粹的，纯真的）→ 虔诚的，尽职的
例 1. He was brought up by pious female relatives. 他是由虔诚的女性亲属带大的。
2. His attitude is compassionate without being pious. 他的态度是真心实意的同情。
扩 impious *adj.* 不虔诚的
piety *n.* 虔诚

supersede
[ˌsuːpər'siːd]
v. 更新，取代
记 super (=above) + sede (=sit) → 代替
例 The theory has been superseded by more recent research. 这一理论已为新近的研究所取代。

inexorable
[ɪn'eksərəbl]
adj. 1. 不为所动的；2. 无法改变的
记 in (=not) + ex (=out) + ora (=pray) + ble → 不能被说动的
例 1. The judgment is inexorable; it is absolute and eternal. 法官不为所动，判决是板上钉钉的事。
2. Either accept that reality, or accept the continued inexorable decline of the American middle class. 要么接受现实，要么眼看着美国中产阶级无可避免地继续衰落。

ineffectual
[ˌɪnɪ'fektʃuəl]
adj. 无能的，达不到目的的
记 in (=not) + effect + ual → 无法产生预期效果的
例 The mayor had become ineffectual in the struggle to clamp down on drugs. 市长打击毒品的努力未见成效。
扩 ineffectuality *n.* 无能

wrath
[ræθ]
n. 盛怒，怒火
例 He incurred the wrath of the authorities in speaking out against government injustices. 他直言批评政府的不公正做法，招致当局震怒。
扩 wrathful *adj.* 怒气冲冲的

sedate
[sɪ'deɪt]
adj. 镇静的，不慌不忙的；*v.* 给…服镇静剂
例 1. We followed the youngsters at a more sedate pace. 我们跟在年轻人后面，步子稍慢一点。
2. The animal was heavily sedated during the procedure. 在整个过程中这只动物被注射了大量镇静剂。
扩 sedative *n.* 镇定剂

wanton
['wɑːntən]

adj. 残忍的，恶毒的，肆意的

记 wan (=lacking) + ton (=discipline) → 缺乏控制的，无限制的 → 肆意的

例 He showed a wanton disregard for his friend's feelings. 他毫不顾忌朋友的感情。

扩 wantonly *adv.* 肆意地，恶意地

imminent
['ɪmɪnənt]

adj. 即将发生的，迫在眉睫的

记 im (=in, upon) + min (=mount) + ent → 泰山压顶的 → 迫在眉睫的

例 The species is in imminent danger of extinction. 这个物种的灭绝迫在眉睫。

扩 imminently *adv.* 逼近地

infamous
['ɪnfəməs]

adj. 声名狼藉的

例 1. Blackwater became infamous in 2007 when its employees opened fire on Iraqi civilians, killing 17. 黑水公司在 2007 年变得声名狼藉，因为它的员工朝伊拉克平民开枪，打死了 17 个人。
2. We experienced some of the city's infamous weather. 我们见识了该城的糟糕天气。

扩 infamy *n.* 声名狼藉；罪行

insuperable
[ɪn'sjuːpərəbl]

adj. 无法克服的，不可逾越的

记 in (=not) + super (=over) + able → 不能超过的

例 They succeeded despite some nearly insuperable difficulties. 尽管困难似乎不可逾越，他们还是完成了任务。

同 insurmountable

rectify
['rektɪfaɪ]

v. 矫正，纠正

记 rect (=right) + ify → 使变正确 → 纠正

例 We must take steps to rectify the situation. 我们一定要采取措施整顿局面。

taint
[teɪnt]

v. 污染，使腐坏，玷污

记 与 touch 同源 → 因接触而污染

例 1. The administration was tainted with scandal. 丑闻使得政府声名狼藉。
2. The water had been tainted by pesticides. 水被农药污染了。

扩 tainted *adj.* 污染的

subtlety
['sʌtlti]

n. 1. 细微，微妙；2. 微妙之处

记 sub (=under) + tle (=web, text) + ty → 编织得很仔细 → 细微

例 1. It's a thrilling movie even though it lacks subtlety. 这部电影虽说不算精巧，但还是扣人心弦的。
2. When a book gets translated, all those linguistic subtleties get lost. 一部书被翻译后就失去了语言上的精妙之处。

List 3

unequivocal
[ˌʌnɪˈkwɪvəkl]

adj. 毫不含糊的，不容置疑的
记 un (=not) + equi (=equal) + vocal (=call) → 同一个声音 → 不容置疑的
例 He told them in unequivocal terms what was expected of them. 他明确告诉他们应该做什么。

sophistry
[ˈsɑːfɪstri]

n. 诡辩（术）
记 sophi (=clever) + stry → 聪明人 → 会辩论的人
例 Political selection is more dependent on sophistry and less on economic literacy. 政治选举更多地取决于诡辩的能力，而不在于是否懂经济。
扩 sophist *n.* 哲学家；古希腊时代的学者

sanguine
[ˈsæŋgwɪn]

adj. 1. 充满信心的，乐观的；2. 健康红润的
记 原意"血"，根据古希腊医学家希波克拉底的观点，多血质的人通常精力充沛，遇事乐观；另外三种体质为 choleric、phlegmatic 和 melancholic
例 1. Google is sanguine about Android's prospects, and said the company's original vision for Android was never solely about huge profits. 谷歌对安卓的前景非常乐观，并且说该公司对安卓的初衷并不仅是获取巨额利润。
2. The violence of his cough had a powerful effect on his sanguine complexion, and he grew exceedingly red in the face. 他剧烈的咳嗽在他潮红的脸上留下了明显的效果，他的脸越来越红了。
扩 sanguinary *adj.* 杀戮的，血腥的

sentinel
[ˈsentɪnl]

n. 哨兵，岗哨
记 sent (=sense) + inel → 感知 → 哨兵
例 Large dark pines stood like sentinels guarding the wintry garden. 巨大的黑松像哨兵一样保卫着冬日花园剧场的入口。

surmise
[sərˈmaɪz] *v.*
[ˈsɜːrmaɪz] *n.*

v. 推测；*n.* 猜测
例 1. From the looks on their faces, I surmised that they had had an argument. 看他们的脸色，我猜想他们之间发生了争执。
2. This is pure surmise on my part. 这纯粹是我的猜测。

rectitude
[ˈrektɪtuːd]

n. 公正，诚实
记 rect (=right) + itude → 正确 → 正直，诚实
例 Mr. Awlaki preached rectitude but conducted his private life on other terms. 奥拉奇先生满口仁义道德，在私生活中又是另一码事。

fervor
[ˈfɜːrvər]

n. 热情，热烈
记 与 fever（发烧）同源近义
例 Some commentators have noted that the rise of Trump has coincided with white nationalist fervor. 一些评论家注意到，特朗普的崛起恰逢白人民族主义热情高涨之际。

materialism [mə'tɪriəlɪzəm]	*n.* 1. 物质主义；2. 唯物主义 例 1. He wanted to warn them against the temptations of capitalism, individualism and materialism. 他想警告他们提防资本主义、个人主义和物质主义的诱惑。 2. A friend once asked me how I could reconcile my creed of African nationalism with a belief in dialectical materialism. 一位朋友曾问我如何把非洲民族主义和辩证唯物主义结合起来。 扩 materialist *n.* 物质享乐主义者 materialistic *adj.* 物质主义的，享乐的
martial ['mɑːrʃl]	*adj.* 军事的，战争的 记 源于古罗马神话中的战神 Mars 例 Not only does he become an expert in martial arts, but he also dresses in Chinese garb like Lee. 他不仅成了武术高手，而且还学李小龙一样穿衣打扮。
ostensible [ɑː'stensəbl]	*adj.* 表面的，宣称的 记 与 ostentatious 同源近义 例 The ostensible reason for his absence was illness. 他假托生病缺勤。 扩 ostensibly *adv.* 假装地
mandate ['mændeɪt] *n.* [ˌmæn'deɪt] *v.*	*n.* 1. 授权；2. 委托书；*v.* 强迫，强制执行 记 与 manual 同源；man (=hand) + date (=give) → 放入某人手中 → 委托，托付 → 授权 例 1. The election victory gave the party a clear mandate to continue its program of reform. 选举获胜使得这个政党拥有了明确的继续推行改革的权力。 2. The bank had no mandate to honor the check. 银行没有得到指令来承兑这张支票。 3. The law mandates that imported goods be identified as such. 法律规定进口货物必须如实标明。 扩 mandatory *adj.* 强迫的
humane [hjuː'meɪn]	*adj.* 1. 善良的，人道的；2. 人文主义的 例 1. The Pope plans to hold a mass at the U.S.-Mexico border next week to call for a more humane approach to immigration. 教皇还打算下周在美墨边境举行弥撒，呼吁对移民更加人道。 2. It would involve the replacement of the humane ideal at the center of the party and its history. 这将会取代该党的人文主义理想，并且改变它的历史。 扩 humanely *adv.* 人道地 反 inhuman
valor ['vælər]	*n.* 英勇，勇气 记 与 value 同源 → 值得尊敬的（品质）→ 勇气 例 The true warrior thinks only of honor and his code of valor. 真正的勇

士只在乎荣誉和勇气。

扩 valorous *adj.* 英勇的

prophetic
[prə'fetɪk]

adj. 有预见的，预言的

记 pro (=before) + phet (=speak) + ic → 提前说的 → 预言的

例 1. His cough was prophetic of an early death. 他的咳嗽预示着早亡。

2. The same prophetic power was attributed in India to virgins. 印度人相信这种预言的能力在处女身上。

扩 prophet *n.* 先知，预言家，倡导者

prophesy *v.* 预言

tenacious
[tə'neɪʃəs]

adj. 1. 紧握的；2. 顽强的，坚韧的

记 tenac (=hold) + ious → 抓住不放的 → 坚持的

例 1. But the drill could not punch through those tenacious layers. 但是钻头无法穿透密实的地层。

2. Ever since surgeons amputated Mary's legs, she has been tenacious in her recovery. 自从做了外科截肢手术后，玛丽在恢复期一直很顽强。

subjugate
['sʌbdʒugeɪt]

v. 1. 征服；2. 使次要，让位于

记 sub (=under) + jud (=rule) + ate → 在上面统治 → 征服，使屈服

例 1. "We must stand together," he urged Congress, "to stop Iran from subjugating the region, then the world." 他敦促国会说："我们必须团结一致，阻止伊朗征服该地区，然后是全世界。"

2. Gay couples for too long have been wrongly subjugated and isolated. 同性伴侣长期以来受到不公平的贬抑和孤立。

扩 subjugation *n.* 征服

invincible
[ɪn'vɪnsəbl]

adj. 不可战胜的

记 in (=not) + vinc (=victory) + ible → 不能战胜的

例 He always seemed invincible, with firm, broad shoulders and lots of teeth. 他有着紧实宽阔的肩膀和密集的牙齿，看上去永远都是那么的不认输。

imperceptible
[ˌɪmpər'septəbl]

adj. 难以察觉的

记 im (=not) + percept (=feel, perceive) + ible →（小到）无法察觉的

例 Symptoms of infection often are mild or imperceptible. 受感染后的症状通常很温和，甚至难以察觉。

fugitive
['fjuːdʒətɪv]

n. 逃亡者；*adj.* 1. 逃跑的，流浪的；2. 短暂的，易逝的

记 fugi (=flee) + tive → 逃跑的人 → 逃亡者

例 1. U.S. fugitive Edward Snowden told Mr. Bush to delete his account. 美国逃亡者爱德华·斯诺登告诉（杰布·）布什删除他的推特内容。

2. She has been charged with helping a fugitive slave

from justice. 她被控帮助逃亡奴隶逃避法律。.
3. As he daydreamed, fugitive thoughts passed through his mind. 在他做白日梦的时候，短暂的思绪在他心里闪过。

vindictive
[vɪn'dɪktɪv]

adj. 想复仇的，报复性的
例 And narcissists are among the most vindictive people you'll ever meet. 自恋的人可能是你见过的最容易睚眦必报的人。

vigilance
['vɪdʒɪləns]

n. 机警，警惕
例 Officials advised U.S. citizens to "exercise vigilance" in public places or on mass transportation. 美国官员提醒本国公民在公共场合及交通工具上要"提高警惕"。
扩 vigilant *adj.* 警惕的

transparent
[træns'pærənt]

adj. 1. 透明的，清澈的；2. 公开的，显而易见的；3. 易懂的
记 trans (=through) + parent (=appear) → 透过能看到的 → 透明的
例 1. The insect's wings are almost transparent. 这昆虫的翅膀几乎是透明的。
2. Protesters are demanding a transparent probe into the missing money and a new election. 抗议者要求对丢失的钱进行公开透明的调查以及重新选举。
3. Their motives were transparent. 他们的电影非常容易懂。

potent
['poʊtnt]

adj. 1. 强有力的；2. 有效的
记 pot (=power) + ent → 有力的
例 1. The drug is extremely potent, but causes unpleasant side effects. 这种药药效极强，但会产生不良的副作用。
2. Her story serves as a potent reminder of the dangers of drug abuse. 她的故事非常有力地说明了滥用毒品的危害。
扩 impotent *adj.* 无力的，无能的

preclude
[prɪ'kluːd]

v. 阻止，预防
记 pre (=before) + clude (=close) → 提前关上 → 阻止
例 1. Lack of time precludes any further discussion. 由于时间不足，不可能作深入的讨论。
2. His religious beliefs precluded him serving in the army. 他的宗教信仰不允许他服兵役。

generality
[ˌdʒenə'ræləti]

n. 1. 概论，概述；2. 主体，大多数；3. 一般性，普遍性
例 1. As usual, he confined his comments to generalities. 他像往常一样，只作了笼统的评论。
2. This view is held by the generality of leading scholars. 大多数知名学者都持这种观点。
3. An account of such generality is of little value. 这种一般性描述没有什么价值。

overbearing
[ˌoʊvərˈberɪŋ]

adj. 1. 压倒一切的；2. 专横的，盛气凌人的

例 1. This race should be about which candidate will best protect you from an overbearing government. 这场竞争将决定哪位候选人最能保护你免受强大政府的压迫。

2. Uber is not an overbearing employer using its bargaining power to impose poor terms on drivers. 优步并不是一个专横的雇主，它没有用它的定价权强迫司机接受不公平的条款。

protracted
[prəˈtræktɪd, proʊˈ-]

adj. 延长的，拖延的

记 pro (=front) + tract (=draw) + ed → 拉长的

例 They reached an agreement after protracted negotiations. 经过漫长的谈判之后，他们终于达成了一项协议。

List 4

justification
[ˌdʒʌstɪfɪˈkeɪʃn]

n. 正当理由，合理解释

例 I can see no possible justification for any further tax increases. 我看不出还能提出什么理由来加税了。

扩 justifiable *adj.* 有理由的，情有可原的
unjustifiable *adj.* 无法接受的

reprisal
[rɪˈpraɪzl]

n. 1. 报复；2. 夺回

例 1. Most who spoke about it did so on the condition of anonymity, fearing reprisals. 多数愿意谈论此事的人都要求匿名，他们害怕报复。
2. It is true that the business economy of the world is mainly a system of reprisals. 确实，这个世界上的商业经济无非就是一个交换系统。

invalidate
[ɪnˈvælɪdeɪt]

v. 1. 证明…错误；2. 使无效

例 1. This new piece of evidence invalidates his version of events. 这项新的证据证明他对事情的描述是错误的。
2. An official decree invalidated the vote in the capital. 一份官方法令宣布在首都举行的投票无效。

trite
[traɪt]

adj. 陈腐的，老一套的

例 The movie is teeming with obvious and trite ideas. 这部电影充斥着平铺直叙的陈腐观点。

officious
[əˈfɪʃəs]

adj. 爱指手画脚的

记 offic (=office) + ious → 办公 → 干预，指手画脚

例 After the boss told his workers what to do, his officious assistant stepped in to supervise. 当老板给员工布置完任务后，他那爱指手画脚的助理进来监督大家。

penury
[ˈpenjəri]

n. 贫困

记 联想 penny（便士）→ 不名一文 → 贫困

例 He was brought up in penury, without education. 他从小一贫如洗，没有受过教育。

扩 penurious *adj.* 贫穷的

labyrinth
[ˈlæbərɪnθ]

n. 迷宫，曲径

记 源于古希腊神话中的米诺斯迷宫，传说里面住着一头半人半牛的怪物。（见插图）

例 We lost our way in the labyrinth of streets. 我们在

迷宫式的街道上迷了路。
扩 labyrinthine *adj.* 迷宫般的

insipid
[ɪn'sɪpɪd]

adj. 1. 无味道的；2. 枯燥乏味的，无聊的
记 in (=not) + sip (=taste) + id → 不能喝的 → 无味道的
例 1. It tasted indescribably bland and insipid, like warmed cardboard. 这东西尝起来淡而无味至极，像加热过的纸板一样。
2. The group is an insipid imitation of the Beatles. 这个乐团不过是枯燥无味地模仿了甲壳虫乐队。

forestall
[fɔːr'stɔːl]

v. 先发制人，阻止
记 fore (=before) + stall (=stand) → 提前占据 → 预防
例 1. Women who forestall or forgo childbearing are also at higher risk for breast and other gynecological cancers. 女性若避孕或放弃抚育孩子，还将面临更高的乳腺和其他妇科癌症风险。
2. Today we need a new round of deep decarbonization to forestall climate change. 如今我们需要新一轮深入的去碳化来防止气候变化。

recapitulate
[ˌriːkə'pɪtʃuleɪt]

v. 概括
例 We understood your point, there's no need to recapitulate. 我们明白你的要点，没必要再重述。
扩 recapitulation *n.* 概括

persevere
[ˌpɜːrsə'vɪr]

v. 坚持，孜孜以求
记 per (=very) + severe (=strict) → 非常坚定地（进行）→ 坚持
例 Despite a number of setbacks, they persevered in their attempts to fly around the world in a balloon. 尽管面临很多挫折，他们还是坚持乘气球环游世界。
扩 persevering *adj.* 坚持不懈的
persevernce *n.* 毅力

profane
[prə'feɪn]

adj. 1. 亵渎的；2. 非宗教的；*v.* 亵渎，诋毁
记 谐音"泼粪"→ 亵渎
例 1. When Burns told the crowd that Trump is "pro-faith," someone shouted out from the audience "Trump is profane." 当伯恩斯告诉人群特朗普"有信仰"时，听众中有人喊"特朗普很恶心"。（见插图）

2. Cardinal Daly has said that churches should not be used for profane or secular purposes. 戴利主教已经说过，教堂不应该用于非宗教或世俗的目的。
3. They have profaned the long upheld traditions of the Church. 他们亵渎了教会长期以来的传统。

indelible
[ɪn'deləbl]

adj. 1. 难以忘怀的；2. 擦不掉的
记 in (=not) + del (=delete) + ible → 不能删除的 → 不能忘掉的
例 1. Her unhappy childhood left an indelible mark. 她不幸的童年留下了不可磨灭的痕迹。
2. While my time in Hong Kong was finite, its impression, and this ink, is indelible. 虽然我在香港呆的时间有限，但它给我留下的印象就像这墨水一样难以抹掉。

revert
[rɪ'vɜːrt]

v. 恢复
记 re (=back) + vert (=turn) → 变回去 → 恢复
例 After her divorce she reverted to her maiden name. 离婚以后，她重新用起娘家的姓氏。
扩 revertible *adj.* 可恢复的

inflated
[ɪn'fleɪtɪd]

adj. 1. 夸张的；2. 过高的，离谱的；3. 中空的，膨胀的
记 in + flat (=blow) + ed → 往里吹气的 → 夸张的，中空的

例 1. Fiat Chrylser is also facing a lawsuit from U.S. dealers alleging it inflated sales. 菲亚特·克莱斯勒目前还面临一桩法庭诉讼，美国的经销商指责它的销售量水分太大。
2. He has an inflated sense of his own importance. 他自视过高。
3. A football is shaped like an inflated pig's bladder. 足球被做成形似充气的猪膀胱。
扩 inflation *n.*（通货）膨胀

provident
['prɑːvɪdənt]

adj. 1. 审慎的，未雨绸缪的；2. 节俭的
记 pro (=before) + vid (=vision) + ent → 提前看到的 → 审慎的
例 1. He meant to go thoroughly armed, for he was a very provident old gentleman. 他本想全副武装，因为他是个非常审慎的老人。
2. Good harvests make men prodigal, bad ones provident. 好年景让人挥霍，坏收成让人节俭。
辨 providential *adj.* 天缘巧合的，及时的
improvident *adj.* 不节俭的，挥霍的

oligarchy
['ɑːləgɑːrki]

n. 1. 寡头政治，寡头国家；2. 寡头集团
记 把 olig 看作 only + archy (=rule) → 只有少数人的统治 → 寡头政治
例 1. We have the illusion of control, because some of us still exercise the franchise, but we live in an oligarchy. 我们误以为自己仍然有控制力，因为我们有些人还在行使选举权，但其实我们国家早已变成了寡头政治了。
2. The American government, which I would call the American oligarchy, is afraid of the American people. 我把美国政府称作美国寡头，它是害怕美国人民的。

fraudulent ['frɔːdʒələnt]	*adj.* 欺骗的 记 fraud (=cheat) + ulent → 欺骗的 例 Corrupt leaders were chosen in a fraudulent election. 腐败的领导人通过舞弊选举当选。 扩 fraudulence *n.* 欺骗
thwart [θwɔːrt]	*v.* 反对，阻挠 例 1. She was thwarted in her attempt to take control of the party. 她控制这个政党的企图受阻了。 2. Her ambition to become an artist was thwarted by failing eyesight. 她想成为艺术家的梦想由于视力衰减而破灭了。
innate [ɪ'neɪt]	*adj.* 天生的，本质的 记 in + nate (=born) → 一出生就有的 → 天生的 例 The findings were exhilarating, suggesting an innate regenerative mechanism in the body. 这一发现令人兴奋，它表明体内有一种天生的再生机制。
temperament ['temprəmənt]	*n.* 1. 气质，性情；2. 冲动，暴躁 记 temper (=mix) + a + ment → 各种性格的混合 → 气质 例 1. She's a dreamer and a romantic by temperament. 她生性异想天开，浪漫多情。 2. Mark does have a habit of allowing his temperament to get the better of him. 马克的确经常由着自己的性子来。 扩 temperate *adj.* 气候温和的；心平气和的 temperance *n.* 禁酒；节欲
prowess ['praʊəs]	*n.* 造诣，高超的技艺 例 Now Israel is looking to harness their technological prowess for the fight to protect Israel's international image. 现在以色列正试图利用它们的技术打击能力来保护其国际形象。
stringent ['strɪndʒənt]	*adj.* 1. 严格的；2. 银根紧的 记 string (=tight) + ent → 紧的 例 1. Its drug-testing procedures are the most stringent in the world. 其药物检测程序是世界上最严格的。 2. Argentina introduced stringent capital controls three years ago in order to protect its fast-dwindling foreign reserves. 阿根廷在 3 年前引入了紧缩的资本管控以保护其迅速减少的外汇储备。 扩 stringency *n.* 财政紧张
remorse [rɪ'mɔːrs]	*n.* 懊悔，自责 记 re (=back) + morse (=bite) → 反咬 → 懊悔 例 He was filled with remorse for not believing her. 他因为没有相信她而懊悔不已。 扩 remorseful *adj.* 懊悔的

sustenance
[ˈsʌstənəns]

n. 1. 食物，营养；2. 维持，保持

记 sustain（维持）的名词

例 1. There's not much sustenance in a bowl of soup. 一碗汤没多少营养。
2. Elections are essential for the sustenance of parliamentary democracy. 选举制度是维持议会民主所必不可少的。

insolence
[ˈɪnsələns]

n. 1. 粗野，傲慢；2. 无礼的行为

例 1. Her insolence cost her her job. 她的蛮横态度使她丢了工作。
2. Pupils could be excluded from school for insolence. 学生可能会因目无师长而被开除。

扩 insolent *adj.* 傲慢的，粗野的

stipulate
[ˈstɪpjuleɪt]

v. 规定，明确要求

记 可能与 staple（钉书钉）同源 → 钉在一起 → 规定

例 A delivery date is stipulated in the contract. 合同中规定了交货日期。

扩 stipulation *n.* 规定

timidity
[tɪˈmɪdəti]

n. 畏缩，懦弱

记 timid (=fear) + ity → 胆怯，缺乏勇气

例 He was soon disillusioned by the government's timidity on social reform. 他不久就因政府在进行社会改革时缩手缩脚而不抱幻想了。

扩 timid *adj.* 羞怯的，胆怯的

ramble
[ˈræmbl]

v. 1. 漫步；2. 漫谈，闲扯；3. 蔓生

记 与 roam（漫游）同源同义 → 漫谈，蔓生

例 1. We spent the summer rambling in Ireland. 我们花了一个夏天漫游爱尔兰。
2. He had lost track of what he was saying and began to ramble. 他忘了原先的话题，开始瞎扯起来。
3. Climbing plants rambled over the front of the house. 攀缘植物贴着房子正面的墙到处长。

muse
[mjuːz]

n. 1. 灵感，源泉；2. 沉思

记 来源于古希腊罗马神话中的九位文艺女神缪斯 Muse；music, museum, amusement 都是源于此

例 1. He felt that his muse had deserted him. 他觉得他已失去了创作灵感。
2. I sat quietly, musing on the events of the day. 我静静地坐着，沉思一天中所发生的事。

sober
[ˈsoʊbər]

adj. 1. 未醉的，清醒的；2. 冷静的；*v.* 变得冷静

例 1. I promised him that I'd stay sober tonight. 我答应过他，今晚我不会喝醉。
2. On sober reflection, I don't think I really need a car after all. 冷静地想了想以后，我觉得我其实并不需要车。

3. Stay here with us until you've sobered up. 你就待在我们这儿，等酒醒了再走。

扩 sobriety *n.* 未醉，清醒；持重，冷静

revoke
[rɪˈvoʊk]

v. 取消，废除

记 re (=back) + voke (=voice, call) → 唤回，取消

例 1. The EU is demanding that Canada revoke the legislation. 欧盟要求加拿大废除这一法律。

2. After the third accident, her driving license was revoked. 经过第 3 起事故后，她的驾驶证被吊销了。

扩 revocation *n.* 取消

irrevocable *adj.* 无法改变的

malicious
[məˈlɪʃəs]

adj. 恶毒的，怀有恶意的

例 He took malicious pleasure in telling me what she had said. 他幸灾乐祸地告诉我她说的那些话。

扩 malice *n.* 恶意，怨恨

indulgent
[ɪnˈdʌldʒənt]

adj. 1. 纵容的，放纵的；2. 宽容的

例 1. Sending people into space was too expensive, indulgent and, frankly, what was the point? 把人类送往太空代价太高，甚至有点太为所欲为了，但坦率说，有什么意义呢？

2. He could have shaved, and trimmed his indulgent mop of hair. 他可能刮过胡子了，并且剪了剪那一堆乱糟糟的（肆无忌惮地生长的）头发。

3. The law can be as weirdly indulgent as it is harsh. 法律可能是严酷的，但也同样可能宽容得离谱。

扩 indulgence *n.* 纵容；宽容

indulge *v.* 沉迷；放纵

peremptory
[pəˈremptəri]

adj. 1. 霸道的，不容分说的；2. 傲慢的

例 1. With a brief, almost peremptory gesture he pointed to a chair. 他做了一个简单的手势，近乎霸道地指着椅子。

2. Her peremptory tone angered me. 她傲慢的语气激怒了我。

irrational
[ɪˈræʃənl]

adj. 1. 不合逻辑的；2. 非理性的；*n.*［数］无理数

例 1. He became irrational as the fever got worse. 当高烧恶化的时候，他开始变得迷糊起来。

2. She had an irrational fear of cats. 她莫名其妙地害怕猫。

vindicate
[ˈvɪndɪkeɪt]

v. 1. 证明有理；2. 澄清，证明无罪

记 vin (=force) + dic (=say) + ate → 强有力的说 → 证明，澄清

例 1. I have every confidence that this decision will be fully vindicated. 我完全相信这一决定的正确性将得到充分证明。

2. New evidence emerged, vindicating him completely. 新证据出现了，证明他完全是无辜的。
扩 vindication *n.* 证实

kindred ['kɪndrəd]
n. 家人，亲属；*adj.* 类似的，相似的
记 kind + red → 同一种类的 → 亲属
例 1. He went out to sea, and never saw his kindred again. 他出海后再没看到过家人。
2. I knew I'd found a kindred spirit. 我知道我找到了志同道合的人。

rhetoric ['retərɪk]
n. 1. 花言巧语；2. 修辞（技巧）；3. 话语
例 1. It's not rhetoric to say that college students are not customers and that the university is not a business. 要说大学生不是顾客、大学也不是企业，这并不是花言巧语。
2. They seem to be waging a war of rhetoric, using anecdotes as ammunition. 他们好像发动了一场修辞的战争，用了大量的典故做弹药。

3. Tim Cook has pinned a lot of rhetoric on privacy and security. 提姆·库克说了很多关于隐私和安全的话。
扩 rhetorical *adj.* 反问的；花言巧语的；修辞的

rebuke [rɪ'bjuːk]
v. 指责，批评
例 The company was publicly rebuked for having neglected safety procedures. 公司因忽略了安全措施而受到公开批评。
同 reprimand

shrewd [ʃruːd]
adj. 1. 精明的，有眼光的；2. 判断得准的
例 1. She is a shrewd judge of character. 她看人看得很准。
2. I have a shrewd idea who the mystery caller was. 这个神秘的来访者是谁，我能猜个八九不离十。

multiplicity [ˌmʌltɪ'plɪsəti]
n. 多样性，很多
例 This situation can be influenced by a multiplicity of different factors. 当前的形势可能受到各种不同因素的影响。

refute [rɪ'fjuːt]
v. 反驳，否认
例 She refutes any suggestion that she behaved unprofessionally. 谁要是表示她不在行，她都予以反驳。
扩 refutation *n.* 反驳

retort [rɪ'tɔːrt]
v. 反驳，顶嘴；*n.* 回应，顶嘴
记 re (=back) + tort (=twist) → 拧回去 → 顶嘴
例 1. Sam retorted that it was my fault as much as his. 萨姆反驳说我和他同样有错。

2. Rose flushed with annoyance and seemed about to make a sharp retort. 罗斯恼红了脸，好像要准备说点什么反驳。

pique
[piːk]

n. 怨恨；*v.* 使恼怒，刺激
记 西班牙国家足球队队员皮奎（Pique）
例 1. When he realized nobody was listening to him, he left in a fit of pique. 他发觉他说话无人理睬，就愤然离去。
2. I was piqued by his rudeness. 我被他的无礼惹恼了。
扩 piqued *adj.* 不高兴的

serenity
[səˈrenəti]

n. 安详
记 女子名 Serena 本意“清晰、明亮、欢乐”
例 The hotel offers a haven of peace and serenity away from the bustle of the city. 酒店是一个宁静安详的好去处，让人远离市井的喧嚣。
扩 serene *adj.* 宁静的，平静的

headstrong
[ˈhedstrɔːŋ]

adj. 固执的，倔强的
例 He's young, very headstrong, but he's a good man underneath. 他年轻、任性，但骨子里是个好人。

synthetic
[sɪnˈθetɪk]

adj. 人造的，合成的；*n.* 合成物
例 1. Boots made from synthetic materials can usually be washed in a machine. 合成材料制成的靴子通常可以机洗。
2. The drug is a synthetic. 这种药是合成品。

constitution
[ˌkɑːnstəˈtuːʃn]

n. 1. 宪法，章程；2. 体质，体格；3. 构造
例 1. The right to free speech is guaranteed by the (U.S.) Constitution. 言论自由在（美国）宪法中获得了保证。
2. Only animals with strong constitutions are able to survive the island's harsh winters. 只有体格强壮的动物才能挺过岛上严寒的冬天。
3. What is the molecular constitution of the chemical? 这种化学品的分子构成是什么？
扩 constitutional *adj.* 宪法的；体格的
constitutionally *adv.* 符合宪法地；体质方面地

passion
[ˈpæʃn]

n. 1. 冲动；2. 激情；3. 非理性，盛怒；4. 喜好
例 1. The crime was committed in a fit of passion. 罪行是出于一时冲动。
2. She argued her case with considerable passion. 她相当激动地为自己的主张提出论据。
3. She flies into a passion if anyone even mentions his name. 哪怕是有人提到他的名字，她也会勃然大怒。
4. The English have a passion for gardens. 英国人酷爱花园。
扩 passionate *adj.* 情意绵绵的；狂热的

affair
[ə'fer]

n. 1. 公共或个人事务；2. 公共事件，新闻；3. 私通

例 1. She wanted to put her affairs in order before she died. 她想在去世前把自己的事务安排妥当。
2. The newspapers exaggerated the whole affair wildly. 报章毫无根据地夸大了整个事件。
3. She is having an affair with her boss. 她跟老板有暧昧关系。

aristocratic
[əˌrɪstə'krætɪk]

adj. 贵族的

记 Aristotle（亚里士多德）本指最好的；aristo (=best) + crat (=rule) + ic → 最好的统治的 → 贵族的

例 He laughed it off with aristocratic indifference. 他带着贵族式的漠然对其一笑置之。

扩 aristocracy *n.* 贵族统治
aristocrat *n.*（一个）贵族

remark
[rɪ'mɑːrk]

n. 1. 评述，言论；2. 引人注目；*v.* 评论

记 re (=again) + mark → 一再标记 → 引人注目

例 1. He made a number of rude remarks about the food. 关于这里的食物他说了许多无礼的评论。
2. The exhibition contains nothing that is worthy of remark. 这次展览没有任何值得看的东西。
3. The judges remarked on the high standard of entries for the competition. 众评委说参赛作品水准很高。

扩 remarkable *adj.* 引人注目的，非凡的

magistrate
['mædʒɪstreɪt]

n. 地方执法官，治安官

例 A U.S. magistrate ordered Apple to produce software that would give investigators access to the iPhone at issue. 一名美国法官命令苹果公司推出软件让调查人员能够获取 iPhone 中的数据。（见插图）

扩 magisterial *adj.* 地方法官的；威严的
magistracy *n.*（统称）地方行政官

necessity
[nə'sesəti]

n. 1. 必要；2. 必需品；3. 必然性

例 1. We were discussing the necessity of employing more staff. 我们在讨论是否需要雇用更多员工。
2. Many people cannot even afford basic necessities such as food and clothing. 许多人甚至买不起食物和衣服之类的基本必需品。
3. Living in London, he felt, was an unfortunate necessity. 他觉得在伦敦生活是迫于无奈。

supreme
[suː'priːm]

adj. 1. 至高无上的；2. 最大的，最终的

记 supre (=super, above) + me → 最高级的

例 1. The Constitution vests in the President the power to appoint judges to the Supreme Court.（美国）宪法赋予总统任命最高法院大法官的权力。

2. She smiled with supreme confidence. 她充满自信地微微一笑。

扩 supremacy *n.* 至高无上；最高地位

scarcely
['skersli]

adv. 1. 几乎不，勉强；2. 刚一…就；3. 不可能

例 1. Scarcely a week goes by without some new scandal in the papers. 报上几乎周周都会登出新的丑闻。

2. Scarcely had the game started when it began to rain. 比赛才开始就下起雨来了。

3. She could scarcely complain, could she? 她压根儿没什么好抱怨的，是不是？

provision
[prə'vɪʒn]

n. 1. 提供；2. 准备；3. 供应，粮食；4. 规定，条款

记 provide 的名词

例 1. There is no provision for anyone to sit down here. 这里没有可坐的地方。

2. You should make provision for things going wrong. 你要采取措施，以防不测。

3. We brought enough provisions to last the entire trip. 我们带的食物够吃一路的。

4. Under the provisions of the lease, the tenant is responsible for repairs. 按契约规定，房客负责房屋维修。

扩 provisional *adj.* 暂时的；临时的

oblige
[ə'blaɪdʒ]

v. 1. 强迫，迫使；2. 帮忙，效劳；3. 感激

例 1. Broadcasters are obliged to provide due impartiality, and the BBC's guidelines require a "broad balance" of views. 广播公司有义务维持适度的公正，而 BBC 的信条要求对观点保持"宽泛的平衡"。

2. Would you oblige me with some information? 拜托您给我透露点消息好吗？

3. I would be obliged if you could read it to us. 您若能把它读给大家听，我将不胜感激。

扩 obligation *n.* 义务，责任

obliging *adj.* 乐于助人的

jurisdiction
[ˌdʒʊrɪs'dɪkʃn]

n. 1. 司法权；2. 管辖范围

记 juris (=jury, judge) + dict (=order, speak) + ion → 裁决 → 司法权

例 1. The Court of Appeals exercised its jurisdiction to order a review of the case. 上诉法庭行使司法权，要求对案件进行重审。

2. Practice varies between different state jurisdictions. 不同的州法律在此事上的做法不同。

扩 jurist *n.* 法学家

jurisprudence *n.* 法学

assembly
[ə'sembli]

n. 1. 立法机构（尤指下院）；2. 集会，集会者；3. 组装，装配

例 1. The national assembly has voted to adopt the budget. 国民议会已表决通过预算。

2. He was to address a public assembly on the issue. 他要对公众集会发表演说谈论这个问题。
3. Putting the bookcase together should be a simple assembly job. 组装书橱应该是个简单的装配活。
扩 assemble *v.* 聚集；组装
assemblage *n.* 聚焦

consent
[kən'sent]

n. 1. 允许，批准；2. 同意，一致意见；*v.* 允许，批准
记 con (=together) + sent (=sense) → 共同的感觉 → 一致意见，同意
例 1. Children under 16 cannot give consent to medical treatment. 16 岁以下的儿童不得自行同意接受治疗。
2. She was chosen as leader by common consent. 大家一致同意选她为领导人。
3. He reluctantly consented to his daughter's marriage. 他勉强同意了女儿的婚事。

confederate
[kən'fedərət]

n. 同谋，同伙；*v.* 结盟；*adj.* 联盟的，同盟的
记 con (=together) + federate (=league) → 共同的同盟
例 The city was the last major Atlantic port to remain under confederate control, before falling to union forces in January 1865. 该城在 1865 年 1 月落入联邦军手中之前，曾是南部邦联控制的最后一个大西洋主要港口。

扩 confederation *n.* 联盟，联邦
confederacy *n.* 联盟，联邦

conceive
[kən'siːv]

v. 1. 想出，相像；2. 怀孕；3. 怀有，持有…想法，理解
记 con (=com-) + ceive (=hold, take) → 持有，怀有
例 1. He conceived the idea of transforming the old power station into an arts center. 他想出了把旧发电站改造为艺术中心的主意。
2. Their first child was conceived on their wedding night. 他们的第一个小孩是在新婚之夜怀上的。
3. The ancients conceived the earth as afloat in water. 古人认为地球飘浮在水里。
扩 conceivable *adj.* 可想像的，可信的
misconception *n.* 误解

treaty
['triːti]

n. 条约，协定
记 treat (=handle) + ty → 对事情的处理 → 协定
例 The country's warring factions have signed a peace treaty. 该国的交战双方签订了和平条约。

affection
[ə'fekʃn]

n. 1. 喜爱，钟爱；2. 爱情
例 1. She was held in deep affection by all her students. 她的学生都十分爱戴她。

2. Anne had two men trying to win her affections. 安妮有两个男人追求。
辨 affectation *n.* 假装，做作
扩 affectionate *adj.* 表示关爱的
affectionately *adv.* 关切地

tribunal
[traɪˈbjuːnl]

n. 裁判所，特别法庭
记 trib (=tribe) + unal → 部落首领 → 法官的座位 → 法庭
例 His case comes before an industrial tribunal in March. 他的讼案将于 3 月在劳资法庭受审。
扩 tribune *n.*（古罗马）保民官；讲坛

multitude
[ˈmʌltɪtuːd]

n. 1. 众多，大量；2. 群众；3. 人群
记 multi (=many) + tude → 很多
例 1. The region attracts tourists in their multitudes. 这个地区吸引大批游人。
2. It was an elite that believed its task was to enlighten the multitude. 精英阶层会认为自己的职责是启迪群众。
3. He preached to the assembled multitude. 他向聚集在那里的民众布道。

execution
[ˌeksɪˈkjuːʃn]

n. 1. 处决；2. 实行，执行；3. 表演，制作
例 1. He faced execution by hanging for murder. 他因谋杀罪要以绞刑处死。
2. He had failed in the execution of his duty. 他未能履行职责。
3. Her execution of the piano piece was perfect. 她把那段钢琴曲演奏得非常完美。

inquiry
[ˈɪnkwəri, ɪnˈkwaɪəri]

n. 1. 研究；2. 探寻，审问；3. 调查
记 in (=into) + quiry (=ask) → 深入询问 → 探寻
例 1. Further inquiry showed that he had visited the city twice before. 进一步的调查表明他之前曾去过该市两次。
2. She refused to answer inquiries from the media about her marriage. 她拒绝回答媒体提出的婚姻问题。
3. The police are conducting an inquiry into his death. 警方正在调查他的死因。
扩 inquire *v.* 审问；调查

sentiment
[ˈsentɪmənt]

n. 1. 观点，看法；2. 伤感，哀伤
记 sent (=sense) + iment → 感觉到的东西 → 看法，伤感（的感情）
例 1. Public sentiment is against any change to the law. 公众反对对该法律作任何修改。
2. There is no room for sentiment in business. 在生意场上心肠不能软。
扩 sentimental *adj.* 伤感的；情感的

amendment
[ə'mendmənt]

n. 1. 修改，修订；2.（美国宪法的）修正案

例 1. Parliament passed the bill without further amendment. 议会未作进一步修改便通过了法案。

2. The 19th Amendment gave women the right to vote. 第 19 修正案赋予妇女选举权。

defect
['di:fekt, dɪ'fekt] *n.*
[dɪ'fekt] *v.*

n. 缺陷；*v.* 背叛，投敌

记 源于 desert（抛弃）→ 抛弃一党（国）投向另一方

例 1. This small defect greatly reduces the diamond's value. 这个小瑕疵降低了这枚钻石的价值。

2. The reporter defected to another TV network. 这名记者转投了另一家电视台。

扩 defection *n.* 背叛，投敌

defective *adj.* 有缺点的，有瑕疵的

disposed
[dɪ'spoʊzd]

adj. 1. 倾向于，乐意；2. 对…有好感（或恶感）

例 1. You're most welcome to join us if you feel so disposed. 你若有意参加，我们非常欢迎。

2. She seems favorably disposed to the move. 她似乎对这一行动持赞同态度。

扩 disposition *n.* 性情；倾向，意向

indisposed *adj.* 不能做某事的，不愿的

acquaint
[ə'kweɪnt]

v. 使熟悉，使了解

例 You will first need to acquaint yourself with the filing system. 你首先需要熟悉文件归档方法。

扩 acquaintance *n.* 泛泛之交；认识；了解

inferior
[ɪn'fɪriər]

adj. 1. 较差的，次的；2. 低级别的

例 1. Modern music is often considered inferior to that of the past. 现代音乐常被认为不如过去的。

2. The judges voted to overturn a ruling made by an inferior court. 法官们表决推翻了下级法院的一项判决。

扩 inferiority *n.* 劣质；低等

despotism
['despətɪzəm]

n. 1. 暴政，独裁；2. 暴政国家

例 1. The people have had to endure many years of despotism. 人民不得不忍受多年的暴政。

2. Greece is more properly viewed as the child of Byzantine and Ottoman despotism than of Periclean Athens. 希腊更像是拜占庭和奥斯曼独裁政权的后代，而不像伯里克利统治下雅典的后代。

扩 despot *n.* 暴君，专制君主

despotic *adj.* 残暴的

militia
[məˈlɪʃə]

n. 民兵组织，国民卫队

记 mil (=miles, soldier) + itia → 士兵 → 民兵组织

例 The troops will not attempt to disarm the warring militias. 部队并不打算解除战斗中的民兵武装。

enlightened
[ɪnˈlaɪtnd]

adj. 开明的，有见识的

记 en + lighten (=illuminate) + ed → 被照亮（启发）的 → 开明的

例 Their parents took an enlightened approach to child-rearing. 他们的父母采取了开明的教子方式。

扩 enlightenment *n.* 启发，开导

merit
[ˈmerɪt]

n. 1. 美德，优点；2. 功绩，长处；*v.* 应得，值得

例 1. I want to get the job on merit. 我要凭才能得到这份工作。

2. Qualifications and merit should carry the most weight in this and all other nominations. 在这次提名及其他提名中，资历和成就应该占最大的比重。

3. The case does not merit further investigation. 这个案子不值得进一步调查。

扩 meritocracy *n.* 精英领导体制

List 5

endeavor
[ɪn'devər]

v. 努力，尝试；*n.* 努力，尝试

例 1. They endeavored to create a government that truly serves its people. 他们努力要创造一个能真正为人民服务的政府。
2. Technology is the fastest-changing field of human endeavor. 技术领域是人类事业中变化最快的。

proceeding
[prə'siːdɪŋ]

n. 1. 诉讼（程序）；2. 过程

例 1. McLean did not appear in court during a proceeding related to the case on Monday. 麦考林周一并未出现在与此案有关的法庭上。
2. Each wore headphones during the proceeding to listen through a translator. 在整个进行过程中每个人都戴着耳机听译员的翻译。

pursuit
[pər'suːt]

n. 1. 追求；2. 追捕；3. 消遣，爱好

例 1. The upshot is that there are no signs that North Korea is thinking about giving up its pursuit of nuclear weapons. 结果表明朝鲜并无迹象要放弃追求核武器。
2. We drove away with two police cars in pursuit. 我们驾车离开，后面有两辆警车跟着追赶。
3. Whole cookbooks have been devoted to this arcane pursuit. 整本食谱书都在谈论这项难懂的兴趣（烹饪）。

扩 pursue *v.* 追求；探讨

undertake
[ˌʌndər'teɪk]

v. (undertook, undertaken) 1. 承担，从事；2. 承诺

例 1. It's part of the obligations you willingly undertake when you decide to have a family. 当你组建家庭时，你就会心甘情愿地承担这种责任。
2. He undertook to finish the job by Friday. 他答应星期五或之前完成这一工作。

扩 undertaking *n.* 任务；承诺

vest
[vest]

n. 背心，坎肩；*v.* 授予，赋予

例 1. One officer was struck in his bulletproof vest and suffered blunt force trauma. 一名警官被击中防弹背心，受到钝物击伤。
2. Congress is vested with the power to declare war. 国会有宣战权。

扩 vested *adj.* 无条件赋予的

confer
[kən'fɜːr]

v. (conferred, conferred) 1. 商讨，协商；2. 授予，颁发

记 con (=together) + fer (=bear) → 共同承受 → 商讨

例 1. They also complained that McAuliffe had not conferred with House or Senate leaders before making his pick. 他们还抱怨说麦克奥利弗在

作出选择之前并没有征询众议院或参议院领袖的意见。
2. Having the disease does not confer lifelong immunity. 患过这种病并不会带来终生的免疫。
扩 conference *n.* 大会
conferment *n.* 授予

attachment
[ə'tætʃmənt]

n. 1. 依恋，爱慕；2. 忠诚，拥护；3.（电子邮件的）附件
记 at (=to) + tach (=post) + ment → 粘在一起
例 1. They all have a deep attachment to the old house. 他们都很依恋老房子。
2. Scottish firms need to lose their attachment to Scotland to succeed. 苏格兰公司要想成功，应该要放弃死守在苏格兰。
3. A typical attack starts when a person opens an emailed link or attachment. 当有人打开带链接的电子邮件或者附件时，就会发生网络攻击。

扩 attached *adj.* 依恋的；附属的

restrain
[rɪ'streɪn]

v. 1. 阻止，管制；2. 自我约束
例 1. A judge decided that prosecutors didn't have enough evidence for a restraining order. 法官判定检察官没有足够的证据申请限制令。
2. She had to restrain herself from crying out in pain. 她只得忍住疼痛，不哭出来。
扩 restraint *n.* 约束力

subsist
[səb'sɪst]

v. 1. 维持生计；2. 存在，有效
例 1. They were subsisting on instant noodles and fruit, she said. 她说，他们（地震难民）当时正以速食面和水果充饥。
2. The terms of the contract subsist. 合同条款有效。
扩 subsistence *n.* 勉强维持生活

estate
[ɪ'steɪt]

n. 1. 私有土地，地产；2. 房地产；3. 个人财产，遗产
例 1. She receives rent from all the people whose cottages are on estate land. 她从地产上的农户那里收租金。
2. Wang made his fortune building real estate developments throughout China, mainly shopping malls and hotels. 王（健林）在中国各地建设房地产而致富，这些房地产主要是购物中心和酒店。
3. Her estate was left to her daughter. 她的遗产全部留给了女儿。

applicable
[ə'plɪkəbl, 'æplɪkəbl]

adj. 合适的，适用的
例 1. Much of the form was not applicable to me. 表格中很多部分不适用于我。
2. Businesses must comply with all applicable laws. 企业必须遵守所有相关法律。

hitherto
[ˌhɪðər'tuː]

adv. 迄今，直到某时

例 1. Robots are also becoming capable of manual labor that hitherto could be carried out only by dexterous humans. 机器人还能够完成一些迄今只能由熟练工人完成的手工作业。
2. Hitherto peaceful protest then developed into an armed revolt. 到那时为止和平的抗议活动演变成了武装暴动。

morality
[mə'ræləti]

n. 1. 道德，道义；2. 道德问题，道德程度

例 1. The morality of one society can seem alien to outsiders. 某个社会的道德可能在外人看来是很奇怪的。
2. The decision may be legally justified, but I question its morality. 这一决定可能是合法的，但我质疑它的道德层面。

扩 moral *adj.* 道德的
mores *n.* 风俗习惯，传统
moralist *n.* 卫道士，道德学家

precaution
[prɪ'kɔːʃn]

n. 预防措施

记 pre (=before) + caution (=care) → 提前小心 → 预防

例 1. Several leopards were later spotted in the city, causing 142 schools to shut down as a precaution. 城里又发现了几只猎豹，导致有142所学校关闭以防万一。
2. If Apple took precautions in applying the software, it wouldn't necessarily leak out. 如果苹果公司在安装这种软件时采取预防措施，就不一定会造成信息泄露。

obedience
[ə'biːdiəns]

n. 遵从，服从

例 1. Confucius stressed values such as filial piety and obedience to foster subservience to the emperors. 孔子强调的价值观是孝顺和服从，以培养对君主的恭顺。
2. He said that "we owe respect" to the country's laws, but "obedience" to God's law. 他（主教）说"我们应尊重"国家法律，但对上帝之法应"表示顺从"。

扩 obedient *adj.* 顺从的，服从的
disobedience *n.* 违抗

exert
[ɪg'zɜːrt]

v. 1. 运用，施加；2. 努力

例 1. On the one hand, there is plenty of evidence that the wealthy exert overwhelming influence over politics. 反言之，有大量证据证明富裕阶层对政治有绝对影响。
2. The magazine wrote, "he exerts himself fully by standing in front of an audience for an hour."（《时代》）杂志写道："他（特朗普）努力地在观众面前站立了一个小时。"

扩 exertion *n.* 努力；运用

perpetually
[pər'petʃuəli]

adv. 1. 持久地；2. 不断反复地

记 per (=through) +pet (=seek) + ual + ly → 彻底追求地 → 持久地

例 1. The lack of sunlight means the abyss is perpetually cold—usually

a degree or two above freezing. 缺少阳光意味着深海永远都是冷冰冰的——通常只比冰点高上一两度。
2. But in a city that is perpetually rebuilding itself, who controls the remnants buried underfoot? 但在一个反复重建的城市里，又是谁控制着脚下的废墟呢？

savage
['sævɪdʒ]

adj. 1. 凶恶的，损害严重的；2. 猛烈的；3. 野蛮的，未开化的

例 1. She had been badly hurt in what police described as "a savage attack". 她遭受袭击而身受重伤，警方称这是一次"野蛮的袭击"。
2. The article was a savage attack on the government's record. 文章对政府的业绩进行了猛烈的抨击。
3. It was the first time I had seen a brown man in a Hollywood film who was neither a servant nor a savage. 那曾是我第一次在好莱坞电影里看到一个既非奴仆亦非野蛮人的棕肤色人。

suffice
[sə'faɪs]

v. 1. 满足，足够；2. 胜任

记 sufficient 的动词

例 1. Suffice it to say we got to Mars 124 days later without strangling each other. 无须赘述，我们在 124 天后抵达火星，而没有互相掐死对方。
2. On Twitter on Monday, the Bataclan's owners wrote: "No words suffice to express the magnitude of our grief. 周一在推特上，巴塔克兰剧院的老板写道："没有言语能够表达得出我们的悲伤。"

notwithstanding
[ˌnɑːtwɪð'stændɪŋ, ˌnɑːtwɪθ'-]

prep./adv. 虽然，尽管

例 1. Notwithstanding some major financial problems, the school has had a successful year. 虽然有些重大的经费问题，这所学校一年来还是很成功。
2. Although there are some who oppose the plan, we will go through with it notwithstanding. 虽然有人反对这个方案，我们还是要把它执行下去。

thereof
[ˌðer'ʌv]

adv. 在其中，由此

例 Is the property or any part thereof used for commercial activity? 这一财产或其中任何部分是用于商业活动吗？

tranquil
['træŋkwɪl]

adj. 宁静的，安静的

记 tran (=over) + quil (=quiet) → 过度安静 → 宁静

例 She led a tranquil life in the country. 她过着恬静的乡村生活。

扩 tranquilly *adv.* 宁静地
tranquility *n.* 安静，安宁

ignorance
['ɪgnərəns]

n. 无知

记 i (=not) + gno (=know) + rance → 不知道 → 无知

例 She was kept in ignorance of her husband's activities. 关于丈夫的活

动，她一直蒙在鼓里。
扩 ignorant *adj.* 无知的

agreeable
[ə'griːəbl]

adj. 1. 愉悦的，宜人的；2. 欣然同意的；3. 可接受的
例 1. We spent a most agreeable day together. 我们在一起度过了非常愉快的一天。
2. Do you think they will be agreeable to our proposal? 你认为他们会爽快同意我们的提议吗？
3. The deal must be agreeable to both sides. 处理方法必须是双方都可以接受的。

dictate
['dɪkteɪt]

v. 1. 决定，支配；2. 强行规定；3. 口述
记 dict (=speak) + ate → 说话 → 命令，决定
例 1. It's generally your job that dictates where you live now. 一般说来，你住在什么地方是由你的工作决定的。
2. What right do they have to dictate how we live our lives? 他们有什么权利强行规定我们该怎样生活？
3. He dictated a letter to his secretary. 他向秘书口授信稿。
扩 dictation *n.* 口述；听写
dictatorship *n.* 独裁，专政

oppression
[ə'preʃn]

n. 1. 压迫，压制；2. 抑郁
例 1. I thought then that when people rise up against oppression they are bound ultimately to win. 我当时认为，当人民起来反抗压迫的时候，他们就一定会赢。
2. While observing her face, the dreams of the night before came back to mind, and without knowing why, I felt an oppression in my heart. 当我看着她的脸时，那天晚上的梦境又出现在我的脑海中，不知为什么，我感到心里很压抑。
扩 oppressive *adj.* 压迫的；闷热的

recollect
[ˌrekə'lekt]

v. 回忆
记 re (=again) + collect (=gather) → 再次收集 → 回忆
例 She could no longer recollect the details of the letter. 她想不起那封信的细节了。
扩 recollection *n.* 回忆，记忆力

distress
[dɪ'stres]

n. 1. 忧虑，疼痛；2. 遇险，遇难；*v.* 使忧虑，使疼痛
例 1. The newspaper article caused the actor considerable distress. 报上的文章给这位演员带来极大的痛苦。
2. It is a rule of the sea to help another boat in distress. 救助别的遇难船是海上的规则。
3. It was clear that the letter had deeply distressed her. 这封信显然使她极为悲伤。
扩 distressing *adj.* 令人苦恼的
distressed *adj.* 烦恼的，痛苦的

apprehend
[ˌæprɪˈhend]

v. 1. 逮捕；2. 理解，领会

记 ap (=to) + prehend (=hold) → 抓住（人、意思）

例 1. The boy threw the weapon down and was apprehended nearby with the help of a police dog. 那个男孩放下武器，在警犬的协助下受到逮捕。
2. According to Karasick, Watson can recognize irony and sarcasm—and properly apprehend the intended meaning. 根据卡拉思克的说法，沃森（电脑）能够听出讽刺，而且能正确理解其中的意思。

扩 apprehensive *adj.* 忧虑的，恐惧的
misapprehension *n.* 误会

suffrage
[ˈsʌfrɪdʒ]

n. 投票权

例 Women's suffrage was granted by the 19th Amendment in 1920. 在1920 年通过的（美国宪法）第 19 修正案赋予了女性选举权。

扩 suffragist *n.* 主张妇女参政者

indifference
[ɪnˈdɪfrəns]

n. 1. 不关心，无偏见；2. 不重要，无影响

例 1. Students were protesting what some saw as indifference to racial issues on the Columbia campus. 学生们抗议哥伦比亚大学校内对种族问题的漠视。
2. What she said is a matter of complete indifference to me. 她的话对于我来说完全无关紧要。

扩 indifferent *adj.* 漠不关心的；不很好的

superiority
[suːˌpɪriˈɔːrəti, -ˈɑːrəti]

n. 1. 优越性；2. 优越感，盛气凌人

例 1. Apple achieved its dominant market position thanks largely to the superiority of products like the iPhone. 苹果公司今天之所以能取得市场主导地位，很大程度上应归功于 iPhone 这类产品的优越性。
2. Feminism is about giving the sexes respect and equal treatment, not replacing male superiority with female superiority. 女性主义是给予两性尊重与平等对待，而不是用女性至上来取代男性至上。

扩 superior *adj.* 占优势的；高傲的

engagement
[ɪnˈgeɪdʒmənt]

n. 1. 约定；2. 战斗，交战；3. 了解，密切关系

例 1. He never turned down a speaking engagement or told a booster he was too busy to chat. 他从未拒绝过演讲邀约，或者告诉支持者说自己太忙无暇闲聊。
2. The general tried to avoid an engagement with the enemy. 将军竭力避免与敌军交火。
3. The president has said repeatedly the way to rebuild the U.S.-Cuba relationship is by people-to-people engagement. 总统一再强调说，重建美国 - 古巴关系依赖于人民之间的互相了解。

扩 engaging *adj.* 有趣的，迷人的

anarchy
[ˈænərki]

n. 1. 无政府状态；2. 混乱，无序

记 an (=without) + arch (=leader) + y → 没有统治者的 → 无政府状态

例 1. It appears no one is safe from a growing state of anarchy. 似乎没人能在一种无政府状态中幸免。

2. Clinton fatigue among Democrats is one thing, but the total anarchy in the Republican Party is quite another.（希拉里·）克林顿在民主党内的审美疲劳是一回事，而共和党内部的混乱又是另一回事。

扩 anarchical *adj.* 无政府的

administer
[əd'mɪnɪstər]

v. 1. 管理，治理；2. 执行；3. 给予，提供；4. 施用（药物）

记 ad (=to) + minister (=serve) → 提供服务 → 管理，执行

例 1. The document stipulated that henceforth this area should be administered by Egypt. 这一文件约定自此以后该地区由埃及管理。

2. The College Board said that 58 percent of the students who took the SAT when it was last administered in January paid for test preparation. 美国大学理事会说，在一月份主办的考试中有 58% 的学生参加过付费培训。

3. The teacher has the authority to administer punishment. 老师有权处罚。

4. The study focused on 20 cancer drugs that are infused—administered intravenously or injected—by doctors' offices or hospitals. 这一研究着重于医生或医院使用的 20 种癌症药物，包括静脉注射和打针给药。

扩 administrative *adj.* 管理的，行政的

maladministration *n.* 管理不善

utility
[juː'tɪləti]

n. 1. 公用事业；2. 实用，效用

记 比反义词 futility（无效）只少一个字母 f

例 1. Many of these people are in danger of having their utilities shut off for nonpayment. 有些人由于付不起帐而面临断水断电。

2. Some experts question the utility of the procedure. 一些专家质疑这一程序的有效性。

扩 utilize *v.* 使用，运用

peculiarly
[pɪ'kjuːliərli]

adv. 1. 特别，不寻常地；2. 独特地；3. 奇怪地

例 1. At its core, the company remains a peculiarly German enterprise. 这家公司的内在仍然是一个非常德国化的企业。

2. Air pollution caused by diesel engines is, for now, a peculiarly European problem. 柴油发动机造成的空气污染目前是欧洲独有的问题。

3. Here is a selection of photos of some peculiarly shaped fruits and vegetables. 这些照片上都是些奇形怪状的水果蔬菜。

livid
['lɪvɪd]

adj. 1. 暴怒的，狂怒的；2. 乌青色的

例 1. My parents would be livid if they found out I'd had this conversation and might end contact with me altogether. 如果让我父母知道我跟你说过这番话，他们一定会暴跳如雷，甚至跟我断绝关系。

2. He looked carefully at Harry, his eyes lingering on the scar that stood out, livid, on Harry's forehead. 他（马人）仔细地看着哈利·波特，他的目光停留在哈利前额突起而乌青的疤痕上。

presume
[prɪˈzuːm]

v. 1. 假定，假设；2. 推定

例 1. Jeb Bush, once a presumed favorite for the nomination, bowed to reality and suspended his campaign. 杰布·布什这位之前被认定的提名热门人选向现实屈服了，退出了竞选。

2. She is presumed dead, but her body has never been found. 虽然她被推定死亡，但她的尸体还未被找到。

扩 presumption *n.* 假设；可能的事

presumable *adj.* 可假设的

gratification
[ˌɡrætɪfɪˈkeɪʃn]

n. 满足，满意

记 grat (=grace) + ifi + cation → 使高兴 → 满足

例 There's no denying that we live in a world full of instant gratification. 毫无疑问，在我们生活的世界中，到处都是只顾眼前利益。

扩 gratified *adj.* 满足的

qualification
[ˌkwɑːlɪfɪˈkeɪʃn]

n. 1. 资格，学历；2. 限定条件

例 1. The clock is ticking on her Olympic dream and the next few events are crucial to gain the necessary points for qualification. 距她实现奥运会梦想的时间紧迫，而接下来的几次赛事对获得奥运资格至关重要。

2. Previous teaching experience is a necessary qualification for this job. 过往的教学经验是担任这项工作的必备条件。

扩 qualified *adj.* 有条件的；具备学历的

disqualification *n.* 取消资格

session
[ˈseʃn]

n. 1. 一段时间；2. 开庭，会议；3. 学年

例 1. Belgium have canceled Tuesday's training session out of respect for the victims of the Brussels attacks. 比利时队已经取消了周二的训练时间，向布鲁塞尔恐怖袭击的遇难者致哀。

2. Georgia's House and Senate have full calendars as they near the end of the legislative session. 佐治亚州参众两院在立法会议即将结束之前议程满满当当。

3. School will be back in session at the beginning of September. 学校将在九月份开学。

functionary
[ˈfʌŋkʃəneri]

n. 公职人员，官员

例 Reporters are not so unlike functionaries after all. 毕竟，记者也并不是跟公职人员完全两样。

civility
[səˈvɪləti]

n. 1. 礼貌，客气；2. 客气话

记 civil 除了表“国内的”，还表示“平民的”、“有礼貌的”

例 1. Staff members are trained to treat customers with civility at all times. 员工经过培训，要做到任何时候都以礼待客。

2. They greeted each other with the usual exchange of civilities. 他们像平时那样互相说着客套话。

扩 civilly *adv.* 民事方面；礼貌地

uncivil *adj.* 失礼的，粗鲁的

procure
[prəˈkjʊr]

v. 设法获得
记 与 secure 同根同义
例 Travel agencies offer to procure passports and visas for hundreds of dollars apiece. 旅行社承诺以每人几百美元的价格办好护照和签证。
扩 procurable *adj.* 可获得的

compliment
[ˈkɑːmplɪmənt]

n. 1. 赞扬；2. 致意，问候；*v.* 赞美
例 1. Never underestimate the power of a simple compliment. 绝不要低估赞美的力量。
2. Please accept these flowers with the compliments of the manager. 请接受经理送的鲜花。
3. People should not compliment others for weight loss unless the person losing weight is happy about it and wants to talk about it. 人们不应恭喜别人减肥成功，除非那个减肥的人对此乐意而且愿意就此讨论。
扩 complimentary *adj.* 赞美的；赠送的

patriot
[ˈpeɪtriət]

n. 爱国者，爱国精神
记 patri (=father) + ot → 爱父亲，爱国家
例 They deserve to be laid to rest in one of our nation's most prominent cemeteries with their fellow patriots. 他们值得与同样的爱国者们一起葬在我国最显赫的公墓里。
扩 patriotic *adj.* 爱国的
patriotism *n.* 爱国主义，爱国精神

vanity
[ˈvænəti]

n. 1. 自负，虚荣；2. 渺小，不重要
记 vain（虚荣的）的名词
例 1. The lion was often a symbol of vanity and masculine power. 狮子通常代表虚荣和雄性力量。
2. His story demonstrated the vanity of human ambition in the face of death. 他的事迹表明了个人抱负在死亡面前的微不足道。
辨 vein *n.* 静脉；纹理
扩 vainly *adv.* 徒劳地

bestow
[bɪˈstoʊ]

v. 给予，授予
记 be + stow (=stand, put) → 放在 → 给予
例 Green tea, one of those tested, bestowed no health or life span benefits, despite its popularity. 其中受测的绿茶并不会带来什么健康或寿命方面的好处，尽管它很受欢迎。
扩 bestowal *n.* 授予

liable
[ˈlaɪəbl]

adj. 1. 有法律责任的；2. 可能的；3. 可能受…影响
例 1. Guidelines from Europe's governing body state that host clubs are liable for order and security inside and around the stadium. 欧洲管理部门的准则说，主办方俱乐部有责任维持赛场内外的安全和秩序。
2. We're all liable to make mistakes when we're tired. 人在疲劳时都可

能出差错。
3. You are more liable to injury if you exercise infrequently. 不经常运动就更容易受伤。
扩 liability *n.* 责任；债务

dispense
[dɪ'spens]

v. 1. 分配；2. 施予，提供
记 dis (=out) + pens (=pay) → 花出去 → 分配，分发
例 1. The machine dispenses a range of drinks and snacks. 这台机器发售各种饮料和小吃。
2. Working machines dispense hot cans of coffee or tea and cold soft drinks. 这些运行的机器可以提供罐装热咖啡、热茶及冰镇软饮料。
扩 dispensable *adj.* 可有可无的
indispensable *adj.* 不可或缺的，必要的

resort
[rɪ'zɔːrt]

n. 1. 诉求，求助；2. 应急措施；*v.* 诉诸
记 re (=again) + sort (=go out) → 向外寻求 → 诉诸
例 1. There are hopes that the conflict can be resolved without resort to violence. 冲突有望不需要诉诸武力而得到解决。
2. The warnings emphasize that prescription painkillers should be used only when necessary, and as a last resort. 警示语强调，处方镇痛片只能在必要时使用，并且只能作为应急措施。
3. We may have to resort to using untrained staff. 我们也许只能使用未受过训练的员工了。

exceedingly
[ɪk'siːdɪŋli]

adv. 极其，非常
例 1. The ore mined by the native workers and African slaves made many Spaniards exceedingly wealthy. 由当地工人和非洲奴隶开采的矿石曾让许多西班牙人极其富有。
2. I have a case that troubles me exceedingly. 我有一件非常棘手的案子。

deliberation
[dɪˌlɪbə'reɪʃn]

n. 1. 考虑，细想；2. 从容，审慎
记 de (=entirely) + liber (=scale) + ation → 象秤一样平衡、衡量 → 思量
例 1. Jurors weren't shown the video during the trial but were permitted to see it during deliberations. 陪审员们在审判期间并未看到录像，但获准在商议时观看。
2. She signed her name with great deliberation. 她非常审慎地签上了自己的名字。
扩 deliberative *adj.* 审议的，起审议作用的

municipal
[mjuː'nɪsɪpl]

adj. 市政的，地方政府的
记 muni (=community) + cipal → 社区的 → 市政的
例 Last year women in Saudi Arabia cast their votes for the first time in municipal elections. 去年沙特阿拉伯女性首次在地方举行中投票。
扩 municipality *n.* 自治区，自治市

whence
[wens]

adv. 从何处

例 They returned whence they had come. 他们从哪里来又回到哪里去了。

sway
[sweɪ]

v. 1.（使）摇摆；2. 说服，使相信；*n.* 控制，影响

例 1. They danced rhythmically, swaying their hips to the music. 他们伴着音乐扭动屁股，有节奏地跳舞。

2. She wasn't swayed by his good looks or his clever talk. 他相貌不凡，谈吐风趣，但她不为其所动。

3. Rebel forces hold sway over much of the island. 该岛很大一部分控制在叛军手里。

intrigue
[ɪn'tri:g]

v. 1. 激起兴趣；2. 密谋；*n.* 1. 密谋；2. 神秘气氛

记 in (=to) + trig (=trick, cheat) + ue → 骗来 → 使产生

例 1. The novelty of the situation intrigued him. 周围环境的独具一格令他着迷。

2. They were arrested for intriguing against the government. 他们因密谋反对政府而被捕。

3. For decades, law firms have been portrayed on television as realms of glamor and intrigue. 数十年以来，律师事务所在电视中一直被刻画成光彩与阴谋的国度。

4. Clinton's string of recent primary wins added another element of intrigue to the Supreme Court fight.（希拉里·）克林顿一连串的初选胜利给最高法院的斗争增加了一些神秘气氛。

inflict
[ɪn'flɪkt]

v. 打击，使遭受打击

记 in (=on) + flict (=strike) → 打在上面 → 打击

例 An autopsy determined more than 50 wounds had been inflicted on the toddler. 验尸报告表明这个孩子受到了至少 50 处外伤。

扩 infliction *n.* 打击

gratitude
['grætɪtu:d]

n. 感谢

记 grat (=grace) + itude → 感谢（grace 也有"恩典"之意）

例 I want to say particular words of gratitude today to the women of the wartime generation. 我今天想说一些特别的话来感谢战争年代的女性们。

扩 ingratitude *n.* 忘恩负义

misery
['mɪzəri]

n. 1. 痛苦；2. 穷困

例 1. The centurion stabs a crucified man to put him out of his misery. 百夫长刺向十字架上的人，了结了他的痛苦。

2. The vast majority of the population lives in utter misery. 这里的人绝大多数生活在极度贫困之中。

扩 miserable *adj.* 痛苦的；可怜的；脾气坏的

miserably *adv.* 可怜地，痛苦地

List 5

concurrence
[kən'kɜːrəns]

n. 1. 同意，一致；2. 同时发生

记 con (=together) + cur (=run, happen) + rence → 共同发生

例 1. In the last term, he filed 30 dissents and concurrences, far more than any other justice. 在最后一个任期内，他发出了30份异议和同意的意见，比其他法官都多。
2. The concurrence of their disappearances had to be more than coincidental. 他们同时失踪肯定不仅仅是巧合。

despair
[dɪ'sper]

n. 绝望；*v.* 绝望

例 1. With this faith, we will be able to hew out of the mountain of despair a stone of hope. 带着这种信仰，我们将能够从绝望之山上采下希望之石。（马丁·路德·金）
2. It's easy to despair about this election season—to think that Trump voters are all psychopaths. 一想到特朗普的支持者们都是精神病，我们很容易对这次选举感到绝望。

扩 desperate *adj.* 绝望的；铤而走险的
desperado *n.* 亡命之徒

spiritual
['spɪrɪtʃuəl]

adj. 1. 精神的；2. 宗教的

例 1. Doctors must consider the emotional and spiritual needs of their patients. 医生必须考虑病人心理和精神上的需求。
2. I regularly consult our pastor about spiritual matters. 我时常向牧师寻求宗教事务的帮助。

扩 spiritually *adv.* 精神方面地

irresistible
[ˌɪrɪ'zɪstəbl]

adj. 1. 不可遏止的；2. 极诱人的

例 1. Globalization was irresistible, the argument went, and free trade was always and in all situations a good thing. 辩论称，全球化是不可遏止的，并且自由贸易无论在哪方面来说都是好事。
2. The bright colors were irresistible to the baby. 那些鲜艳的色彩逗得婴儿直想去抓。

扩 irresistibly *adv.* 不可遏止地

dominion
[də'mɪniən]

n. 1. 管辖，支配；2. 领土

记 与 dominate（主宰）同根

例 1. At one point, the Spanish king even claimed sole dominion over snow so he could enjoy sorbet. 曾经一度西班牙国王甚至宣布所有的雪都是他的，这样他就可以享受雪糕了。
2. The whole island is the king's dominion. 整座岛屿都是国王的领土。

decree
[dɪ'kriː]

n. 1. 法令，政令；2. 判决；*v.* (decreed, decreed) 颁布，决定

记 与 decide 同源

例 1. Almost all who addressed the council spoke in favor of signing the decree. 几乎所有在议会上发言的人都赞同签署这项法令。
2. She tried to have the court's decree reversed. 她试图推翻法院的判决。

3. Sometimes I just pick the nearest Friday or Saturday and decree that to be my "non-birthday". 有时我（2月29日出生的人）随便挑个最近的周五或周六，把它定为我的"非生日"。

caste
[kæst]

n. 1. 社会等级；2.（印度的）种姓

记 cast + e → 塑造出来的 → 等级

例 1. Caste is defined primarily by social honor attained through personal lifestyle. 社会等级制度主要是通过个人生活方式赢得的社会荣誉来确定。

2. The unrest was led by a privileged group in India's society, still stratified by its ancient caste system. 这场骚乱由印度社会的特权阶层发起，它仍被古代的种姓制度所分化。

utter
[ˈʌtər]

adj. 完全的，十足的；*v.* 出声，说

记 ut (=out) + ter → 发出 → 出声

例 1. A black woman standing next to him gave him a look of utter disbelief. 一位站在他旁边的黑人妇女以一种完全不信任眼神看了他一眼。

2. It's OK to utter the names of Jesus, Moses and Mohammed in front of school children, for education's sake. 出于教育目的，在学生面前说出耶稣、摩西和穆罕默德的名字是允许的。

扩 utterly *adv.* 完全地，彻底地

utterance *n.* 话语；表达

feeble
[ˈfiːbl]

adj. (feebler, feeblest) 1. 虚弱的；2. 无效的，无力的

例 1. Inside a rodent's nose are up to 1,000 different types of olfactory receptors, whereas humans only have a feeble 100 to 200 types. 在啮齿类动物的鼻腔内有多达1000种不同的嗅觉接收器，而人类只有屈屈100至200种。

2. McConnell's feeble explanation is that he does not want to limit the next president's options. 麦康内尔蹩脚的解释就是他并不想限制下任总统的选择。

辨 fable *n.* 寓言

扩 feebly *adv.* 虚弱地

feebleness *n.* 虚弱

agitation
[ˌædʒɪˈteɪʃn]

n. 1. 焦虑不安；2. 骚动

记 agi (=act) + tation → 动来动去的 → 骚动

例 1. As the election draws near, intrigues intensify, and agitation increases and spreads. 随着选举临近，紧张加剧，焦虑不安增加、扩散。

2. Some members of the union have been agitating for a strike. 部分工会成员一直骚动不安准备罢工。

扩 agitated *adj.* 焦虑不安的

List 5

marrow
['mæroʊ]

n. 1. 骨髓；2. 精华

例 1. Transplant ultimately destroys not only the marrow's cancerous cells but healthy tissue as well. 移植最终不仅破坏了骨髓中的癌细胞，同时也破坏了健康细胞。

2. We're getting into the marrow of the film. 我们就要进入这部电影最精彩的部分了。

bosom
['bʊzəm]

n. 1. 胸部；2. 心底，怀抱；*adj.* 心爱的，亲爱的

例 1. Her index finger cradles the baby's head, a tiny foot rests on her bosom. 她的食指摇着婴儿的头，小脚靠在她的胸前。

2. He never spoke of his childhood as an orphan, but kept dark memories of those days in his bosom. 他从未提及过自己的孤儿童年，而把黑暗的记忆埋在心底。

3. Close friends of the PM's are not necessarily bosom buddies of the Parliamentary party. 首相的密友并不一定是议会里的亲密伙伴。

antiquity
[æn'tɪkwəti]

n. 1. 古代（古希腊古罗马）；2. 古老；3. 古董，文物

例 1. The statue was brought to Rome in antiquity. 这座雕像是古时运到罗马的。

2. A number of the monuments are of considerable antiquity. 有些历史遗迹相当古老。

3. The western appetite for antiquities has always been a motivation for others to loot them. 西方对文物的需求导致文物的偷盗行为。

扩 antique *adj.* 古老的；*n.* 古董

peril
['perəl]

n. 1. 危险；2. 危险的事，险情

例 1. Among people of color, economic peril has no effect on attitudes of racial resentment. 在有色人种当中，经济危险并不会影响他们对种族仇恨的态度。

2. They faced many perils in their journey through the region. 他们在此地的行程面临许多险情。

扩 perilous *adj.* 危险的，艰难的

dwell
[dwel]

v. 1. 居住，栖身；2. 思索，纠结于

例 1. For ten years she dwelled among the nomads of North America. 她在北美游牧民中生活了十年。

2. She says she is a person who does not like to dwell on bad things. 她说她并不是个喜欢去想坏事的人。

扩 dweller *n.* 居民

bound
[baʊnd]

adj. 1. 一定会的；2. 有义务的；3. 去往某地的；*v.* 跳跃

记 谐音“绑的”→为义务所缚的；谐音“蹦的”→跳跃

例 1. This fissure is bound to widen as IS comes under heavier pressure in Iraq and Syria. 随着“伊斯兰国”在伊拉克和叙利亚的压力越来越大，

这种裂缝定会加大。
2. You are bound by the contract to pay before the end of the month. 按照合同规定，你必须在月底前付款。
3. They both boarded the number 73 bus bound for Belgrade's northwestern suburbs. 他们都登上了去往贝尔格莱德西北郊区的 73 路汽车。
4. We saw three deer bound over the fence into the woods. 我们看见三只鹿跳过篱笆进了树林。

institute
[ˈɪnstɪtuːt]

v. 建立，实行；*n.* 机构
例 1. Bourguiba instituted universal education and advanced women's rights beyond those in other Arab countries. 布尔吉巴（突尼斯总统）推行了全民教育，并把妇女权益推进到其他阿拉伯国家未达到的高度。
2. They founded an institute for research into the causes of mental illness. 他们成立了一家机构来研究心理疾病。
扩 institution *n.* 机构；制度

anticipate
[ænˈtɪsɪpeɪt]

v. 1. 预料；2. 期盼；3. 早于…行动
记 anti (=before) + cip (=take) + ate → 提前掌握 → 预料
例 1. And no one anticipated the strength of the eruption, which spewed 540 million tons of ash into the air and killed 57 people. 没人曾料到火山喷发的威力，它向大气中喷出了 5.4 亿吨火山灰，致 57 死亡。
2. But there's been no hint of any blockbuster developments, such as last year's highly anticipated Apple Watch debut. 但此次（发布会）并未暗示有任何夺人眼球的新技术，比如像去年那个众所期待的苹果手机的发布。
3. When Scott reached the South Pole he found that Amundsen had anticipated him. 斯科特到达南极时发现阿蒙森已先到过那里。
扩 anticipation *n.* 预期；盼望

perfection
[pərˈfekʃn]

n. 1. 完美；2. 最后完善
记 perfect 本身有动词“完善”之意
例 1. "You are always searching for perfection, always learning, always growing, inside and outside," he said. 他说：“你一直在追求完美，总是在学习，成长，在各个方面。”
2. They have been working on the perfection of the new model. 他们一直在努力完善新型号。
扩 perfectionist *n.* 完美主义者
imperfection *n.* 缺点，瑕疵

List 6

caprice
[kə'priːs]

n. 任性，反复无常

例 1. Talent and intelligence never inoculated anyone against the caprice of the fates. 天才和智慧绝不能让任何人免受命运的捉弄。

2. Its fortune is subject to fashion and whim, weather and the caprice of travelers. 它（安提瓜）的命运取决于流行趋势，天气还有旅行者一时的兴致和想法。

扩 capricious *adj.* 任性的，变幻莫测的

mingle
['mɪŋgl]

v. 1. 使混合；2. 相交往，混杂其中

记 ming (=among) + le → 在其中 → 混合，混杂

例 1. The sounds of laughter and singing mingled in the evening air. 笑声和歌声交织在夜空中。

2. The princess was not recognized and mingled freely with the crowds. 公主没有被人认出，随意混杂在人群之中。

扩 intermingle *v.* 混合

commingle *v.* 混合，掺和

behold
[bɪ'hoʊld]

v. (beheld, beheld) 看见

记 be + hold → 抓住 → 看见

例 1. Watching reports on the caucus felt much like beholding a fiery sports match. 观看政党会议的新闻犹如看一场激烈的体育比赛。

2. In painting and sculpture, the eye of the beholder lingers on the face and body of the beheld. 在绘画和雕塑作品中，观看者的眼睛在被观看者的脸上和身上流连。

扩 beholder *n.* 目击者

surrender
[sə'rendər]

v. 1. 投降；2.（被迫）交出，放弃；*n.* 投降

记 sur (=over) + render (=give back) → 交上去 → 投降

例 1. If Apple surrenders, Cook would have to assemble a new software team to carry out a government-mandated task. 如果苹果公司投降，那么库克不得不重新组建一支软件队伍，以执行政府要求的任务。

2. He agreed to surrender all claims to the property. 他同意放弃对那笔财产的一切权利要求。

3. They demanded (an) unconditional surrender. 他们要求无条件投降。

vacancy
['veɪkənsi]

n. 1.（职位的）空缺；2. 空房间

记 vacan (=void) + cy → 空缺

例 1. A vacancy may not be filled until after the next president takes office in January. 只有等一月新总统就职后这个空缺的（大法官）职位

才能补上。
2. This year hotels that usually are jammed had vacancies all summer. 今年那些往常爆满的旅店整个夏天都有空客房。
扩 vacant *adj.* 空着的；空缺的

lodge
[lɑːdʒ]

n. 小屋；*v.* 1. 正式提出（声明）；2. 寄住，借宿；3. 提供住宿
记 lodge (=log) → 木头 → 小木屋 → 借宿
例 1. Harry Truman, who was closest to the volcano, became nationally and even internationally famous for his refusal to leave his lodge. 住得离火山最近的人叫哈里·杜鲁门，他因为拒绝离开自己的小屋，而成了全国甚至全世界最著名的人。
2. His extradition is due to go ahead soon unless he lodges an appeal. 除非他提出上诉，否则他的认罪就要生效。
3. He lodged with Mrs. Brown when he arrived in the city. 他初到这座城市时租房住在布朗太太的家里。
4. The tourism industry took the biggest hit, losing some $45 million in hotel and lodging cancelations. 旅游业受到的打击最大，酒店和住宿取消造成了 4500 万美元的损失。
扩 lodging *n.* 住处

entrust, intrust
[ɪn'trʌst]

v. 委托，交付
记 en (=make) + trust → 给予信任 → 委托
例 Many Republicans were simply unwilling to entrust the presidency to a young first-term senator. 许多共和党人只是不愿意把总统之职交给一个年轻的只当过一届的参议员。
扩 entrustment *n.* 委托

boast
[boʊst]

v. 1. 自夸；2.（自豪地）拥有；*n.* 夸耀
例 1. Obama boasts that U.S. trade with the region has doubled during his presidency. 奥巴马吹嘘说在他的任期内，美国与该地区的贸易已经翻了一番。
2. Though it has not spread beyond Brazil's borders, it now boasts 2.8 million followers. 虽然它（教会）并没有超出巴西的国界，但它现在已经有 280 万信众了。
3. It was her proud boast that she had never missed a day's work because of illness. 她所引以自豪的是她从未因病而耽误过一天工作。
扩 boastful *adj.* 自吹自擂的

charter
['tʃɑːrtər]

n. 1. 宪章；2. 租赁（飞机、船）；*v.* 1. 包租（飞机、船）；2. 特许设立

记 charter = paper 文件 → 宪章；许可
例 1. *The Olympic Charter* forbids sex discrimination. 《奥林匹克宪章》禁止性别歧视。
2. From the visas to the charter flights, there is little that is straightforward about travel to Cuba for Americans. 美国人到古巴旅游，从签证到包机，什么都不方便。

3. They flew to Athens and then chartered a boat to the island. 他们先飞到雅典，然后租船去往该岛。
4. The city was chartered in 1837. 该市设立于 1837 年。

abide
[əˈbaɪd]

v. 1. 容忍；2. (abode, abode) 逗留，居住；3. (– by) 遵守

例 1. She lives easily with nature and not only abides squirrels in the attic but also aids and abets them. 她与大自然相处和谐，不仅能忍受阁楼里的松鼠，而且还帮助它们。
2. May joy and peace abide in us all. 愿我们大家都欢乐平安。
3. They are under surveillance and if they do not abide by the law, they will be charged. 他们处于监督之下，如果他们不遵守法律，他们将被指控。

扩 abiding *adj.* 持久的
abode *n.* 住所

nobility
[noʊˈbɪləti]

n. 1. 贵族；2. 高贵的品质

记 nob(le) (=knowable) + ility → 生来就闻名的 → 贵族

例 1. The ruler tried to convince the Roman people, particularly the nobility, to follow him—but it didn't work. 统治者试图劝服古罗马民众顺从，尤其是贵族们，但没什么用。
2. Even when under extreme stress, Armstrong projected an air of embattled nobility. 即便处于重压之下，阿姆斯特朗也能表现出一种受困时的高贵。

扩 noble *adj.* 高贵的；崇高的
ignoble *adj.* 不光彩的，卑劣的

barbarous
[ˈbɑːrbərəs]

adj. 1. 残酷的；2. 粗野的

记 barbar 是古希腊罗马人对蛮族的称呼，因听不懂对方的语言，拟声表示为 bar-bar-

例 1. The Democrats cry out for gun control as the solution to stop the barbarous killing. 民主党人呼吁控枪来制止这种残酷的枪击行为。
2. He thought the poetry of Whitman barbarous. 他认为惠特曼的诗歌太粗俗。

扩 barbarism *n.* 残酷；野蛮
barbarian *n.* 野蛮人
barbarity *n.* 暴行，残忍

constrain
[kənˈstreɪn]

v. 1. 强迫；2. 限制

记 con (=together) + strain (=draw tight) → 拉紧 → 限制

例 1. The evidence was so compelling that he felt constrained to accept it. 证据是那样的令人折服，他觉得不得不接受。
2. The GRE is much less time constrained, and most people are able to answer all questions in the time allowed. GRE 考试时间限制相对较少，多数人都能在规定的时间内答完题。

扩 constraint *n.* 限制；约束

fleet
[fliːt]

n. 舰队，船队；*adj.* 快速移动的

记 fleet (=flow)，形似 flee（逃跑）

例 1. The fleet will be decommissioned at the end of the month. 这支舰队将在本月底退役。

2. She is very fleet of foot. 她的脚步飞快。

扩 fleeting *adj.* 短暂的，闪现的

treasure
[ˈtreʒər]

v. 珍藏；*n.* 财富，珠宝

例 1. Dad says, you boys ought to treasure your mother's love. 老爸常说，你们这些男孩子们应该珍惜母爱。

2. Central Park is one of New York City's many treasures. 中央公园是纽约城的财富之一。

扩 treasurer *n.* 财务主管，财政部长

treasury *n.* 财政部；宝库

rouse
[raʊz]

v. 1. 唤醒；2. 使活跃，激起；3. 激怒

例 1. He states that the noise from passing wagons would "rouse a dozing seal—or an emperor." 他声称过往车辆的噪音能够"吵醒一个瞌睡的海豹，或者一个皇帝。"

2. In the early part of the twentieth century, nationalists used verse to rouse those who struggled for independence from Great Britain. 二十世纪早期，民族主义者用诗歌来唤起人们争取摆脱英国的独立运动。

3. Chris is not easily roused. 克里斯很少激动。

扩 rousing *adj.* 充满活力的；激励的

arouse *v.* 唤醒，激起，激发

complexion
[kəmˈplekʃn]

n. 1. 面色，肤色；2. 性质

记 complex (=mix) + ion → 各种气质的混合 → 肤色

例 1. Dark spots prevent your skin from reflecting light and gives you a dull complexion. 黑点会防止皮肤反射光线，能让你的肤色暗淡无光。

2. The complexion of the neighborhood has changed over the years. 多年来社区的面貌有所改变。

avail
[əˈveɪl]

v. 1. 有帮助，有益；2. 利用；*n.* 帮助

记 available 的动词

例 1. This knowledge availed her little. 知道这一点对她并无帮助。

2. To avail all these benefits, just register online. 要想得到所有这些好处，就在线注册吧。

3. I have tried several products to remove the stains, to no avail. 我试过了好几种产品来洗掉这些污渍，但没什么用。

扩 unavailing *adj.* 徒劳的

divine
[dɪˈvaɪn]

adj. 天赐的，神的；*v.* 猜测，领悟

记 本义为"解说神的旨意"→ 神的；猜测

例 1. Perhaps divine intervention slipped that ball between his fingers. 或许是出于神助让球从他的指缝间溜走了。

2. It is hard to divine the justices' thinking, but there are several reasons, beyond pure partisanship, that could have motivated them. 很难猜测大法官们的想法，但除了单纯的党派之见以外，还有其他原因。

扩 divinity *n.* 神性；神

consul
['kɑːnsl]

n. 1. 领事；2.（古罗马）执政官

例 1. The British Consul in Zurich has confirmed that a British man was among the people killed. 英国驻苏黎世领事证实被害人中有一名英国籍男子。
2. When Cicero ran for consul around 63 B.C., his brother Quintus wrote a fascinating manual of political advice. 当西塞罗（见插图）竞选公元前63年的执政官时，他的弟弟昆图斯写了一本建言录。

扩 consular *adj.* 领事的

overthrow
[ˌoʊvər'θroʊ]

v. (overthrew, overthrown) 推翻，打倒；*n.* 推翻

例 1. The president was overthrown in a military coup. 总统在军事政变中被赶下台。
2. They were charged with plotting the overthrow of the state. 他们被控阴谋颠覆国家政权。

expressly
[ɪk'spresli]

adv. 1. 清楚地，明确地；2. 特意，专程

记 express 本有"快递、特快的"之意

例 1. Any rights not expressly granted herein are reserved. 未明确规定的权利在此都予以保留。
2. But investigation led to an astonishing discovery: the tomb had been built expressly to trick relic hunters. 但调查发现了一个惊人的结论：这座坟墓是故意用来迷惑盗宝者的。

idle
['aɪdl]

adj. 1. 懒惰的；2. 闲散的，空闲的；*v.* 混时间，使空转

例 1. There was a group of idle boys standing on the corner. 墙角站着一堆懒散的男孩子。
2. Much of the idle land where tomatoes and cotton normally grow is equipped with water-efficient drip irrigation. 通常种植番茄和棉花的许多空闲土地现在装备了节水的滴灌设备。
3. As traffic jams increased, overall emissions were boosted even more because cars were forced to idle, experts say. 专家们说，随着交通拥堵增加，总体的排放量将增加得更快，因为车子不得不空转。

扩 idleness *n.* 闲散

disgrace
[dɪs'greɪs]

n. 耻辱（的事）；*v.* 使蒙羞

记 dis (=opposite of) + grace → 优雅的反面 → 耻辱

例 1. Mr. Trump was repeatedly interrupted by the protesters, who he called a "disgrace". 特朗普不断被抗议者打断，那人喊着"耻辱"。
2. He says they "disgraced themselves, they disgraced this badge, they disgraced their oaths of office." 他说他们"玷污了自己，玷污了

这个警徽，也玷污了这个职业的誓言。”
扩 disgraceful *adj.* 不光彩的

pronounced
[prə'naʊnst]

adj. 显著的，明确表明的
例 As fuel was consumed, the ship got lighter, and the acceleration more pronounced. 随着燃料的消耗，飞船变得更轻了，而加速度也变得更明显了。
扩 pronouncedly *adv.* 显著地

feudal
['fjuːdl]

adj. 封建的
例 The lack of women in rural China resurrected the old, feudal practice of a bride price, or *chai li*. 中国农村缺乏妇女，这导致旧式的封建做法死灰复燃，即给新娘标价，或者叫“彩礼”。
扩 feudalism *n.* 封建制度
feudatory *adj.* 附庸的

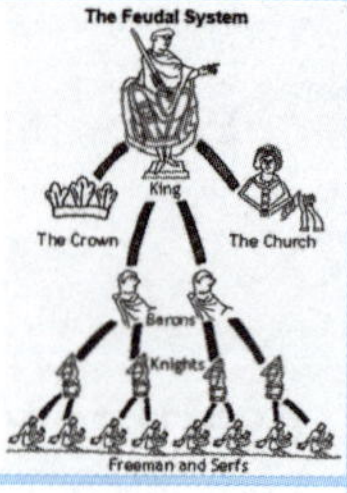

invariably
[ɪn'veriəbli]

adv. 始终如一地
例 These games are played on neutral courts, and fans invariably adopt the underdog. 这些比赛是在第三方场地举行的，因此球迷们自然而然同情弱者。
扩 invariable *adj.* 永无变化的

weary
['wɪri]

adj. 1. 疲劳的；2. 使人厌烦的；*v.* 使疲惫
例 1. The miners were weary after a long shift. 上了长时间的班后，矿工们很疲惫了。
2. I wanted a world weary Batman…someone who has had experiences, and Ben has really hit that.（导演：）我想塑造一个对世界厌烦了的蝙蝠侠，一个有过经历的人，而本（·阿弗莱克）正好符合这一点。
3. He quickly wearied of answering their questions. 他很快就懒得回答他们的问题。
扩 wearily *adv.* 疲惫地
wearisome *adj.* 乏味的，令人疲劳的

scorn
[skɔːrn]

n. 轻蔑；*v.* 轻蔑
例 1. They had nothing but scorn for his political views. 他们对他的政治观点只有鄙夷。
2. She scorned their views as old-fashioned. 她对他们的观点嗤之以鼻，认为陈腐过时。
扩 scornful *adj.* 轻蔑的

infinitely
['ɪnfɪnətli]

adv. 1. 非常；2. 极其，无限
例 1. His bearing was infinitely more patrician than the Beatles', but he grew up working class. 他的气质比甲壳虫乐队更高贵，但他其实成长于工人阶层家庭。

2. If you prepare and file your own tax forms, using software will make your life infinitely easier. 如果你自己准备和提交税务表，使用软件就会让你的生活极其容易。

repose
[rɪˈpoʊz]

n. 休息，睡眠；*v.* 1. 位于，搁置；2. 休息

记 re (=back) + pose (=put) → 放回去 → 搁置

例 1. Reagan will lie in repose Wednesday and Thursday at the library. 星期三和星期四两天里根夫人（的遗体）将存放在（里根）图书馆中。
2. I need you to be very responsible with the trust I have reposed in you. 我需要你非常负责，对得起我对你的信任。
3. For some time we reposed upon the velvet sward, beneath Margaretta's favourite tree. 有时我们躺在丝绒般的草地上，躺在玛格丽特最钟爱的树下。

treason
[ˈtriːzn]

n. 叛国罪

例 After four years of plots, Elizabeth lost patience and had her cousin Margaret and her husband arrested for treason and witchcraft. 经历了四年的阴谋诡计之后，伊丽莎白（一世）失去了耐心，以叛国罪和巫术罪逮捕了她的堂姐玛格丽特及其丈夫。

扩 treasonable *adj.* 叛国的
treasonist *n.* 叛国者

mischief
[ˈmɪstʃɪf]

n. 1. 淘气；2. 恶意；3. 伤害

记 mis (=badly) + chief (=happen) → 做坏事

例 1. Those children are always getting into mischief. 那些孩子总是淘气。
2. Her eyes were full of mischief. 她眼睛里满是使坏的神情。
3. Police reported a handful of arrests, mainly for criminal mischief. 警方逮捕了很多人，多数是因为毁坏财物。

扩 mischievous *adj.* 顽皮的；恶意的

providence
[ˈprɑːvɪdəns]

n. 上帝，苍天

记 美国罗德岛州（Rhode Island）州府 Providence（普罗维登斯）

例 How much does history hinge on character, how much on providence? 历史在多大程度上取决于人为、多大程度上取决于天意呢？

扩 providential *adj.* 天缘巧合的，及时的

impart
[ɪmˈpɑːrt]

v. 1. 传授，透露；2. 赋予

记 im (=in) + part → 分成部分 → 分享，传授

例 1. "She knew that teaching was way more than just imparting information and that it was really important to know students," Walton says. 沃顿说："她早知道教学并不仅仅是传授知识，了解学生也很重要。"
2. The spice imparts an Eastern flavor to the dish. 这种调味品给菜肴添加了一种东方风味。

扩 impartment *n.* 传授；赋予

pretension
[prɪ'tenʃn]

n. 1. 虚饰，自命不凡；2. 自命，标榜

例 1. Pretension is tied up with class, which is not just a question of money and how you spend it. 自命不凡跟阶级有关，它不仅仅是钱的问题，或者如何花钱的问题。

2. Then again, last year Google didn't have any pretensions of low cost with the Nexus 6, a huge device with a pretty large price tag. 去年谷歌并没有假装 Nexus 6 的成本很低，它的价格标得很高。

扩 pretentious *adj.* 炫耀的，虚夸的

pretense *n.* 假象，伪装；标榜

folly
['fɑːli]

n. 1. 愚蠢；2. 愚蠢的事

记 fol (=fool) + ly → 愚蠢的行为

例 1. It would be folly to expect peace already this year, he said, "however, five years is certainly a realistic timeline" . 他说，指望今年就能迎来和平是愚蠢的，"但五年时间是很现实的"。

2. Their pranks were just youthful folly. 他们的恶作剧只不过是年轻人的把戏。

prejudicial
[ˌpredʒu'dɪʃl]

adj. 1. 有害的，不利的；2. 有偏见的

例 1. The delay is likely to be prejudicial to the child's welfare. 这一耽搁很可能不利于孩子。

2. The appeals court ruled that the testimony was unfairly prejudicial to the defendant. 上诉法院判定证词明显偏袒被告人。

扩 prejudiced *adj.* 偏心的，带成见的

hearth
[hɑːrθ]

n. 1. 壁炉前；2. 家或家庭生活

例 1. The cat dozed in its favorite spot on the hearth. 猫躺在壁炉前它最喜欢的地方打盹。

2. Protecting hearth and home is still the essential function of government. 保护家庭生活仍然是政府的基本职能。

procession
[prə'seʃn]

n. 1. 行列，游行；2. 一队人

例 1. A procession led by bagpipers escorted the casket out of the church in Roseville, near Taylor's hometown. 在泰勒的家乡附近，由风笛手们引导的行列护卫着灵柩走出罗斯韦尔的教堂。

2. A procession of waiters appeared bearing trays of food. 一长列服务生端着一盘一盘饭菜出现了。

扩 processional *adj.* 列队行进的

partake
[pɑːr'teɪk]

v. (partook, partaken) 1. 享用；2. 参与

记 与 participate（参加，参与）同根

例 1. Mr. Martin said he knew that the Beatles at the time were heavily into drugs, but he did not partake. 马丁说他早就知道甲壳虫乐队当时吸毒很厉害，但他并没有参与。

2. They preferred not to partake in the social life of the town. 他们不想参加这个镇的社交活动。

List 6

obscurity
[əbˈskjʊrəti]

n. 1. 默默无闻；2. 费解，晦涩

例 1. The latter half of his life was spent in obscurity and loneliness. 他在默默无闻中孤独地度过了后半生。

2. If they get their way, the struggle, despite its technical obscurity, may be one of the most consequential court cases of our time. 如果他们（FBI）得逞的话，尽管在技术层面很让人难以理解，但这可能是这个时代最有影响力的法庭案件（FBI 诉苹果公司）。

扩 obscure *v.* 使模糊；*adj.* 模糊的

veil
[veɪl]

n. 1. 面纱；2. 借口，掩饰；*v.* 掩饰

例 1. She swathes her face in a veil of decorative muslin. 她用装饰性的薄纱遮住了脸。

2. Their work is carried out behind a veil of secrecy. 他们的工作是在秘密掩护下进行的。

3. Former U.S. secretary of state Henry Kissinger gave thinly veiled approval to Argentina's military for the use of violence against leftwing activists. 前美国国务卿基辛格几乎不加掩饰地同意了阿根廷使用武力对付左翼活动分子的行为。

扩 unveil *v.* 揭幕；展示

incur
[ɪnˈkɜːr]

v. (incurred, incurred) 招致，引来

记 in (=on) + cur (=run, happen) → 发生于 → 招来

例 1. She had incurred the wrath of her father by marrying without his consent. 她结婚未获父亲同意，这可能招致父亲的怒火。

2. You will need to wait until age 59 ½ to withdraw the money without incurring the early withdrawal penalty. 你得等到 59 岁半的时候提取退休金才不会招致过早提取的罚金。

扩 incurrence *n.* 招致；引来

plunge
[plʌndʒ]

v. 1. 使突然前冲；2. 暴跌；*n.* 1. 突然跌落；2. 暴跌

例 1. The earthquake plunged entire towns over the edge of the cliffs. 地震将整座城镇掀到悬崖之下。

2. Whereas Taiwan's total exports fell by 12% year on year in February, display screens and other "optical instruments" plunged by 34%. 虽然台湾二月份的总出口额环比下降了 12%，但显示屏和其他"光学设备"却猛跌了 34%。

3. The calm water ends there and the river begins a headlong plunge. 平静的河水突然中断，开始奔腾直泻而下。

4. Market analysts predicted a price plunge. 市场分析人员预计将有价格暴跌。

observance
[əbˈzɜːrvəns]

n. 1. 遵守，奉行；2. 宗教仪式

记 observe 作动词也有"遵守"的意思

例 1. Within two years, Women's Day had grown into an international observance that spread through Europe. 两年内，妇女节就在整个欧洲变成国际性节日。

2. The carnival will end on 9 February, marking the start of the Christian observance of Lent. 嘉年华将于2月9日结束，即基督教大斋期仪式的开始。

profess [prə'fes]

v. 1. 妄称，伪称；2. 宣称，公开表明

记 pro (=forth) + fess (=speak) → 说出来

例 1. I don't profess to be an expert in this subject. 我不敢自诩为这方面的专家。

2. She professed herself satisfied with the progress so far. 她表示对目前为止的进度很满意。

扩 profession *n.* 行业；声明，宣称

confide [kən'faɪd]

v. 吐露（秘密、隐私等）

记 与 confidence（信心）同根 → 相信 → 吐露

例 The episodes can feel like watching new friends telling you their deepest thoughts, confiding in you their secrets. 这一剧集仿佛让我们观看新朋友向你吐露内心最深处的想法，吐露他们的秘密。

扩 confidant *n.* 知己，密友

vulgar ['vʌlgər]

adj. 粗俗的，不雅的

例 She found their laughter and noisy games coarse and rather vulgar. 她觉得他们的笑声和吵吵闹闹的游戏趣味低下，俗不可耐。

扩 vulgarity *n.* 粗野，下流

tolerable ['tɑːlərəbl]

adj. 1. 还凑合的；2. 可忍受的

例 1. When he says a "tolerable English writer," he's being humble. 他说自己是个"还凑合的英语作家"，这是在自谦。

2. At times, the heat was barely tolerable. 有时天气炎热得几乎令人难以忍受。

扩 intolerable *adj.* 难以容忍的

innumerable [ɪ'nuːmərəbl]

adj. 很多的，数不清的

例 1. Although the countries share innumerable family and cultural ties, this will be the first Canadian state visit to the U.S. for 19 years. 虽然两国拥有很多跨国家庭及文化联系，但这将是19年来首次加拿大官方访问美国。

2. He has invented innumerable excuses, told endless lies. 他编造了数不清的借口和谎话。

chaste ['tʃeɪst]

adj. 1. 贞洁的；2. 纯洁的；3. 简朴的

例 1. Abramov did not live a chaste life. 阿布拉莫夫生活不检点。

2. There is zero nudity or sex, just one chaste forehead kiss. 这其中不涉及任何的裸体或性，只是纯洁的额头一吻。

3. She wore a chaste gold chain around her neck. 她脖子上戴着简式的金项链。

扩 chastity *n.* 忠贞，贞操

forfeit
[ˈfɔːrfət]

v. 丧失，没收；*n.* 罚金

记 for (=outside) + feit (=do) → 越过边界 → 违规，没收

例 1. I trained hard as a ballet dancer, forfeited my childhood, because that's what dancers do. 我当芭蕾舞演员训练很辛苦，没有童年，因为舞蹈演员都是如此。

2. The judge declared the property a forfeit. 法官宣布罚没财产。

扩 forfeiture *n.* 丧失，没收

enumerate
[ɪˈnuːməreɪt]

v. 列举

记 e (=from) + numer (=number, count) + ate → 使数 → 列举

例 In her two-page letter, Cook enumerated prison problems from a mother's perspective. 在她的这两页信中，库克从母亲的角度列举了监狱里存在的问题。

扩 enumeration *n.* 列举

moderate
[ˈmɑːdərət]

v. 1. 缓和；2. 主持；*adj.* 1. 中等的，适度的；2. 不激烈的

记 mod (=measure) + er + ate → 使可衡量 → 适度

例 1. We agreed to moderate our original demands. 我们同意降低我们原先的要求。

2. And I moderated an hourlong conversation with *This American Life* host Ira Glass. 我主持了一个一小时长的对话节目，采访《美国生活》的主持人伊拉·格拉斯。

3. I pointed out that the scientific research said moderate drinking isn't bad for you; indeed, it might even offer some benefits. 我指出，科学研究证明适度饮酒无害；相反，它还能带来一些好处。

4. She holds a moderate position on the subject of taxes. 她在税务问题上的立场比较温和。

扩 moderation *n.* 适中，中庸

hasty
[ˈheɪsti]

adj. 草率的，考虑不周的

例 Perhaps I was too hasty in rejecting his offer. 我拒绝他的提议也许过于草率了。

扩 haste *n.* 匆忙

hastily *adv.* 匆忙地

patrician
[pəˈtrɪʃn]

adj. 贵族的，上流社会的；*n.* 贵族

记 patr (=father) + ician → 父亲高贵的 → 贵族

例 1. She comes from an old patrician family. 她出身贵族家庭。

2. Even the most dignified patrician deserves to have a bit of fun now and again. 即使是最尊贵的上流人士也应该时不时多少找点乐子。

扩 patriciate *n.* 贵族阶层

persuasion
[pərˈsweɪʒn]

n. 1. 说服；2. 信仰

例 1. It didn't take much persuasion to get her to tell us where he was. 我们没费什么口舌就让她说出了他的下落。

2. The longstanding belief among parents of all persuasions is that

sugar makes their kids crazy. 各种信仰的父母都持有同样的传统观念，即糖类会让孩子发疯。

扩 persuasive *adj.* 有说服力的

insensible
[ɪn'sensəbl]

adj. 1. 无感觉的，麻木的；2. 昏迷的

例 1. I first encountered the insensible power of nature during a two-week sailing trip with my wife in the Greek isles. 我在跟妻子去希腊岛的两周航行中，首次见识了大自然无情的力量。

2. It was already past 10 pm, by which time the crowd was completely insensible with drink. 当时已经是夜里十点多了，大家都完全喝晕了。

扩 insensibility *n.* 无知觉

insensibly *adv.* 未察觉地

pledge
[pledʒ]

n. 1. 保证；2. 抵押品；*v.* 1. 保证；2. 典当

例 1. Will the government honor its election pledge not to raise taxes? 政府会履行其竞选诺言，不增加税收吗？

2. He left his car as a pledge that he would return with the money. 他以车抵押，承诺拿钱回来。

3. The group has pledged that they will continue campaigning. 这个组织发誓他们将继续投入运动。

4. He pledged his paintings as collateral for a loan. 他抵押他的绘画来贷款。

wretched
['retʃɪd]

adj. 1. 难受的；2. 恶劣的；3. 可怜的

记 可能与 wizard（巫师）有关 → 格格巫 → 可恶的

例 1. I felt wretched about the way things had turned out. 事情落了这么个结局，我感到很难受。

2. The animals are kept in the most wretched conditions. 这些动物的饲养条件极其恶劣。

3. She finally agreed to have the wretched animal put down. 她最后同意把这头可怜的动物人道毁灭。

扩 wretch *n.* 可怜的人；坏蛋

wretchedness *n.* 可怜；穷困

ridicule
['rɪdɪkjuːl]

v./n. 嘲笑，奚落

例 1. The other kids ridiculed him for the way he dressed. 别的孩子嘲笑他的穿着。

2. Images of the castle before and after the restoration have recently fueled outrage and ridicule on social media.（西班牙）城堡在修复前后的照片最近在社交媒体上引发了愤怒和嘲笑。

扩 ridiculous *adj.* 愚蠢的

ridiculously *adv.* 离谱地

honorary
[ˈɑːnəreri]

adj. 1. 荣誉的；2. 无报酬的

例 1. At commencement, he will receive an honorary doctor of humane letters degree. 在毕业典礼上，他将被授予名誉文学博士学位。

2. The honorary position, founded in 1626, is traditionally conferred on a musician of distinction by the monarch. 这一虚职始于 1626 年，通常由君主授予杰出的音乐家。

扩 honorarium *n.* 酬金

honorable *adj.* 可敬的；体面的

beget
[bɪˈget]

v. (begot, begot) 招致

例 Violence is never the answer. Violence only begets violence. 暴力从来不能解决问题。暴力只能带来暴力。

wit
[wɪt]

n. 1. 才思，风趣；2. 机智的人；3. 理解力

记 witness（目击者）中的 wit 即为“知道”之意

例 1. His latest book doesn't have the same wit as his earlier books. 他新出的书不如之前的书有才气。

2. She was a famous writer and wit. 她是一位有名的作家，也是个机智的人。

3. He needed all his wits to find his way out. 他需要绞尽脑汁找到出路。

扩 witting *adj.* 知道的，故意的

witty *adj.* 言辞诙谐的，机智的

populace
[ˈpɑːpjələs]

n. 民众

例 1. The populace at large is/are opposed to sudden change. 民众普遍反对突然的改变。

2. He had the support of large sections of the local populace. 他受到当地大部份百姓的拥护。

辨 populous *adj.* 人口密集的

fixation
[fɪkˈseɪʃn]

n. 1. 依恋，癖；2. 固定

记 fix + ation → 固定的感情 → 依恋

例 1. He's got this fixation with cleanliness. 他有洁癖。

2. I asked the zoo's staff to explain the public fixation on pandas. 我要求动物园的人解释为何公众都只关注大熊猫。

3. The process that makes nitrogen easier for organisms to use, called nitrogen fixation, did not emerge until 2 billion years ago. 固氮是把氮化为有机物所用，这一过程到 20 亿年前才出现。

扩 fixate *v.* 使固定；凝视

fixedly *adv.* 凝视地

effectually
[ɪˈfektʃuəli]

adv. 奏效地

例 The law would effectually bar new development in the neighborhood. 这项法律将有效地阻止这一地区的发展。

tariff
['tærɪf]

n. 1. 关税；2. 收费表

例 1. America wants to eliminate tariffs on items such as electronics. 美国打算取消电子产品等的关税。
2. The daily tariff includes accommodation and unlimited use of the pool and gymnasium. 日常费用包括住宿以及游泳池和健身房的不限时使用。

console
['kɑːnsoʊl] *n.*
[kən'soʊl] *v.*

n. 操纵台；*v.* 安慰

例 1. A video game console is a device that outputs a video signal or visual image to display a video game. 电脑游戏仪表台是输出视频信号或视频图像的地方。
2. Nothing could console him when his wife died. 他妻子去世后，什么事情也不能使他感到宽慰。

扩 consolation *n.* 使感到安慰的人（或物）；慰藉

attainment
[ə'teɪnmənt]

n. 1. 成就，造诣；2. 达到，获得

记 at (=to) + tain (=touch) + ment → 达到

例 1. She is a young woman of impressive educational attainments 她是位学业成就斐然的年轻女子。
2. The attainment of his ambitions was still a dream. 他要实现的抱负仍然是一个梦想。

扩 attainable *adj.* 可达到的，可获得的

abolish
[ə'bɑːlɪʃ]

v. 废除

例 In 2016, a hundred and five countries have abolished the death penalty, and another sixty have not used it in a decade. 到 2016 年，有 105 个国家已经废除了死刑，还有 60 个国家在十年内都未判过死刑。

扩 abolition *n.* 废除

delicacy
['delɪkəsi]

n. 1. 娇嫩；2. 美味；3. 棘手，微妙

记 "美味" 之意与 delicious 同根

例 1. Her skin had the delicacy of a flower. 她的肌肤像花一样娇嫩。
2. The restaurant serves delicious sausages and other regional delicacies. 这家餐馆有美味的腊肠和其他一些地方特产。
3. I need to talk to you about a matter of some delicacy. 我需要与你谈个有点棘手的问题。

padlock
['pædlɑːk]

n. 挂锁；*v.* 锁住

例 1. They'll start to see a gray padlock next to conversations within the next two weeks or so. 在接下来的两周左右时间里，他们（用户们）将会开始见到（手机 app 的）谈话框旁边出现了一把灰色的挂锁（标志）。
2. She always padlocked her bike to the railings. 她总是用挂锁把自行车锁在栏杆上。

throne
[θroʊn]

n. 1. 御座；2. 王权，帝位

例 1. And directly across from me, his fiery gaze burning into mine, is the king, sitting on a diamond throne carved into an inferno. 国王在我对面用火热的眼神看着我，他坐在一个用钻石雕成火海的宝座上。

2. The creators of *Game of Thrones* have made it clear that no character is safe on the show. 《权力的游戏》制片人曾表明，该剧中的角色没人是安全的。

degrade
[dɪˈgreɪd]

v. 1. 降低身份，侮辱；2. 退化，分解

记 de (=down) + grade (=step) → 走下坡路 → 退化

例 1. This poster is offensive and degrades women. 这张海报冒失无礼，有辱女性尊严。

2. The United States formed a global coalition to "degrade and ultimately destroy" the Islamic State back in September 2014. 美国在 2014 年 9 月形成了全球联盟以"分化和最终瓦解""伊斯兰国"。

扩 degrading *adj.* 侮辱的

degradation *n.* 堕落；恶化

swell
[swel]

v. 膨胀，肿胀；2. 增大，扩大；*n.* 膨胀

例 1. Her arm was beginning to swell up where the bee had stung her. 她胳膊给蜜蜂蜇了，肿了起来。

2. We are looking for more volunteers to swell the ranks of those already helping. 我们期盼有更多的志愿者加入，以壮大目前已在提供帮助的队伍。

3. The boat was caught in a heavy swell. 船遇上了大浪涌。

thence
[ðens]

adv. 从那里，随后

例 They made their way from Spain to France and thence to England. 他们从西班牙去了法国，再从那里去了英国。

同 thenceforth, thenceforward, therefrom

dissent
[dɪˈsent]

n. 异议；*v.* 持异议

记 dis (=different) + sent (=sense, feel) → 不同的感觉 → 异议

例 1. He did everything in his power to suppress political dissent. 他竭尽所能压制政治异见。

2. Only two ministers dissented from the official view. 只有两位部长与官方持不同的观点。

扩 dissension *n.* 意见不和

counteract
[ˌkaʊntərˈækt]

v. 抵制，抵消

例 These exercises aim to counteract the effects of stress and tension. 这些运动旨在抵消压力与紧张的影响。

扩 counteractive *adj.* 抵消的

List 7

onward
[ˈɑːnwərd, ˈɔː-]

adj. 向前的，继续的；*adv.* 向前地

例 1. Ticket prices include your flight and onward rail journey. 票价包括您的飞行航程和接续的铁路旅费。
2. They have lived in that house from 1983 onward. 他们从 1983 年以后就一直住在那座房子里。

reckon
[ˈrekən]

v. 1. 想，认为；2. 被看作是；3. 指望，预计

例 1. I reckon (that) I'm going to get that job. 我认为我会得到那份工作。
2. Children are reckoned to be more sophisticated nowadays. 人们认为今天的孩子比过去世故。
3. We reckon to finish by ten. 我们预计十点钟以前结束。

commonwealth
[ˈkɑːmənwelθ]

n. 1. 英联邦；2.（美国的某几个）州；3. 自治区

例 1. Other documents show Mrs. Thatcher refused to bail out the 1986 Commonwealth Games despite being asked to contribute £1m by media tycoon Robert Maxwell. 其他文件表明撒切尔夫人拒绝救助 1986 年的英联邦运动会，尽管媒体大亨罗伯特·马克斯韦尔要求她投入一百万英镑。

2. Bottom line is the commonwealth of Virginia should not be allowed to discriminate. 我们的底线是弗吉尼亚州不能容许歧视。
3. Puerto Rico remains a U.S. commonwealth, not a state. 波多黎各仍是美国的一个自治区，不是州。

parish
[ˈpærɪʃ]

n. 1. 教区；2. 教区教徒；3.（英国）乡村

例 1. He is vicar of a large rural parish. 他是乡下一个大教区的代牧。
2. The parish has grown significantly in the last three years. 过去三年教区居民增加很多。
3. He was elected to the parish council. 他当选进入乡村公会。

辨 perish *v.* 死亡，丧失

emolument
[ɪˈmɑːljumənt]

n. 薪水，工资

记 谐音“一毛钱留下”→ 薪水

例 He could earn up to £1m a year in salary and emoluments from many directorships. 他每年的薪水加上担任许多董事职务的报酬高达一百万英镑。

endow [ɪn'daʊ]

v. 1. 捐赠，资助；2. 天生具有，赋予

记 en (=in) + dow (=donate, give) → 放进去 → 捐赠

例 1. The wealthy couple endowed a new wing of the hospital. 这对富有的夫妇向医院捐建了一个新的翼厅。

2. Human beings are endowed with reason. 人类拥有天赋的理性。

扩 endowment *n.* 捐款；天赋

astonish [ə'stɑːnɪʃ]

v. 使吃惊

例 Developing nations have experienced an astonishing boom in urbanization in the past few decades. 在过去几十年间，发展中国家经历了一个令人吃惊的城市化的发展。

扩 astonishment *n.* 惊讶

astonished *adj.* 感到吃惊的

proprietor [prə'praɪətər]

n. 业主

记 proprie (=property) + tor → 拥有财产的人 → 业主

例 The proprietor of Windows, David Emil, had pledged to help his former employees find work. 窗口（餐厅）的业主大卫·埃米尔发誓要帮助他以前的员工们找到工作。

扩 proprietorship *n.* 所有权，拥有

revolt [rɪ'voʊlt]

n. 反抗；*v.* 1. 反抗；2. 使惊骇，令人厌恶

记 与 revolve（旋转）同源 → 翻过来 → 推翻，反抗

例 1. Attempts to negotiate peace ended in armed revolt. 和谈的努力最后以武装叛乱告终。

2. Finally the people revolted against the military dictatorship. 人民最终起来反抗军事独裁。

3. All the violence in the movie revolted me. 电影里的各种暴力场面令我非常震惊。

辨 revolve *v.* 旋转

扩 revolution *n.* 革命；旋转

rejoice [rɪ'dʒɔɪs]

v. 非常高兴

记 "飘柔"洗发水的商标为 Rejoice

例 Hollywood rejoices as Supreme Court rules same-sex marriage legal across U.S.. 当美国最高法院宣判同性婚姻在全国合法时，好莱坞一片欢腾。

Rejoice 飘柔

扩 rejoicing *n.* 喜庆

evade [ɪ'veɪd]

v. 1. 躲避；2. 逃避；3. 使想不出

记 谐音"一味地"逃避困难

例 1. For two weeks they evaded the press. 他们有两周一直避而不见记者。

2. She is trying to evade all responsibility for her behavior. 她在试图逃避应为自己的行为承担的所有责任。

3. The answer evaded him. 他答不上来。

扩 evasive *adj.* 回避的，推托的

evasion *n.* 躲避；借口

subdue
[səb'duː]

v. 1. 制伏；2. 抵制，压抑

例 1. Troops were called in to subdue the rebels. 军队被调来镇压反叛者。
2. Julia had to subdue an urge to stroke his hair. 朱莉娅得克制住自己，不去抚摩他的头发。

辨 subduce *v.* 减去

ballot
['bælət]

n. 1. 投票选举；2. 投票总数；*v.* 无记名投票

记 ball- 来源于早期投票所用的小球

例 1. The chairperson is chosen by secret ballot. 主席是通过无记名投票选举产生的。
2. She won 58.8% of the ballot. 她赢得了投票总数的 58.8%。
3. The workers balloted for a strike. 工人对是否罢工进行无记名投票表决。

vicious
['vɪʃəs]

adj. 1. 狂暴的，残酷的；2.（动物）凶猛的；3. 严厉的

记 可看作 vice（罪行、堕落）的形容词

例 1. She has a vicious temper. 她性情暴虐。
2. Three dogs have attacked residents and pets, leaving residents frightened that the vicious dogs might hound their neighborhoods again. 三只狗袭击了居民和宠物，让居民们担忧恶犬会再次骚扰他们的社区。
3. She wrote me a vicious letter. 她给我写了一封严厉的信。

扩 viciously *adv.* 恶毒地

melancholy
['melənkɑːli]

n. 忧郁，伤悲；*adj.* 令人悲哀的

记 参见 sanguine 的记忆法

例 1. There is a brooding melancholy in his black and white photography. 他的黑白照片中有种幽然的伤感。
2. He became quiet and melancholy as the hours slowly passed. 随着时间慢慢流逝，他变得安静而伤感。

扩 melancholic *adj.* 忧郁的

heretofore
[ˌhɪrtu'fɔːr]

adv. 在这之前

例 1. This technology has created heretofore unimaginable possibilities. 这种技术创造了史无前例的可能性。
2. Heretofore her writing has never displayed such depth of feeling. 之前他的作品从未表现出如此深的感情。

infuse
[ɪn'fjuːz]

v. 1. 使具有，注入；2. 全面影响

记 in (=into) + fuse (=pour) → 倒入 → 注入，输入

例 1. Her novels are infused with sadness. 她的小说充满哀伤。
2. In America, in modernity, money is an entire and pervasive symbolic realm that infuses almost everything else. 在美国，在现代，金钱成了一个无处不在的标志性的领域，它影响了几乎所有的东西。

辨 defuse *v.* 缓和；拆除引信
扩 infusion *n.* 注入

imposition [ˌɪmpəˈzɪʃn]

n. **1. 颁布，征收；2. 不公平（或不合理）的要求**
记 im (=in, on) + pos (=put) + ition → 放在上面 → 施加，颁布
例 1. The U.S. has been pushing for the imposition of sanctions following its Jan. 6 nuclear test. 在 1 月 6 日的核试验以后，美国一直在要求对该国进行制裁。
2. I'd like to stay if it's not too much of an imposition. 如果不会给您增添太多麻烦，我倒愿意留下。

opulent [ˈɑːpjələnt]

adj. **1. 豪华的；2. 阔气的**
例 1. We sat in the opulent surroundings of the Ritz Hotel. 我们坐在豪华的利兹酒店里。
2. Most of the cash went on supporting his opulent lifestyle. 大部分现金都花在了维系他挥金如土的生活方式上。
扩 opulence *n.* 豪华

forgo [fɔːrˈɡoʊ]

v. (forwent, forgone) **放弃**
记 for (=away) + go → 走开 → 放弃
例 No one was prepared to forgo their lunch hour to attend the meeting. 谁都不愿意放弃午餐时间出席会议。
辨 forge *v.* 伪造，假冒；炼成

ardor [ˈɑːrdər]

n. **激情，热情**
记 与 ash（灰烬）同源 → 燃烧 → 热情
例 They also believe that nothing cools a customer's ardor like seeing a new model and having to wait months to buy. 他们还相信，见到新款或者等待数月才能购买，这些都不会浇灭消费者的热情。
辨 adore *v.* 热爱；爱慕
arduous *adj.* 艰苦的，费力的
扩 ardent *adj.* 热烈的
ardently *adv.* 热烈地

solitary [ˈsɑːləteri]

adj. **1. 独自的，单独的；2. 独处的；3. 单个的**
记 sol (=sole, alone) + itary → 单独的
例 1. She enjoys long solitary walks. 她喜欢独自长距离散步。
2. A hawk is solitary, Macdonald explains, and almost always frightened of you until you convince the creature that you're a friend and food source. 麦当劳解释说，鹰是独居的，它几乎总是害怕人类，除非你让它相信你是朋友或者食源。
3. A solitary light burned dimly in the hall. 大厅里点着一盏孤灯，发出昏暗的光。
扩 solitude *n.* 独居，独处

odious
['oʊdiəs]

adj. 令人作呕的，可憎的
例 Herr Schmidt is certainly the most odious man I have ever met. 赫尔·施密特无疑是我见过的最让人作呕的人。
扩 odium *n.* 憎恶，公愤

personage
['pɑːrsənɪdʒ]

n. 1. 要人，名人；2. 历史、戏剧人物
例 1. Some even went down upon their knees, so I knew her to be a personage of great power. 有些人甚至为她下跪，这样我就知道她肯定是个有权力的人物。
2. There is no evidence for such a historical personage. 没有证据表明存在这样一位历史人物。
辨 parsonage *n.* 教区牧师的住所

terminate
['tɜːmɪneɪt]

v. 1. 使停止；2. 到达终点站
例 1. Your contract of employment terminates in December. 你的聘约十二月份到期。
2. This train terminates at London Victoria. 这趟列车的终点站是伦敦维多利亚火车站。
扩 terminal *adj.* 致命的；末端的；*n.* 终点站，航站楼
termination *n.* 末端，终止；结果，结局

turbulent
['tɜːrbjələnt]

adj. 1. 动荡的；2. 汹涌的
记 turb (=stir) + ulent → 搅动的 → 动荡的
例 1. The sixties were a turbulent period in American history. 六十年代是美国历史上的动荡时期。
2. This week's turbulent ocean activity is the result of a strong storm over the Central Pacific, bringing a long-period swell. 本周剧烈的海洋活动源于太平洋中部上空的风暴，它带来了长期的涌浪。
扩 turbulence *n.* 骚乱，动荡；涡流

encroach
[ɪn'kroʊtʃ]

v. 1. 侵占，扰乱；2. 侵蚀，蚕食
记 en (=in) + croach (=crook, hook) → 钩住，抓住 → 侵占
例 1. He never allows work to encroach upon his family life. 他从不让工作扰乱他的家庭生活。
2. The growing town soon encroached on the surrounding countryside. 这个不断扩大的城镇不久便将周围的农村变成了市区。
扩 encroachment *n.* 侵占

extravagant
[ɪk'strævəgənt]

adj. 1. 奢侈的，挥霍的；2. 过于昂贵的；3. 放肆的
例 1. I felt very extravagant spending £100 on a dress. 我觉得花 100 英镑买一条连衣裙太奢侈了。
2. We're going on a less extravagant vacation this year. 我们今年度假不会花那么多钱了。
3. The company has been making extravagant claims/promises about

the drug's effectiveness. 该公司对药品的疗效一直夸大其辞。
扩 extravagance *n.* 奢侈；豪华

grieve
[gri:v]

v. 1. 悲伤；2. 使悲伤
记 与 grave（沉重；坟墓）同源
例 1. The Belgians are hurt and scared and grieve the terrible loss of their dead, but the world shouldn't be surprised anymore. 比利时人民受伤了，害怕了，哀悼他们死去的亲人，但世界不应对此感到惊讶。
2. It grieved him that he could do nothing to help her. 他因无法帮助她而伤心。
扩 grief *n.* 悲伤，忧虑
grievous *adj.* 极严重的，使人痛苦的

commence
[kə'mens]

v. 开始，着手
例 A year after my father commenced his journey into illness, he collapsed in the middle of the night. 在我父亲与病魔斗争了一年以后，他在夜里去世了。
扩 commencement *n.* 开端；毕业典礼

yoke
[jouk]

n. 1.（牛）轭；2. 束缚，奴役；*v.* 使联合
例 1. Every morning he put on the heavy wooden yoke, and trudged over to North Square for drinking water. 每天早上他都要套上沉重的牛轭，去北广场打水。
2. The country has struggled to free itself from the yoke of foreign rule. 该国努力想摆脱外国的控制。
3. The Hong Kong dollar was yoked to the American dollar for many years. 港元多年来与美元挂钩。
扩 yokel *n.* 乡下人

dreadful
['dredfl]

adj. 1. 讨厌的，令人不快的；2. 极坏的；3. 可怕的
例 1. It's dreadful the way they treat their staff. 他们对待雇员的方式糟糕透了。
2. She's making a dreadful mess of things. 她把事情搞得一塌糊涂。
3. They suffered dreadful injuries. 他们严重受伤。
扩 dread *n.* 恐惧；*v.* 担心

detain
[dɪ'teɪn]

v. 1. 拘留；2. 耽搁，阻留
记 de (=away) + tain (=hold) → 留住 → 拘留
例 1. Currently 18 people detained in six countries are suspected of helping the Paris attackers. 目前在 6 个国家共有 18 名拘留者疑与巴黎恐怖袭击者有关。
2. I'm sorry—he'll be late; he's been detained at a meeting. 对不起——他要晚点到，他因会议耽搁了。
扩 detainee *n.* 被拘留者

ordain
[ɔːr'deɪn]

v. 1. 授予圣职；2. 主宰，掌握

记 与 order 同根

例 1. He was ordained (as) a priest last year. 他去年接受任命为神父。
2. Fate had ordained that they would never meet again. 他们命里注定永远不会再相见。

扩 preordained *adj.* 命中注定的

discern
[dɪ'sɜːrn]

v. 1. 识别；2. 看出，分辨

例 1. He discerned a certain coldness in their welcome. 他觉察到他们的接待有点冷淡。
2. We could just discern the house in the distance. 我们只能勉强分辨出远处的房子。

扩 discernible *adj.* 可分辨的
discernment *n.* 识别力，洞察力

immunity
[ɪ'mjuːnəti]

n. 1. 免疫力；2. 豁免，受保护

记 im (=not) + muni (=common) + ty → 不共通 → 免疫

例 1. The vaccine provides longer immunity against flu. 这种疫苗对流感的免疫效力时间较长。
2. Officials of all member states receive certain privileges and immunities. 各成员国的官员均享有某些特权和豁免权。

扩 immune *adj.* 有免疫力的；不受影响的

seduce
[sɪ'duːs]

v. 诱骗，唆使

记 se (=sub) + duce (=lead) → 使坠落 → 唆使

例 1. The promise of huge profits seduced him into parting with his money. 高额利润的许诺诱使他把钱交了出来。
2. Clever advertising would seduce more people into smoking. 巧妙策划的广告会引诱更多的人吸烟。

扩 seductive *adj.* 诱人的，令人神往的
seduction *n.* 魅力，吸引力

lapse
[læps]

n. 1. 小错误；2. 间隔时间；*v.* 1. 失效；2. 衰退

例 1. A momentary lapse in the final set cost her the match. 她最后一盘一走神儿，输掉了整场比赛。
2. After a lapse of six months we met up again. 相隔六个月之后我们又相遇了。
3. She had allowed her membership to lapse. 她的会员资格期满终止，没有再续。
4. His concentration lapsed after a few minutes. 几分钟后他的注意力就下降了。

扩 elapse *v.* 时间流逝
relapse *n.* 旧病复发；*v.* 故态复萌

List 7

involuntary
[ɪnˈvɑːlənteri]

adj. 1. 不自觉的，无意识的；2. 非自愿的

例 1. Breathing and circulation are involuntary processes. 呼吸与循环都是无意识的行为。

2. The lawyer argued that the client's confession was involuntary. 律师辩称委托人的认罪是被迫的。

ascend
[əˈsend]

v. 1. 上升，登高；2. 高升，高就

例 1. The air became colder as we ascended. 随着我们往上攀登，空气就寒冷起来。

2. John Adams ascended to the presidency in 1797. 约翰·亚当斯于 1797 年升任总统（之前为副总统）。

扩 ascent *n.* 上升；进步

ascendant *n.* 越来越大，日益受欢迎

therein
[ˌðerˈɪn]

adv. 在那里，在其中

例 1. The insurance policy covers the building and any fixtures contained therein. 保险单为这座大楼及其中所有的设施保了险。

2. He works extremely hard and therein lies the key to his success. 他工作极其努力，这就是他成功的关键。

stern
[stɜːrn]

adj. 1. 严厉的；2. 难对付的

例 1. Buckingham Palace has issued a stern denial of a newspaper report claiming the Queen of England supported Britain's departure from the European Union. 白金汉宫发布了一项措辞严厉的声明，否认报纸所称的英国女王支持脱欧的报道。

2. We face stern opposition. 我们遇到激烈的反对。

扩 sternness *n.* 严厉，严峻

infringe
[ɪnˈfrɪndʒ]

v. 1. 违背，触犯；2. 侵犯

例 1. The material can be copied without infringing copyright. 这份材料可以复制，不会侵犯版权。

2. She refused to answer questions that infringed on her private affairs. 她拒绝回答侵犯她隐私的问题。

扩 infringement *n.* 侵犯

affirmative
[əˈfɜːrmətɪv]

adj. 1. 肯定的，同意的；2. 积极的，赞同的；*n.* 肯定

例 1. Republicans do not have the votes to override Mr. Obama's veto, but say that their affirmative vote is symbolic. 共和党人并没有足够的票数来推翻奥巴马的否决，而是说他们投赞同票只是象征性的。

2. The case before the court, Fisher vs. University of Texas at Austin, is likely to affect the future of affirmative action nationwide. 法庭上的这桩“费舍尔诉得州大学奥斯汀分校案”很可能影响全国的（照顾少数种族学生的）种族倾斜政策。（见插图）

3. Clinton, when asked if she supported

capital punishment, answered in the affirmative.（希拉里·）克林顿在被问及她对死刑的态度时作了肯定的回答。

superintend
[ˌsuːpərɪnˈtend]

v. 主管，监督

例 During the interval, Linton superintended a prize draw. 中间休息时，林顿组织了一次抽奖。

扩 superintendent *n.* 主管人；警察局长
superintendence *n.* 监督

deity
[ˈdeɪəti, ˈdiːəti]

n. 神，女神

例 This time of year, many families will go and pray not only to deities but to their ancestors as well. 每年(春节)这个时候，许多（中国）家庭会敬神，也会敬自己的祖先。

sensibility
[ˌsensəˈbɪləti]

n. 1. 感受能力；2. 感情

例 1. The writer is remembered most for his sensibility. 这位作家的情感表达能力众所周知。
2. The article offended her religious sensibilities. 那篇文章伤害了她的宗教感情。

eminence
[ˈemɪnəns]

n. 1. 卓越，著名；2. 高地，山丘

例 1. Many of his students have achieved eminence in their fields. 他的许多学生都在各自的领域有所成就。
2. He built his home on an eminence overlooking the city. 他在俯看城市的山丘上建造了自己的房子。

扩 eminent *adj.* 卓越的，杰出的
eminently *adv.* 卓越地

inculcate
[ɪnˈkʌlkeɪt]

v. 谆谆教诲

例 The teacher inculcated in her students the importance of good study habits. 老师向学生们强调养成好的学习习惯的重要性。

扩 inculcation *n.* 教导

subscribe
[səbˈskraɪb]

v. 1. 定期订阅；2. 捐款；3. 支持

记 sub (=underneath) + scribe (=write) → 写下（名字）→ 同意（购买）→ 订阅

例 1. We subscribe to several sports channels. 我们付费收看好几个体育频道。
2. She subscribes to various different charitable organizations. 她给几个不同的慈善机构捐款。
3. The authorities no longer subscribe to the view that disabled people are unsuitable as teachers. 当局不再支持残疾人不适宜做教师的观点。

扩 subscriber *n.* 订户
subscription *n.* 订阅（款）；会员费

banish ['bænɪʃ]

v. 1. 放逐；2. 驱散

例 1. He was banished to Australia, where he died five years later. 他被流放到澳大利亚，五年后在那里去世。

2. The sight of food banished all other thoughts from my mind. 看到吃的，我别的什么都忘记了。

revere [rɪ'vɪr]

v. 尊敬

例 He's a well-known believer in judicial restraint, the quality Republicans claim to revere in judges. 众所周知他坚信司法应有所克制，这正是共和党人所看重的法官品质。

扩 reverence *n.* 尊敬，崇敬

ameliorate [ə'miːliəreɪt]

v. 改善

例 Progressives favor governments that widely distribute economic growth and work to ameliorate power imbalances. 进步主义者支持政府广泛分享经济发展成果，以改善权力分布不均衡。

扩 amelioration *n.* 改善

indebted [ɪn'detɪd]

adj. 1. 感激的；2. 负债的

记 in (=enter) + debt + ed → 进入负债状态 → 欠人情 → 感激的

例 1. I am deeply indebted to my family for all their help. 我深深感激我的家人给我所有的帮助。

2. America's treasury secretary identified the most heavily indebted countries. 美国财政部长指出了负债最多的那些国家。

interpose [ˌɪntər'poʊz]

v. 1. 插话；2. 夹进，介入

记 inter (=between) + pose (=put) → 放在两者中间 → 插话

例 1. Please allow me to interpose a brief observation. 请允许我插入一段简短的观察内容。

2. He quickly interposed himself between Mel and the doorway. 他迅速挡在梅尔和门口之间。

扩 interposition *n.* 介入

patronage ['pætrənɪdʒ, 'peɪ-]

n. 1. 资助；2. 互惠互利；3. 光顾

记 patron (=father, support) + age → 给予支持 → 顾客，光顾

例 1. Patronage of the arts comes from businesses and private individuals. 对艺术的资助来自企业和个人。

2. The reforms are intended to halt political patronage and corruption. 这些改革旨在阻止政治交易和腐败。

3. The city should do more to encourage patronage of local businesses. 该市应该采取措施鼓励大家光顾本地商店。

扩 patron *n.* 资助人；顾客

patronize *v.* 经常光顾；资助

denote
[dɪˈnoʊt]

v. 1. 标志，预示；2. 表示
记 de (=completely) + note (=mark) → 标记清楚
例 1. And in a country where accent can still denote social class, his problems included the rather fundamental one of how to speak. 在一个口音仍然代表社会阶层的国家，他的问题包括基本的说话方式。
2. The red triangle denotes danger. 红色三角形表示危险。

corps
[kɔːr]

n. (*pl.* corps) 1. 兵团；2. 特种部队；3. 一群人
记 本意为 body，引申为“一群人”
例 1. Peace Corps recently announced the suspension of its operations there. 维和部队最近宣布暂停那里的军事行动。
2. A spokesman for Portland says the Army Corps hopes to begin the work in the spring of 2017. 波特兰的发言人称陆军特种部队希望能在 2017 年春天开始动工。
3. Sanders travels with his press corps and sometimes wanders to the back of the plane to answer a few questions. 桑德斯与记者团同行，有时还会走到飞机后部回答一些（记者们提出的）问题。
辨 corpse *n.* 尸体

modesty
[ˈmɑːdəsti]

n. 1. 谦虚；2. 庄重，朴素；3. 中庸
记 mode (=measure) + sty → 可测量，有限度 → 谦虚，中庸
例 1. He accepted the award with characteristic modesty. 他以他一贯的谦逊态度接受了奖项。
2. The male demand for female modesty, she argued, is implicitly backed by the threat of violence. 她说，男性要求（穆斯林）女性着装朴素，这其中暗藏着暴力的威胁。
3. They tried to disguise the modesty of their achievements. 他们成就不大，所以力图掩盖这一点。

nourish
[ˈnɜːrɪʃ]

v. 1. 养育；2. 助长
记 nour (=nurse) + ish → 养育
例 1. All the children were well nourished and in good physical condition. 所有这些孩子都营养良好，身体健康。
2. By investing in education, we nourish the talents of our children. 我们通过教育投资，培养孩子们的才能。
扩 nourishment *n.* 营养品

recess
[rɪˈses, ˈriːses] *n.*
[rɪˈses] *v.*

n. 1. 休会，休庭，课间休息；2. 隐蔽处；*v.* 暂停
记 re (=back) + cess (=go) → 停止 → 休会，课间休息
例 1. The judge called a short recess. 法官宣布短暂休庭。
2. The doubt was still there, in the deep recesses of her mind. 在她的内心深处依然存有疑虑。
3. The hearing was recessed for the weekend. 听证会周末暂停。
扩 recessive *adj.*（基因）隐性的

gloom
[gluːm]

n. 1. 忧郁; 2. 昏暗

例 1. The gloom deepened as the election results came in. 选举结果陆续传来，失落的情绪越来越重。

2. We watched the boats come back in the gathering gloom. 我们注视着船只在朦胧暮色中返航。

扩 gloomy *adj.* 前景黯淡的；忧郁的

accordance
[əˈkɔːrdns]

n. 依照，依据

例 His funeral will be private, in accordance with his wishes. 他的葬礼将不对外开放，这是他生前的愿望。

elude
[iˈluːd]

v. 1. 避开; 2. 使不记得

记 谐音“一路的”逃跑 → 避开

例 1. The two men managed to elude the police for six weeks. 这两个男人想方设法逃避警方追捕达六个星期。

2. Finally he remembered the tiny detail that had eluded him the night before. 他终于想起了前一天晚上想不起来的细节。

扩 elusive *adj.* 难找的，难解释的

gradation
[grəˈdeɪʃn]

n. 1. 等级，渐度; 2. 刻度

记 grade（年级，梯度）→ 等级；刻度

例 1. But TV images require subtle gradations of light and shade. 但是，电视影像要求有十分细微的光影变化。

2. It has a trough compass, and the gradations around the edge of the semicircle are marked with tiny brass pins. 它有个槽状的罗盘，而半圆形的边缘刻度标着小的铜针。

aloof
[əˈluːf]

adj. 冷漠的，漠不关心的

例 I liked the people, who were politely aloof at first, but who were lovely once they warmed up to you. 我喜欢这样的人，他们开始时保持客气的距离，但跟你熟络起来后就变得很可爱。

扩 aloofness *n.* 冷漠

zeal
[ziːl]

n. 激情

例 In their zeal to industrialize, they got rid of too many farms. 伴随着工业化的热潮，他们解散了太多的农场。

扩 zealous *adj.* 有热情的

censorship
[ˈsensərʃɪp]

n. 审查制度

记 censor 谐音“审 sir”→ 审查员 → 审查制度

例 The decree imposed strict censorship of the media. 这个法令强制实行严格的媒体审查制度。

扩 censor *n.* 审查员；*v.* 删剪
censorial *adj.* 审查的

mold
[məʊld]

n. 1. 模具；2. 类型，风格；3. 霉菌；*v.* 塑造
记 与 model（模特）同源 → 模具 → 塑造
例 1. They broke the mold when they made you. 你是世上独一无二的。
2. She doesn't fit (into) the traditional mold of an academic. 她不像一个传统的学者。
3. She's allergic to mold, cigarette smoke, and dust. 她对霉菌、香烟和灰尘过敏。
4. The experience had molded and colored her whole life. 这次经历影响了她的一生。

entreat
[ɪn'triːt]

v. 恳求，乞求
记 en (=make) + treat → 使对待 → 恳求
例 My mother said a prayer before I left and entreated my ancestors to guide and protect me. 我动身之前，母亲作了番祷告，祈求祖先们指引并保护我。
扩 entreatment *n.* 恳求
entreaty *n.* 恳求

subdivide
['sʌbdɪvaɪd, ˌsʌbdɪ'vaɪd]

v. 再分割
例 The people who attend the conference can be subdivided into three distinct groups. 参加大会的人群可以分成三个不同的组。
扩 subdivision *n.* 细分；分支

exquisite
[ɪk'skwɪzɪt, 'ekskwɪzɪt]

adj. 1. 精美的，精致的；2. 非常的，剧烈的；3. 微妙的
例 1. Her wedding dress was absolutely exquisite. 她的婚妙极其精美。
2. He chose his words with exquisite care. 他非常仔细地斟酌字句。
3. The room was decorated in exquisite taste. 这个房间的装饰情趣高雅。
扩 exquisitely *adv.* 精致地

gospel
['gɑːspl]

n. 1. 福音；2. 信念；3. 绝对真理
记 谐音"高射炮"→ 弘扬福音
例 1. I didn't shirk my duties. I visited the sick and I preached the gospel. 我没有逃避职责，我探望病人，也宣讲福音。
2. He preached a gospel of military strength. 他鼓吹军事实力主义。
3. Don't take his word as gospel. 别把他的话当作绝对真理。

axiom
['æksiəm]

n. 公理
例 I'm reminded of an axiom we're all familiar with: objects in the rearview mirror may appear closer than they are. 我想起一个大家都很熟悉的谚语：后视镜看东西更近。
扩 axiomatic *adj.* 不证自明的

List 7

sullen
['sʌlən]

adj. 1. 闷闷不乐的；2. 阴沉的

例 1. Geniuses can be sullen introverts like Michelangelo or garrulous extroverts like Titian. 天才可能是阴郁的内向性格，比如米开朗琪罗；也可能是饶舌的外向性格，比如提香。

2. The sullen wet heat of Volantis sapped his strength and left him feeling dirty. 瓦兰提斯阴沉湿热的天气让他无精打采，感觉浑身肮脏。

duly
['du:li]

adv. 1. 恰当地；2. 按时地

记 due 的副词

例 1. The document was duly signed by the inspector. 这份文件已由检查员签妥。

2. They duly arrived at 9:30 in spite of torrential rain. 尽管下着倾盆大雨，他们仍在 9:30 准时到达了。

扩 undue *adj.* 不适当的，过分的

unduly *adv.* 过分，过度

fetish
['fetɪʃ]

n. 1. 迷恋，癖；2. 神物，圣物

例 1. What began as a postwar fetish for sunbathing is rapidly developing into a world health crisis. 战后兴起的对日光浴的迷恋后来迅速演变成全球范围内的健康问题。

2. The tribal leader wore a rabbit's foot around his neck as a fetish. 部落首领脖子上戴着兔脚作为圣物。

urchin
['ɜ:rtʃɪn]

n. 1. 流浪儿；2. (sea urchin) 海胆

例 1. We were in the bazaar with all the little urchins watching us. 我们在集市里，周围一大帮衣衫褴褛的小孩盯着我们看。

2. Sea urchins and sea cucumbers are harvested off of Maine and both are sold to buyers in Asia. 人们在缅因州海岸捕捞海胆和海参卖给亚洲买家。

preponderate
[prɪ'pɑ:ndəreɪt]

v. 主导，压倒

记 pre (=before) + pond (=pound, weight) + er + ate → 提前压倒 → 主导

例 Looking backwards, I can now perceive how my love for science gradually preponderated over every other taste. 回首过去，我现在才明白我对理科的偏爱如何逐渐压倒了我对别的兴趣。

扩 preponderant *adj.* 主导的

preponderance *n.* 优势，多数

allot
[ə'lɑ:t]

v. (allotted, allotted; allotting) 分配（时间、钱财等）；分派（任务）

记 lot 有“一块（土地）、抓阄”之意 → 分配

例 1. I completed the test within the time allotted. 我在限定的时间内完成了测试。

2. The newspaper will allot a full page to each of the three mayoral candidates. 报纸将给每位市长候选人一整版的报道。

扩 allotment *n.* 小块土地；分配额

List 8

saga
['sɑːɡə]

n. 1. 长篇小说；2. 经历，记述

记 本意“萨迦”原指北欧神话 → 故事；记述

例 1. *Downton Abbey* is smart to bring its saga to a close before it lets more time pass.《唐顿庄园》很巧妙地在短时间内把故事带到观众面前。

2. The front page is devoted to the continuing saga of the hijack. 头版是对劫持事件的连续报道。

sage
[seɪdʒ]

n. 哲人，圣人；*adj.* 贤明的

例 1. A virtue advocated by the ancient Chinese sage and philosopher Confucius, it promotes absolute respect to elders, particularly parents and ancestors. 作为中国古圣贤孔子推崇的美德，它（磕头）能促进尊老敬长，尤其是对父母和祖先。

2. Looking back, that was obviously sage advice, but I thought the sooner I started a Ph.D. the better. 回想起来，那个建议很明智，但我当时认为越早读博士越好。

扩 sagacious *adj.* 洞察事理的

sagacity *n.* 贤明

upright
['ʌpraɪt]

adj. 1. 直立的；2. 正直的；*adv.* 垂直着

例 1. Gradually raise your body into an upright position. 慢慢起身，成直立状态。

2. Barty Crouch was a stiff, upright, elderly man, dressed in an impeccably crisp suit and tie. 巴蒂·克劳奇是位刻板、正直的老人，穿着挺括的西装和领带。

3. There wasn't enough room to stand upright, so we had to bend over. 空间太低直不起腰，我们只能弯着腰。

delineate
[dɪ'lɪnieɪt]

v. 1. 描画；2. 解释

记 de (=completely) + line (=draw) + ate → 全部刻画 → 描画

例 1. The ship's route is clearly delineated on the map. 这条船的航线清楚地标在地图上。

2. The report clearly delineates the steps that must be taken. 报告很清楚地解释了必要的步骤。

扩 delineation *n.* 描述，解释

accost
[ə'kɔːst, ə'kɑːst]

v.（贸然）搭讪

记 ac (=to) + cost (=coast, side) → 走到身边 → 搭讪

例 She was accosted in the street by a complete stranger. 在街上，一个

完全陌生的人贸然走到她跟前搭讪。

gleam
[gliːm]

v. 1. 闪烁，发微光；2. 闪现，流露；*n.* 1. 微光；2. 表露

例 1. The moonlight gleamed on the water. 月光照在水面上泛起粼粼波光。
2. His eyes gleamed with amusement. 他眼睛里流露出愉悦的神情。
3. A few gleams of sunshine lit up the gloomy afternoon. 几线阳光使阴暗的下午亮了起来。
4. The gleam in his eye made her uncomfortable. 他闪烁的眼神令她感到不舒服。

attentive
[əˈtentɪv]

adj. 1. 专心的；2. 关心的

记 与 attention 同源

例 1. Attentive readers might notice some mistakes in the book. 细心的读者可能会注意到书中一些错误。
2. The hotel staff are friendly and attentive. 旅馆人员友好而且照顾周到。

扩 attentively *adv.* 专注地；关心地

jeopardy
[ˈdʒepərdi]

n. 危险，威胁

例 The wrong decision could place your career in jeopardy. 这个错误决定可能会让你的职业受到威胁。

扩 jeopardize *v.* 危及

insupportable
[ˌɪnsəˈpɔːrtəbl]

adj. 难以接受的，棘手的

例 Their debt had become an insupportable burden. 他们的债务已经变成了难以忍受的重负。

haughty
[ˈhɔːti]

adj. 傲慢的

例 He replied with haughty disdain. 他的回答充满了不屑。

扩 haughtily *adv.* 傲慢地

convulse
[kənˈvʌls]

v. 1. 使痉挛；2. 全身抖动

例 1. A violent shiver convulsed him. 剧烈的颤抖使他抽搐不已。
2. The audience was convulsed with/by laughter. 全体观众都笑得抖动起来。

扩 convulsion *n.* 抽搐；骚动

retard
[rɪˈtaːrd] *v.*
[ˈriːtaːrd] *n.*

v. 阻碍，减缓；*n.* 弱智

例 1. The progression of the disease can be retarded by early surgery. 早期手术可以抑制病情的发展。
2. That made me crack up a little, even though I know there's nothing funny about being a mental retard. 那让我有点想笑，虽然我知道当弱智并没有什么好笑之处。

扩 retardation *n.* 阻碍

menace ['menəs]

n. 1. 威胁，危险的人（或物）；2. 恐吓；*v.* 威胁

例 1. Those dogs are a menace to the neighborhood. 这些狗对社区是个威胁。

2. They were accused of demanding money with menaces. 他们被控勒索钱财。

3. The forests are being menaced by major development projects. 大型开发项目正在危及森林。

actuate ['æktʃueɪt]

v. 1. 开动（机器）；2. 激励，驱使

记 act (=do) + u + ate → 使做 → 开动

例 1. The pump is actuated by the windmill. 水泵是由风车驱动的。

2. He was actuated entirely by malice. 他完全是出于恶意。

扩 actuation *n.* 激励；驱动

dogma ['dɔːgmə]

n. 教条

记 dog (=doc, document) + ma → 文件，教义 → 教条

例 1. These new findings challenge the current dogma in the field. 这些新发现挑战了这一领域的固有观念。

2. Their opposition to the reforms is based on pure dogma. 他们反对这些改革纯粹是出于教条。

扩 dogmatical *adj.* 教条的，武断的

Protestant ['prɑːtɪstənt]

n. 新教教徒；*adj.* 新教的

例 1. The Pilgrims were dissenting Protestants who sided closely with Cromwell in the English Civil War. 这些（赴北美）朝圣者都是持异见的新教教徒，他们在英国内战中曾坚决支持克伦威尔。

2. Nine Protestant civilians were killed in the 1993 attack in Belfast, as well as one of the IRA bombers. 有九名新教平民在 1993 年贝尔法斯特的袭击中丧生，此外还有一名爱尔兰共和军“人体炸弹”。

扩 Protestantism *n.* 新教

debase [dɪ'beɪs]

v. 降低价值，败坏名誉

记 de (=down) + base (=low) → 使低 → 贬低

例 Sport is being debased by commercial sponsorship. 体育运动因受商业赞助而降低了声誉。

扩 debasement *n.* 贬低

knit [nɪt]

v. 1. (knitted, knitted; knitting) 编织，针织；2. (knit, knit) 使紧密结合；3. (knit, knit) 使愈合

例 1. I knitted this cardigan myself. 我自己织的这件开襟毛衣。

2. Society is knit together by certain commonly held beliefs. 社会是靠某些共同的信念来维系的。

3. The bone failed to knit correctly. 骨头愈合得不好。

attire
[ə'taɪər]

n. 服装，礼服；*v.* 着装，穿衣

例 1. Proper attire is required at the restaurant. 该餐馆要求正式着装。
2. Sunday will be TV's biggest night, with formally attired celebrities ambling through the familiar red-carpet gantlet at the 67th Primetime Emmy Awards. 星期日将是电视台最重要的一晚，穿着正式的名人走上第 67 届艾美奖的红地毯。

detach
[dɪ'tætʃ]

v. 1. 拆卸，分开；2. 挣脱，离开；3. 派遣

记 de (=apart) + tach (=touch, unite) → 使分开 → 拆卸

例 1. Detach the coupon and return it as soon as possible. 将表格撕下后尽快寄回。
2. She detached herself from his embrace. 她挣脱了他的拥抱。
3. Five destroyers were detached to carry out a bombardment of the port. 五名爆破手被派去执行港口爆炸任务。

扩 detached *adj.* 不带感情的；公正的
detachable *adj.* 可拆卸的

chancellor
['tʃænsələr]

n. 1.（德国或澳大利亚）总理；2. 校长

记 chancell (=channel, lead) + or → 引导者 → 总理，校长

例 1. Germany's chancellor, Angela Merkel, is expected to address the refugee crisis in Europe, which could hurt her party in regional elections this month. 人们期望德国总理默克尔解决欧洲难民危机，但这可能危及本月该党和地区性选举。
2. Mark Wrighton, the university's thoughtful chancellor, and I were chatting before the ceremony. 该校校长马克·怀顿深思熟虑，他与我在仪式前闲聊了一会。

frantic
['fræntɪk]

adj. 1. 手忙脚乱的；2. 发狂的

例 1. Things are frantic in the office right now. 现在办公室里忙作一团。
2. Let's go back. Your parents must be getting frantic by now. 咱们回家吧。你的父母现在肯定快要急死了。

扩 frantically *adv.* 发狂地；忙乱地

adduce
[ə'duːs]

v. 引证，举证

记 ad (=to) + duce (=lead) → 引导，推导

例 Several factors have been adduced to explain the fall in the birth rate. 已经有几个因素可以说明出生率降低的原因。

injunction
[ɪn'dʒʌŋkʃn]

n. 1. 强制令；2. 警告，命令

例 1. The court granted an injunction against the defendants. 法庭对被告发出了禁制令。
2. We hear endless injunctions to build a sense of community among staff. 我们听到上面没完没了地讲要在员工中培养一种集体归属感。

扩 injunctive *adj.* 强制的

commotion
[kə'moʊʃn]

n. 喧闹，骚动

记 com (=together) + mot (=move) + ion → 群体运动 → 骚动

例 1. I heard a commotion and went to see what was happening. 我听到一阵喧闹便去看看发生了什么事情。

2. The crowd waiting outside was causing a commotion. 在外面等待的人群眼看就要发生骚乱。

paralyze
['pærəlaɪz]

v. 1. 使瘫痪；2. 使失灵，失效

例 1. The accident left him paralyzed from the waist down. 那场事故使他腰部以下都瘫痪了。

2. The federal bureaucracy is completely paralyzed right now; for lack of money, for lack of knowing where all of this is headed. 联邦政府机构现在完全失灵了，因为缺钱，也因为不知道怎么办。

扩 paralysis *n.* 瘫痪

plea
[pliː]

n. 1. 恳求；2. 答辩，辩护

记 与 please 同源 → 由“请”联想到“恳求”

例 1. She made an impassioned plea for help. 她恳切地求助。

2. He was charged with murder, but got off on a plea of insanity. 他被指控犯了谋杀罪，但以精神错乱为由逃过惩罚。

扩 plead *v.* (pleaded, pleaded; or pled, pled) 恳求；申辩

matrimony
['mætrɪmoʊni]

n. 婚配

例 Domestic partnership can be a creative alternative to matrimony. 民事结合或许是代替结婚的一种创造性的方式。

扩 matrimonial *adj.* 婚姻的

vassal
['væsl]

v. 1. 封臣，家臣；2. 附庸国

例 1. Feudal society's scheme of estates was bound by chains of oaths between lords and vassals. 封建社会的财产结构是由主仆盟誓联结起来的。

2. “The United States doesn't need allies; it needs vassals,” Putin said. 普京曾说过：“美国不需要联盟国，它需要的是附庸。”

辨 vessel *n.* 轮船；容器

befall
[bɪ'fɔːl]

v. (befell, befallen)（坏事）降临到

例 1. They were unaware of the fate that was to befall them. 他们并不知道即将降临到他们头上的厄运。

2. The drought was only one of many hardships to befall the small country. 干旱只是该国面临的诸多困难之一。

stride
[straɪd]

v. (strode, stridden) 大步走；*n.* 1. 大步；2. 进展

例 1. We strode across the snowy fields. 我们大步流星地穿过雪封的旷野。
2. I was gaining on the other runners with every stride. 我正一步步赶上其他运动员。
3. We're making great strides in the search for a cure. 在探索治疗办法方面，我们正不断取得重大进展。

felony
[ˈfeləni]

n. 重罪

例 He faces up to a decade behind bars because of prior felony convictions that prosecutors say include theft and burglary. 由于之前的重罪判决，包括检察官所说的偷盗和入室偷窃，他将面临最多十年的有期徒刑。

扩 felonious *adj.* 重罪的
felon *n.* 重罪犯

suspense
[səˈspens]

n. 担心，焦虑，兴奋，悬念

记 suspend（悬挂、暂停）的名词 → 悬心，担心

例 1. Don't keep us in suspense. Tell us what happened! 别让我们心老悬着了，告诉我们出了什么事！
2. I couldn't bear the suspense a moment longer. 这样提心吊胆，我一刻也受不了。

扩 suspenseful *adj.* 充满悬疑的
suspensive *adj.* 暂停的，悬而未决的

antagonist
[ænˈtæɡənɪst]

n. 对立者，对手

例 Indeed, if Trump were a figure in a movie or television series, he'd be the antagonist, not the protagonist. 确实，如果特朗普出现在影视剧中，那么他应该是个反面人物，而非主人公。

扩 antagonistic *adj.* 对抗的，对立情绪的

tact
[tækt]

n. 老练，圆滑

记 tact (=touch) → 接触，打交道 → 圆滑

例 On this occasion the press have not been intrusive and they have shown great tact. 媒体此次并没有过多纠缠，表现十分得体。

辨 tactile *adj.* 触觉的

扩 tactful *adj.* 得体的，圆滑的
tactic *n.* 手段，策略

expedite
[ˈekspədaɪt]

v. 加快，加速

记 ex (=out) + pedite (=chain for the feet) → 去掉脚镣 → 加快

例 We have developed rapid order processing to expedite deliveries to customers. 我们已开发了快速处理订单的方法以便迅速将货物交给顾客。

扩 expedient *adj.* 得当的，适宜的；*n.* 权宜之计
expeditious *adj.* 迅速完成的

physiognomy
[ˌfɪzi'ɑːnəmi]

n. 容貌，相貌

例 He was fascinated by her physiognomy—the prominent nose, brooding eyes and thick hair. 他被她的外表——高挺的鼻梁、深邃的双眸和浓密的秀发——迷住了。

mortal
['mɔːrtl]

adj. 1. 终将死亡的；2. 致命的；*n.* 普通人，凡人

例 1. We are all mortal. 我们都总有一死。
2. Her reputation suffered a mortal blow as a result of the scandal. 这一丑闻毁了她的名声。
3. Such things are not for mere mortals like ourselves. 这种事不会落在我们这样的凡夫俗子身上。

扩 mortality *n.* 死亡率
immortal *adj.* 长生的；流芳百世的；*n.* 不朽的人物

royalty
['rɔɪəlti]

n. 1. 王室成员；2. 版税

例 1. The gala evening was attended by royalty and politicians. 王室成员和政坛要人参加了这个晚会。
2. All royalties from the album will go to charity. 这张音乐专辑的全部版税收入将捐给慈善机构。

扩 royal *adj.* 王室的；庄严的

acquit
[ə'kwɪt]

v. (acquitted, acquitted; acquitting) 1. 宣判无罪；2. 表现（好或坏）

记 ac (=to) + quit (=free) → 使自由 → 宣判无罪

例 1. The jury acquitted him of murder. 陪审团裁决他谋杀罪不成立。
2. He acquitted himself brilliantly in the exams. 他在考试中表现出色。

扩 acquittal *n.* 宣布无罪

falsehood
['fɔːlshʊd]

n. 1. 虚假，说谎；2. 谎言

例 1. She called the verdict a victory of truth over falsehood. 她将这一判决称为真理对谬误的胜利。
2. He accused them of knowingly spreading falsehoods about him. 他指责他们故意散布有关他的谎言。

expound
[ɪk'spaʊnd]

v. 详述，解释

记 ex (=forth, out) + pound (=put, position) → 说出立场 → 解释

例 He expounded his views on the subject to me at great length. 他详细地向我阐述了他在这个问题上的观点。

fallible
['fæləbl]

adj. 会犯错误的

记 fall (=fail) + ible → 出错的

例 *Making a Murderer* reinforces what we already believe: that power structures are fallible and often corrupt.《制造杀手》这部纪录片强化了我们的认识，即权力结构有时会出错，而且通常有腐败行为。

扩 infallible *adj.* 一贯正确的；万无一失的
fallibility *n.* 犯错

grievance
[ˈgriːvəns]

n. 委屈，牢骚

例 He had been nursing a grievance against his boss for months. 他几个月来一直对老板心怀不满。

brethren
[ˈbreðrən]

n. 1.（教友）弟兄们；2. 同仁

记 brother 的古英语复数

例 1. Sri Lankans share a common ancestry with their Indian brethren. 斯里兰卡人和他们的印度兄弟有共同的祖先。
2. We should do all we can to help our less fortunate brethren. 我们应当尽力帮助那些不幸的兄弟姐妹。

beset
[bɪˈset]

v. (beset, beset; besetting) 困扰，威胁

例 It's one of the most difficult problems besetting our modern way of life. 那是困扰我们现代生活方式的一个最棘手的问题。

扩 besetment *n.* 困扰

complaisance
[kəmˈpleɪzəns]

n. 殷勤，顺从

记 com + plais (=please) + ance → 使高兴 → 殷勤

例 "Voltaire, like the French in general," said Dr. Young, "showed the greatest complaisance outwardly, and had the greatest contempt for us inwardly." 杨博士说："伏尔泰像多数法国人一样，外表很顺从，但内心对我们非常不屑。"

辨 complacency *n.* 自满，自鸣得意

扩 complaisant *adj.* 顺从的，殷勤的

conspire
[kənˈspaɪər]

v. 1. 密谋；2. 共同导致

记 com (=together) + spire (=breathe) → 同呼吸 → 密谋

例 1. They were accused of conspiring against the king. 他们被指控密谋反对国王。
2. Circumstances had conspired against them. 各种情况都凑在一起和他们作对。

扩 conspiracy *n.* 阴谋

rue
[ruː]

v. 懊悔

例 He rued the day they had bought such a large house. 他懊悔他们买了这样大的一所房子。

扩 rueful *adj.* 悲伤的，懊悔的

covet
[ˈkʌvət]

v. 渴望，觊觎

例 1. He had long coveted the chance to work with a famous musician. 他一直渴望有机会与著名音乐家一起工作。
2. They are this year's winners of the coveted trophy (=that everyone would like to win). 他们是人人都向往的本年度获奖者。

扩 covetous *adj.* 贪求的
covetousness *n.* 贪婪

enervate
['enərveɪt]

v. 使衰弱

记 e (=ex, out) + nerv (=spirit) + ate → 去掉精神 → 衰弱

例 Andy Murray said he tried a gluten-free diet but gave up, feeling enervated. 安迪·穆雷说，他尝试过无谷蛋白食物，但后来放弃了，因为感觉衰弱无力。

扩 enervation *n.* 虚弱

plurality
[plʊ'ræləti]

n. 1. 众多，大量；2.（未超过半数的）最多数票

记 plu (=plus) + ral + ity → 增加 → 众多

例 1. The researchers studied a plurality of approaches. 研究人员尝试了很多方法。

2. In order to be elected, a candidate needs only a plurality of the votes cast. 候选人只需要得票最多就能当选。

扩 pluralism *n.* 多元化；兼职

promulgate
['prɑːmlgeɪt]

v. 1. 传播，宣传；2. 颁布

例 1. Her theories have been widely promulgated on the Internet. 她的理论已经在网上得到广泛传播。

2. The law was promulgated in April 1988. 该法于 1988 年颁布。

扩 promulgation *n.* 散布，传播

pervert
[pər'vɜːrt]

v. 1. 败坏，误导；2. 腐蚀，侵害

记 per (=away) + vert (=turn) → 变坏 → 败坏

例 1. Some scientific discoveries have been perverted to create weapons of destruction. 某些科学发明被滥用来生产毁灭性武器。

2. Some people believe that television can pervert the minds of children. 有些人认为，电视能腐蚀儿童的心灵。

3. He was charged with conspiring to pervert the course of justice. 他被控谋划妨碍司法公正。

扩 perversion *n.* 颠倒，歪曲；变态

trample
['træmpl]

v. 1. 踩碎；2. 摧残

例 1. The campers had trampled the corn down. 野营的人践踏了庄稼。

2. Their most cherished traditions have been trampled. 他们最珍视的传统受到了破坏。

perplex
[pər'pleks]

v. 使困惑

记 per (=through) + plex (=complex) → 复杂化 → 困惑

例 The cures for some of the world's most perplexing diseases might be closer than we think. 对于当今世界最令人头疼的一些疾病，其治疗有望来得出乎意料的快。

扩 perplexity *n.* 困惑

cabal
[kə'bæl, - 'bɑːl]

n. 政治阴谋小集团

例 He had been chosen by a cabal of fellow senators. 他已被一个由一些参议员同仁组成的小集团选中。

crave
[kreɪv]

v. 1. 渴望；2. 恳求

例 1. That middle class also craves better housing, however, generating an insatiable thirst for land among developers. 然而，中产阶层渴望更好的住房条件，这将让开发商对土地的渴求更加难以满足。
2. I must crave your pardon. 我必须恳求您原谅。

扩 craving *n.* 强烈的愿望

tout
[taʊt]

v. 1. 标榜，吹捧；2. 招徕，兜售

记 与 shout 形似 → 叫喊 → 吹捧

例 1. She's being touted as the next leader of the party. 她被吹捧为该党的下一任领导人。
2. He's busy touting his client's latest book around London publishers. 他正忙于向伦敦多家出版商兜售他的委托人的一部新书。

commend
[kə'mend]

v. 1. 称赞；2. 推荐；3. 委托给

记 与 recommend 近义

例 1. His designs were highly commended by the judges. 他的设计受到了评委的高度赞扬。
2. The movie has little to commend it. 这部电影乏善可陈。
3. We commend her soul to God. 我们把她的灵魂托付给上帝。

扩 commendation *n.* 赞扬；奖励
commendable *adj.* 值得赞扬的

emancipate
[ɪ'mænsɪpeɪt]

v. 解放

记 e (=ex, out) + man (=hand) + cip (=take) + ate → 放开手 → 解放

例 Slaves were not emancipated until 1863 in the United States. 美国奴隶直到 1863 年才获得自由。

扩 emancipation *n.* 解放

afflict
[ə'flɪkt]

v. 使痛苦

记 af (=to) + flict (=strike) → 打 → 使痛苦

例 About 40% of the country's population is afflicted with the disease. 全国 40% 左右的人口患有这种疾病。

扩 affliction *n.* 痛苦

exalt
[ɪg'zɔːlt]

v. 1. 提拔，提升；2. 表扬

记 ex (=out) + alt (=high) → 使高 → 提升

例 1. His behavior has exalted the power and prestige of his office. 他的行为提升了他职务的权力和声誉。
2. The essay exalts the simple beauty of the country. 这篇文章颂扬了乡村的简朴之美。

扩 exaltation *n.* 兴奋；提拔

alienate
['eɪliəneɪt]

v. 1. 使疏远；2. 使格格不入

记 alien (=foreign) + ate → 使陌生

例 1. His comments have alienated a lot of young voters. 他的评论使许多年轻选民离他而去。
2. Very talented children may feel alienated from the others in their class. 天才出众的孩子可能觉得与班上的同学格格不入。

扩 alienation *n.* 疏远
alienated *adj.* 不合群的，不亲密的

dismember
[dɪs'membər]

v. 1. 肢解；2. 分割，瓜分

例 1. The victims' bodies had been dismembered and buried in the basement. 受害人的尸体被肢解后埋进了地窖。
2. The American railroad network has gradually been dismembered. 美国铁路系统已经逐步被瓜分了。

扩 dismemberment *n.* 肢解；瓦解

litigate
['lɪtɪgeɪt]

v. 打官司，诉讼

例 The company's unwillingness to make a deal increased her desire to litigate. 该公司不愿和解，逼得她想打官司。

扩 litigation *n.* 诉讼
litigant *n.* 诉讼当事人

mortify
['mɔːrtɪfaɪ]

v. 使难堪，使羞愧

记 mort (=death) + ify → 使想死 → 使难堪

例 She was mortified to realize he had heard every word she said. 她意识到自己的每句话都被他听到了，羞得无地自容。

扩 mortification *n.* 屈辱感，窘迫感

abominable
[ə'bɑːmɪnəbl]

adj. 令人憎恶的，极讨厌的

例 1. The judge described the attack as an abominable crime. 法官称那次袭击是一桩令人发指的罪行。
2. We were served the most abominable coffee. 给我们喝的是最劣质的咖啡。

扩 abominate *v.* 憎恨，厌恶
abominably *adv.* 憎恶地

etiquette
['etɪket, - kət]

n. 礼节，礼仪

例 Her failure to respond to the invitation was a serious breach of etiquette. 她没回复邀请函是一件非常失礼的事。

deplore
[dɪ'plɔːr]

v. 公开谴责，强烈反对

例 Like everyone else, I deplore and condemn this killing. 我同所有人一样强烈谴责这桩凶杀案。

扩 deplorable *adj.* 令人震惊的，糟透了的

dignify
['dɪgnɪfaɪ]

v. 1. 使有尊严，使显贵; 2. 美化

例 1. The mayor was there to dignify the celebrations. 市长的光临为庆祝活动增辉。
2. I'm not going to dignify his comments by reacting to them. 我才不会理睬他的评论以抬高其身价呢。

扩 dignity *n.* 庄重，尊严
dignitary *n.* 达官贵人
indignity *n.* 侮辱

emanate
['emənеɪt]

v. 产生，表现

例 1. He emanates power and confidence. 他表现出力量和信心。
2. The proposal originally emanated from the UN. 这个建议最初是由联合国提出的。

扩 emanation *n.* 显示，表现

garrison
['gærɪsn]

n. 守备总队 *v.* 驻防

例 1. Half the garrison is/are on duty. 卫戍部队有半数人在执勤。
2. Two regiments were sent to garrison the town. 派了两个团驻守在那个城镇。

pulpit
['pʊlpɪt]

n. 1. 布道坛; 2.（宗教）教职（人员）

例 1. Speaking from the pulpit of a black church there, she demands: "We need action now." 她站在黑人教堂的布道坛上说："我们需要立即采取行动。"
2. The war crimes were denounced from the pulpit. 战争罪行受到教会的谴责。

doom
[du:m]

n. 毁灭; *v.* 使遭殃

例 1. She had a sense of impending doom. 她预感到厄运已经逼近。
2. The marriage was doomed from the start. 这桩婚姻从一开始就注定要破裂。

扩 doomsday *n.* 世界末日
doomsayer *n.* 凶事预言者

wicked
['wɪkɪd]

adj. 1. 邪恶的; 2. 调皮的; 3. 严重的，危险的

例 1. Many Republican politicians think of Mrs. Clinton as actively wicked. 许多共和党政客认为（希拉里·）克林顿居心叵测。
2. Jane has a wicked sense of humor. 简有一种恶作剧的幽默感。
3. I had two fractures, two torn tendons, some wicked road rash and a concussion. 我当时有两处骨折，两处肌腱撕裂，几处严重的皮肉擦伤，还有脑震荡。

扩 wickedness *n.* 邪恶；邪恶的东西

edifice
['edɪfɪs]

n. 1. 大厦，宏伟的建筑; 2. 复杂系统

例 1. The American consulate was a magnificent edifice in the center of Bordeaux. 美国领事馆是位于波尔多市中心的一座宏伟的大厦。

2. The whole edifice of EU environmental policy is threatened by this bill. 欧盟环境政策的整个体系都受到该法案的威胁。

affront
[ə'frʌnt]

v./n. 侮辱，冒犯

记 af (=to) + front → 使面对 → 冒犯

例 1. He hoped they would not feel affronted if they were not invited. 他希望如果他们没有获得邀请也不要感到受辱。

2. He regarded her rude behavior as a personal affront. 他把她的粗鲁行为视作侮辱。

preliminary
[prɪ'lɪmɪneri]

adj. 预备性的，初步的；*n.* 初步行动

记 pre (=before) + limin (=limit) + ary → 进入之前 → 初步的

例 1. After a few preliminary remarks he announced the winners. 说了几句开场白之后，他即宣布优胜者名单。

2. I'll skip the usual preliminaries and come straight to the point. 闲话少说，我就直接进入正题。

treacherous
['tretʃərəs]

adj. 1. 背叛的；2. 有潜在危险的

例 1. He was weak, cowardly and treacherous. 他软弱、胆怯、奸诈。

2. The ice on the roads made driving conditions treacherous. 路上的冰对驾车构成了隐患。

扩 treachery *n.* 背叛，变节

List 9

reprove
[rɪ'pruːv]

v. 责备，非难

例 I was the first one to giggle, and on my second giggle I got a sternly reproving look from the man sitting ahead of me. 我是第一个笑的，我第二次笑的时候，前排的人给了我一个严厉责备的眼神。

扩 reproof *n.* 责备；责备的话

faction
['fækʃn]

n. 1. 派系，小集团；2. 内讧

例 1. The committee soon split into factions. 该委员会很快便分裂成几个派系。

2. Faction and self-interest appear to be the norm. 派系之争和自私自利看来非常普遍。

辨 fraction *n.* 分数

扩 factious *adj.* 派系的；内乱的

draft
[dræft]

n. 1. 通风；2. 一饮；*adj.* 散装的，零售的

例 1. A cold draft of air blew in from the open window. 一股寒气从敞开的窗户吹了进来。

2. He took a deep draft of his beer. 他喝了一大口啤酒。

3. Draft beers high in alcohol make up four-fifths of the local market. 高度的散装啤酒占当地市场的 4/5。

辨 drought *n.* 干旱

pervade
[pər'veɪd]

v. 渗透，弥漫

记 per (=through) + vade (=go) → 到处走 → 渗透

例 But gender-based violence and discrimination remains a major problem in the country, which is known for a pervading "machista" culture. 但性暴力和性歧视仍然是该国（墨西哥）的一个主要问题，这源于一种普遍存在的"男权"文化。

扩 pervasive *adj.* 遍布的，弥漫的

recede
[rɪ'siːd]

v. 1. 逐渐远离；2. 逐渐减弱；3. 变秃顶

记 re (=back) + cede (=go) → 退回去 → 远离，减弱

例 1. The sound of the truck receded into the distance. 卡车的声音渐渐在远处消失了。

2. The prospect of bankruptcy has now receded. 破产的可能性现已减少了。

3. His hair started receding when he was in his thirties. 他三十多岁时发际线开始后退了。

扩 recession *n.* 经济衰退；撤回

condescend
[ˌkɑːndɪˈsend]

v. 1. 屈尊，俯就；2. 傲慢，表现得高人一等

记 com (=together) + descend (=go down) → 下降到现一高度 → 俯就

例 1. We had to wait almost an hour before he condescended to see us. 我们等了几乎一小时他才屈尊大驾来见我们。
2. When giving a talk, be careful not to condescend to your audience. 发表讲话时，注意别对听众表现出高人一等的样子。

扩 condescension *n.* 傲慢，俯就

overwhelm
[ˌoʊvərˈwelm]

v. 1.（感情）充溢；2. 压倒，征服；3. 淹没，漫过

例 1. She was overwhelmed by feelings of guilt. 她感到愧疚难当。
2. The army was overwhelmed by the rebels. 军队被叛乱者完全击败了。
3. The boat was overwhelmed by a huge wave. 这艘船被大浪淹没了。

扩 overwhelming *adj.* 压倒性的，巨大的

rapture
[ˈræptʃər]

n. 狂喜，兴高采烈

记 由 rapt 联想到 rap → 狂喜

例 1. Charles listened with rapture to her singing. 查尔斯兴致勃勃地听她演唱。
2. The children gazed at her in rapture. 孩子们欣喜若狂地看着她。

扩 rapturous *adj.* 狂喜的，兴高采烈的

ascribe
[əˈskraɪb]

v. 1. 把…归因于；2. 认为…具有

记 a (=to) + scribe (=write) → 写上去 → 归因于

例 1. He ascribed his failure to bad luck. 他认为自己的失败是运气不好。
2. We ascribe great importance to these policies. 我们认为这些政策十分重要。

toil
[tɔɪl]

v. 1. 苦干，劳作；2. 跋涉，缓慢移动；*n.* 苦干

例 1. He's been toiling (away) in his workshop. 他一直在车间里苦干。
2. They toiled up the hill in the blazing sun. 他们冒着炎炎烈日艰难地一步一步爬上山冈。
3. After three days of toil, he hopes to fill at least nine 50 kg bags with charcoal blocks made from the red-colored wood. 经过三天的苦干后，他希望能装满 9 袋 50 公斤装的红木木炭。

circumspect
[ˈsɜːrkəmspekt]

adj. 小心谨慎的，慎重的

记 circum (=around) + spect (=look) → 四下环顾 → 小心的

例 He was very circumspect in his financial affairs. 他对自己的金融事务非常谨慎。

扩 circumspection *n.* 谨慎

abhor
[əb'hɔːr]

v. (abhorred, abhorred; abhorring) 憎恨，厌恶
记 ab (=away) + hor (=horror) → 吓跑 → 憎恨
例 Silicon Valley abhors a ceiling, and Twitter has never quite been willing to admit that it might have one. 硅谷（高科技企业）憎恨“天花板”（增长见顶），而推特从来不愿意承认它已经没有增长空间了。
扩 abhorrent *adj.* 令人憎恶的
同 loathe

pathogen
['pæθədʒən]

n. 病原体
记 path (=disease) + o + gen (=produce) → 产生疾病的物质 → 病原体
例 One of its jobs is to act as a protective barrier, but sometimes pathogens sneak past. 它（胎盘）的作用就是充当防御机制，但有时病原体会偷偷潜入。
扩 pathogenic *adj.* 病原体的
pathogenesis *n.* 发病机理

writ
[rɪt]

n.（法庭）令状
记 古英语中是 write 的过去分词
例 The company has been served with a writ for breach of contract. 这家公司因违约已接到法院令状。

rash
[ræʃ]

n. 1. 皮疹；2. 大量，许多；*adj.* 鲁莽的
例 1. I come out in a rash if I eat chocolate. 我一吃巧克力就长皮疹。
2. There has been a rash of burglaries in the area over the last month. 近一个月这一带发生了很多起入室行窃案。
3. It would be rash to assume that everyone will agree with you on this. 你要是认为在这件事上谁都会同意你的看法，那就太欠考虑了。
扩 rashly *adv.* 鲁莽地

glitter
['glɪtər]

v. 1. 闪光，闪耀；2. 闪现，流露出；*n.* 1. 闪光；2. 魅力
例 1. Badges and medals glitter on his breast, a testament to things he's never done. 胸章和奖章在他胸前闪光，但他其实并未做出过这些成就。
2. His eyes glittered with greed. 他眼睛里闪现出贪婪的神色。
3. Since his death, the pavement outside his Soho penthouse has turned into a shrine of flowers and glitter. 他（大卫·鲍威）死后，他在梭霍的豪华公寓外的人行道上就堆满了鲜花和装饰品。
4. Though all four members attended the Oscars, they were not necessarily enamored of the glitter and the attention. 虽然四个成员都参加了奥斯卡颁奖礼，但他们并不一定享受它的魅力和别人的关注。
扩 glittering *adj.* 闪光的，有魅力的

soothe
[suːð]

v. 1. 安慰；2. 减轻
例 1. The music soothed her for a while. 音乐让她稍微安静了一会儿。
2. Take a warm bath to soothe tense, tired muscles. 洗个热水澡，让紧张疲劳的肌肉放松一下。
扩 soothing *adj.* 令人安慰的

conversant
[kən'vɜːrsnt]

adj. 1. 熟悉的，通晓的；2. 通晓外语的

记 与 converse（相反的）同根

例 1. You need to become fully conversant with the company's procedures. 你得对公司的程序了如指掌。
2. She's conversant in several languages. 她能晓好几门外语。

incontestable
[ˌɪnkən'testəbl]

adj. 无可否认的

记 in (=not) + con (=together) + test (=witness) + able → 不能证实（有理）→ 无可否认的

例 The evidence against him is incontestable. 这件对他不利的证据是无可置疑的。

扩 incontestably *adj.* 无可否认地

devour
[dɪ'vaʊər]

v. 1. 狼吞虎咽地吃；2. 如饥似渴地读；3. 吞没

例 1. The lions devoured their prey. 狮群啃光了猎物。
2. She devoured everything she could lay her hands on: books, magazines and newspapers. 无论是书、杂志，还是报纸，只要能弄到手，她都看得津津有味。
3. She was devoured by envy and hatred. 她心中充满嫉妒和憎恨。

fascist
['fæʃɪst]

n. 1. 法西斯主义者；2. 极右分子；*adj.* 法西斯的

例 1. Delmer Berg, the last known American survivor who fought fascists in 1930s Spain, has died in northern California. 狄姆·伯格，1930 年代反西班牙法西斯主义的最后一名美国幸存者，近日于加利福尼亚北部去世。

2. They point to fascist or racist undertones in his campaign. 他们指出了他竞选活动中的极右或种族主义倾向。
3. The thing is, Sanders wasn't wrong about the right-wing lunatics or the fascist dictatorships. 事实是，桑德斯对右翼狂人或法西斯独裁者的看法并没有什么错误。

扩 fascism *n.* 法西斯主义

detest
[dɪ'test]

v. 憎恶

记 de (=down) + test (=witness) → 让上天来见证 → 诅咒 → 憎恶

例 A drama about identical twins who detest each other was recorded in stereo, with the same actor playing both roles. 录影棚里录制了一出孪生兄弟互相厌恶的戏剧，由一个演员分饰两角。

扩 detestable *adj.* 可憎的

hue
[hjuː]

n. 1. 颜色，色调；2. 信仰

例 1. Her paintings capture the subtle hues of the countryside in autumn. 她的油画捕捉到了秋天乡村的微妙色调。
2. Further cuts in welfare have raised a hue and cry among the public. 进一步减少福利激起了公众的强烈抗议。

asunder
[ə'sʌndər]

adv. 碎，散
记 谐音“散的”
例 1. The government was torn asunder by scandal. 政府被丑闻搞得四分五裂。
2. The debate is tearing Wall Street asunder. 这场争论令华尔街分崩离析。

denomination
[dɪˌnɑːmɪ'neɪʃn]

n. 1. 教派；2. 面值，面额
例 1. Christians of all denominations attended the conference. 基督教所有教派的人都出席了这次会议。
2. The kidnappers asked for bills in small denominations. 绑架者要求得到小额面值的钞票。

foliage
['foʊliɪdʒ]

n. 枝叶
例 In Autumn, New England foliage turns vibrant shades of red, yellow, and orange. 秋天新英格兰的枝叶变成鲜艳的红色、黄色和桔黄色。

deduce
[dɪ'duːs]

v. 推论，演绎
记 de (=down) + duce (=lead) → 向下推导 → 推论
例 We can deduce a lot from what people choose to buy. 从人们选购的东西可以作出多方面的推断。
辨 deduct *v.* 减去，扣除
扩 deduction *n.* 演绎
deducible *adj.* 可推断的

persecute
['pɜːrsɪkjuːt]

v. 1. 迫害，压迫；2. 骚扰
例 1. Throughout history, people have been persecuted for their religious beliefs. 人们因宗教信仰而受迫害的情况贯穿了整个历史。
2. Why are the media persecuting him like this? 新闻媒体为什么总这样揪住他不放？
辨 prosecute *v.* 控告，检举
扩 persecution *n.* 迫害

pagan
['peɪgən]

n. 1. 异教徒；2. 追求享乐的人；*adj.* 教外的，异教的
例 1. The new religion was eager to convert the pagan world. 那种新宗教急于使异教徒皈依本教。
2. It is possible that the association of Valentine's Day with love is rooted in a tradition dating back to pagan Rome. 很可能圣瓦伦丁日（情人节）与爱情的关联要追溯到古罗马多神教（基督教之前）时期的传统。
扩 paganism *n.* 异教

gallant
['gæl**ə**nt]

adj. 1. 勇敢的，英勇的；2. 对女子殷勤的

例 1. She made a gallant attempt to hide her tears. 她强掩住泪水。
2. He offered her his seat in a gallant gesture. 他殷勤地把自己的座位让给她。

扩 gallantry *n.* 勇敢；殷勤

deride
[dɪ'raɪd]

v. 嘲笑，愚弄

记 de (=down) + ride (=laugh) → 嘲笑

例 One critic derides the book as dull and predictable. 有批评家嘲笑这本书枯燥老套。

扩 derision *n.* 嘲笑

intermission
[ˌɪntər'mɪʃn]

n. 1. 幕间休息；2. 间歇

记 inter (=between) + miss (=send) + ion → 放在中间 → 间歇

例 1. Coffee was served during the intermission. 幕间休息时有咖啡供应。
2. This state of affairs lasted without intermission for a hundred years. 这种局面从未间断地持续了一百年。

扩 intermittent *adj.* 间歇的，断断续续的

refresh
[rɪ'freʃ]

v. 1. 使恢复精力；2. 提醒，提示；3. 刷新，更新

例 1. He refreshed himself with a cool shower. 他冲了个凉水澡凉快凉快。
2. He had to refresh his memory by looking at his notes. 他不得不看笔记提醒自己。
3. The page refreshes automatically. 页面会自动更新。

扩 refreshment *n.* 小食，饮料；恢复活力

testament
['testəmənt]

n. 1. 证明；2. 遗嘱，遗言

记 test (=witness) + a + ment → 见证 → 证明

例 1. Scipio, in Washington, agreed: "This is indeed a testament to Apple's incredibly strong encryption." 西比奥在华盛顿赞同地说："这确实证明了苹果公司超凡的加密能力。"
2. At the back of all their minds exists one anxiety—the dispositions of my last will and testament. 他们内心深处有一种焦虑，那就是对我的遗嘱进行处置。

subservient
[səb'sɜːrviənt]

adj. 1. 恭顺的，驯服的；2. 次要的，从属于

记 sub (=under) + serv + ient → 在下面服务 → 恭顺的

例 1. The press was accused of being subservient to the government. 有人指责新闻界一味迎合政府的旨意。
2. The needs of individuals were subservient to those of the group as a whole. 个人的需要服从于整个集体的需要。

扩 subservience *n.* 驯服

delinquent
[dɪ'lɪŋkwənt]

adj. 1. 有违法倾向的；2. 欠债的

例 1. His delinquent behavior could lead to more serious problems. 他的违法行为可能会带来更严重的问题。

2. Delinquent power bills have been piling up for years and are one of the reasons cited by the electrical utility for its financial woes. 欠缴电费已经积累多年，成了电力公司财务困难的原因之一。

扩 delinquency *n.* 犯罪，违法行为

contingent
[kən'tɪndʒənt]

adj. 1. 依情况而定的；2. 临时工作的；*n.* 代表团

记 conting (=contact) + ent → 接触的 → 依赖的

例 1. All payments are contingent upon satisfactory completion dates. 所有的付款须视乎是否如期完成。

2. Understanding how to better utilize contingent and part-time workers is ranked as one of the top priorities for executives. 理解如何更好地利用临时和兼职工人这个问题，这是执行官的第一要务。

3. The largest contingent was from the United States. 最大的会议代表团来自美国。

扩 contingency *n.* 可能发生的事，偶发事件

extort
[ɪk'stɔːrt]

v. 敲诈，强夺

记 ex (=out) + tort (=twist) → 拧出来，挤出来 → 敲诈

例 The gang extorted money from over 30 local businesses. 这帮歹徒向当地30多家企业勒索过钱财。

扩 extortion *n.* 敲诈

inasmuch as
[ˌɪnəz'mʌtʃ əz]

conj. 鉴于…，在…范围内

例 1. He was a very unusual musician inasmuch as he was totally deaf. 他是完全失聪的，从这点上来说，他是个很了不起的音乐家。

2. They abide by the rules only inasmuch as it suits them. 只要合他们的意，他们还是遵守规则的。

dazzle
['dæzl]

v. 1. 使眼花；2. 使倾倒，使赞叹

例 1. He was momentarily dazzled by the strong sunlight. 强烈的阳光使他一时睁不开眼。

2. He was dazzled by the warmth of her smile. 她那温柔的微笑使他神魂颠倒。

扩 dazzling *adj.* 令人赞叹的，使人眼花的

contrive
[kən'traɪv]

v. 1. 设法做到；2. 促成；3. 巧妙策划

例 1. She contrived to spend a couple of hours with him every Sunday evening. 每周星期日晚上她都设法与他待上几个小时。

2. I decided to contrive a meeting between the two of them. 我决定设法让他们双方见上一面。

3. They contrived a plan to defraud the company. 他们精心策划要欺诈那家公司。

扩 contrivance *n.* 精巧装置；计谋

recoil
[rɪ'kɔɪl]

v. 1. 退缩；2. 反冲；*n.* 反冲力，后坐力

记 re (=back) + coil (=roll) → 向后卷 → 反冲

例 1. He recoiled in horror at the sight of the corpse. 他一见到尸体就吓得往后缩了。

2. The rifle recoiled and bruised my shoulder. 步枪产生后坐力，把我肩膀擦破了。

3. The gun has a sharp recoil. 这支枪的后坐力很大。

omnipotent
[ɑːm'nɪpətənt]

adj. 万能的，全能的

记 omni (=all) + potent (=power) → 万能的

例 Doug lived in the shadow of his seemingly omnipotent father. 道格生活在他那看似权威至高无上的父亲的阴影里。

扩 omnipotence *n.* 万能，全能

"I just don't feel very omnipotent today."

hypocrite
['hɪpəkrɪt]

n. 伪君子

例 Would God think I was a hypocrite, praying every time I was scared? 我每次害怕时都要祈祷，上帝会不会觉得我太伪善？

扩 hypocrisy *n.* 伪善

hypocritical *adj.* 伪善的

astray
[ə'streɪ]

adv. 1. 丢失地；2. 误入歧途地

记 a (=on) + stray (=street) → 在大街上 → 丢失地

例 1. We locked up our valuables so they would not go astray. 我们把贵重物品锁了起来以免被盗。

2. Jack's parents thought the other boys might lead him astray. 杰克的父母认为，其他的男孩可能会把他引入歧途。

perch
[pɜːrtʃ]

v. 1.（鸟）栖息；2.（使）坐，放置于；*n.* 栖息处，高处

例 1. A robin was perching on the fence. 一只知更鸟落在篱笆上。

2. We perched on a couple of high stools at the bar. 我们坐在酒吧的几张高脚凳上。

3. He watched the game from his precarious perch on top of the wall. 他无视安全，高坐在墙头上观看比赛。

bounty
['baʊnti]

n. 1. 慷慨之举，大量；2. 奖金，赏金

记 bount (=bonus) + y → 奖金，奖赏

例 1. The cottage is filled with a bounty of fresh flowers. 小木屋里摆满了鲜花。

2. A bounty of 500 dollars was put on his head. 有人悬赏 500 美元要他的人头。

apprise
[ə'praɪz]

v. 通知，告知

例 1. He wasn't on shift, but he was kept apprised at all times. 他当时并不当班，但他一直会接到通知。

2. At first, he thought it was an earthquake but now is apprised of the nuclear test conducted not that far across the border. 起初他以为是场地震，但现在他被告知是在边境附近进行了一次核试验。
辨 apprize *v.* 珍视

austere
[ɔː'stɪr]

adj. 1. 朴素的；2. 严肃的；3. 苦行的，禁欲的
例 1. They choose austere furnishings for the office. 他们为办公室选了朴素的装修。
2. My father was a distant, austere man. 我父亲是个难以接近的严肃的人。
3. They lived an austere life in the country. 他们在乡下过着苦行的生活。
扩 austerity *n.* 朴素，艰苦，（经济）紧缩

subvert
[səb'vɜːrt]

v. 1. 颠覆（政权）；2. 破坏，使失常
记 sub (=under) + vert (=turn) → 打翻 → 颠覆
例 1. They conspired to subvert the government. 他们密谋颠覆政府。
2. Tesla has issued a software update for its model S car after two researchers found a way to subvert its onboard systems. 在两名研究人员破解其操作系统之后，特斯拉发布了一款软件来更新其 S 型轿车。
扩 subversion *n.* 颠覆罪
subversive *adj.* 颠覆性的

judicature
['dʒuːdɪkətʃər]

n. 1. 司法系统；2. 审判人员
记 jud (=judge) + icature → 司法，裁判
例 1. In the Yamen of Judicature at Seoul I saw a few small private cells reserved for the better class. 在首尔的审判衙门，我看到一些留给上层阶层用的小单间。
2. In place of the monastic judicature a jury of six bachelors and six maidens appear in the 16th century. 取代修道院审判团的是 16 世纪由 6 名单身男士和 6 名单身女士组成的陪审团。
扩 judicatory *n.* 司法人员，审判人员

herald
['herəld]

v. 1. 预示；2. 宣称；*n.* 1. 预兆；2. 信使，传令官
记 谐音"海螺的"→ 吹号角 → 宣称，预示
例 1. These talks could herald a new era of peace. 这些谈判可能预示着新的和平时代的来临。
2. The report is being heralded as a blueprint for the future of transport. 这份报告被宣称是未来运输的蓝图。
3. The government claims that the fall in unemployment is the herald of economic recovery. 政府宣称失业人数减少是经济复苏的先兆。
4. A consultant created a coat of arms for the group featuring a herald's horn with blue background to represent "blue-sky thinking." 一名顾问为该团体创造了一个袖章，上面是蓝底的信使号角，寓意"天马行空式思维"。

sparkle
['spɑːrkl]

v. 1. 闪烁；2. 生气勃勃；*n.* 闪烁

例 1. Her jewellery sparkled in the candlelight. 烛光下，她的首饰光彩熠熠。
2. He always sparkles at parties. 在各种聚会上，他总是光芒四射。
3. There was a sparkle of excitement in her eyes. 她眼里闪耀着激动的光芒。

tangible
['tændʒəbl]

adj. 1. 有形的，实际的；2. 可触摸的，可感知的

记 tang (=touch) + ible → 可接触的

例 1. There is no tangible evidence to support her claim. 她的说法没有实际证据。
2. The tension between them was almost tangible. 他们之间的紧张关系几乎让人都感觉得出来。

preamble
[pri'æmbl]

adj. 序言，前言

记 pre (=before) + amble (=walk) → 走在前面 → 前言

例 She gave him the bad news without preamble. 她开门见山地把坏消息告诉了他。

fortuitous
[fɔːr'tuːɪtəs]

adj. 1. 偶然发生的；2. 幸运的

记 fortu (=fortune) + itous → 幸运的

例 1. His presence there was entirely fortuitous. 他出现在那里完全是偶然。
2. You could not have arrived at a more fortuitous time. 你到达的时间真是再好不过了。

扩 fortuitously *adv.* 偶然地；幸运地

succinct
[sək'sɪŋkt]

adj. 简明的

例 He also tweeted a more succinct statement after the verdict was made. 在裁决宣判以后，他也在推特上发表了一则更简短的声明。

扩 succinctly *adv.* 简明地

obliterate
[ə'blɪtəreɪt]

v. 覆盖，清除

记 ob (=against) + liter (=letter) + ate → 去掉字母 → 清除

例 The building was completely obliterated by the bomb. 炸弹把那座建筑物彻底摧毁了。

扩 obliteration *n.* 覆盖，毁掉

inclusive
[ɪn'kluːsɪv]

adj. 1. 包含全部费用的；2. 包含在内的；3. 包容广阔的

例 1. The rent is inclusive of water and heating. 租金包括水费和暖气费。
2. The castle is open daily from May to October inclusive. 这个古堡从五月起每天开放，直至十月尾。
3. The party must adopt more inclusive strategies and a broader vision. 这个党必须采取更广泛的策略和更远大的视野。

List 9

generic
[dʒəˈnerɪk]

adj. 1. 普通的，通用的；2.（药品）无商标的，无厂家的

记 gene (=kind) + ric → 同一种类的，非特殊的 → 普通的

例 1. 'Vine fruit' is the generic term for currants and raisins. vine fruit 是有核和无核葡萄干的通称。
2. The doctor offered me a choice of a branded or a generic drug. 医生让我选择用有商标的还是没有商标的（便宜）药物。

homogeneous
[ˌhoumәˈdʒiːniәs, hәˈmɑːdʒәnәs]

adj. 同种类的

记 homo (=same) + gene (=kind) + ous → 同一种类的

例 The unemployed are not a homogeneous group. 失业者不能一概而论。

transitory
[ˈtrænsətɔːri]

adj. 暂时的，片刻的

例 A key reason for the low inflation was the decline in energy prices, whose effects the Fed predicted would be "transitory." 低通胀的一个关键因素是能源价格下降，而美联储预测这种影响将是"暂时的"。

扩 transit *v.* 穿过；*n.* 运输；中转

同 fleeting, temporary

reprimand
[ˈreprɪmænd]

v. 训斥；*n.* 训斥

记 repri (=reprove) + mand (=command) → 命令般地谴责 → 训斥

例 1. The officers were severely reprimanded for their unprofessional behavior. 军官们因违反专业操守而受到了严厉的斥责。
2. He received a severe reprimand for his behavior. 他的行为受到了严厉谴责。

quench
[kwentʃ]

v. 1. 解渴；2. 扑灭，熄灭

例 1. He quenched his thirst by drinking a bottle of water. 他喝了一瓶水解渴。
2. Firemen tried to quench the flames raging through the building. 消防队员奋力扑救大楼中熊熊的火焰。

扩 quenchable *adj.* 可熄灭的

同 slake; extinguish

torpor
[ˈtɔːrpər]

n. 迟钝，死气沉沉

例 When I had first visited, India was only slowly waking from decades of economic torpor. 在我初次来访时，印度还在从几十年的经济萧条中缓慢苏醒过来。

同 lethargy

retribution
[ˌretrɪˈbjuːʃn]

n. 严惩，报应

记 re (=back) + tribut (=assign) + ion → 回馈 → 报复

例 People are seeking retribution for the latest terrorist outrages. 人们在设法对恐怖分子最近的暴行进行严惩。

扩 retributive *adj.* 报应的

inimical
[ɪ'nɪmɪkl]

adj. 1. 不利的；2. 敌意的，不友好的

记 inimi (=enemy) + cal → 敌意的

例 1. These policies are inimical to the interests of society. 这些政策有损于社会的利益。

2. The emperor slightly bit his lips, and a hard, almost an inimical look, flashed upon the empress. 皇帝轻咬着嘴唇，朝皇后恨恨地瞪了一眼。

crunch
[krʌntʃ]

n. 1. 压碎声；2. 困境，症结；3. 不足，短缺

例 1. The car drew up with a crunch of gravel. 那辆汽车在沙砾路上嘎吱一声停了下来。

2. He always says he'll help but when it comes to the crunch he does nothing. 他口口声声说一定帮忙，然而到关键时候却不会行动。

3. A number of unusual factors contributed to the cash crunch in March. 几个异常的因素导致了三月份出现了现金短缺。

volition
[və'lɪʃn, voʊ'-]

n. 意志力，自愿选择

例 A U.S. soldier—acting on his own volition—helped walk freed hostages to safety. 一名美军士兵自愿地陪同获释人质走到安全区域。

扩 volitional *adj.* 自愿的，自主的

precocious
[prɪ'koʊʃəs]

adj. 早熟的

记 pre + coc (=cook) + ious → 早熟的

例 From an early age she displayed a precocious talent for music. 她年纪轻轻就表现出不凡的音乐天赋。

扩 precocity *n.* 早熟

lax
[læks]

adj. 1. 马虎的，不严格的；2. 松散的

记 与 relax 同根

例 1. In Iran, a country of 80 million people, road accidents annually claim nearly 17,000 lives, which many blame on lax safety standards. 伊朗拥有 8000 万人口，而交通事故每年致死 1.7 万人，这要归咎于马虎的安全标准。

2. Were the ties of old friendship so lax as all this? 老朋友之间的联系都像这样松散吗?

扩 laxity *n.* 马虎，松散

penetrate
['penətreɪt]

v. 1. 穿过，进入；2. 渗透，混入；3. 被领悟

例 1. The war penetrates every area of the nation's life. 战争波及到全国国民生活的各个领域。

2. They had penetrated airport security. 他们已渗透机场保安组织。

3. I was at the door before his words penetrated. 我走到门口才听懂了他说的话。

扩 penetration *n.* 渗透

impenetrable *adj.* 不可进入的；高深莫测的

List 9

profuse [prəˈfjuːs]

adj. 1. 大量的，丰富的；2. 过多的，不吝惜的

记 pro (=forth) + fuse (=flow) → 多得流出 → 大量的

例 1. Complications include profuse bleeding in the digestive system that can lead to death. 并发症包括消化系统大量出血，并导致死亡。

2. His news conference began with a profuse apology, even to his children. 他在记者招待会开头不断地道歉，包括对他的孩子们道歉。

扩 profusion *n.* 大量，众多

profusely *adv.* 大量地

levity [ˈlevəti]

n. 轻佻，轻浮

记 levi (=light) + ty → 轻的 → 轻浮

例 1. She would not tolerate any levity in the classroom. 她不会允许课堂上有轻率的举动。

2. The joke provided a moment of levity in an otherwise dreary meeting. 这个笑话给原本枯燥的会议增添了一点轻松。

扩 levitate *v.* 升空，使飘浮

同 frivolity

headlong [ˈhedlɔːŋ, -lɑːŋ]

adv. 1. 轻率地；2. 莽撞地，慌张地

例 1. The government is taking care not to rush headlong into another controversy. 政府现在很谨慎，以防不慎陷入另一场争端。

2. He ran headlong into a police car. 他一头撞上了一辆警车。

latent [ˈleɪtnt]

adj. 潜在的，隐藏的

记 lat (=lay, lie) + ent → 放在下面的 → 潜在的

例 These children have a huge reserve of latent talent. 这些孩子蕴藏着极大的潜在天赋。

扩 latency *n.* 潜力

monotonous [məˈnɑːtənəs]

adj. 单调乏味的

记 mono (=single) + ton (=tone) + ous → 一个声调的 → 单调的

例 1. Students complained that the meals were monotonous. 学生们抱怨饭菜单调。

2. The job could be both monotonous and highly pressured, with work going on around the clock. 这份工作要求争分夺秒，因此可能单调而且压力很大。

扩 monotony *n.* 单调乏味，千篇一律

precipitate [prɪˈsɪpɪteɪt]

v. 1. 使突然降临，加速；2. 析出，结晶；*adj.* 鲁莽的，仓促的

例 1. Hera lost this beauty contest to Aphrodite, and it is claimed to be one of the precipitating events of the Trojan War. 赫拉在这场美貌之争中输给了阿芙罗狄特，据说这是加速特洛伊战争的原因之一。

2. Bile lingering in the organ may become stagnant and stones may precipitate out. 留在器官内的胆汁可能停滞不动，进而析出变成结石。

3. I don't think we should make precipitate decisions. 我认为我们不应该贸然作出决定。

扩 precipitation *n.* 降水；沉淀

malefactor
[ˈmælɪfæktər]

n. 犯罪分子，作恶之人

记 male (=bad) + fact (=do) + or → 做坏事的人

例 Microsoft provides security from malefactors, not privacy from corporate and governmental monitoring. 微软提供的安全措施能预防犯罪分子，阻止公司和政府获取个人隐私。

扩 malefaction *n.* 罪行

reprehensible
[ˌreprɪˈhensəbl]

adj. 不道德的，应受谴责的

记 re (=back) + prehens (=grasp) + ible → 反过来被抓住（把柄）的→ 不道德的

例 Mr. Cramer said the violence by anti-government protestors was reprehensible. 克拉默先生说反政府示威者的暴力活动应该受到谴责。

扩 reprehend *v.* 谴责

02

CHANG PIN CI HUI

LIST 10 ------ LIST 20

常频词汇

List 10

reiterate
[ri'ɪtəreɪt]

v. 重申，反复说

例 Let me reiterate that we are fully committed to this policy. 我再说一遍，我们对这项政策是全力以赴、坚定不移的。

扩 reiteration *n.* 重申

heresy
['herəsi]

n. 1. 宗教异端；2. 离经叛道的观点

例 1. He was burned at the stake for heresy. 他因为信奉异端思想而被火刑处死。
2. The idea is heresy to most employees of the firm. 这种想法有悖于公司大多数员工的意见。

扩 heretic *n.* 犯异端罪者
heretical *adj.* 异端的

"Heretic!"

petulant
['petʃələnt]

adj. 闹脾气的，任性的

记 pet (=seek) + ulant → 追求自己想要的 → 任性的

例 He behaved like a petulant child and refused to cooperate. 他表现得像个任性的孩子，拒绝合作。

扩 petulance *n.* 任性，发脾气

palliate
['pælieɪt]

v. 减轻，缓和

记 pall (=cover) + iate → 掩盖 → 减轻；pall 本身是一个单词，意为"浓烟，柩布"

例 He palliates his ignorance by pretending that his taste lies another way. 他假装说他的兴趣在别处，借以掩饰自己的无知。

扩 palliative *n.* 缓解剂；权宜之计

impeccable
[ɪm'pekəbl]

adj. 无错误的，完美的

记 im (=not) + pecc (=sin) + able → 无罪过的 → 完美的

例 He was dressed in a suit and an impeccable white shirt. 他身穿一套礼服和一件洁白的衬衣。

扩 peccadillo *n.* 过失

soliloquy
[sə'lɪləkwi]

n. 独白

记 soli (=single) + loqu (=speak) + y → 一个人说

例 There's not a single soliloquy that doesn't shed fresh insight into how Hamlet thinks. 所有的独白都表现了哈姆雷特的内心。

扩 soliloquize *v.* 独白

List 10

frugal
[ˈfruːgl]

adj. 1. 节俭的；2. 简单廉价的

例 1. I went in and perused the menu and, while it looked fantastic, it was a bit beyond my frugal budget. 我进去仔细看了看菜单，虽然菜看上去不错，但有点超出我紧张的预算了。

2. However you choose to celebrate the month, there are plenty of options for frugal fun. 不论你怎么庆祝这个月，总有几种方法找到简单的快乐。

扩 frugality *n.* 节俭

legacy
[ˈlegəsi]

n. 1. 遗产；2. 遗留问题；*adj.* 老化的

例 1. They each received a legacy of $5000. 他们每人得到了 5000 元的遗产。

2. Future generations will be left with a legacy of pollution and destruction. 留给子孙后代的将是环境的污染与破坏。

3. How can we integrate new technology with our legacy systems? 我们该如何将新技术整合到我们老化的系统上？

voluminous
[vəˈluːmɪnəs]

adj. 1. 肥大的，宽松的；2. 冗长的

记 volum (=volume) + inous → 很大容量的 → 宽松的

例 1. I sank down into a voluminous armchair. 我一下子坐在了宽大的扶手椅里。

2. They carried on a voluminous correspondence. 他们坚持写很长的信。

proletariat
[ˌproʊləˈteriət]

n. 工人阶级，普罗大众

记 中文词汇“普罗大众”是该词的法语或英语音译

例 Marx wrote of the class struggle between the bourgeoisie and the proletariat. 马克思曾写过资产阶级和工人阶级之间的斗争。

扩 proletarian *adj.* 无产者的

malign
[məˈlaɪn]

adj. 有害的；*v.* 诽谤，中伤

记 mal (=bad) + ign (=gene, born) → 骨子里坏的 → 有害的

例 1. Straw said at the time that the west had to recognize it had often had a malign influence on Iran. 当时，斯多说西方国家必须认识到它们通常对伊朗有不好的影响。

2. And Nixon's ugly attempt to malign her character left her shaken. 而尼克松试图诋毁她的人格让她很震惊。

扩 malignant *adj.*（疾病）恶性的；恶毒的
malignity *n.* 恶意

tantalize
[ˈtæntəlaɪz]

v. 招惹

记 源于希腊神话，宙斯之子 Tantalos 因泄漏天机而被罚站于齐下巴深的水中，头顶悬有结满美果的树枝。他口渴时水即减退，腹饥想吃果实时，树枝即升高。

例 She was tantalized by the possibility of earning a lot of money quickly. 能快速赚很多钱，这让她很受诱惑。

扩 tantalizing *adj.* 挑逗的，诱人的

fret
[fret]

v. (fretted, fretted; fretting) 苦恼，烦躁；*n.* 担心，烦恼

记 可能与 fetter（脚镣）同源

例 1. Her baby starts to fret as soon as she goes out of the room. 她一走出房间，婴儿就躁动起来。
2. Don't get in (such) a fret! We won't miss the plane. 别担心！我们不会赶不上飞机的。

扩 fretful *adj.* 烦躁的，不舒服的

glut
[glʌt]

v. (glutted, glutted; glutting) 超量供应，充斥；*n.* 供过于求

例 1. Soldiers returning from the war had glutted the job market. 从战场返乡的士兵挤爆了劳动力市场。
2. There's a glut of agricultural products in Western Europe. 西欧的农产品供过于求。

扩 glutton *n.* 贪吃者；吃苦耐劳的人

indigent
[ˈɪndɪdʒənt]

adj. 十分贫穷的

例 Because he was indigent, the court appointed a lawyer to defend him. 由于他十分贫穷，法庭为他指定了一名律师。

同 impoverished

intractable
[ɪnˈtræktəbl]

adj. 1.（人）难对付的；2.（问题）难处理的

记 in (not) + tract (=treat, handle) + able → 难以处理的

例 1. What may be done to reduce the influence of intractable opponents? 能做些什么来减少那些难缠的反对者的影响呢？
2. The economy still faces intractable problems. 经济仍然面临着一些棘手的问题。

扩 tractable *adj.* 易处理的

repudiate
[rɪˈpjuːdieɪt]

v. 1. 拒绝；2. 否认，驳斥；3. 断绝往来

记 re (=away) + pud (=ped-, foot) + iate → 走开 → 断绝来往

例 1. He has publicly repudiated the government's policies. 他已经公开拒绝支持政府的政策。
2. He published an article that repudiates the study's claims. 他发文反驳这项研究的结论。
3. He repudiated his first wife and married her sister. 他和第一个妻子离了婚，又娶了她的妹妹。

扩 repudiation *n.* 拒绝；驳斥

laud
[lɔːd]

v. 称赞，赞美

记 与 applaud 同根 → 赞美

例 Dickens was lauded for his social and moral sensitivity. 狄更斯以其敏锐的社会和道德触觉为人称道。

扩 laudable *adj.* 值得赞美的

fruition
[fruˈɪʃn]

n. 完成，实现

例 1. After months of hard work, our plans finally came to fruition. 经过几个月的艰苦工作，我们的计划终于完成了。
2. His extravagant ideas were never brought to fruition. 他不切实际的想法从来没有实现过。

扩 fruitful *adj.* 成果丰硕的；富饶的

prosaic
[prəˈzeɪɪk]

adj. 1. 平庸的，非诗歌化的；2. 乏味的，平淡的

记 prosa (=prose) + ic → 散文的，不押韵的 → 平淡的

例 1. More prosaic, according to *Time* magazine, *Dreams from My Father* is "the best-written memoir ever produced by an American politician". 在《时代》杂志看来，（奥巴马的）《父亲的梦想》更加平实，它是“由美国政治家写的最好的回忆录”。
2. For the Mets, the night had the feel of giddy hope colliding with prosaic reality. 对于美国 Met 棒球队来说，这天晚上交织着令人头晕目眩的希望和平淡的现实。

jargon
[ˈdʒɑːrgən]

n. 行话，术语

记 jar 原指鸟的声音“喳喳”→ 听不懂的话 → 行话

例 This jargon is common in the technology and defense industries, but scarcely understood in mainstream society. 这个术语在技术和安全行业很常见，但主流社会很少有人理解。

lethargic
[ləˈθɑːrdʒɪk]

adj. 慵懒的，无精打采的

例 He felt too miserable and lethargic to get dressed. 他心情低落，无精打采，完全没有心思穿衣整装。

扩 lethargy *n.* 无精打采，冷漠

temporize
[ˈtempəraɪz]

v. 拖延时间

记 tempor (=time) + ize → 拖延

例 Pressured by voters on both sides of the issue, the congressmen temporized. 国会议员们受到问题双方的压力，只好拖延时间。

扩 temporary *adj.* 短暂的，临时的

heed
[hiːd]

v. 注意，留心；*n.* 留心

例 1. We must heed the words of our leaders and make peace. 我们必须留意领导人的话，努力维持和平。
2. She does not pay their concerns any heed. 她并没有留意他们的诉求。

扩 heedless *adj.* 不加注意的

perpetrate
['pɜːrpətreɪt]

v. 犯罪，干坏事

例 He vowed revenge for the crime perpetrated on his family. 他们对他的家人犯下了罪行，他发誓要报复。

辨 penetrate *v.* 穿过，渗透

扩 perpetration *n.* 罪行，坏事
perpetrator *n.* 罪犯，坏人

swerve
[swɜːrv]

v. 急转弯；*n.* 转向

例 1. She swerved sharply to avoid a cyclist. 她猛地急转弯，以避开一个骑自行车的人。
2. He swung the car to the left and that swerve saved Malone's life. 他猛地将车头转向左边，这才保住了马隆的性命。

fuse
[fjuːz]

v. 融合，熔接；*n.* 保险丝，导火线

例 1. Our different ideas fused into a plan. 我们不同的想法融合成一项计划。
2. The bombs inside were on a one-hour fuse. 炸弹内装有一小时起爆的引信。

扩 fusion *n.* 熔接，融化

secession
[sɪ'seʃn]

n. 退出，脱离

记 se (=apart) + cess (=go) + ion → 分开

例 1. Spain's 1978 constitution prohibits secession, he said, and two of its seven authors are Catalan. 他说，西班牙的 1978 年宪法禁止地区独立，况且该宪法的 7 位起草人，有两位正是加泰罗人。
2. Defenders of secession and states' rights use "occupied" to describe places recaptured by U.S. forces. 州权和脱邦支持者使用"占领"一词来描述被美军占据的地区。

retrospective
[ˌretrə'spektɪv]

adj. 1. 回顾的；2. 有追溯力的

记 retro (=back) + spect (=look) + ive → 回顾的

例 1. Afterwards, retrospective fear of the responsibility would make her feel almost faint. 后来，回想起要负的责任她几乎会吓晕过去。
2. Bankers are quick to condemn retrospective tax legislation. 银行家们立即声讨有追溯力的税收立法。

扩 retrospection *n.* 回顾

succumb
[sə'kʌm]

v. 屈服，屈从

例 1. His career was cut short when he succumbed to cancer. 他的事业随着他死于癌症而中断。
2. He finally succumbed to Lucy's charms and agreed to her request. 他最终为露西的魅力所倾倒，答应了她的请求。

stipend
['staɪpend]

n. 1. 生活津贴，薪俸；2. 奖学金

例 1. The program provides a monthly stipend for qualifying families with children. 这一项目给符合资质的有孩子的家庭每月提供生活津贴。
2. The program also offers financial support and a monthly stipend to reduce the costs of college. 该学位还提供经济支持及月度奖学金以减少大学费用。

superfluous
[suː'pɜːrfluəs]

adj. 过剩的，过多的

记 super (=over) + flu (=flow) + ous → 溢出来的 → 过多的

例 She gave him a look that made words superfluous. 她看了他一眼，这已表明一切，无须多言了。

扩 superfluity *n.* 过剩

scrupulous
['skruːpjələs]

adj. 1. 仔细的，细致的；2. 恪守道德规范的

例 1. You must be scrupulous about hygiene when you're preparing a baby's feed. 给婴儿准备食物时，对卫生丝毫马虎不得。
2. He was scrupulous in all his business dealings. 他在所做的一切商业交易中都是清白的。

扩 scrupulously *adv.* 仔细地；正直地
scruple *n.*（道德上的）顾忌，顾虑

virulent
['vɪrələnt, 'vɪrjə-]

adj. 1. 致命的，剧毒的；2. 狠毒的，恶毒的

例 1. A very virulent form of the disease appeared in Belgium. 比利时出现了这种疾病的一种极其危险的变体。
2. The country seemed to be returning to the virulent nationalism of its past. 该国似乎正回到过去残酷的民族主义中去。

扩 virulence *n.* 狠毒，残忍

prototype
['proʊtətaɪp]

n. 1. 原型，雏形；2. 榜样，典型

记 proto (=first) + type → 最初的形式 → 雏形

例 1. He is developing a prototype for his invention. 他正在开发一个小发明的雏形。
2. He is the prototype of a conservative businessman. 他是保守商人的典范。

扩 prototypical *adj.* 原型的，原始的

woe
[woʊ]

n. 1. 麻烦，困难；2. 痛苦，悲伤

例 1. She may have found a remedy to her financial woes. 她当时可能已经找到解决经济困难的方法。
2. Thanks for listening to my woes. 谢谢您听我诉说不幸的遭遇。

扩 woeful *adj.* 糟糕的；悲惨的

preposterous
[prɪ'pɑːstərəs]

adj. 1. 荒唐的；2. 古怪的

记 pro (=before) + posterous (=behind) → 前后颠倒 → 荒唐的

例 1. These claims are absolutely preposterous! 这些要求简直荒谬绝伦！
2. The band were famous for their preposterous clothes and haircuts. 这支乐队以怪异的服装和发式而闻名。

inveterate
[ɪn'vetərət]

adj. 1.（人）难改的，上瘾的；2.（习惯）根深蒂固的

记 in (=into) + veter (=old) + ate → 变老的 → 难改的

例 1. She's an inveterate reader. 她是个非常喜欢读书的人。
2. The U.S. government's allegations reveal "its inveterate bitterness" toward North Korea, the spokesman said. 这位发言人说，美国政府的声明表明了它对朝鲜"时来已久的仇恨"。

扩 inveterately *adv.* 根深蒂固地；上瘾地

ordeal
[ɔːr'diːl]

n. 磨难，煎熬

记 谐音"熬到底"→ 煎熬

例 1. They are to be spared the ordeal of giving evidence in court. 他们将免受出庭作证的难堪。
2. The hostages spoke openly about the terrible ordeal they had been through. 人质公开陈述了他们所遭受的非人的折磨。

temerity
[tə'merəti]

n. 鲁莽，冒失

例 A young man's mobile had rung and he had the temerity to answer it. 一个年轻人的电话响了，而他居然有脸接听电话。

扩 temerarious *adj.* 胆大的，冒失的

trepidation
[ˌtrepɪ'deɪʃn]

n. 惊恐，不安

记 trepid (=tremble, afraid) + ation → 害怕

例 He felt some trepidation about agreeing to their proposal. 他对赞同他们的建议心存不安。

grapple
['græpl]

v. 1. 扭打，搏斗；2. 努力设法解决

记 grap (=grasp, hold) + ple → 抓住打 → 扭打

例 1. Passers-by grappled with the man after the attack. 袭击发生之后，过路人便与这男人扭打起来。
2. The new government has yet to grapple with the problem of air pollution. 新政府还需尽力解决空气污染问题。

industrious
[ɪn'dʌstriəs]

adj. 勤奋的，忙碌的

记 industry 本义也有"勤奋"之意

例 The project gave him a new respect for beekeepers as well as the industrious insects. 除了勤劳的昆虫之外，这项工作也让他对养蜂人产生了新的敬意。

扩 industriously *adv.* 忙碌地

discreet [dɪ'skriːt]

adj. （言行）谨慎的，考虑周到的

例 You ought to make a few discreet enquiries before you sign anything. 你应该审慎地询问清楚再签字。

辨 discrete *adj.* 分离的，各自的

扩 discretion *n.* 慎重
discretionary *adj.* 自行决定的，酌情行事的
indiscreet *adj.* 鲁莽的

menial ['miːniəl]

adj. 枯燥的，报酬低的；*n.* 仆人

例 1. She thought household chores were menial and unimportant. 她觉得家务事枯燥、无足轻重。
2. But that finely-distilled aristocrat did not condescend to notice such trivial matters as the coming and going of menials. 但是高高在上的贵族们不会屈尊纡贵地去关注仆人去留之类的小事。

扩 menially *adv.* 枯燥地

pacifist ['pæsɪfɪst]

n. 反战者，和平主义者；*adj.* 反战的

记 paci (=peace) + f + ist → 追求和平的人

例 1. His campaign spokesman told ABC News that he was a pacifist then but isn't now. 他的竞选活动发言人在全美广播公司的新闻中说，他当时是个反战者，但现在不是了。
2. Japan and Germany went from highly militarized societies to highly pacifist and staunchly democratic societies in the last fifty years. 日本和德国在过去五十年中从高度军事化的社会变成高度和平、坚定的民主社会。

stigma ['stɪgmə]

n. 耻辱

记 stig (=stick) + ma → 粘在上面的（污点、标记）→ 耻辱

例 Nurses worry they might lose their own jobs in retaliation, or they fear the stigma of being perceived by colleagues as a whistleblower. 护士们担心他们可能受到报复而失去工作，或者被同事当成告密者。

扩 stigmatic *adj.* 耻辱的

quiescent [kwi'esnt]

adj. 1. 静态的，沉寂的；2.（病）静止状态的

记 quie (=quiet) + scent → 静的，静止的

例 1. A heretofore quiescent problem was suddenly catapulted into the national consciousness. 一个到目前为止沉寂的问题突然进入了全国人民的视野。
2. Some cancer cells are quiescent during the tumour's boom times but can become reactivated if left behind after surgery. 有些癌细胞在肿瘤的高发期是静止的，但如果手术时没有除掉，反而可能重新活跃起来。

扩 acquiescent *adj.* 默认的，默许的

quail
[kweɪl]

n. 鹌鹑；v. 恐惧，胆怯

例 1. Two of the five pigeons and four of the 20 chickens tested positive for H7N9, but none of the ducks or quails. 五只鸽子中的两只和 20 只鸡中的 4 只检出 H7N9 呈阳性，而鸭子和鹌鹑都没有检出。
2. Most people quail at the idea of shoving the man to his death. 多数人对把人推下摔死这种做法会感到恐惧。

mischance
[ˌmɪsˈtʃæns]

n. 不幸，厄运

记 mis (=bad) + chance → 坏运气 → 不幸

例 In Geoffrey Chaucer's famous *Canterbury Tales*, written in the 14th century, he says "and on a Friday fell all this mischance". 在 14 世纪乔叟著名的《坎特伯雷故事集》中，他说："这种不幸终于在星期五发生了"。

construe
[kənˈstruː]

v. 理解，领会

记 与 construct 同根，建造 → 构建，领会

例 But he was reluctant to construe his paper as an indictment of psychology. 但他拒绝把他的论文解读为心理学的衰落。

扩 misconstrue v. 误解

subterfuge
[ˈsʌbtərfjuːdʒ]

n. 诡计，秘密手段

记 subter (=beneath, under) + fuge (=flee) → 偷偷逃跑 → 诡计

例 He accused the media of targeting him and said his supporters would see through the "subterfuge." 他指责媒体针对他，并且说他的支持者会看穿这个"诡计"。

replete
[rɪˈpliːt]

adj. 1. 充满的，充足的；2. 饱食的

记 re + plete (=complete) → 使充满 → 充足的

例 1. The country's history is replete with stories of people who became successful by working hard. 该国历史上有很多通过勤奋而成功的例子。
2. Replete, guests can then retire to the modern conservatory for coffee. 吃饱喝足后，宾客们可以到现代化的暖房里享受一杯咖啡。

扩 repletion n. 充足，满足

impetuous
[ɪmˈpetʃuəs]

adj. 鲁莽的，轻率的

记 in + pet (=seek) + uous → 内心驱动的，冲动的 → 鲁莽的

例 Mr. Cameron, meanwhile, is prone to last-minute fixes and can be both imperious and impetuous. 同时，卡梅隆（首相）善于在最后关头出手，这既危险又鲁莽。

扩 impetuosity n. 鲁莽，轻率

replenish
[rɪˈplenɪʃ]

v. 补充，重新装满

例 There, the spacecraft will dock with the ISS and replenish the crew with food, water, and other important inventory. 太空船将与国际空间站对接，为空间站成员补充食物、水和其他重要物资。

ominous
[ˈɑːmɪnəs]

adj. 不祥的，恶兆的

例 While coal has been declining over the last several years, Wall Street's broad retreat is an ominous sign for the industry. 虽然煤炭产业在过去几年间都在下降，但华尔街的大规模撤资对这个行业是个不祥的兆头。

扩 omen *n.* 预兆

rave
[reɪv]

v. 1. 热烈谈论；2. 咆哮；3. 胡扯

例 1. The critics raved about his performance in *Hamlet*. 评论家们热情赞扬了他在《哈姆雷特》中的表演。
2. She was shouting and raving at them. 她冲着他们大喊大叫。
3. He wandered the streets raving at passers-by. 他在街上闲逛，跟过路的人瞎扯。

fitful
[ˈfɪtfl]

adj. 断断续续的，一阵阵的

记 fit 作名词有"一阵阵"之意

例 The financial crisis was a uniquely painful event and the recovery has been slow and fitful. 经济危机是个尤其痛苦的事件，而经济复苏缓慢而且断断续续。

扩 fitfully *adv.* 断断续续地

stint
[stɪnt]

n. 从事某项工作的时间；*v.* 节省，吝惜

例 1. He did a stint abroad early in his career. 他刚参加工作时在国外干过一段时间。
2. She never stints on the food at her parties. 她举办聚会准备吃的东西时从不小气。

rabid
[ˈræbɪd, ˈreɪbɪd]

adj. 1.（人）极端的，疯狂的；2.（物）激烈的，非理性的；3. 患狂犬病的

例 1. And I quickly identified a certain kind of woman at the convention who I actively disliked: the rabid Hillary supporter. 我很快就在大会上发现了那种我很讨厌的妇女，那就是极端的希拉里支持者。
2. It appears Apple's days of rabid growth are over. 看上去苹果公司极速增长的时代已经结束了。
3. Authorities in Arlington are warning that a rabid raccoon was on the loose in the area last week. 阿灵顿当局警告人们，上周本地一只患狂犬病的浣熊逃跑了。

扩 rabidly *adv.* 极端地；激烈地

surveillance
[sɜːrˈveɪləns]

n. 监视

记 sur (=over) + veill (=watch) + ance → 从上面看 → 监视

例 1. The police are keeping the suspects under constant surveillance. 警方正对嫌疑人实施不间断监视。
2. The bank robbery was recorded by surveillance video cameras. 银行抢劫案被监控探头拍了下来。

slovenly
['slʌvnli]

adj. 疏忽的，衣冠不整的

例 Some high school students who've been slovenly about studying and their grades should not go to college until or if they are ready. 一些对学习和分数不上心的高中生不应该上大学，除非他们准备好了。

ruthless
['ru:θləs]

adj. 残酷无情的，残忍的

记 ruth (=rue, regret) + less → 不怜惜的，不后悔的 → 残忍的

例 1. The way she behaved towards him was utterly ruthless. 她对待他真是无情至极。
2. He has a ruthless determination to succeed. 他有不获成功绝不罢休的坚定决心。

seclude
[sɪ'klu:d]

v. 使与…隔离，隐居

记 se (=apart) + clude (=close) → 单独关起来 → 隐居

例 As their wall secludes them from other nations, so do their mental habits prevent them from a free interchange of ideas with foreigners. 当他们的城墙把他们与外界隔绝时，他们的心理习惯也阻止他们与外国人进行交流。

扩 seclusion *n.* 清静，隐居
secluded *adj.* 清静的，隐居的

credulous
['kredʒələs]

adj. 轻信的，易受骗的

记 cred (=credit, trust) + ulous → 信任过多的 → 轻信的

例 1. Few people are credulous enough to believe such nonsense. 很少有人会相信这种废话。
2. Television now is more credulous; the supernatural has become a natural part of storytelling. 如今的电视节目更容易让人相信了；超自然力量变成了讲故事的必要部分。

扩 incredulous *adj.* 不能相信的，表示怀疑的

outstrip
[ˌaʊt'strɪp]

v. (outstripped, outstripped; outstripping) 1. 超过，胜过；2.（跑得）快过

例 1. The scale and severity of this crisis is expected to far outstrip available resources. 这次危机的规模和程度预计将超过现存资源的承受范围。
2. The fullback outstripped the defenders and scored a touchdown. 这名后卫跑过了防守队员，成功地持球触地。

veracity
[və'ræsəti]

n. 真实性

记 ver (=very, truth) + acity → 真实

例 Historians continue to debate the historical veracity of this account. 历史学家们不断争论这种说法的真实性。

扩 veracious *adj.* 真实的，准确的

List 10

postulate
[ˈpɑːstʃəleɪt]

v. 假定，假设；*n.* 假定，假设

例 1. They postulated a 500-year lifespan for a plastic container. 他们假定塑料容器的寿命为 500 年。

2. Einstein's theory of relativity was deduced from two postulates. 爱因斯坦的相对论得自于两个假设。

peripheral
[pəˈrɪfərəl]

adj. 1. 次要的，附带的；2. 外围的，周边的

例 1. Fund-raising is peripheral to their main activities. 相对于他们的主要活动，筹集资金是次要的。

2. He saw in his peripheral vision that a car was trying to pass him. 他从眼睛的余光中看到有辆车想超越他。

retrograde
[ˈretrəgreɪd]

adj. 倒退的，退化的

记 retro (=backward) + grade (=go) → 往后走 → 倒退的

例 Wilson was perhaps the most retrograde racist ever to occupy the White House. 威尔逊总统可能是入主白宫的人中最反动的种族主义者。

oblivion
[əˈblɪviən]

n. 1. 无意识，昏迷；2. 被遗忘；3. 被摧毁

记 有人在该词的形容词 oblivious 前加了 m 造出新词 moblivious（指沉迷于手机忘了周围环境）

例 1. He often drinks himself into oblivion. 他常常喝酒喝得不省人事。

2. An unexpected victory saved him from political oblivion. 一次意外的胜利使得他在政治上不再默默无闻。

3. Hundreds of homes were bombed into oblivion during the first weeks of the war. 在战争的最初几周内，数以百计的房屋被炸毁。

stealth
[stelθ]

n. 秘密行动；*adj.* 隐形的，偷偷摸摸的

例 1. The government was accused of trying to introduce the tax by stealth. 有人指责政府想不事声张地开征这种税。

2. Michael C. Hall just pulled off a stealth wedding, marrying his girlfriend in a private ceremony. 麦克·豪尔秘密举行了婚礼，在一个私密的仪式上迎娶了他的女友。

扩 stealthy *adj.* 偷偷摸摸的，不声张的

ignominious
[ˌɪgnəˈmɪniəs]

adj. 耻辱的，不光彩的

记 ig (=not) + nomin (=name, fame) + ious → 不名誉的 → 不光彩的

例 He made one mistake and his career came to an ignominious end. 他犯了一个错误，他的事业就很不体面地结束了。

扩 ignominy *n.* 耻辱，不光彩

intangible
[ɪnˈtændʒəbl]

adj. 1. 难以形容的，不易度量的；2. 无形的

记 in (=not) + tang (=tact, touch) + ible → 触不到的 → 无形的

例 1. The old building had an intangible air of

sadness about it. 那座旧建筑笼罩着一种说不出的悲凉气氛。
2. Goodwill is an intangible asset that is often difficult to measure, but there are valuations of it somewhere every day. 信誉是通常难以衡量的无形资产，但日常生活中大家都很看重它。

mediocre
[ˌmiːdiˈoʊkər]

adj. 平庸的，普通的

例 I thought the play was only mediocre. 我认为这部戏剧只是平庸之作。

扩 mediocrity *n.* 平庸；碌碌无为者

whimsical
[ˈwɪmzɪkl]

adj. 异想天开的，滑稽可笑的

例 We say whimsical mostly because the performance involves a barbecue grill used as a percussion instrument. 我们之所以说它“异想天开”是因为演出中用烤肉的架子充当打击乐器。

扩 whim *n.* 突发的奇想
whimsy *n.* 随心所欲

negligence
[ˈneɡlɪdʒəns]

n. 疏忽，失误

例 Suspects could be charged with negligence after the investigation ends in about a month. 在经过一个月的调查之后，嫌疑人可能以疏忽之罪被起诉。

pliant
[ˈplaɪənt]

adj. 1. 柔顺的；2. 容易摆布的

记 pli (=fold, bend) + ant → 容易弯曲的 → 柔顺的

例 1. She lay pliant in his arms. 她顺从地偎依在他的怀中。
2. He was deposed and replaced by a more pliant successor. 他被赶下台，由一个比较容易摆布的继任者取代。

vogue
[voʊɡ]

n. 流行，风尚

例 1. His art seems to be enjoying a vogue these days. 他的艺术作品最近又开始流行了。
2. Sixties music has come back into vogue. 六十年代的音乐又开始流行了。

辨 vague *adj.* 含糊的，不详细的

List 11

oscillate
['ɑːsɪleɪt]

v. 1.（人）摇摆，波动；2.（物）摆动，振动

例 1. Her moods oscillated between depression and elation. 她的情绪时而抑郁，时而亢奋。

2. Watch how the needle on the dial oscillates. 仔细看仪表盘上的指针如何摆动。

扩 oscillation *n.* 摆动，浮动

placid
['plæsɪd]

adj. 1.（人）温和的，文静的；2.（物）安静的

记 plac (=please) + id → 满足的 → 温和的

例 1. Marcus remained placid in the face of her outburst. 马库斯面对她的发作保持平静。

2. He had been leading a placid life for the past eight years. 他 8 年来一直过着平静的生活。

扩 placidly *adv.* 平静地

incorrigible
[ɪn'kɔːrɪdʒəbl, ɪn'kɑː-]

adj. 无法改正的

例 He is always the class clown and his teachers say he is incorrigible. 他一直在班上出洋相，老师说他屡教不改。

扩 incorrigibly *adv.* 屡教不改地

foible
['fɔɪbl]

n. 怪癖，小缺点

例 Enthusiasts for the rise of robots argue that they can overcome the foibles and fallibilities of human workers. 机器人崛起的乐观者认为，它们能够克服人工的缺点和错误。

parity
['pærəti]

n. 1. 平等，对等；2.（货币的）平价

记 可看作 pair 的名词

例 1. Prison officers are demanding pay parity with the police force. 狱警正要求与警察部队同工同酬。

2. The government was ready to let the pound sink to parity with the dollar if necessary. 政府准备在必要的时候将英镑降到与美元平价。

stagnant
['stægnənt]

adj. 1.（水或空气）不流动的；2. 停滞的，不发展的

例 1. Few fish survive in the stagnant waters of the lake. 死水湖中很少有鱼类存活。

2. The housing market has been largely stagnant over the past few months. 过去几个月房地产市场一直停滞不前。

扩 stagnancy *n.* 停滞不前

tenet
[ˈtenɪt]

n. 原则，教义

记 tene (=hold) + t → 坚持的东西 → 教义

例 Non-violence and patience are the central tenets of their faith. 非暴力和忍耐是他们的信仰的核心原则。

辨 tenant *n.* 房客，佃户

goad
[ɡoʊd]

v. 1. 招惹，激怒；2. 驱赶，放牧；*n.* 刺激

例 1. Even the most responsible kid can get goaded into doing stupid things. 即便最有责任感的孩子也可能受刺激去做傻事。

2. The researchers placed some tuna out of frame, farther up the trail, to goad the ants out of their hill. 研究人员在架子上放了些金枪鱼，沿途摆在路上，想把蚂蚁赶出窝。

3. The threat of legal action is a powerful goad to companies that have ignored the regulations. 法律威胁对于无视规定的公司来说是个有力的刺激。

incipient
[ɪnˈsɪpiənt]

adj. 刚开始的，早期的

记 in (=upon) + cip (=take) + ient → 从事，拿起 → 开始的

例 The Obama administration issued an order allowing exports of building materials, car parts and farm machinery to Cuba's incipient private sector. 奥巴马政府下令允许出口建筑材料、汽车配件和农业机械给古巴新兴的私营部门。

propitiate
[prəˈpɪʃieɪt]

v. 使息怒

例 She was famously jealous and violent, and Hawaiians tried to propitiate her with offerings of pork, fish and liquor. 女神善妒而残暴，夏威夷人尽量用猪肉、鱼和酒来使她息怒。

扩 propitious *adj.* 吉利的，吉祥的
propitiation *n.* 安抚；献祭

hoard
[hɔːrd]

n. 聚藏，秘藏；*v.* 囤积

例 1. The case involves a hoard of silver and jewels valued at up to $40m. 此案涉及密藏的一批价值高达 4000 万美元的银子和珠宝。

2. They've begun to hoard food and gasoline and save their money. 他们已经存钱并开始储存食物和汽油。

扩 hoarder *n.* 囤积者，收集者

myriad
[ˈmɪriəd]

n. 无数，大量；*adj.* 大量的

例 1. Designs are available in a myriad of colors. 各种色彩的款式应有尽有。

2. Today we remember the myriad ways she helped others in her lifetime. 我们今天还记得她生前曾无数次地帮助过别人。

infinitesimal
[ˌɪnfɪnɪˈtesɪml]

adj. 极小的，微量的

例 The gravitational waves, in theory, should contract or expand space by an almost infinitesimal amount. 理论上，引力波应该能极小地压缩或拉伸空间。

扩 infinitesimally *adv.* 极小地

satire
[ˈsætaɪr]

n. 讽刺（作品）

例 The novel is a stinging satire on American politics. 这部小说是对美国政治的尖锐讽刺。

incapacitate
[ˌɪnkəˈpæsɪteɪt]

v. 使失去正常生活（或工作）能力

例 1. The class teaches you how to incapacitate an attacker. 这门课教大家如何制服歹徒。
2. The stroke left her completely incapacitated. 这次中风让她完全失去了自理能力。

indefatigable
[ˌɪndɪˈfætɪgəbl]

adj. 不屈不挠的，不知疲倦的

记 in (=not) + de (=away) + fatig (=tired) + able → 不知疲倦的

例 He was genuinely passionate about social justice and indefatigable in trying to achieve results. 他真心实意地追求社会公平，为达目标不屈不挠。

扩 fatigue *n.* 疲劳，劳累

loathe
[loʊð]

v. 厌恶

例 Apple loathes to use customer data to deliver targeted advertising or personalized recommendations. 苹果公司厌恶使用用户数据发送目标广告或个性化内容。

扩 loath *adj.* 不情愿的，不乐意的

prod
[prɑːd]

v. (prodded, prodded; prodding) 1. 捅，戳；2. 催促，鼓动；*n.* 1. 捅；2. 催促

记 与 probe（探测）形近义近

例 1. She prodded him in the ribs to wake him up. 她用手指捅他肋部把他叫醒。
2. She finally prodded him into action. 她终于催促他行动起来。
3. She gave him a sharp prod with her umbrella. 她用雨伞使劲捅了他一下。
4. If they haven't replied by next week, you'll have to call them and give them a prod. 如果下周他们还没答复，你就得打电话催催他们。

rapacious
[rəˈpeɪʃəs]

adj. 贪婪的，强取的

记 rapac (=rape, graspe) + ious → 夺取的

例 This is the standard model of rapacious capitalism, fueled and developed in the tech sector. 这正是贪婪的资本主义的典型，在科技行业尤其如此。

扩 rapacity *n.* 贪婪

procrastinate
[proʊˈkræstɪneɪt]

v. 拖延，耽搁

例 He procrastinated and missed the submission deadline. 他因为拖延而错过了提交的截止日期。

扩 procrastinator *n.* 拖延者

retaliate
[rɪˈtælieɪt]

v. 报复，反击

例 The boy hit his sister, who retaliated by kicking him. 男孩打了他妹妹，妹妹则回敬了他一脚。

扩 retaliation *n.* 报复

impregnable
[ɪmˈpregnəbl]

adj. 1. 坚不可摧的；2. 不可战胜的，难以改变的

记 im (=not) + pregn (=take, grasp) + able → 不能抓住的 → 不可战胜的

例 1. In those impregnable mountains, the guerrillas could hold out for years. 在那些易守难攻的大山里，游击队可以坚守很多年。
2. The team built up an impregnable 5–1 lead. 这个队以 5:1 的绝对优势领先。

reprieve
[rɪˈpriːv]

n. 1. 死刑缓刑令；2. 延缓；*v.* 1. 暂缓执行死刑；2. 取消，暂缓

记 re (=back) + prieve (=take) → 拿回去 → 缓刑，暂缓

例 1. He won/got a (temporary) reprieve from his death sentence. 他获得了死刑暂缓令。
2. Campaigners have won a reprieve for the hospital threatened with closure. 活动家们为这家受关闭威胁的医院赢得了喘息的机会。
3. He was sentenced to death but then reprieved. 他被判死刑，但被暂缓执行了。
4. The library has been reprieved and will remain open for at least another year. 图书馆暂缓关闭，并将继续开放至少一年。

untenable
[ʌnˈtenəbl]

adj. 难以捍卫的，站不住脚的

记 un (=not) + ten (=hold) + able → 把持不住的 → 难以捍卫的

例 His position had become untenable and he was forced to resign. 他的地位已难以维持，因此他被迫辞职。

frail
[freɪl]

adj. 1. 瘦弱的；2. 易损的，易碎的

例 1. Mother was becoming too frail to live alone. 母亲已逐渐衰弱到无法独居。
2. Human nature is frail. 人性脆弱。

扩 frailty *n.* 虚弱；弱点

ostentatious
[ˌɑːstenˈteɪʃəs]

adj. 浮华的，卖弄的

例 He wore ostentatious chains around his neck, including a very large crucifix. 他（李云迪）脖子上戴着夸张的链子，上面系着一个很大的耶稣受难像。

扩 ostentation *n.* 炫耀，卖弄

A NEW OPERA-GLASS.

stratagem
['strætədʒəm]

n. 计策，计谋

例 Trade discounts may be used as a competitive stratagem to secure customer loyalty. 商业折扣可以用作维护顾客忠诚度的一种竞争手段。

overt
[oʊ'vɜːrt, 'oʊvɜːrt]

adj. 公开的，不隐瞒的

例 In America, nothing casts a darker shadow than slavery and racial segregation, so that overt anti-black racism is uniquely taboo. 在美国没有什么比奴隶制和种族隔离更痛苦的回忆了，所以公开歧视黑人是绝对的禁忌。

扩 overtly *adv.* 公开地

remiss
[rɪ'mɪs]

adj. 疏忽的，玩忽职守的

例 1. It was remiss of them not to inform us of these changes sooner. 他们太粗心大意了，没有早一些通知我们这些变化。

2. She had clearly been remiss in her duty. 她在工作中显然马马虎虎。

辨 remission *n.* 缓解期；减刑

repute
[rɪ'pjuːt]

n. 名誉，名声

例 My parents were artists of (some) repute. 我的双亲是具有（一定）知名度的艺术家。

扩 reputed *adj.* 号称的，所谓的

同 reputation

sham
[ʃæm]

n. 1. 假象，伪善；2. 假冒者；3. 虚假的行为；*adj.* 虚假的

例 1. The latest crime figures are a complete sham. 最新的犯罪统计数字完全是捏造的。

2. Many people believed he could help them, but I knew he was a sham. 许多人以为他可以帮助大家，但我知道他是个冒牌货。

3. Their promises turned out to be full of sham and hypocrisy. 他们的许诺到头来全是假的、骗人的。

4. Foggy at that hour and shirtless, the owner answered the door and was told he was the target of a sham marriage investigation. 房主当时一头雾水并且光着上身，开门以后被告知，他正接受假结婚调查。

inscrutable
[ɪn'skruːtəbl]

adj. 难以捉摸的，神秘莫测的

记 in (=not) + scrut (=examine) + able → 无法检查的 → 神秘的

例 The woman was in the back, quiet and inscrutable, gazing out the window and writing in a journal. 这个女人穿着黑衣服，安静又难以捉摸，她望着窗外，写着日记。

knotty
['nɑːti]

adj. 1. 复杂的，棘手的；2. 有节的

记 knot (=knob) + ty → 打成结的，难解决的

例 1. Tsai built a career by handling knotty intellectual property cases. 沙通过处理复杂的知识产权案件建立了一份事业。

2. A piano sat in the corner and a painting of a cellist hung on the knotty pine walls. 一架钢琴放在墙角，一幅演奏大提琴的画挂在松木墙上。

phlegmatic
[fleg'mætɪk]

adj. 冷静的，不易冲动的

记 参见 sanguine 记忆法

例 She was phlegmatic even during the most difficult moments of the crisis. 她甚至在这场危机最困难的时候仍然很冷静。

扩 phlegm *n.* 冷静，自制力；痰

magnanimous
[mæg'nænɪməs]

adj. 宽宏的，大度的

例 He was magnanimous in defeat and praised his opponent's skill. 他对失败表现得很洒脱，并且赞扬了对手的才能。

扩 magnanimity *n.* 宽宏大量的行为

vapid
['væpɪd]

adj. 枯燥的，愚蠢的

记 可能与 vapor（汽）有关 → 酒散了汽的 → 无味的，枯燥的

例 Lincoln was not making any vapid campaign speech when he uttered those words in 1862. 林肯在 1862 年发表这番讲话的时候并不是在作出无聊的竞选演说。

扩 vapidity *n.* 枯燥，无聊

impromptu
[ɪm'prɑːmptuː]

adj. 无准备的，即兴的；*n.* 即兴创作

记 im (=upon) + prompt (=prompt) + u → 迅速做出来的 → 即兴的

例 1. He made an impromptu speech about honor and responsibility. 他就荣誉和责任感作了即兴演讲。
2. There were three encores each night, including Schubert impromptus and Beethoven bagatelles. 每晚上都有三首加演曲子，包括舒伯特的即兴曲和贝多芬的钢琴小品。

sardonic
[sɑːr'dɑːnɪk]

adj. 轻蔑的，嘲弄的

记 古希腊人认为吃了萨丁岛上的某种植物，能引起面部扭曲，类似嘲弄别人的样子。

例 The movie is a sardonic look at modern life. 这部电影是对现代生活的嘲弄。

扩 sardonically *adv.* 讽刺地

pensive
['pensɪv]

adj. 忧伤的，深思的

记 pens(e) (=pend, weigh) + ive → 沉思

例 He looked suddenly somber and pensive. 他突然看起来很阴郁，一副忧虑的样子。

inadvertently
[ˌɪnəd'vɜːrtəntli]

adv. 无意地

记 in (=not) + advert (=attention) + ent + ly → 没有注意地

例 We had inadvertently left without paying the bill. 我们无意之中未付账就离开了。

扩 inadvertent *adj.* 不经意的

stanza
['stænzə]

n. (诗的)节，段

例 Pointing to the later stanzas, Share praised some of the rhythmic musicality that emerges in certain lines. 雪儿指着最一个诗节，称赞某些行中出现的韵律。

taciturn
['tæsɪtɜːrn]

adj. 不苟言笑的，沉默寡言的

记 罗马历史学家 Tacitus（塔西佗）可能就是根据 tacit（缄默）一词取的外号

例 A taciturn man, he replied to my questions in monosyllables. 他寡言少语，回答我的问题时只是往外蹦单字。

trespass
['trespəs]

v. 1. 非法侵入；2. 做错事；*n.* 1. 非法侵入；2. 罪过

记 tres (=beyond) + pass → 越界 → 非法侵入

例 1. He told me I was trespassing on private land. 他说我在擅闯私人土地。
2. I mustn't trespass on your time any longer. 我不能再占用你的时间了。
3. He was arrested for trespass. 他因非法入侵而被捕。
4. Forgive us our trespasses. 原谅我们的过错。

扩 trespasser *n.* 不法入侵者

tentative
['tentətɪv]

adj. 1. 不确定的，暂定的；2. 踌躇的，不果断的

例 1. We made a tentative arrangement to meet on Friday. 我们暂定星期五见面。
2. I'm taking the first tentative steps towards fitness. 我试探性地开始实施健身计划。

rig
[rɪg]

v. (rigged, rigged; rigging) 1. 操纵，控制；2.（秘密地）安装，装配

例 1. He said the election had been rigged. 他说选举被人操纵了。
2. The car had been rigged with about 300 lbs of explosives. 有人暗中在车上放了大约 300 磅炸药。

punctual
['pʌŋktʃuəl]

adj. 按时的，守时的

记 punct (=point) + ual → 准点的

例 I liked the clean streets, the amazing, punctual public transportation and the lovely public spaces. 我喜欢干净的街道，良好的、准时的公交系统以及可爱的公共空间。

扩 punctually *adv.* 守时地
punctuality *n.* 守时

defiance
[dɪ'faɪəns]

n. 违抗，反抗

例 Nuclear testing was resumed in defiance of an international ban. 尽管国际上明令禁止，核试验又在进行了。

扩 defy *v.* 反抗；使不可能

outset
['aʊtset]

n. 开始

记 来源于动词词组 set out

例 I made it clear right from the outset that I disapproved. 从一开始我就明确地说我不赞成。

辨 onset *n.* 开端，发作

fallacy
['fæləsi]

n. 1. 谬论；2. 错误的思维方式

记 fall (=fail) + acy → 失败，错误

例 1. It is a fallacy to say that the camera never lies. 说照相机绝不骗人，这是谬见。

2. He detected the fallacy of her argument. 他发觉了她论据中的推理谬误。

扩 fallacious *adj.* 谬误的

imputation
[ˌɪmpju'teɪʃn]

n. 归咎，转嫁罪责

记 im (=in) + put (=put) + ation →放在里面→归咎

例 Meanwhile, it also expounds the principle of contract breaking imputation in China. 同时，还分析了中国合同中违约责任的归责原则。

impertinent
[ɪm'pɜːrtnənt]

adj. 粗鲁无礼的，不敬的

例 Would it be impertinent to ask why you're leaving? 唐突问一下，你为什么要离开？

扩 impertinence *n.* 无礼

evince
[ɪ'vɪns]

v. 表明，显示

例 He evinced a strong desire to be reconciled with his family. 他表现出与家人和好的强烈愿望。

扩 evincible *adj.* 明显的，表露无遗的

emphatic
[ɪm'fætɪk]

adj. 1. 强调的；2. 明确表示的；3. 明显的

记 与 emphasize 同根

例 1. Her answer was an emphatic "Yes!" 她的回答是很坚定的"是"。

2. He was emphatic that he could not work with her. 他明确表示不能与她共事。

3. Yesterday's emphatic victory was their fifth in succession. 昨天的大胜是他们连续第 5 场胜利。

扩 emphatically *adv.* 强调地

earthly ['ɜːrθli]

adj. 1. 人间的，世俗的；2. 可能的

例 1. They lived in an earthly paradise. 他们生活在人间天堂。

2. He didn't have an earthly chance of getting the job. 他根本就不可能得到这份工作。

同 worldly

luster ['lʌstər]

n. 1. 光泽；2. 荣耀

记 与 illustrate 中的 lustr 同根

例 1. Her hair had lost its luster. 她的头发失去了光泽。

2. The presence of the prince added luster to the occasion. 王子的出现给那场面增添了光彩。

prepossess [ˌpriːpə'zes, -'ses]

v. 积极影响，熏陶

例 Laud was greatly prepossessed in Margaret's favor; he had heard much of her at Ipswich, and had been long anxious to see her. 劳德对玛格丽特尤其心想神往，他之前在伊普斯威奇曾多次听说过她，并且一直很想见她。

扩 prepossession *n.* 偏见

inverse [ˌɪn'vɜːrs]

adj. 相反的，反向的；*n.* 反面

例 1. A person's wealth is often in inverse proportion to their happiness. 一个人的财富常常与他的幸福成反比。

2. There is no sign that you bothered to consider the inverse of your logic. 你根本就不想把你的逻辑反过来考虑。

扩 inversion *n.* 颠倒，倒置

testify ['testɪfaɪ]

v. 1. 出庭作证；2. 证明

记 test (=witness) + ify → 给出证据

例 1. She refused to testify against her husband. 她拒绝出庭作证指控丈夫。

2. Too many young people are unable to write or spell well, as employers will testify. 写作或拼写不好的年轻人太多了，这一点雇主都会证明。

demeanor [dɪ'miːnər]

n. 外表，风度

例 He maintained a professional demeanor throughout. 他始终保持着专业的风度。

同 bearing

stoop [stuːp]

v. 1. 俯身，弯腰；2. 弓背

记 与 steep 同源 → 因陡峭而弯腰

例 1. She stooped down to pick up the child. 她俯身抱起孩子。

2. He tends to stoop because he's so tall. 他个子太高了，所以时常弓着背。

conjugal
[ˈkɑːndʒəgl]

adj. 婚姻的，夫妻间的

例 Household harmony is valued above all else, including conjugal relationships. 家庭和睦是最重要的，包括夫妻之间的关系。

snare
[sner]

n. 1. 陷阱，罗网；2. 骗局；*v.* 设陷阱

例 1. The rabbit's foot was caught in a snare. 这只兔子的脚被卡在陷阱里了。

2. City life can be full of snares for young people. 城市生活对年轻人来说可能到处是陷阱。

3. He found himself snared in a web of intrigue. 他发现自己中了圈套。

辨 sneer *v.* 嘲笑

infest
[ɪnˈfest]

v. 大量滋生

例 The university's president and his wife moved out of the house a year ago after they complained it had become infested by bats. 大学校长和妻子一年前搬出了这所房子，他们抱怨说房子里有很多蝙蝠。

扩 infestation *n.* 滋生

puritan
[ˈpjʊrɪtən]

n. 1. 禁欲者；2. [P-] 清教徒；*adj.* 禁欲的，苦行的

例 1. We must be careful we don't create a world only puritans can inhabit. 我们必须小心，不能创造一个只有禁欲者才能生存的社会。

2. And while we're not living in a Puritan society—or are we?—the shadows of the past live on today. 虽然我们并未生活在清教徒时代（抑或是这样），过去的影子在今天仍然存在。

3. Modernist design is puritan, but its fruits are Epicurean. 现代派设计是朴素的，但它的成果却是享乐主义的。

扩 puritanical *adj.* 清教徒式的，道德极严格的

puritanism *n.* 清教主义；十分严格的道德观

exempt
[ɪgˈzempt]

v. 免除；*adj.* 豁免的

例 1. His bad eyesight exempted him from military service. 他因视力不好而免服兵役。

2. Some students are exempt from certain exams. 有些学生可免除某些考试。

扩 exemption *n.* 豁免

annihilate
[əˈnaɪəleɪt]

v. 1. 消灭；2. 彻底击败

记 an (=to) + nihil (=nothing) + ate → 使消失 → 消灭

例 1. The human race has enough weapons to annihilate itself. 人类拥有的武器足以使自己灭绝。

2. She annihilated her opponent, who failed to win a single game. 她大获全胜，对方连一局也没有赢。

扩 annihilation *n.* 毁灭

interdict
[ˈɪntərdɪkt] *n.*
[ɪntərˈdɪkt] *v.*

n. （法庭）禁令；*v.* 下达禁令

记 inter (=between) + dict (=speak) → 裁决，禁令

例 1. They are trying to get an interim interdict to stop construction of the road. 他们试图得到暂时的法庭禁令阻止道路施工。

2. Troops could be ferried in to interdict drug shipments. 可以把军队渡运过来阻截毒品的装运。

扩 interdiction *n.* 禁运，封锁

gig
[gɪg]

n. 1. 现场演奏会；2. 短时的工作

例 1. He was finally able to book a gig at the nightclub. 他最终得以在夜店预订一场演奏会。

2. I have a part-time job, but I really need a full-time gig. 我现在有一份兼职工作，但我的确需要一份全职工作。

seminary
[ˈsemɪneri]

n. 神学院，修道院

记 semin (=seed) + ary (=place) → 传播（种子）→ 传播教义的地方 → 修道院

例 He said the seminary was eager to cooperate with law enforcement authorities in the investigation. 他说神学院很期待与执法部门合作进行调查。

adjourn
[əˈdʒɜːrn]

v. 休会，延期；*n.* 休会

记 ad (=to) + journ (=day) → 指定一天 → 休会

例 1. The trial has been adjourned until next week. 审判延期至下周。

2. The judge granted us a short adjournment. 法官允许我们暂时休庭。

扩 adjournment *n.* 休会期

inward
[ˈɪnwərd]

adj. 1. 内心的，精神的；2. 向内的，中心的；*adv.* 向内

例 1. Her calm expression hid her inward panic. 她平静的外表掩盖了内心的恐慌。

2. The athlete takes off from one leg from an inward twist. 这名运动员向内转体一周单腿起跳。

3. The door opens inwards. 门向里开。

扩 inwardly *adv.* 在内心；秘密地

susceptible
[səˈseptəbl]

adj. 1. 易受影响的，敏感的；2. 好动感情的；3. 允许……的

记 sus (=under) + scept (=take) + ible → 居下接受 → 受影响的

例 1. Salt intake may lead to raised blood pressure in susceptible adults. 盐的摄入可能导致易病的成年人血压升高。

2. She was both charming and susceptible. 她迷人而多情。

3. Is this situation not susceptible of improvement by legislation? 这种状况有没有可能通过立法加以改善？

扩 susceptibility *n.* 易受影响，敏感性；感情脆弱处

conceit
[kən'siːt]

n. **1. 自负；2. 弄巧成拙的设计；3. 比喻，言辞**

例 1. His conceit has earned him many enemies. 他的自负给他树立了很多敌人。
2. Since so much time has passed, the original conceit has been deftly warmed over for the 21st century. 因为时间过去太久了，最初的设计已经经过精巧改造以适应 21 世纪。
3. That the animals largely have jobs that match their customary traits proves one of the narrative's most fertile conceits.（《疯狂动物城》中的）动物们大多都有符合各自特性的工作，这一点表明了编剧丰富的想像力。

扩 conceited *adj.* 自负的

elope
[ɪ'loʊp]

v. **私奔**

记 e (=away) + lope (=run, leap) → 跑远 → 私奔

例 She loved him and despite her parents' objections, she ran away and they eloped. 她爱着他，尽管家人反对，她还是跑出来跟他私奔了。

扩 elopement *n.* 私奔

paltry
['pɔːltri]

adj. **1. 微小的；2. 无价值的，无用的**

例 1. This account offers a paltry 1% return on your investment. 这个账户给你投资的回报仅是微不足道的 1%。
2. The parents had little interest in paltry domestic concerns. 那些家长对家里鸡毛蒜皮的小事没什么兴趣。

triumph
['traɪʌmf]

n. **1. 巨大成就；2. 喜悦；** *v.* **战胜，成功**

例 1. It was a personal triumph over her old rival. 这是她对老对头的个人胜利。
2. The winning team returned home in triumph. 球队凯旋而归。
3. As is usual in this kind of movie, good triumphs over evil in the end. 像这类电影的一贯结局一样，善良战胜了邪恶。

扩 triumphant *adj.* 大获全胜的，扬扬得意的

invaluable
[ɪn'væljuəbl]

adj. **极有用的，极宝贵的**

例 The research should prove invaluable in the study of children's language. 这项调查对于儿童语言的研究应该极有价值。

辨 unvalued *adj.* 无价值的

comtempt
[kən'tempt]

n. **1. 轻视；2. 不顾**

例 1. Politicians seem to be generally held in contempt by ordinary people. 百姓似乎普遍看不起从政者。
2. The firefighters showed a contempt for their own safety. 那些消防队员已把他们自己的安全置之度外。

扩 contemptible *adj.* 可鄙的，卑劣的

repulse
[rɪˈpʌls]

v. 1. 使反感；2. 击退，打垮；3. 回绝，拒绝

例 1. I was repulsed by the horrible smell. 这种可怕的气味让我恶心。
2. The troops repulsed the attack. 部队击退了进攻。
3. Each time I tried to help I was repulsed. 每次我想要帮忙都遭到了拒绝。

扩 repulsive *adj.* 令人厌恶的

fetter
[ˈfetər]

v. 1. 束缚，抑制；2. 戴上脚镣；*n.* 束缚，脚镣

例 1. He felt fettered by petty rules and regulations. 他感觉受到规则的束缚。
2. A man lay fettered on the floor of the prison cell. 一个男人躺在监狱地板上，戴着脚镣。
3. They were at last freed from the fetters of ignorance. 他们终于从愚昧无知的束缚中解脱出来。

扩 fettered *adj.* 受束缚的

List 12

slaughter
['slɔːtər]

n./v. 1. 屠宰；2. 杀戮

例 1. Thousands of cows are sent to (the) slaughter every day. 每天都有数千头牛送去屠宰。
2. Men, women and children were slaughtered and villages destroyed. 村庄被毁，男人、女人和儿童惨遭杀戮。

stately
['steɪtli]

adj. 1. 宏大的；2. 优雅从容的

例 1. Along the seafront are restaurants, clubs, cafés and the stately municipal casino. 沿着海边座落着餐馆、俱乐部、咖啡馆和宏伟的城市赌场。
2. The procession made its stately progress through the streets of the city. 游行队伍缓慢而庄严地穿过城市的街道。

vivacious
[vɪ'veɪʃəs, vaɪ'-]

adj. 可爱的，动人的

例 Many people in China consider this profession a type of “Qingchunfan”, meaning a kind of job exclusively open to vivacious young women. 许多中国人认为这一行（跳嘻哈舞）是“青春饭”，这意味着这种工作是留给可爱的年轻女性的。

扩 vivacity *n.* 可爱，活泼

solace
['sɑːləs]

n. 安慰，慰藉；*v.* 安慰

例 1. His grandchildren were a solace in his old age. 他晚年从孙儿们身上得到了安慰。
2. She smiled, as though solaced by the memory. 她笑了，仿佛在往事的回忆中得到了安慰。

misconduct
[ˌmɪs'kɑːndʌkt]

n. 1. 失职，行为不端；2. 管理不善；*v.* 不当操作

例 1. There have been reports of misconduct by several employees. 曾有过员工行为不当的报告。
2. The bank's results have been repeatedly dragged down by misconduct. 银行的结果不断被管理不善所拖累。
3. If we made them all share the consequences when research is misconducted, they would try harder to prevent it. 如果我们要求他们每个人都承担研究不当的后果，他们就会更加努力去避免这种情况的发生。

premise ['premɪs]

n. 前提，假定；*v.* 以…为前提

记 pre (=before) + mise (=send) → 提前拿来的东西 → 前提

例 1. His reasoning is based on the premise that all people are equally capable of good and evil. 他的推理是基于这样的假设，即所有人都同样有能力分辨是非。

2. The Florida Supreme Court's opinion, however aberrant it might be, was premised mostly on state rather than federal law. 佛罗里达最高法院的观点，不论它多么反常，都是基于州法而非联邦法律的。

empathy ['empəθi]

n. 同感，共鸣

记 em (=in) + path (=feeling) + y → 感受到的 → 同感

例 Campbell knew that a lack of empathy often translated into an inability to listen. 坎贝尔深知缺乏共鸣就不会善于倾听。

扩 empathize *v.* 有同感，产生共鸣

empathetic *adj.* 移情的，能共鸣的

aggrandize [ə'grændɪz]

v. 使…更辉煌，使高大

记 ad (=to) + grand (=great) + ize → 使更大

例 1. They use religion to aggrandize themselves. 他们利用宗教来为自己贴金。

2. And television is a double-edged enabler; the camera can aggrandize normal people, but it can also undo grandiosity. 电视是一个双刃剑，摄像机既能美化普通人，也能揭露浮华。

扩 aggrandizement *n.* 美化，贴金

masculine ['mæskjəlɪn]

adj. 1. 男子汉的；2. 阳性的

例 1. He was handsome and strong, and very masculine. 他英俊强壮，富有男子汉气概。

2. 'He' and 'him' are masculine pronouns. he 和 him 都是阳性代词。

pristine ['prɪstiːn]

adj. 1. 崭新的，清新的；2. 原始的，未开发的

例 1. The car is in pristine condition. 这辆汽车是全新的。

2. The sea here is pristine, and the slopes and cliffs are dramatic. 这里的海是原始的，山坡和峭壁令人印象深刻。

insolent ['ɪnsələnt]

adj. 粗野的，无礼的

例 The cloven-foot beast is usually described as carrying a bundle of birch switches, a chain or even a whip for punishing insolent children. 这个张牙舞爪的野兽（圣诞怪兽）据说背着桦木条、链子或者鞭子以惩罚不听话的孩子。

扩 insolence *n.* 粗鲁，无礼

brute
[bru:t]

n. 1. 暴君；2. 牲畜，野兽；*adj.* 1. 蛮干的；2. 赤裸裸的

记 与 cruel 形近

例 1. His father was a drunken brute. 他父亲是个蛮横的醉鬼。
2. If he becomes irritated, he turns into a vicious brute. 如果他被惹怒，就会变成狠毒的野兽。
3. They used brute force to open the door. 他们使用蛮力去开门。
4. Their desire for independence has to do with brute economics. 他们对独立的渴望纯粹是出于经济考虑。

扩 brutal *adj.* 残暴的；冷酷的

wholesome
['hoʊlsəm]

adj. 1. 有益健康的；2. 有道德的

例 1. What could be more wholesome than Johnson & Johnson's talcum powder? 还有什么比强生的爽身粉更有益健康的呢？
2. Compared to the dank corners of the Internet, *Playboy* was positively wholesome. 与互联网上的一些阴暗角落相比，《花花公子》绝对更有道德。

blaze
[bleɪz]

v. 1. 熊熊燃烧；2. 闪耀，发光；3. 怒视

记 可能源自 blow → 使劲吹 → 怒吼 → 怒视，发光

例 1. Within minutes the whole building was blazing. 不消几分钟整个大楼便成了一片火海。
2. The sun blazed down from a clear blue sky. 耀眼的阳光从清澈蔚蓝的天空中照射下来。
3. Her eyes were blazing with fury. 她的双眼燃烧着怒火。

cupidity
[kju:'pɪdəti]

n. 贪婪

记 源于丘比特 Cupid → 爱欲 → 贪婪

例 The evidence revealed the cupidity of the company's directors. 证据揭露了公司董事们的贪婪。

同 greed

imbecile
['ɪmbəsl]

n. 笨蛋；*adj.* 蠢的，低能的

例 1. It is hard to accept that these imbeciles represent the people in our government. 我们真难以接受这些笨蛋就是我们政府的代表。
2. Hitherto we did not believe there were people stupid and imbecile enough to write such things. 迄今为止我们并不相信有人会傻到写出这些东西来。

扩 imbecility *n.* 愚蠢

indolent
['ɪndələnt]

adj. 懒惰的，好逸恶劳的

例 If you detect an indolent cancer early, there's no life to save. 如果你及早检查出惰癌，还不至于威胁到生命。

扩 indolence *n.* 懒惰

List 12

consummate
[ˈkɑːnsəmət] *adj.*
[ˈkɑːnsəmeɪt] *v.*

adj. 完美的；*v.* 使完美，完成
记 com (=together) + sum (=sum, total) + m + ate → 使完成
例 1. He played the shot with consummate skill. 他以高超的技巧投球进篮。
2. If revenge is just a natural emotion, what happens when it's successfully consummated? 如果复仇只是一种自然的感情，那么当成功复仇以后会怎么样呢？
扩 consummation *n.* 完美，完整

perfidy
[ˈpɜːrfədi]

n. 背叛
记 per (=through) + fid (=faith, trust) + y → 通过信任（骗取）→ 背叛
例 It depicts God accusing Adam and Eve of perfidy in the Garden of Eden. 它描绘了上帝谴责亚当和夏娃在伊甸园里背信弃义的故事。
扩 perfidious *adj.* 不可信任的，背叛的
同 treachery

admiral
[ˈædmərəl]

n. 海军上将
记 源于 admire
例 The admiral visited the ships under his command. 海军上将视察了自己所指挥的船。

lattice
[ˈlætɪs]

n. 格子木架，斜条结构
例 We were crawling along the narrow steel lattice of the bridge. 我们沿着桥上狭窄的钢制格架往前爬。

disguise
[dɪsˈɡaɪz]

v. 1. 伪装；2. 掩饰；*n.* 伪装物，伪装
记 dis (=away) + guise (=appearance) → 去掉外表 → 伪装
例 1. They got in disguised as security guards. 他们装扮成保安人员混了进去。
2. She made no attempt to disguise her surprise. 她没有掩饰自己惊奇的心情。
3. A vote for the Liberal Democrats is just a Labour vote in disguise. 投自由民主党的票不过是改头换面投工党的票。

"Global Warming" © Felipe Galindo (Feggo)

remunerate
[rɪˈmjuːnəreɪt]

v. 付酬劳
例 What is needed are changes in how jobs are structured and remunerated, enhancing the flexibility of work schedules. 我们需要做的是改变工作的结构、酬劳，以及提高工作时间的灵活性。
扩 remuneration *n.* 酬劳

hone
[hoʊn]

v. 1. 磨练；2. 磨刀
记 谐音"霍霍"→ 磨刀霍霍
例 1. She honed her debating skills at college. 她在大学时便练就了辩论技巧。

2. The hook should be honed to a needle-sharp point. 这只钩子应该磨成针尖状。

sneer
[snɪr]

v./n. 嘲笑，讽刺

记 源于 snort（鼻子出气，类似 snore），表示轻笑时的身体动作

例 1. He sneered at people who liked pop music. 他嘲笑喜欢流行音乐的人。
2. A faint sneer of satisfaction crossed her face. 她的脸上掠过一丝得意的冷笑。

辨 snare *v.* 设陷阱

nuisance
[ˈnuːsns]

n. 1. 麻烦事，讨厌的人；2. 非法妨害，滋扰行为

例 1. I don't want to be a nuisance, so tell me if you want to be alone. 我不想讨人嫌，你要是想一个人待着就说一声。
2. He was charged with causing a public nuisance. 他被控滋扰生事。

intermix
[ˌɪntərˈmɪks]

v.（使）混合，混杂

例 1. Grass fields were intermixed with areas of woodland. 草地和林地相互交错。
2. When they talk, they often intermix English and/with Spanish. 他们交谈时，常常用英语混杂西班牙语。

扩 intermixture *n.* 混合

steward
[ˈstuːərd]

n. 1. 乘务员；2. 统筹者；3. 管家

例 1. A steward offered me a pot of tea, which I took in the reading room on the lower deck, protected from the morning chill. 管家给我上了一壶茶，我拿到阅读室的矮桌上，避开早晨的寒气。
2. The race stewards are reviewing the results. 比赛监理人正在评判比赛的结果。
3. The Earl didn't have the money or good judgement to employ a steward to manage the place for him. 这位伯爵既没钱也没有良好的判断力去雇用一名管家替自己管理这所房子。

扩 stewardess *n.* 女乘务员

henceforward
[ˌhensˈfɔːrwərd]

adv. 此后

例 Henceforward France and Britain had a common interest. 自此法国和英国有了共同的利益。

awhile
[əˈwaɪl]

adv. 片刻，一会儿

例 The rumor had been around awhile. 流言已经传播一段时间了。

tenor
[ˈtenər]

n. 1. 男高音；2. 大意，要旨

例 1. She asked the tenors to sing the line again. 她请求男高音歌唱家们再唱一遍这首歌。
2. I was surprised by the angry tenor of her letter. 我惊讶于她信中的怒意。

List 12

maneuver
[mə'nuːvər]

n. 1. 策略，花招；2. 军事演习；*v.* 1. 移动；2. 操纵

例 1. The amendment was somehow introduced by political maneuver. 这项修正案是通过政治策略得以通过的。
2. The army is on maneuvers in the desert. 军队在沙漠中进行军事演习。
3. She maneuvered the car carefully into the garage. 她小心翼翼地将车开进了车库。
4. The new laws have left us little room to maneuver. 新法律没给我们留下多少回旋的余地。

strife
[straɪf]

n. 冲突，争斗

例 During the years of vicious civil strife that followed, Afghan farmers raised the only crop that ensured instant profits, the opium poppy. 在之后残酷的内战期间，阿富汗农民只能种植赚钱快的作物，那就是罂粟。

wherein
[wer'ɪn]

adv./conj. 其中，在那里

例 1. Wherein lies the difference between conservatism and liberalism? 保守主义和自由主义的区别在哪里?
2. There was a period in her life wherein she took no active part in politics. 有段时期她没参加过政治活动。

overtake
[ˌoʊvər'teɪk]

v. (overtook, overtaken) 1. 赶上，超过；2. 大于，胜过；3. 使遭遇

例 1. He pulled out to overtake a truck. 他驶出车流，为的是超过一辆卡车。
2. We mustn't let ourselves be overtaken by our competitors. 我们决不能让竞争对手超过我们。
3. The climbers were overtaken by bad weather. 登山者突然遭遇了恶劣天气。

辨 take over 接管，控制

perverse
[pər'vɜːrs]

adj. 任性的，执拗的

记 per (=away) + verse (=turn) → 远离（正轨）的 → 任性的

例 She finds a perverse pleasure in upsetting her parents. 她让父母担惊受怕，从中获得任性的快乐。

扩 perverseness *n.* 任性

oracle
[ˈɔːrəkl]

n. 1. 牧师，女祭司；2. 神谕；3. 智囊

记 甲骨文 (Oracle) 公司的中文名和英文名均有“神谕”之意

例 1. They consulted the oracle at Delphi. 他们在德尔斐神示所向神请示。(见插图)
2. We leave the church, and I ask him whether he feels satisfied with the oracle. 我们离开神庙后，我问他是否对神谕感到满意。
3. My sister's the oracle on investment matters. 我姐姐是个万无一失的投资顾问。

扩 oracular *adj.* 神谕般的

similitude
[sɪˈmɪlɪtuːd]

n. 相似，类似

记 similar 的另一个名词

例 Does a mountain or a rock bear similitude to the figures of human beings or of animals? 是否有一座山或者一块岩石酷似人类或者动物的轮廓呢?

appertain
[ˌæpərˈteɪn]

v. 属于，涉及，关系到

例 These figures appertain to last year's sales. 这些数字指的是去年的销售额。

扩 pertain *v.* 存在，适用

cloak
[kloʊk]

n. 1. 斗篷，披风；2. 遮盖物；*v.* 遮盖

记 源于 clock，因"斗篷"的外形类似古代的大钟。

例 1. An invisibility cloak would stop working when travelling near to light speed. 当接近光速穿越时，隐形披风就失效了。

2. They left under the cloak of darkness. 他们在夜色的掩护下离开了。

3. The meeting was cloaked in mystery. 会议笼罩着神秘的气氛。

velvet
[ˈvelvɪt]

n. 天鹅绒，丝绒；*adj.* 天鹅绒的，丝滑的

例 1. She looked pretty and rather fragile, dressed in black velvet. 她穿着黑色的天鹅绒礼服，看上去娇小美丽。

2. My favorite is probably a pair of black velvet ones, although I don't wear them all the time. 我最喜欢的一双鞋可能是黑丝绒的，虽然我并不是总是穿着它。

lurk
[lɜːrk]

v. 1. 埋伏；2. 潜在；3. (网络论坛上)"潜水"，隐身

例 1. A crocodile was lurking just below the surface. 有条鳄鱼就潜伏在水面下。

2. A ninth large planet may lurk deep in the outer solar system. 第九大行星可能存在于外太阳系的深处。

3. I lurked for four and a half years before finally taking the plunge. 我在论坛里潜水了四年半之后才开始发言。

pirate
[ˈpaɪrət]

n. 1. 海盗；2. 盗版者；*v.* 盗印，窃用

例 1. Pirates have attacked tankers to either rob crew members or take the crude or fuel products for sale elsewhere in the region. 海盗们袭击油轮，要么抢劫船员，要么把原油或燃料拿到当地出售。

2. A software pirate made bootleg copies of the computer program. 软件盗版者会非法复制电脑程序。

3. He was accused of pirating their invention. 他被指控盗用别人的发明。

扩 piracy *n.* 海上抢劫；盗版行为

rev [rev]

v. (revved, revved)（使）快速运转；*n.*（发动机）旋转

记 revolution 的简写

例 1. The taxi driver revved up his engine. 出租车司机把发动机发动起来。

2. The needle on the rev counter soared. 转数指针快速上升。

brink [brɪŋk]

n. 1. 边缘，初始状态；2. 危险的边缘

例 1. Scientists are on the brink of making a major new discovery. 科学家很快就会有新的重大发现。

2. The two nations are on the brink of war. 两国处于战争的边缘。

wield [wiːld]

v. 1. 拥有，运用；2. 挥，使用

例 1. She wields enormous power within the party. 她操控着党内大权。

2. He was wielding a large knife. 他挥舞着一把大刀。

iniquitous [ɪ'nɪkwɪtəs]

adj. 很不公正的，不正当的

记 in (=not) + iquit (=equate) + ous → 不公平的

例 We should look at their corruption as a byproduct of a very iniquitous system. 我们应当把他们的腐败看作一个有失公允的系统的副产物。

扩 iniquity *n.* 不公正的事

gratuitous [grə'tuːɪtəs]

adj. 无正当理由的，无谓的

例 The film was criticized for its gratuitous violence. 这部电影因不当暴力而受到批评。

扩 gratuitously *adv.* 不正当地

overhear [ˌoʊvər'hɪr]

v. (overheard, overheard) 偶然听到

例 We talked quietly so as not to be overheard. 我们低声交谈，以免别人听到。

同 eavesdrop

decidedly [dɪ'saɪdɪdli]

adv. 1. 确实，显然；2. 果断地，坚决地

例 1. Amy was looking decidedly worried. 埃米看上去显然是忧心忡忡的。

2. She answered the question decidedly: "No, I will not lie for him." 她非常坚决地说："我是不会替他撒谎的。"

poetical [poʊ'etɪkl]

adj. 1. 诗意的；2. 理想化的

例 1. Looking at the sea can turn the mind poetical. 观海令人心旷神怡。

2. It was more gymnastic than esthetic, more realistic than poetical. 它更加物质而非审美，更加现实而非理想化。

brook [brʊk]

v. 允许；*n.* 小河

例 1. The tone in his voice brooked no argument. 他的声音里透露着一种不容争辩的语调。

2. I followed the trail for a while, until it was crossed by a brook. 我沿着小路走了一段，直到小路被小河切断。

bequest
[bɪ'kwest]

n. 遗产

例 Perhaps Dickens' best-loved novel, *Great Expectations* is the story of the orphan Pip, who receives a bequest from a mysterious benefactor. 《远大前程》可能是狄更斯最受欢迎的小说，它讲述了孤儿皮普收到神秘慈善家遗产的故事。（见插图）

扩 bequeath *v.* 遗赠给

nullify
['nʌlɪfaɪ]

v. 1. 废止；2. 使无效，抵消

例 1. Judges were unwilling to nullify government decisions. 法官们不愿废止政府决定。
2. An unhealthy diet will nullify the effects of training. 不健康的饮食会抵消锻炼的效果。

扩 nullification *n.* 废止

irritate
['ɪrɪteɪt]

v. 1. 使烦恼；2. 刺激

例 1. The way she puts on that accent really irritates me. 她故意操那种口音的样子实在令我恼火。
2. Some drugs can irritate the lining of the stomach. 有些药物可能刺激胃内壁。

扩 irritable *adj.* 易怒的
irritation *n.* 生气，恼怒

lieu
[luː]

prep./n. 替代

例 1. They took cash in lieu of the prize they had won. 他们没有领奖品而是领了现金。
2. We work on Saturdays and have a day off in lieu during the week. 我们每周星期六上班，用其他的日子补休一天。

desolate
['desələt]

adj. 1. 荒凉的；2. 不幸的，忧伤的；*v.* 使悲惨

记 de (=completely) + sola (=alone) + te → 完全一个人的 → 忧伤的

例 1. We drove for hours along a desolate stretch of road. 我们沿着一条荒凉的小路开了好几个小时。
2. The thought that her husband did not want the baby made her feel utterly desolate. 想到丈夫并不想要这个孩子，她很伤心。
3. She had been desolated by the death of her friend. 朋友的去世使她感到十分悲伤。

扩 desolation *n.* 忧伤；荒凉

hospitable
[hɑː'spɪtəbl, 'hɑːspɪtəbl]

adj. 1. 好客的；2. 舒适的，适宜的

例 1. The local people are very hospitable to strangers. 当地人对外来客人十分友好热情。
2. The climate here is hospitable to many species. 这里的气候对许多物种都很适宜。

扩 hospitality *n.* 好客；舒适
inhospitable *adj.* 荒凉的；不好客的

sanctity
['sæŋktəti]

n. 1. 神圣不可侵犯；2. 圣洁性
记 sanct (=saint) + ity → 神圣
例 1. I believe in the sanctity of human life. 我相信人类生命的神圣不可侵犯。
2. Abydos was a place of sanctity for the ancient Egyptians. 阿比多斯对古埃及人来说是个圣洁之地。
扩 sanctify *v.* 使圣洁

cordial
['kɔːrdʒəl]

adj. 热情友好的
记 cord (=core, heart) + ial → 发自内心的 → 热情的
例 We received a cordial greeting from our hostess at the party. 我们在聚会上受到了女主人热情的招待。
扩 cordiality *n.* 热情友好
cordially *adv.* 热情友好地；非常

grove
[groʊv]

n. 1. 树丛；2. 果园
例 1. Through the early morning fog, I make out a red-brick temple nestled in a grove of palm trees. 透过清晨的雾，我认出在一丛棕榈树中坐落着一座红砖庙宇。
2. At an orange grove, where most of the fruit-pickers are from the European Union nation of Bulgaria, six women had no contracts at all. 在一个桔子园，多数采摘者来自欧盟国家保加利亚，其中 6 名妇女都没有签合同。

duke
[duːk]

n. 公爵
例 Images of the Duke of Windsor meeting Adolf Hitler during a 1937 visit remain controversial. 温莎公爵在 1937 年会见阿道夫·希特勒的照片仍然备受争议。

benevolent
[bə'nevələnt]

adj. 慈善的
例 He belonged to several benevolent societies and charitable organizations. 他隶属于几家慈善团体。
扩 benevolence *n.* 慈善

traverse
[trə'vɜːrs] *v.*
['trævɜːrs] *n.*

v. 横越；*n.* 横过
例 1. The candidates traversed the state throughout the campaign. 竞选人在整个竞选活动中走遍了全国。
2. The climbers made a dangerous traverse across the glacier. 登山者在冰川上进行了危险的穿越。

avarice
['ævərɪs]

n. 贪婪
例 The corporate world is plagued by avarice and a thirst for power. 商场里充斥着贪婪和权力争夺。
扩 avaricious *adj.* 贪财的

nugatory
[ˈnuːɡətɔːri]

adj. 无目的的，无价值的

例 Walt wants to argue that the terror threat is both nugatory and worse than it was before 9/11. 沃尔特想证明恐怖威胁既无价值，也比 911 之前更糟糕。

adultery
[əˈdʌltəri]

n. 通奸

例 Adultery remains a misdemeanor in Alabama, but has a one-year statute of limitations and almost never is prosecuted. 通奸在阿拉巴马州仍是一项罪行，但有一年的诉讼时效，并且几乎没人受到起诉。

扩 adulterous *adj.* 通奸的

hideous
[ˈhɪdiəs]

adj. 十分丑陋的

例 The whole experience had been like some hideous nightmare. 整个经历就像一场可怕的噩梦。

counterfeit
[ˈkaʊntərfɪt]

adj. 伪造的；*v.* 伪造；*n.* 假币

记 counter (=against) + feit (=fact, make) → 制造假的 → 伪造的

例 1. The troop did not immediately realize the cash was counterfeit and gave the man $75 in change. 士兵并未立即认出现金是伪造的，就找给了该男子 75 美元的零钱。

2. The decree is intended to regulate penalties for counterfeiting olive oil and its origins. 这一法令的目的在于规范对伪造橄榄油及产地的处罚。

3. The couple used that information to create counterfeit checks they cashed at other Wal-Marts. 这对夫妇利用那些信息伪造支票，然后在另一个沃尔玛提现。

proffer
[ˈprɑːfər]

v. 1. 递上，端上；2. 提出

记 pro (=forth) + (o)ffer → 提供出来 → 端上

例 1. He rose and proffered a silver box full of cigarettes. 他站起身，伸手递过一个装满香烟的银盒子。

2. What advice would you proffer to someone starting up in business? 您对初入商界的人有何建议？

deviate
[ˈdiːvieɪt]

v. 背离，偏离

记 di (=de, away) + via (=way) + te → 离开正轨 → 背离

例 The bus had to deviate from its usual route because of a road closure. 因为道路封闭，公共汽车只得绕道而行。

扩 deviation *n.* 背离，偏离

superstition
[ˌsuːpərˈstɪʃn]

n. 迷信

记 super (=above) + stit (=stand) + ion → 站在上面（的神）→ 迷信

例 According to superstition, breaking a mirror brings bad luck. 按照迷信

的说法，摔碎镜子会带来噩运。

扩 superstitious *adj.* 迷信的

commune
['kɑːmjuːn]

n. 1. 群体，公社；2. 行政区；*v.* 与（动物或大自然等）交流

例 1. He's living in a religious commune. 他住在宗教群体当中。
2. The commune can trace its history back more than a hundred years. 这一地区的历史可以追溯到一百多年前。
3. Reading a forgotten book can seem a little like communing with ghosts; it helps acquaint you with oblivion. 读小众的书有点像跟鬼魂交流；它能让你想起过往的事。

辨 commute *v.* 通勤

扩 communion *n.* 交流；教派，教会

nook
[nʊk]

n. 僻静处

记 美国图书零售企业 Barnes & Noble 出品的电子书阅读器名为 nook，取"静静阅读"之意

例 He knows every nook and cranny of that engine. 他对发动机了解得一清二楚。

affectation
[ˌæfek'teɪʃn]

n. 假装，做作

记 affect 本身也有"做作"之意

例 He raised his eyebrows with an affectation of surprise. 他扬起双眉，装出一副吃惊的样子。

strained
[streɪnd]

adj. 1. 紧张的，憔悴的；2. 不友好的；3. 不自然的

例 1. He spoke in a low, strained voice. 他焦虑地低声说话。
2. There was a strained atmosphere throughout the meeting. 会议自始至终气氛紧张。
3. She gave a strained laugh. 她勉强笑了一下。

stout
[staʊt]

adj. 1. 肥胖的；2. 粗壮结实的；3. 顽强的

例 1. He was a tall, stout man with grey hair. 他是个又高又胖、头发灰白的男子。
2. The old man picked up a stout stick that lay by his feet. 老头捡起脚边的一根粗棍子。
3. He put up a stout defense in court. 他在法庭上进行了顽强的辩护。

辨 tout *v.* 吹捧；兜售

relapse
[rɪ'læps, 'riːlæps] *n.*
[rɪ'læps] *v.*

n. 旧病复发；*v.* 故态复萌

记 re (=back) + lapse (=slip) → 滑回，倒退 → 旧病复发

例 1. Everyone thought she was well until a sudden relapse sent her back to the hospital. 大家都以为她好了，直到她再次发病进了医院。

2. Two days after leaving the hospital she relapsed into a coma. 出院两天后，她再度昏迷。

bondage
[ˈbɑːndɪdʒ]

n. 奴役

记 bond (=connect) + age → 被束缚的状态 → 奴役

例 1. He delivered the slaves from bondage. 他释放了奴隶。

2. He struggled in the bondage of drug addiction. 他在毒瘾中挣扎。

gall
[gɔːl]

n. 1. 鲁莽；2. 怨恨；*v.* 使烦恼，使恼怒

例 1. Then they had the gall to complain! 那时他们居然还有脸抱怨！

2. Why did he put words of gall into my mouth? 他为什么要让我说出怨恨的话呢？

3. It galls me that such a small group of people can have so much power. 这么小的一撮人居然有这么大的权力，真让我愤怒。

List 13

horrid
['hɔːrɪd, 'hɑː-]

adj. 非常讨厌的

记 horr (=horror) + id → 害怕的 → 令人反感的

例 But I hope the kids I went to school with can forgive me for being a horrid, bullying brat. 但我希望跟我一起上过学的孩子们能原谅我当时那么让人讨厌、爱欺负人。

grope
[groʊp]

v. 1. 搜寻; 2. 摸索

记 与 grasp 同源

例 1. He groped around in the dark for his other sock. 他在黑暗中到处瞎摸找另一只袜子。

2. He groped his way up the staircase in the dark. 他摸黑走上楼梯。

avid
['ævɪd]

adj. 1. 热衷的; 2. 渴望的

例 1. She has taken an avid interest in the project. 她对这个项目入了迷。

2. He was avid for more information. 他渴望知道更多信息。

扩 avidity *n.* 热衷

trinity
['trɪnəti]

n. 1.[T-]（基督教）三位一体; 2. 三件套

例 1. The old lady lived two blocks north of Trinity Church, the one with spires that scraped the sky. 这位老太太住在三一教堂两个街区以北的地方，就是有尖顶的那个教堂。

2. Since the days of Ronald Reagan, Republican presidential aspirants have claimed fealty to conservatism's holy trinity of free markets, traditional values and a strong military. 自从里根时代以来，共和党总统竞选人就一直宣称忠实于保守派神圣的三驾马车：自由市场、传统价值观和强有力的军队。

picturesque
[ˌpɪktʃə'resk]

adj. 1. 优美的; 2. 生动的

例 1. The view of the mountains was very picturesque. 山景很优美。

2. He gave a picturesque account of his travels. 他生动地描述了旅行的见闻。

disfigure
[dɪs'fɪgjər]

v. 使变丑，毁容

例 Her face was disfigured by a long red scar. 她脸上一条红色的长疤使她破相了。

phantom
['fæntəm]

n. 1. 鬼魂；2. 幻觉；*adj.* 1. 像鬼魂的；2. 幻觉的

记 与 fantasy 同源 → 幻想出来的东西 → 鬼魂

例 1. The book is about the phantoms that are said to haunt the nation's cemeteries. 这本书写的是出没于全国墓地的幽灵。

2. The crisis is merely a phantom made up by the media. 这场危机只是媒体捏造出来的幻觉。

3. People claim to have seen a phantom ship floating on the lake. 很多人宣称见过湖上有幽灵船。

4. She was always taking days off for what her colleagues considered phantom illnesses. 她老请病假，同事们认为她所说的病纯属无中生有。

deprave
[dɪ'preɪv]

v. 使堕落，败坏

例 In my research, I've documented how colonial Americans considered children depraved. 我的研究中记录了殖民地时期的美国人是如何认为儿童邪恶的。

辨 deprive *v.* 剥夺

扩 depravation *n.* 败坏

abrogate
['æbrəgeɪt]

v. 废除，撤销

记 ab (=away) + rog (=rule) + ate → 去掉法律 → 废除

例 The company's directors are accused of abrogating their responsibilities. 人们指责公司的董事们毫不负责。

slumber
['slʌmbər]

n. 睡眠；*v.* 睡眠

记 lumber 指木头，俗语常说“睡得像根木头”，表示沉睡

例 1. She fell into a deep and peaceful slumber. 她睡着了，睡得又沉又香。

2. The older three girls are still slumbering peacefully. 稍大的 3 个女孩还在安静地睡着。

hereby
[ˌhɪr'baɪ]

adv. 特此，以此

例 I hereby declare the Olympic Games officially open. 我特此宣布奥运会正式开幕。

throng
[θrɔːŋ, θrɑːŋ]

n. 一大群人；*v.* 群集

例 1. We pushed our way through the throng. 我们挤过人群。

2. People are thronging to see his new play. 人们成群结队地去看他的新戏。

villain
['vɪlən]

n. 1. 反派主角；2. 恶棍

记 villa (=villa, village) + in → 乡下人 → 无赖，恶棍

例 1. He often plays the part of the villain. 他经常扮演反面人物。

2. Industrialized nations are the real environmental villains. 工业化国家是破坏环境的真正元凶。

List 13

canon
['kænən]

n. 1. 原则；2. 真作，精品

记 佳能（Canon）相机的品牌名

例 1. By the canons of science, the experiment was not valid. 根据科学的原则，该实验是无效的。
2. *Wuthering Heights* is a central book in the canon of English literature.《呼啸山庄》是英国文学原著经典中非常重要的一部作品。（见插图）

torrent
['tɔːrənt, 'tɑː-]

n. 1. 湍流；2. 连发

记 与 current 形似，疑同源

例 1. After the winter rains, the stream becomes a raging torrent. 冬雨过后，溪流湍急。
2. The company receives torrents of e-mails every day. 该公司每天都收到大堆的电子邮件。

扩 torrential *adj.* 倾泻的，如注的

indict
[ɪn'daɪt]

v. 控告，起诉

例 The Justice Department in May 2014 indicted five Chinese military officials suspected of hacking into several major American companies. 美国司法部 2014 年 5 月指控五名中国军官涉嫌入侵几家美洲公司。

扩 indictment *n.* 起诉，公诉书；腐败迹象

counterpoise
['kaʊntərˌpɔɪz]

v./n. 抗衡，抵消

例 1. But it's tough to counterpoise hot-button issues with rationality. 很难用理性去解决棘手的问题。
2. He hoped to find in the German townsmen a counterpoise to the overwhelming power of the Bohemian nobility. 他希望从德国的市民身上找到抗衡波希米亚贵族的力量。

purport
[pɜːr'pɔːrt] *v.*
['pɜːrpɔːrt] *n.*

v. 自称，标榜；*n.* 大意，主旨

记 pur (=pro, forward) + port (=carry) → 拿出（架势）→ 标榜

例 1. The book does not purport to be a complete history of the period. 本书无意标榜为那个时期的全史。
2. The letter was not read aloud, but all present were informed of its purport. 那封信并没有出声地读出来，在场的人只是被告知了它的大意。

devolve
[dɪ'vɑːlv]

v. 1. 移交（钱财）；2. 委托，交给（责任、权力）；3. 退化

记 de (=down) + volve (=turn) → 向后退 → 退化

例 1. Upon his death, the estate devolved to/on/upon a distant cousin. 他死后，财产给了一个远房侄子。
2. The central government devolved most tax-raising powers to the regional authorities. 中央政府将大部份征税权移交给了地方当局。
3. Somehow the debate devolved into

a petty competition to see who could get more applause. 某种程度上这场争论变味了，成了一场赢得掌声的竞争。
扩 devolution *n.* 分权；退化

transgene
[ˌtrænzˈdʒen, ˌtræns-]

n. 转基因
例 Another unresolved aspect concerns the durability of transgene expression over an extended period of time. 另一个悬而未决的问题是关于转基因的长期表征。
扩 transgenic *adj.* 转基因的；*n.* 转基因学，转基因作物

"Don't play with him, he is Wild Type."

crimson
[ˈkrɪmzn]

adj. 1. 深红色的；2. 脸红；*n.* 深红色
例 1. Despite Mars's nickname and its crimson surface, OS did not produce a red map. 尽管它叫"火星"，而且有深红色的外表，英国陆地勘查局（OS）绘制出的（火星）地图却并不是红色的。
2. I knew I'd go crimson every time someone talked to me. 我知道每当有人和我说话时，我就会脸红。
3. Trump tried to talk over him, his face going from ruby to crimson, then crimson practically to magenta. 特朗普试图把他的问题谈开来，他的脸从深红色变成暗红色，又从暗红色变成紫红色。

filial
[ˈfɪliəl]

adj. 子女的
例 His father would accuse him of neglecting his filial duties. 他的父亲会指责他不尽孝道。

admonish
[ədˈmɑːnɪʃ]

v. 1. 责备；2. 劝告
记 ad (=to) + mon (=warn) + ish → 进行告诫 → 劝告
例 1. She was admonished for chewing gum in class. 她在课堂上嚼口香糖，受到了告诫。
2. A warning voice admonished him not to let this happen. 他耳边响起警钟，警告他别让这种事情发生。

sensual
[ˈsenʃuəl]

adj. 1. 感官的；2. 喜欢享受的
例 1. Food is a great sensual experience. 吃东西是一种很好的感官享受。
2. He was darkly sensual and mysterious. 他耽于肉欲，而且让人捉摸不透。
扩 sensuality *n.* 感官享受

whereof
[werˈʌv]

conj. 关于什么，关于那个
例 I know whereof she speaks. 我知道她说的是什么。

List 13

undulate
['ʌndʒəleɪt]

v. 起伏，动荡
例 The countryside undulates pleasantly. 原野起伏，景色宜人。
扩 undulation *n.* 起伏

dilate
[daɪ'leɪt]

v. 扩大，使膨胀
记 di (=apart) + late (=wide) → 宽度变大 → 膨胀
例 1. Red wine can help to dilate blood vessels. 红葡萄酒有助于扩张血管。
2. Her eyes dilated with fear. 她吓得瞪大了眼睛。
扩 dilation *n.* 扩大，膨胀

determinable
[dɪ'tɜːrmɪnəbl]

adj. 可确定的，可查明的
例 During the third month of pregnancy the sex of the child becomes determinable. 孩子的性别在妊娠期第三个月便可查明。
辨 determinate *adj.* 限定的，固定的

intelligible
[ɪn'telɪdʒəbl]

adj. 易懂的
例 His lecture was readily intelligible to all the students. 他的讲课学生们都能轻松地听懂。
同 understandable

admissible
[əd'mɪsəbl]

adj.（法庭）可接受的，受理的
记 源于动词 admit（认可）
例 The judge decided that the confession was admissible in court. 在法庭上法官裁定该供词可以接受。
扩 inadmissible *adj.*（法庭）不可接受的

discompose
[ˌdɪskəm'poʊz]

v. 扰乱，使不安
记 compose 除了“组成”外，还表示“镇静，平静”
例 Of course the failure did not discompose me, nor shake my belief. 当然失败并未使我沮丧，或者动摇我的信念。
辨 decompose *v.* 腐烂，使分解

clot
[klɑːt]

n. 血块；*v.* (clotted, clotted; clotting)（血液）凝结成块
例 1. He needed emergency surgery to remove a blood clot from his brain. 他需要进行紧急手术以清除脑部的一处血块。
2. Aspirin apparently thins the blood and inhibits clotting. 阿司匹林能显著地稀释血液、抑制血液凝结。

philanthropy
[fɪ'lænθrəpi]

n. 博爱，慈善
记 phil (=love) + anthrop (=human) + y → 爱人类 → 博爱
例 The family's philanthropy made it possible to build the public library. 多亏了该家族公众图书馆才得以建造。
扩 philanthropic *adj.* 慈善的

reprobate
['reprəbeɪt]

v. 责备；*n.* 堕落的人，不道德的人；*adj.* 堕落的

例 1. Assembling the people, he reprobated in strong terms the prevailing heresy. 他把人群集合起来，严辞谴责他们中普遍存在的出格行为。
2. If you're looking for a movie about a charming reprobate starring someone cast against type, rent *Dom Hemingway* with Jude Law. 如果你要找一部表现反派魅力又突破演员形象的电影，那就去租一部裘德·洛主演的《唐·海明威》吧。
3. This is thought to be what's behind the behavior of most reprobate athletes because the fact is, they are outside of the rules. 人们认为这正是许多运动员行为堕落的原因，因为他们凌驾于规则之外。

扩 reprobation *n.* 责备

plunder
['plʌndər]

v. 抢劫，掠夺

例 It is possible that Viking raiders stole the Galloway vessel while plundering a wealthy monastery. 很有可能维京强盗在洗劫一座富裕的修道院时偷走了加洛韦的船只。

ripe
[raɪp]

adj. 1.（水果或庄稼）成熟的；2. 时机成熟的

例 1. Pick the tomatoes before they get too ripe. 在番茄熟透之前采摘下来。
2. The conditions were ripe for social change. 社会变革的时机已经成熟。

辨 reap *v.* 收割，收获

扩 ripen *v.* 使成熟
ripeness *n.* 成熟度

adjoin
[ə'dʒɔɪn]

v. 邻接，毗连

例 The blast occurred near the central Guven Park, which adjoins a major transportation hub. 爆炸发生在靠近Guven Park街心公园的地方，那里靠近一个大的公车枢纽。

扩 adjoining *adj.* 相邻的

overrule
[ˌoʊvər'ruːl]

v. 否定，推翻

记 rule over 表示统治…，对…有主导权

例 Tuesday's decision overruled two precedents that had upheld Florida's capital punishment system. 今天的宣判推翻了两宗判例，不再支持佛罗里达州的死刑。

tint
[tɪnt]

n. 1. 色调，浅色；2. 染发（剂）；*v.* 1. 轻微染色；2. 染发

例 1. Its large leaves often show a delicate purple tint. 它的大叶子往往带点紫色。
2. She got a red tint at the salon. 她在美发店染了红色的头发。
3. Glass bottles are filled with water tinted with food colouring. 玻璃瓶中盛满了被食用色素染过色的水。
4. She wanted to have her hair tinted. 她想染发。

ecclesiastical [ɪˌkliːziˈæstɪkl]

adj. 基督教会的，与基督教会有关的

例 My ambition was to travel upwards in the ecclesiastical hierarchy. 我的雄心是在教会中一步一步往上走。

lieutenant [luːˈtenənt]

n. 1.（陆军）中尉；（海空军）上尉；2.（美国）高级警官

例 1. He was promoted to the rank of lieutenant. 他晋升为陆军中尉。

2. A former police lieutenant, Steven Blakeney, was found guilty in January of conspiring with others to falsely arrest a mayoral candidate. 史蒂文·布拉克尼之前是名高级警官，他在一月份被认定有罪，因为他与他人合谋非法逮捕了一名市长候选人。

transgress [trænzˈgres, trænsˈ-]

v. 越轨，违背

记 trans (=across) + gress (=step) → 跨过（界限）→ 越轨

例 There are legal consequences for companies that transgress the rules. 违反规则的公司要负法律责任。

扩 transgression *n.* 越轨

amiss [əˈmɪs]

adj. 不对，不正常；*adv.* 不正常地

例 1. She sensed something was amiss and called the police. 她觉得有点不对头，就叫了警察。

2. A bit of charm and humor would not go amiss. 人有点吸引力和幽默感总是好的。

intrude [ɪnˈtruːd]

v. 1. 闯入，侵入；2. 扰乱

记 in + trude (=thrust) → 伸入 → 闯入

例 1. I'm sorry to intrude, but I need to talk to someone. 对不起打扰了，不过我有话要找人谈。

2. The sound of the telephone intruded into his dreams. 电话铃声把他从梦中吵醒了。

扩 intrusion *n.* 扰乱，闯入

accession [ækˈseʃn]

n. 1. 就职，就任；2. 正式加入；3. 新增藏品

记 不是 access 的名词

例 1. Queen Victoria's accession to the crown/throne occurred in 1837. 维多利亚女王的加冕发生在 1837 年。

2. As a candidate to join the EU, Turkey wants to see real progress in its accession negotiations. 作为加入欧盟的候选国家，土耳其想在入盟谈判中看到实质性的进展。

3. The museum has put its latest accessions on display. 该博物馆已经把最新藏品展示出来了。

扩 accede *v.* 同意；就职

forbidding [fərˈbɪdɪŋ]

adj. 冷峻的，令人生畏的

例 The house looked dark and forbidding. 房子黑森森的，令人望而生畏。

whereby
[wer'baɪ]

adv. 凭此，由于

例 They have introduced a new system whereby all employees must undergo regular training. 他们采用了新的制度，所有的雇员都必须接受正规的培训。

tiresome
['taɪərsəm]

adj. 讨厌的，令人厌烦的

例 Buying a house can be a very tiresome business. 买房子有时是件很麻烦的事。

同 annoying

dreary
['drɪri]

adj. 令人沮丧的，沉闷的

例 She longed to leave her dreary hometown. 她渴望离开沉闷的家乡。

扩 drearily *adv.* 令人沮丧地

licentious
[laɪ'senʃəs]

adj. 放荡的，淫荡的

例 In a heated exchange, DSK accused prosecutors of making exaggerated claims to paint him as a licentious figure. 在一场激烈的交锋中，DSK 指责检察官言辞夸张，把他描述成一个放荡的人。

扩 licentiousness *n.* 放荡

brunt
[brʌnt]

n. 首当其冲

记 词源与“野火”有关，可联想 burnt

例 Schools will bear the brunt of cuts in government spending. 政府削减开支，学校将首当其冲受到影响。

辨 blunt *adj.* 钝的

harangue
[hə'ræŋ]

v. 呵斥，大声谴责；*n.* 谴责

例 1. White men in the crowd repeatedly shoved this young black woman while white women yelled at and harangued her. 人群里的白人男人们不断推搡着这名年轻的黑人妇女，而白人女人们则朝她叫骂。

2. He delivered a long harangue about the evils of popular culture. 他大声地谴责流行文化的邪恶。

antecedent
[ˌæntɪ'siːdnt]

n. 1. 前事，前情；2. 祖先，先人；*adj.* 先前的

记 ante (=before) + cede (=yield) + d + ent → 之前产生的 → 先人

例 1. The events were antecedents of/to the war. 这些事件都是战争的前奏。

2. He is proud of his Scottish antecedents. 他非常为自己的苏格兰先人感到自豪。

3. These antecedent events affected the outcome of the war. 这些之前的事件影响了战争的结局。

vile
[vaɪl]

adj. 1. 糟糕的，极坏的；2. 邪恶的

例 1. The weather was really vile most of the time. 天气大部分时间都糟糕得很。

2. Morgan was evil, wicked and vile, the prosecutor said at trial. 检察官在审判中说，摩根既邪恶又可恶。

pageant
['pædʒənt]

n. 1. 古装游行；2. 选美比赛；3. 盛大场景

例 1. Their church puts on an annual Christmas pageant. 他们教会举行了一年一度的圣诞游行。
2. They disagreed with the pageant judges. 他们不服选美裁判的决定。
3. The museum celebrates the rich pageant of the town's history. 博物馆展示了该城丰富的历史。

扩 pageantry *n.* 盛典，壮观场面

repent
[rɪ'pent]

v. 后悔，忏悔

记 re (=back) + pent (=sorry) → 迟来的伤心 → 后悔

例 She had repented of what she had done. 她对自己所做的事深感懊悔。

扩 repentant *adj.* 后悔的

coquetry
['koʊkɪtri]

n. 卖弄风情

例 Her behavior was mistaken for coquetry. 她的举动被误认为是卖弄风情。

defray
[dɪ'freɪ]

v. 支付，付给

例 The government has committed billions toward defraying the costs of the war. 政府已承诺拨款数十亿支付战争的开支。

chink
[tʃɪŋk]

n. 1. 裂口，缝隙；2. 一缕，一束；3. 叮当声

例 1. We peeked through a chink in the fence. 我们通过篱笆的一道裂缝向外看。
2. A chink of moonlight lit his bedroom. 一缕月光照亮了他的卧室。
3. We heard the chink of coins from the slot machine. 我们听到了投币机里发出的叮当声。

impoverish
[ɪm'pɑːvərɪʃ]

v. 1. 使贫穷；2. 使枯竭

记 im (=em-, to) + pover (=poor) + ish → 使贫穷

例 1. These changes are likely to impoverish single-parent families even further. 这些变革很可能使单亲家庭更加贫困。
2. Intensive cultivation has impoverished the soil. 集约耕作使土壤变得贫瘠。

wreck
[rek]

n. 1.（交通）事故中受损的车船或飞机；2.（交通）事故，失事；*v.* 破坏，毁灭

例 1. Two passengers are still trapped in the wreck. 有两名乘客仍被困在失事的车辆里。
2. Police learned the truck involved in the wreck was registered to Crane. 警察发现事故中的卡车登记在克林的名下。

3. The building had been wrecked by the explosion. 那座楼房被炸毁了。
扩 wreckage *n.* 残骸，废墟

inflame
[ɪnˈfleɪm]
v. 1. 激起强烈感情，激怒；2. 使（局势）恶化
例 1. His comments have inflamed teachers all over the country. 他的评论激怒了全国的教师。
2. The situation was further inflamed by the arrival of the security forces. 保安部队的到达使局势更加难以控制。
扩 inflamed *adj.* 发炎的；愤怒的
inflammatory *adj.* 煽动性的；发炎的

lackey
[ˈlæki]
n. 仆人，听差
例 He was nothing but a spineless lackey of the establishment. 他只不过是个没有骨气的当权派的走狗。

herein
[ˌhɪrˈɪn]
adv. 在此处
例 Neither party is willing to compromise and herein lies the problem. 双方都不愿意妥协，问题就在这里。

progeny
[ˈprɑːdʒəni]
n. 子孙，幼苗
记 pro (=forth) + gen (=produce) + y → 产生出来的 → 子孙
例 He was surrounded by his numerous progeny. 众多的子孙簇拥着他。

votary
[ˈvoʊtəri]
n. 仰慕者，爱好者
记 与 vow 同源 → 宣誓（出家修行）→ 仰慕者
例 Mars' principal votaries were therefore the Roman soldiers and youths, whose exercising ground was called, in his honor, the Campus Martius, or Field of Mars. 因此战神的主要追随者当时正是古罗马的士兵及年轻人，他们操练的场所以他的名字命名，叫做马尔斯广场。

wreath
[riːθ]
n. 花圈，花环，花冠
例 1. The Queen laid a wreath at the war memorial. 女王向阵亡将士纪念碑献了花圈。
2. The ancient Romans awarded laurel wreaths to winners of athletic contests. 古罗马向体育竞赛的获胜者颁赠月桂花环。
辨 wrath *n.* 盛怒，怒火
扩 wreathe *v.* 环绕，缠绕

nostril
[ˈnɑːstrəl]
n. 鼻孔
例 She left in a rage, her nostrils flaring. 她怒气冲冲地离开了，鼻翼翕动。

sequel ['siːkwəl]

n. 1. 续集；2. 后续，结果

例 1. The new film is a sequel to the very successful comedy that came out five years ago. 这部新电影是五年前一部很成功的喜剧片的续集。

2. There was an interesting sequel to these events later in the year. 这几件事发生以后，当年就出现了一种有趣的结果。

扩 sequence *n.* 顺序，次序

despicable [dɪ'spɪkəbl, 'despɪkəbl]

adj. 令人厌恶的，可鄙的

记 de (=down) + spic (=look) + able → 向下看的 → 瞧不起的，厌恶的

例 The Minister said the bombing was a despicable crime. 部长说这次爆炸是一起卑劣的罪行。

扩 despise *v.* 鄙视，看不起

trim [trɪm]

v. (trimmed, trimmed; trimming) 1. 修剪，剪下；2. 装饰，点缀；*n.* 修剪；*adj.* 苗条的

例 1. The training budget had been trimmed by £10,000. 培训预算削减了1万英镑。

2. We trimmed the Christmas tree. 我们装饰了圣诞树。

3. He went to the barber for a trim. 他去理发店理发。

4. He keeps fit and trim by biking. 他骑自行车以保持体形苗条。

congregate ['kɑːŋgrɪgeɪt]

v. 聚焦，集合

记 con (=together) + greg (=gather) + ate → 聚集在一起 → 集合

例 Young people often congregate in the main square in the evenings. 年轻人傍晚时经常聚集在大广场上。

扩 congregation *n.* 教堂的会众

unison ['juːnɪsn]

n. 1. 一起，一齐；2. 一致行动

记 uni (=one) + son (=sound) → 同时发声 → 一致行动

例 1. The children recited the alphabet in unison. 孩子们一起背字母表。

2. Local residents and police are working in unison to make the neighborhood safer. 当地居民与警方一起行动保证社区安全。

sundry ['sʌndri]

adj. 杂项的

例 The club is open to all and sundry. 这个俱乐部什么人都可以加入。

扩 sunder *v.* 分开，割裂

destitute ['destɪtuːt]

adj. 1. 贫困的；2. 缺乏

例 1. When he died, his family was left completely destitute. 他死时家里一贫如洗。

2. They seem destitute of ordinary human feelings. 他们似乎一点人情味都没有。

扩 destitution *n.* 赤贫，贫困

calibrate
[ˈkælɪbreɪt]

v. 1. 标定，校准；2. 精确测量

例 1. These include the ability to calibrate direction by the setting sun and by the patterns of the stars at night. 这些能力包括根据落日及夜空星辰的位置来标定方向的能力。

2. Pesticide levels in food are too difficult to calibrate. 食品中的农药含量很难精确测定。

扩 caliber *n.* 才干；口径

diffuse
[dɪˈfjuːs] *adj.*
[dɪˈfjuːz] *v.*

adj. (more diffuse, most diffuse) 1. 弥漫的；2. 难解的，冗长的；*v.* 1. 传播；2. 扩散，弥漫

记 dif (=dis-, away) + fuse (=flow) → 流走 → 弥漫的

例 1. The forest was filled with a soft, diffuse light. 森林里弥漫着柔和散乱的光线。

2. Trump barely makes an effort to gesture toward economic reform, beyond his diffuse tirades about trade. 特朗普很少去谈论经济改革的问题，而一味沉浸在冗长的对贸易问题的抨击当中。

3. The problem is how to diffuse power without creating anarchy. 问题在于如何将权力分散而不造成无政府状态。

4. The photographer uses a screen to diffuse the light. 摄影师用光板来分散光线。

扩 diffusive *adj.* 散射的

cunning
[ˈkʌnɪŋ]

adj. 1. 狡猾的；2. 灵巧的，精巧的

例 1. He was as cunning as a fox. 他像狐狸一样狡猾。

2. It was a cunning piece of detective work. 那是一篇构思巧妙的侦探作品。

wring
[rɪŋ]

v. (wrung, wrung) 1. 拧（水），绞；2. 拧断，绞死

例 1. I wrung my hair and wrapped it in a towel. 我拧干头发，用毛巾包上。

2. He makes me so mad! I could wring his neck! 他真让我光火！我真想拧断他的脖子。

belle
[bel]

n. 美女

记 belle 是 bene- 词根的变体 → 好的 → 最美的人

例 She was the belle of the ball. 她是人群中的一枝花。

List 14

rustle ['rʌsl]

v. 1. 发出摩擦声；2. 偷窃（牲口）；*n.* 沙沙声

例 1. The sound of the trees rustled in the breeze. 树木在微风中发出沙沙声。

2. She's trying to rustle up some funding for the project. 她正设法尽快为这个项目筹集一些资金。

3. There was a rustle of paper as people turned the pages. 人们翻动书页时发出沙沙的声响。

coerce [koʊ'ɜːrs]

v. 强迫，胁迫

例 They were coerced into negotiating a settlement. 他们被迫通过谈判解决。

扩 coercion *n.* 强迫

blemish ['blemɪʃ]

n. 斑点，疤痕；*v.* 玷污

例 1. His reputation is without a blemish. 他的名誉可以说是白璧无瑕。

2. A series of burn marks blemish the table's surface. 几个烫过的痕迹破坏了桌面。

dejection [dɪ'dʒekʃn]

n. 沮丧，垂头丧气

记 de (=down) + ject (=throw) + ion → 压抑 → 沮丧

例 You could see the dejection on her face. 你能从她脸上看出她的沮丧。

扩 dejected *adj.* 沮丧的

queasy ['kwiːzi]

adj. 1. 恶心的，欲吐的；2. 稍感紧张的，心神不定的

例 1. The boat ride made me a little queasy. 我坐船时有点恶心。

2. She had the queasy feeling that she was being watched. 她感觉到有人正盯着她，因此有些紧张。

扩 queasiness *n.* 恶心；紧张

disquisition [ˌdɪskwɪ'zɪʃn]

n. 专题演讲，专题论文

例 Amanda launched into an authoritative disquisition about contracts. 阿曼达就合约给出了权威性的阐述。

apportion [ə'pɔːrʃn]

v. 分配，分派

例 The program gives the facts but does not apportion blame. 这个节目只摆出事实，并不评论谁是谁非。

扩 appointment *n.* 分配

skepticism
['skeptɪsɪzəm]

n. 怀疑主义，怀疑态度

例 Such claims should be regarded with a certain amount of skepticism. 对这样的说法，大可不必全信。

overflow
[ˌoʊvər'floʊ]

v. 1. 溢出；2. 挤满人；3. 扩展出界；*n.* 容纳不下的人

例 1. Her heart overflowed with love. 她的心里充满了爱。
2. The streets were overflowing with the crowds. 街上到处挤满了人群。
3. The meeting overflowed into the street. 集会的人群延伸到了大街上。
4. A new office block was built to accommodate the overflow of staff. 新建了一座办公大楼以便容纳多出的员工。

swarm
[swɔːrm]

n. 一大群（昆虫或人）；*v.* 成群移动，挤满

例 1. The air was thick with swarms of black flies. 空气中充满了大群密密麻麻的黑苍蝇。
2. Trump canceled a rally in Chicago on Friday over security concerns after protesters swarmed the event, sparking clashes. 特朗普周五取消了在芝加哥的一场公众集会活动，之前有抗议者涌入集会，产生了冲突。

infatuated
[ɪn'fætʃueɪtɪd]

adj. 热恋的，痴情的

记 in + fatuate (=fool) + d → 使变傻，爱得失去理智 → 热恋的

例 She was completely infatuated with him. 她完全迷恋上了他。

扩 infatuation *n.* 迷恋

同 besotted

obstruct
[əb'strʌkt]

v. 1. 阻挡，阻塞；2. 妨碍，阻挠

例 1. First check that the accident victim doesn't have an obstructed airway. 首先要确保事故受伤者的气道通畅。
2. They were charged with obstructing the police in the course of their duty. 他们被指控妨碍警察执行公务。

扩 obstruction *n.* 阻碍

corpus
['kɔːrpəs]

n. (*pl.* corpora) 文集，语料库

记 corp (=body) + us → 一堆（资料）→ 语料库

例 For privacy reasons, humans are not allowed to read Google's vast corpus of e-mail messages. 出于保护隐私的考虑，公众不允许浏览谷歌海量的电子邮件信息。

candor
['kændər]

n. 真诚，坦率

记 cand (=candle, white) + or → 白的 → 直白

例 I was impressed by the candor of his statement. 我对他坦率的说法印象深刻。

pauper
[ˈpɔːpər]

n. 穷人，乞丐

记 马克·吐温的小说《王子与乞丐》(*The Prince and Pauper*)（见插图）

例 He did die a pauper and is buried in an unmarked grave. 他死的时候一文不名，葬在一处无名墓穴中。

overpower
[ˌoʊvərˈpaʊər]

v. 1. 征服，制胜；2. 压倒，令人折服

例 1. The police finally managed to overpower the gunman. 警察最终制服了持枪歹徒。
2. The flavor of the garlic overpowered the meat. 大蒜的味道盖过了肉味。

parody
[ˈpærədi]

n. 1. 滑稽模仿作品；2. 拙劣的模仿

例 1. In the parody of *Love Yourself*, the refrain "Oh, baby, you should go and love yourself" becomes "Pharaoh, you should let my people go." 在一首名为《爱自己》的模仿作品中，叠句"啊，宝贝，你该离开去爱自己"变成了"法老，你该让我的人们离开。"
2. The reality parody genre has been great for startup streaming services. 真人模仿剧这种类型很适合初创的流媒体网站。

soot
[sʊt]

n. 油烟，煤烟

记 源于 sit → 留下的东西 → 煤烟灰

例 The fireplace was blackened with soot. 壁炉被油烟熏黑了。

扩 sooty *adj.* 沾满煤烟的；炭黑色的

docile
[ˈdɑːsl]

adj. 驯服的，易控制的

记 doc (=teach) + ile → 可教的 → 驯服的

例 His students were docile and eager to learn. 他的学生们都很驯服，求知欲强。

扩 docility *n.* 驯服

grudge
[grʌdʒ]

n. 积怨，怨恨；*v.* 1. 勉强做，吝惜；2. 认为…不应得

例 1. He has a grudge against the world. 他对世人心存不满。
2. I grudge having to pay so much tax. 得付这么多的税我很不情愿。
3. You surely don't grudge her her success? 她获得成功，你没有不以为然吧？

warp
[wɔːrp]

v. 1. 扭曲，弯曲；2. 使不合理

例 1. The window frames had begun to warp. 窗框已经开始变形。
2. His judgement was warped by prejudice. 他因偏见而判断有误。

扩 warped *adj.* 扭曲的

duel
['du:əl]

n. 1. 决斗；2. 竞争，斗争；*v.* 决斗

例 1. I challenge you to a duel. 我向你提出决斗的挑战。
2. The baseball game turned into a duel between the teams' pitchers. 这场棒球赛变成了两队投手之间的竞争。
3. The two men dueled to the death. 两个男人双双在决斗中丧命。

pomp
[pɑ:mp]

n. 排场，气派

例 The prime minister was greeted with pomp and circumstance. 首相受到了热情的欢迎。

扩 pompous *adj.* 浮华的，浮夸的

bail
[beɪl]

n. 保释金，保释；*v.* 1. 保释；2. 离开

例 1. He committed another offence while he was out on bail. 他在具保候审期间又犯罪了。
2. He was bailed to appear in court on 15 March. 他获得保释，定于3月15日到庭候审。
3. I'd understand if you wanted to bail out of this relationship. 如果你想从这段关系中摆脱出来，我可以理解。

dexterity
[dek'sterəti]

n. （手）灵巧，熟练

例 You need manual dexterity to be good at video games. 玩好电子游戏手要灵巧。

扩 dexterous *adj.* 灵巧的，熟练的

amenity
[ə'menəti]

n. 生活设施，便利设施

例 Many of the houses lacked even basic amenities. 很多房屋甚至缺乏基本的生活设施。

semblance
['sembləns]

n. 表象，假象，外观

记 sembl (=similar) + ance →（外表）相似 → 假象

例 Life at last returned to some semblance of normality. 生活似乎终于恢复了正常。

扩 resemble *v.* 看起来像

diminutive
[dɪ'mɪnjətɪv]

adj. 极小的，特小的

记 di (=de-, completely) + minut (=small) + ive → 非常小的

例 She was a diminutive figure beside her husband. 她同丈夫比起来就像个小人。

debar
[dɪˈbɑːr]

v. (debarred, debarred; debarring) 阻止，禁止
记 de (=away) + bar → 使远离区域，不让进 → 阻止
例 He was debarred from holding public office. 他被禁止担任公职。
辨 disbar v. 取消律师资格

fervent
[ˈfɜːrvənt]

adj. 热情的，热烈的
记 ferve(r) (=boil) + (e)nt → 滚热的，热烈的
例 They entered a fervent debate over the death penalty. 他们开始对死刑进行热烈的辩论。

probate
[ˈproʊbeɪt]

n. 遗嘱认证；v. 核实
记 prob (=prove) + ate → 证实，核实
例 1. Her will was offered for probate by the relatives. 他的亲属出示了遗嘱进行验证。
2. The court will probate the will. 法庭将核实该遗嘱的真实性。
辨 probation n. 缓刑；试用期

flutter
[ˈflʌtər]

v. 1. 飘动，挥动；2. 拍翅，振翅；3.（心脏）扑腾；n. 1. 振动，飘动；2. 慌乱
例 1. Her eyelids fluttered but did not open. 她的眼皮动了一下，但没有睁开眼。
2. He can seem an agitated moth during lessons, fluttering around his students, peering at the keys. 他看上去就像只受困的飞蛾，在学生中间来回扑动，不时看一眼曲谱。
3. My heart was fluttering like a trapped bird. 我的心像困住的鸟一样扑腾扑腾地跳个不停。
4. Only those of a cast-iron heart wouldn't have felt a flutter of emotion. 只有铁石心肠的人才不会感觉到情感的波动。
5. Her sudden arrival caused quite a flutter. 她的突然来到引起一片慌乱。

bliss
[blɪs]

n. 极乐；v. 欣喜若狂
记 源于 bless
例 1. My idea of bliss is a month in the Bahamas. 我理想中的极乐是在巴哈马群岛度假一个月。
2. Josh is just blissed out, always smiling. 乔什简直乐疯了，总是笑着。

hereof
[ˌhɪrˈʌv, -ˈɑːv]

adv. 关于这个，在本文件中
例 I have warned you hereof again and again, and besought you to turn back to the law and to the testimony. 我已经再三警告过你这一点了，希望你能够遵守法律，提供证据。

waft
[wɑːft, wæft]

v. 飘荡，吹拂；n. 一阵，一股
记 可能是 wave 的变体
例 1. The sound of their voices wafted across the lake. 他们的声音飘过

湖面传到了另一边。
2. A waft of perfume drifted into Ingrid's nostrils. 一股香水味飘进了英格丽德的鼻子里。

deport
[dɪ'pɔːrt]

v. 驱逐出境
记 de (=formally) + port (=carry) → 正式运走 → 驱逐
例 Thousands of immigrants had been illegally deported. 有数千移民曾经被非法驱逐。
扩 deportment *n.* 驱逐出境

umpire
['ʌmpaɪər]

n. 裁判员；*v.* 当裁判，裁决
例 We need someone to umpire. 我们得找个人当裁判。

importunate
[ɪm'pɔːrtʃənət]

adj. 再三要求的，纠缠不休的
例 His secretary shielded him from importunate visitors. 他的秘书替他挡住胡搅蛮缠的来访者。
扩 importunity *n.* 一再要求，纠缠
importune *v.* 再三要求

erroneous
[ɪ'roʊniəs]

adj. 错误的
例 He seems to be under the erroneous impression that she is in love with him. 他似乎误以为她爱上了他。
扩 erroneously *adv.* 错误地

convoke
[kən'voʊk]

v. 召集，召开
记 con (=together) + voke (=call) → 叫到一起 → 召集
例 The assembly was convoked for a special session. 大会召开了特别会议。
扩 convocation *n.* 大会正式会议

mutiny
['mjuːtəni]

n. 哗变，暴动；*v.*（士兵或船员）反抗，反叛
例 1. Discontent among the ship's crew finally led to the outbreak of mutiny. 船员的不满情绪最终酿成了暴乱。
2. The crew was threatening to mutiny. 船员威胁进行暴动。
扩 mutinous *adj.* 不驯服的，有意反抗的

accrue
[ə'kruː]

v. 1. 逐渐增长；2. 积累
例 1. Interest will accrue if you keep your money in a savings account. 如果把钱存入储蓄账户，就会自然生息。
2. The firm had accrued debts of over $6m. 该公司已积欠了 600 多万元的债务。

genteel
[dʒen'tiːl]

adj. 1. 假斯文的，上流社会的；2. 幽静的，古朴的

记 gentle 的变体

例 1. Her genteel accent irritated me. 她那矫揉造作的腔调使我感到恼火。
2. They lived in a more genteel era. 他们曾生活在一个相对古朴简单的时代。

patriarch
['peɪtriɑːrk]

n. 1. 家长，族长；2. 牧首，宗主教

记 patri (=father) + arch (=rule) → 统治的父辈 → 族长

例 1. Our grandfather was the family's patriarch. 我祖父当年是大家庭的族长。
2. The pope and the patriarch issued a global appeal for the protection of Christians under assault in the Middle East. 教皇和宗主教呼吁保护中东地区的基督徒。

"She really does make a good point."

扩 patriarchal *adj.* 男性主宰的；家长的

vestibule
['vestɪbjuːl]

n. 前厅，门厅

例 Goolsby had held the vestibule door open for a woman who was pushing a baby stroller. 高斯比为一位推婴儿车的女士挡住门厅的门。

vouch
[vaʊtʃ]

v. 替…担保

例 I can vouch for her ability to work hard. 我保证她能够努力工作。

同 confirm

languish
['læŋgwɪʃ]

v. 1. 被迫滞留，受煎熬；2. 变衰弱，没有进展

例 1. She continues to languish in a foreign prison. 她继续被囚禁在一所外国的监狱里。
2. The share price languished at 102p. 股票价格停滞在 102 便士。

hew
[hjuː]

v. (hewed, hewed/hewn) 1. 砍，劈；2. 砍成，劈出

例 1. He felled, peeled and hewed his own timber. 他自己砍树、剥皮、劈成木材。
2. The statues were hewn out of solid rock. 这些雕像是在实心岩石上凿出来的。

plausible
['plɔːzəbl]

adj. 1. 有道理的，可信的；2. 巧言令色的，花言巧语的

记 plaus (=plaud, praise) + ible → 值得称道的 → 有道理的

例 1. The only plausible explanation is that he forgot. 唯一合理的解释就是他忘掉了。
2. She was a plausible liar. 她是个巧言令色的说谎高手。

扩 plausibility *n.* 可行性，可信度

thicket
['θɪkɪt]

n. 1. 灌木丛；2. 复杂，盘根错节

例 1. The knife hacked at the thicket surrounding her. 刀子砍向她周围的树丛。

2. He spent the morning trying to work his way through a thicket of statistics. 他整个早晨都在试图弄明白这一大堆统计数据。

insular
['ɪnsələr]

adj. 1. 保守的，思想狭隘的；2. 海岛的，岛屿的

记 insula (=island, isle) + r → 岛的，隔绝的，狭隘的

例 1. The British are often accused of being insular. 英国人常被指责为思想褊狭。

2. Even insular Japan has figured out that it will need guest workers in the future to grow fast enough to finance its aging population. 甚至岛国日本都明白它将来会需要越来越多的外来劳工以应对它的老龄化问题。

扩 insularity *n.* 保守，狭隘

dearly
['dɪrli]

adv. 1. 非常，很；2. 代价极大地，昂贵地

例 1. I would dearly like/love to know what he was thinking. 我很想知道他在想什么。

2. Success has cost him dearly. 他为成功付出了高昂的代价。

stray
[streɪ]

v. 1. 迷路，走失；2. 离题，走神；*adj.* 走失的，离群的

例 1. Her eyes kept straying over to the clock on the wall. 她的目光不时瞟向墙上的钟。

2. My mind kept straying back to our last talk together. 我老走神，一再回想起我们上次在一起交谈的情景。

3. A stray dog came up to him. 一条野狗走近他。

affable
['æfəbl]

adj. 和蔼可亲的

记 af (=to) + fable (=speak) → 可与交流的 → 和蔼可亲的

例 Mr. Brooke is an extremely affable and approachable man. 布鲁克先生极为谦和，平易近人。

扩 affability *n.* 平易近人

confidential
[ˌkɑːnfɪ'denʃl]

adj. 1. 机密的，保密的；2. 隐密的；3. 受信任的

记 confidence 的另一个形容词

例 1. Your medical records are strictly confidential. 你的病历是绝对保密的。

2. He spoke in a confidential tone, his voice low. 他低声用隐密的语气说话。

3. She worked as a confidential secretary to the mayor for many years. 她当了好几年市长的机要秘书。

List 14

shabby
['ʃæbi]

adj. 1.（物）破旧的，破败的；2.（人）衣着破旧的；3. 不公正的

例 1. She wore shabby old jeans and a T-shirt. 她穿着一条破旧的牛仔裤和一件 T 恤衫。
2. The old man was shabby and unkempt. 老头蓬头垢面，衣衫褴褛。
3. She tried to make up for her shabby treatment of him. 她先前待他不好，这时候想弥补一下。

enjoin
[ɪn'dʒɔɪn]

v. 1. 命令，嘱咐；2. 禁止

例 1. The court enjoined the debtors to pay. 法庭命令欠债人还钱。
2. He was enjoined by his conscience from telling a lie. 他的良知禁止他说谎。

efface
[ɪ'feɪs]

v. 消除，抹去

记 ef (=ex-, out) + face → 去掉，抹去

例 The name of the ship had been effaced from the menus. 那艘船的名字已经从选项中删除了。

alloy
['ælɔɪ]

n. 合金；*v.* 铸成合金

例 1. Brass is an alloy of copper and zinc. 黄铜是铜锌合金。
2. Stainless steel is made by alloying steel with chromium. 不锈钢是用钢和铬合成的。

contiguous
[kən'tɪgjuəs]

adj. 相接的，相邻的

记 contig (=contact) + uous → 接触的 → 相邻的

例 Its vineyards are virtually contiguous with those of Ausone. 其葡萄园差不多紧挨着欧颂堡的葡萄园。

辨 contagious *adj.* 接触传染的

扩 contiguity *n.* 相接，相邻

unruly
[ʌn'ruːli]

adj. 难以控制的

记 un (=not) + rul (=rule, control) + y → 不能控制的

例 The bus driver called in the police to deal with an unruly passenger. 公交车司机报警应付一名不服管理的乘客。

contagious
[kən'teɪdʒəs]

adj. 1.（疾病）接触传染的；2.（人）患接触性传染病的

记 contag (=contact) + ious → 接触的 → 传染的

例 1. Scarlet fever is highly contagious. 猩红热的接触传染性很强。
2. I have a cold and I'm still contagious. 我感冒了，会传染别人。

personification
[pərˌsɑːnɪfɪ'keɪʃn]

n. 1. 化身，典型；2. 拟人，人格化

例 1. She was the personification of elegance. 她是典雅的化身。
2. Uncle Sam is the personification of the U.S. government. 山姆大叔是美国政府的人格化形象。

glade
[gleɪd]

n. 林中空地

例 Witsell hopes to conserve some of the glades, where he said scientists are still finding new species of plants. 韦塞尔希望能保留一些林间空地，他说科学家在那里发现了一些新的物种。

parley
[ˈpɑːrli]

n. 和谈，对话；*v.* 会谈

记 parl (=speak) + ey → 对话

例 1. So without further parley he drew his long sword from its sheath. 他不容分说，从剑鞘里拔出剑来。

2. I don't think you've ever tried parleying with Gleed, have you? 我想你没有尝试和格利德谈过，是吗？

apparel
[əˈpærəl]

n. 衣服；*v.* 穿衣

例 1. It also asked Nike, its official supplier, for more long-sleeve apparel to help athletes protect themselves. 它还要求其官方供应商耐克公司提供长袖运动服以助于保护运动员。

2. First of all was Columbus, richly appareled, with the banner of Spain in his hand. 第一个人是哥伦布，衣着华丽，手里拿着西班牙的国旗。

inveigh
[ɪnˈveɪ]

v. 痛骂，抨击

例 Employees inveighed against mandatory overtime. 员工们痛骂强制加班。

outcast
[ˈaʊtkæst]

n. 被抛弃者，被排斥者；*adj.* 被排斥的

记 cast out 扔出去

例 *Glee* began as a show about losers, outcasts, the wretched, slushie-drenched refuse of high school.《欢乐合唱团》开始时是一部关于高中的失败者、受排挤者、可怜鬼的故事。

perforce
[pərˈfɔːrs]

adv. 必须，势必

例 They had perforce to abandon the attempt on the summit. 他们必须放弃尝试登顶。

recompense
[ˈrekəmpens]

n. 赔偿，补偿；*v.* 赔偿

例 1. There must be adequate recompense for workers who lose their jobs. 必须给失业的工人足够的补偿。

2. There was no attempt to recompense the miners for the loss of their jobs. 没有人打算对失业矿工给予补偿。

petite
[pəˈtiːt]

adj. 纤弱的，娇小的

记 与 petty 同源

例 Barbie unveiled three new body types last month: tall, curvy, and petite. 芭比娃娃上月推出了三种新体型的产品：高个版、卷发版和娇小版。

whichever
[wɪtʃ'evər]

pron. 无论哪个，无论哪些

例 The situation is an awkward one, whichever way you look at it. 无论从哪一方面看，这个局面都很尴尬。

scourge
[skɜːrdʒ]

n. 祸害，灾害；*v.* 1. 折磨；2. 鞭打

例 1. Inflation was the scourge of the 1970s. 通货膨胀曾是 20 世纪 70 年代的祸患。
2. He lay awake, scourged by his conscience. 他备受良心的折磨，不能入睡。
3. The prisoner was scourged with a whip. 囚犯受到鞭打。

giddy
['ɡɪdi]

adj. 1. 头晕的；2. 发狂；3. 令人眩晕的

例 1. When I looked down from the top floor, I felt giddy. 我从顶楼朝下看时感到头晕目眩。
2. She was giddy with happiness. 她高兴得忘乎所以。
3. The kids were pushing the roundabout at a giddy speed. 孩子们推动着旋转平台快得令人眩晕。

abjure
[əb'dʒʊr]

v. 公开保证放弃，声明放弃

记 ab (=away) + jure (=swear, law) → 宣誓放弃

例 He abjured the Protestant faith and became King in 1594. 他放弃了新教信仰，于 1594 年登基为王。

同 renounce

almanac
['ɔːlmənæk, 'æl-]

n. 1. 年鉴；2. 年历，历书

例 1. December is historically the best month for the S&P 500 according to data from the Stock Trader's Almanac. 根据股票交易年鉴提供的标普 500 的数据，12 月是历史上最好的月份。
2. Ms. Lee and her husband, Ken Smith, have published the Pocket Chinese Almanac each year since 2010, in English. 李女士和丈夫肯·史密斯自 2010 年以来就一直在出版英文版袖珍中国年历。

concise
[kən'saɪs]

adj. 1. 简洁的；2.（书）简明的

例 1. His answers are concise, but he's always willing to elaborate. 他的回答很简洁，但他总是乐意解释。
2. The "Brief History" part of the title, he jokes, was "based on those *Concise Oxford Dictionaries*—which are always four inches thick". 他开玩笑说，书名中的"简史"，是"从《牛津简明词典》而来的，该词典一直保持 4 英寸的厚度"。

扩 concisely *adv.* 简洁地

peep
[piːp]

v. 1. 偷看；2. 部分出现；*n.* 1. 偷窥；2. 出声音

记 门上的"猫眼" peephole

例 1. We caught her peeping through the keyhole. 她从锁孔偷看时被我们撞着了。

2. The sun peeped out from behind the clouds. 太阳从云层里露了一下脸。
3. Dave took a quick peep at the last page. 戴夫迅速地瞟了一下最后一页。
4. We did not hear a peep out of the baby all night. 我们整夜都没听到婴儿出声。

tinge
[tɪndʒ]

v. 1. 染色；2. 使略带感情；*n.* 微量，少许

例 1. The sky was tinged with red. 天空有点发红。
2. Her days were tinged with sadness. 她生活得有些悲伤。
3. There was a faint pink tinge to the sky. 天空略带一点淡淡的粉红色。

venal
[ˈviːnl]

adj. 贪赃枉法的

例 Ian Trimmer is corrupt and thoroughly venal. 伊恩·特里默贪污受贿，是个彻头彻尾的贪官。

扩 venality *n.* 唯利是图

List 15

emulate
['emjuleɪt]

v. 1. 努力赶上；2. 模仿

例 1. She hopes to emulate her sister's sporting achievements. 她希望在运动成绩方面赶上她姐姐。
2. Sons are traditionally expected to emulate their fathers. 人们历来认为儿子会仿效父亲。

扩 emulation *n.* 模式

transcend
[træn'send]

v. 超出，超越

记 trans (=beyond) + cend (=climb) → 爬上 → 超出

例 She was able to transcend her own suffering and help others. 她能够克服自己的痛苦而去帮助别人。

扩 transcendent *adj.* 卓越的，杰出的

conscript
[kən'skrɪpt] *v.*
['kɑːnskrɪpt] *n.*

v. 征募；*n.* 应征入伍者

记 con (=with) + script (=write) → 写下 → 应征

例 1. He was conscripted into the army in 1939. 他于1939 年应征入伍。
2. Hundreds of British and Argentinian troops—the later mostly young conscripts—died in the conflict. 成百上千名英阿士兵死于这场冲突，而阿根廷士兵中多数是年轻的入伍者。

扩 conscription *n.* 征募

rove
[roʊv]

v. 1. 漫游，流浪；2. 打量，环视

记 与路虎汽车（Landrover）中的 rover 同源，原指北欧的一个四处流浪征战的民族

例 1. A quarter of a million refugees roved around the country. 这个国家有二十五万难民流离失所。
2. His eyes roved the room in search of her. 他的眼睛打量着屋子，寻找她的影子。

juxtapose
[ˌdʒʌkstə'poʊz]

v. 并列放置

记 juxta (=next, near) + pose (=put) → 放在旁边 → 并列放置

例 In the exhibition, abstract paintings are juxtaposed with shocking photographs. 展览会上抽象画与令人震惊的照片并列展出。

扩 juxtaposition *n.* 并列

scion
['saɪən]

n. 1. 望门子弟，名门之后；2. 幼枝

例 1. Bush has now embraced the fact that he's a scion.（杰布·）布什现在已经接受了自己是名门之后这一事实。

2. The other plant or plants, chosen for their fruit, flowers or leaves, are known as scions. 其他的植物叫做幼苗，因其果实、花朵或叶子而入选。

veritable
['verɪtəbl]

adj. 十足的，名副其实的

记 verit (=true) + able → 真的，名副其实的

例 The meal that followed was a veritable banquet. 随后摆上的饭菜俨然是一桌宴席。

同 positive

speculate
['spekjuleɪt]

v. 1. 推测，猜测；2. 投机

记 spec(t) (=look) + ulate → 看（征兆），看（机会）→ 推测，投机

例 1. We all speculated about the reasons for her resignation. 我们大家都推测过她辞职的原因。

2. He likes to speculate on the stock market. 他喜欢炒股。

扩 speculator *n.* 投机商

implacable
[ɪm'plækəbl]

adj. 1.（看法）难以化解的；2.（人）不饶人的，不愿和解的

记 im (=not) + plac (=please) + able → 取悦不了的 → 不愿和解的

例 1. He has an implacable hatred for his political opponents. 他对自己的政治对手有种难以化解的仇恨。

2. Few other compromises are possible between the smoke-free hospital and the hard-core, implacable smoker. 无烟医院和死硬的吸烟者之间很难达成妥协。

pang
[pæŋ]

n. 突然的疼痛

例 Those just seemed like the birth pangs of a new American democracy. 那感觉就像是一种新的美国民主诞生时的阵痛。

stagger
['stæɡər]

v. 1. 蹒跚；2. 使震惊；3. 使交错

例 1. We seem to stagger from one crisis to the next. 我们仿佛在接连不断的危机中举步维艰。

2. It staggers me that the government is doing nothing about it. 政府对此竟然袖手旁观，我觉得不可思议。

3. There were so many runners that they had to stagger the start. 参加赛跑的选手很多，他们不得不把起跑的时间错开。

扩 staggering *adj.* 令人震惊的

salute
[sə'lu:t]

v./n. 1.（军队中）敬礼；2. 致敬，表示敬意

记 salu (=health) + te →（问候）健康 → 致意，致敬

例 1. The sergeant stood to attention and saluted.

中士立正敬礼。
2. The players saluted the fans before leaving the field. 球员在退场前向球迷致意。
扩 salutation *n.* 招呼；称呼语

harmonize
[ˈhɑːrmənaɪz]

v. 1. 协调；2. 相一致
例 1. The new building does not harmonize with its surroundings. 那栋新楼与周围环境不协调。
2. How far will members have progressed towards harmonizing their economies? 各成员国在使彼此经济协调一致的进程上会有多大进展？

beech
[biːtʃ]

n. 1. 山毛榉；2. 山毛榉木材
例 1. The great beeches towered up towards the sky. 一棵棵山毛榉高耸入云。
2. The worktop is made of solid beech. 操作台是由结实的山毛榉木做成的。

yearn
[jɜːrn]

v. 渴望，渴求
例 She yearned to escape from her office job. 她一心想着躲避办公室里的工作。
同 long

encumber
[ɪnˈkʌmbər]

v. 1. 妨碍，阻碍；2. 大得难以移动
记 en (=in) + cumber (=obstacle) → 阻碍
例 1. The police operation was encumbered by crowds of reporters. 警方的行动被成群的记者所妨碍。
2. The frogmen were encumbered by their diving equipment. 沉重的潜水装备使蛙人步履维艰。
扩 encumbrance *n.* 妨碍者，累赘

interweave
[ˌɪntərˈwiːv]

v. (interwove, interwoven) 交织，交错
例 The blue fabric was interwoven with red and gold thread. 蓝布中交织着红色和金色的线。

caress
[kəˈres]

v. 抚摸，爱抚；*n.* 爱抚，亲吻
例 1. His fingers caressed the back of her neck. 他的手指抚摩着她的脖颈。
2. She gave the baby's cheek a gentle caress. 她轻轻摸了摸婴儿的脸蛋。

tableau
[ˈtæbloʊ]

n. (*pl.* tableaux) 1. 舞台造型；2. 群像（雕像）
记 table + au → 画在一块板上 → 群像
例 1. The procession included a tableau of the Battle of Hastings. 游行队伍中包括黑斯廷斯战役的人物造型。
2. I snapped a photo of this multigenerational tableau en route to a visit with longtime friends last fall. 我去年秋天去拜访一位老朋友的途中拍下了这张多代同堂的照片。

dismal [ˈdɪzməl]	*adj.* 1. 忧郁的，凄凉的；2. 不熟练的，差劲的 例 1. The barren landscape looks dismal in winter. 贫瘠的土地在冬天看上去很凄凉。 2. Their recent attempt to increase sales has been a dismal failure. 他们最近努力提高销售量，全是白费劲。
tributary [ˈtrɪbjəteri]	*n.* 支流；*adj.* 支流的 例 1. The reservoir has banked water flows from a major tributary of the Yellow River. 这一水库积蓄了黄河一大支流的水。 2. Each tributary stream is fed by creeks, which are fed, in turn, by rivulets of progressively smaller size. 每条支流都有小溪汇入，这些小溪又由更小的细流汇成。
harry [ˈhæri]	*v.* 1. 烦扰，折磨；2. 反复进攻，不断袭击 例 1. She has been harried by the press all week. 整个星期她都受到新闻界的不断烦扰。 2. They harried the retreating army. 他们不断袭击撤退的军队。 同 harass
imbue [ɪmˈbjuː]	*v.* 使充满，灌输 例 Her voice was imbued with an unusual seriousness. 她的声音里有一种不寻常的严肃语气。
centerpiece [ˈsentərpiːs]	*n.* 1. 主要装饰物；2. 主要内容，核心 例 1. He wants the church to serve as both the dining area and architectural centerpiece. 他想让教堂既变成就餐区域，又当作建筑的中心。 2. He made tax reform the centerpiece of his speech. 他演讲的主要内容是税制改革。
sly [slaɪ]	*adj.* 1. 狡诈的；2. 诡秘的 例 1. You sly old devil! How long have you known? 你这个老滑头！你知道有多久了？ 2. He gave me a sly, meaningful look. 他心照不宣地看了我一眼，意味深长。 扩 slyly *adv.* 诡秘地
regent [ˈriːdʒənt]	*n.* 1. 摄政王；2. 委员会成员，管理成员；*adj.* 摄政的 记 reg (=rule) + ent → 统治的人 例 1. Lord Eddard Stark is herein named Protector of the Realm, to rule as regent until the heir comes of age. 艾德·史塔克因此被任命为王国保护者，以摄政王的身份统治到王储成年。 2. That panel's actions still had to go before regents for approval. 专家小组的行动仍然要经过委员会的同意。 3. Tell the Queen Regent that if she meets my terms, I will sheath this

sword, and make an end to the war between us. 告诉摄政女王，如果她满足我的条件，我将封剑结束我们之间的战争。

扩 regency *n.* 摄政期

hindrance
['hɪndrəns]

n. 1. 造成妨碍的人；2. 妨碍，阻挠

记 hindr (=back) + ance → 往后拉 → 阻挠

例 1. To be honest, she was more of a hindrance than a help. 说实在的，她没帮上忙，反而成了累赘。

2. They were able to complete their journey without further hindrance. 剩下的旅程他们没再受到阻碍。

inquisitive
[ɪn'kwɪzətɪv]

adj. 1. 过分打听他人私事的；2. 好学的，好奇的

记 inqui(re) (=ask) + si + tive → 爱问的，爱打听的

例 1. Don't be so inquisitive. It's none of your business! 别这么追根问底的。这与你无关！

2. Bears are very inquisitive and must be kept mentally stimulated. 熊非常好奇，必须不断地给予其智力上的刺激。

receptacle
[rɪ'septəkl]

n. 1. 容器；2. 插座

记 recept + acle → 接受，接入 → 容器

例 1. The label would also help them decide on the proper public waste receptacles. 这种标签能够帮助人们决定把废物扔在哪种垃圾桶里。

2. As many as 15 strands of lights were plugged into a power strip, which was plugged into a floor receptacle. 多达15支灯连在一个电源线上，电源线接在一个地板插座上。

deceit
[dɪ'siːt]

n. 欺骗

记 de (=from) + ceit (=take) → 拿走 → 欺骗

例 Everyone was involved in this web of deceit. 所有人都牵涉到这起诈骗勾当之中了。

扩 deceitful *adj.* 不诚实的，骗人的

同 deception

operative
['ɑːpərətɪv, -reɪ-]

n. 1. 操作员，工作人员；2. 密探，特工；*adj.* 可使用的

例 1. In an automated car plant there is not a human operative to be seen. 在自动化汽车制造厂看不到一个工人。

2. Naturally the CIA wants to protect its operatives. 美国中央情报局当然想保护其特工。

3. This law becomes operative immediately. 本法规即时生效。

paternal
[pə'tɜːrnl]

adj. 1. 父亲的；2. 父系的

例 1. He gave me a piece of paternal advice. 他给了我慈父般的忠告。

2. Scott spent weekends with his paternal grandparents, who still

lived on the farm. 斯科特与他的祖父母一起过周末，他们仍住在农场里。

inviting
[ɪn'vaɪtɪŋ]

adj. 吸引人的，诱人的
例 The water looks really inviting. 水面看上去真诱人。

imbibe
[ɪm'baɪb]

v. 1. 喝，饮；2. 吸引，接受
例 1. She imbibed vast quantities of coffee. 她喝了大量的咖啡。
2. He imbibed elements of oriental mysticism from the years he spent in India. 他在印度呆的几年中吸收了东方的神秘主义。

homely
['hoʊmli]

adj. (homelier, homeliest) 1. 相貌平平的；2. 亲切的；3. 家常的
例 1. The man was homely and overweight. 该男子其貌不扬，身材肥胖。
2. Mrs. Jones was a pleasant, homely person with a ready smile. 琼斯夫人和蔼亲切，总是面带微笑。
3. Scottish baking is homely, comforting and truly good. 苏格兰烘烤食品简单、温馨，吃起来十分美味可口。
辨 homily *n.* 说教（作品）

marvel
['mɑːrvl]

n. 1. 奇迹，令人惊异的人；2.（人的）成就，不平凡的成果；*v.* 感到惊奇
记 美国著名的漫威（Marvel）系列漫画
例 1. The bridge is an engineering marvel. 这座桥是个工程上的奇迹。
2. The doctors have done marvels for her. 医生为她创造了奇迹。
3. Everyone marveled at his courage. 人人都对他的勇气惊叹不已。

扩 marvelous *adj.* 令人惊奇的

epithet
['epɪθet]

n. 1. 别称，绰号；2. 修饰语
例 1. Many were offended by her use of racial epithets. 许多人被她起的种族主义绰号冒犯了。
2. The film is long and dramatic but does not quite earn the epithet 'epic'. 这部影片篇幅长，戏剧性强，不过还不能誉为"史诗"。

languid
['læŋgwɪd]

adj. 慢悠悠的，慵懒的
记 谐音"懒鬼的"→慢悠悠的
例 Time spent at Jumby Bay can be as energetic or as languid as you wish. 来琼比湾消磨时光，动静皆宜，尽可随心所欲。

turf
[tɜːrf]

n. (*pl.* turfs, *or* turves) 1. 草皮；2. 地盘，势力范围；*v.* 赶（走）
例 1. Synthetic turf was installed in the playing field instead of grass. 运动场上铺着合成草皮而不是真的草。
2. The team beat us on our own turf. 我们在自己的主场被打败。
3. She turfed him out of the house. 她把他赶出了家。

treble ['trebl]	*n.*（音乐的）高音；*adj.* 三重的；*v.* 三倍增长 例 1. My stereo has separate controls for the treble and the bass. 我的立体声音响有独立的高音按钮和低音按钮。 2. More than 7 million shares changed hands, treble the normal daily average. 有 700 多万股换手，是通常日平均成交量的 3 倍。 3. She trebled her earnings in only two years. 她在三年内就让收入增加了两倍。
creditable ['kredɪtəbl]	*adj.* 1. 值得赞扬的；2. 高尚的 记 credit (=trust) + able → 值得信任的，有功劳的 例 1. It was a very creditable result for the team. 对这支参赛队来说，这比赛结果是十分值得称道的。 2. There was nothing very creditable in what he did. 他这事做得可实在不怎么样。
luminous ['luːmɪnəs]	*adj.* 1. 发光的，夜光的；2. 鲜亮的，鲜艳的 例 1. I saw the cat's luminous eyes in my car's headlights. 在车灯的照射下，我看到了猫的发光的眼睛。 2. They painted the door a luminous green. 他们把门漆成了翠绿色。
mirth [mɜːrθ]	*n.* 欢乐，欢笑 记 mir (=merry) + th → 欢乐 例 The performance produced much mirth among the audience. 这场演出使观众笑声不断。 扩 mirthful *adj.* 充满欢乐的
willful ['wɪlfl]	*adj.* 1. 故意的，有意的；2. 任性的，固执的 例 1. Wilful neglect of our manufacturing industry has caused this problem. 故意忽略我们的制造业引起了这个问题。 2. This is a woman who is willful and stubborn and has this innate intelligence. 这是个任性固执的女人，她具有这种天生的智慧。
constable ['kɑːnstəbl]	*n.* 警员，治安官 例 Have you finished your report, Constable? 警察先生，你的报告完成了吗？
perish ['perɪʃ]	*v.* 1. 死亡；2. 丧失 例 1. A family of four perished in the fire. 一家四口死于此次火灾之中。 2. Early buildings were made of wood and have perished. 早期建筑物为木质结构，已经消失殆尽。 扩 perishable *adj.* 易腐烂的
obeisance [oʊ'biːsns]	*n.* 1. 景仰，尊敬；2. 鞠躬示敬 例 1. They paid obeisance to him. 他们向他表示敬意。 2. One by one they came forward, mumbled grudging words of

welcome, made awkward obeisances. 他们挨个儿走上前去，勉强地咕哝出几句欢迎词，生硬地鞠躬致礼。

steadfast
['stedfæst]

adj. 坚定的，不动摇的
例 He remained steadfast in his determination to bring the killers to justice. 他要将杀人凶手绳之以法的决心一直没有动摇。
扩 steadfastly *adv.* 坚定地

transfuse
[træns'fjuz]

v. 1. 灌输；2. 输（血）
记 trans (=across) + fuse (=flow) → 流到另一边 → 输血
例 1. Was it possible to transfuse the peculiar spirit of the Irish native poetry into the English tongue? 有没有可能把爱尔兰语诗歌的某种精神渗透到英语中呢？
2. Battlefield injuries often require large amounts of transfused blood. 战场上的伤员通常需要大量输血。
扩 transfusion *n.* 追加投资；输血

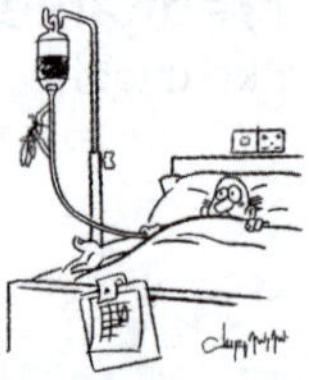

declaim
[dɪ'kleɪm]

v. 慷慨陈词
例 She declaimed the famous opening speech of the play. 她慷慨激昂地朗诵了这出戏中著名的开场白。

plow
[plaʊ]

v. 1. 犁地，耕地；2. 费力地穿过；3. 埋头苦干
例 1. They used oxen to plow the field. 他们用牛来犁地。
2. She plowed her way through the waiting crowds. 她从等候的人群中挤过去。
3. I had to plow through dozens of legal documents. 我得慢慢地埋头阅读几十份法律文件。

fete
[feɪt]

n. 庆祝活动；*v.* 赞誉，欢迎
记 与feast同源
例 1. In fact, the three friends likely won't lack for invites to fetes and parades, big and small. 其实这三个朋友很可能不乏聚会和庆祝活动的邀请，不论大小活动。
2. They were feted back home in Sacramento with a parade. 他们在家乡萨克拉门托受到了游行队伍的欢迎。

haggle
['hægl]

v. 争论，讲价
记 hag (=hack, cut) + gle → 砍掉 → 砍价
例 I left him in the market haggling over the price of a shirt. 我撇下他自己在市场上就一件衬衫讨价还价。

profligate
['prɑːflɪgət]

adj. 挥霍的，浪费的
例 She was very profligate in her spending. 她花钱大手大脚。
扩 profligacy *n.* 浪费，挥霍

List 15

eradicate
[ɪ'rædɪkeɪt]

v. 根除，杜绝
记 e (=out) + radic (=root) + ate → 拔出根 → 根除
例 We are determined to eradicate racism from our sport. 我们决心要杜绝体育竞技活动中的种族歧视现象。

intoxicated
[ɪn'tɑːksɪkeɪtɪd]

adj. 1. 喝醉的; 2. 极其兴奋的
记 in + toxic (=poison) + ate + d → 使中毒 → 喝醉的
例 1. He appeared intoxicated, police said. 他看上去喝醉了，警察说。
2. They seem to have become intoxicated by their success. 他们似乎陶醉在成功的喜悦中。
扩 toxic *adj.* 中毒的

descry
[dɪ'skraɪ]

v. 突然看见
记 与 describe 同源
例 As the sun rose we descried the enemy lying a mile from us. 太阳升起来以后，我们突然发现敌人位于我们一英里以外。

unassuming
[ˌʌnə'suːmɪŋ]

adj. 不爱出风头的，谦逊的
记 assume 有"假装、装出"之义
例 They lived in an unassuming neighborhood. 他们住在一处很不起眼的社区里。

inhuman
[ɪn'hjuːmən]

adj. 1. 无同情心的，冷酷的; 2. 非人的，恐怖的
例 1. The prisoners were subjected to inhuman treatment. 囚犯们遭受了非人的对待。
2. There was a strange inhuman sound. 有一种不像人发出的奇怪声音。

clog
[klɔːg, klɑːg]

v. (clogged, clogged; clogging) 阻塞，堵塞; *n.* 堵塞物
例 1. The narrow streets were clogged with traffic. 狭窄的街道上交通堵塞。
2. There's a clog in the kitchen sink. 厨房水池里有东西堵住了。

preferment
[prɪ'fɜːrmənt]

n. 晋升，提升
记 prefer 作动词本身也有"提拔"之意
例 He was told by the governors that he could expect no further preferment. 他被董事们告之晋升无望了。

torment
['tɔːrment]

n. 折磨，痛苦; *v.* 折磨
记 与 torture 同源
例 1. She suffered years of mental torment after her son's death. 儿子去世后，她多年悲痛欲绝。
2. He was tormented by feelings of insecurity. 他苦于没有安全感。

supplant
[sə'plænt]

v. 取代，替代

例 Older workers are being supplanted by recent college graduates. 年迈的工人正在被新近的大学毕业生取代。

enlist
[ɪn'lɪst]

v. 1. 争取，谋取；2. 征募，从军

记 en (=in) + list → 进入名单 → 争取，从军

例 1. They hoped to enlist the help of the public in solving the crime. 他们希望寻求公众协助破案。
2. He was enlisted into the U.S. Navy. 他应征加入了美国海军。

扩 enlistment *n.* 争取；应征

incite
[ɪn'saɪt]

v. 煽动，鼓动

记 in (=upon) + cite (=move, excite) → 使活跃 → 鼓动

例 They were accused of inciting the crowd to violence. 他们被控煽动群众暴乱。

例 incitement *n.* 煽动

taunt
[tɔːnt]

v. 辱骂，嘲笑；*n.* 嘲笑，奚落

例 1. The other kids continually taunted him about his size. 其他孩子不断地耻笑他的个头儿。
2. Black players often had to endure racist taunts. 黑人运动员经常得忍受种族歧视性的奚落。

辨 tout *v.* 吹捧；招徕

"Just pretend you don't notice him!"

pursuant
[pər'suːənt]

adj. 依照，根据

记 与 pursue 同源 → 追求原则 → 依据

例 A complaint was made pursuant to section 13 of the Act of 1987. 根据 1987 年法案的第 13 款，我们进行了投诉。

execrate
['eksəˌkreɪt]

v. 谴责

例 She came to execrate the hypocritical values of her upper-class upbringing. 她开始谴责她所接受的上层教育的虚伪。

扩 execration *n.* 谴责

corroborate
[kə'rɑːbəreɪt]

v. 证实，确证

记 cor (=thoroughly) + robor (=strong) + ate → 使坚实 → 证实

例 The evidence was corroborated by two independent witnesses. 此证据由两名独立证人提供。

扩 corroboration *n.* 证实，确定

untoward
[ʌn'tɔːrd]

adj. 异常的，意外的

记 un (=not) + toward (=incline) → 没有倾向的 → 异常的

例 He had noticed nothing untoward. 他没有注意到任何特殊情况。

inquisition
[ˌɪnkwɪ'zɪʃn]

n. 1. 宗教裁判所；2. 盘问，责难

例 1. The region had received Jewish refugees from the Spanish inquisition and various European persecutions across the ages. 该地区数年来曾接收过躲避西班牙宗教裁判所及各种欧洲迫害的犹太难民。
2. His political enemies were conducting an inquisition into the details of his personal life. 他的政敌正在盘问他的私生活。

phony
['foʊni]

adj. 假的，冒充的；*n.* 1. 冒充的人，冒牌货；2. 伪装者，伪善者

例 1. Although the fake bills look phony, they're still slipping past inattentive clerks. 虽然这些假钞看上去不像真的，但它们仍然躲过了粗心的职员们的眼睛。
2. The painting is a phony. 这幅画是假的。
3. I don't think she ever meant to help us. What a phony! 我认为她从未想真正帮助我们。真是个虚伪的人！

conflagration
[ˌkɑːnflə'greɪʃn]

n. 1. 大火灾；2. 战争或冲突

记 com + flagrat (=flame) + ion → 强烈的燃烧

例 1. The conflagration prevented her from entering the building when she realized there were people and animals trapped inside. 当她意识到还有人和动物困在里面的时候，大火却让她无法入内。
2. The treaty is the latest attempt to resolve the ten-year conflagration. 该条约是最近一次试图结束十年战争的努力。

扩 conflagrant *adj.* 燃烧的

agglomerate
[ə'glɑːməreɪt] *v.*
[ə'glɑːmərət] *adj.*

v. （使）成团，聚结；*adj.* 成团的，聚结的

记 ag (=to) + glomer (=ball) + ate → 使成团

例 1. It has agglomerated population, centralized means of production, and has concentrated property in a few hands. 它的人口集中，生产集中，而财富也集中在少数人手中。
2. The following are some of the compositions used in the manufacture of agglomerate blocks. 下面就是制造这些团状物的成分。

扩 agglomeration *n.* 团，块，聚焦

encore
['ɑːŋkɔːr]

n. 加演的节目

例 She played a Chopin waltz as an encore. 她应听众的要求又加演了一首肖邦的圆舞曲。

smother
['smʌðər]

v. 1. 闷死；2. 覆盖；3. 抵制，扼杀

例 1. He smothered the baby with a pillow. 他用枕头把婴儿闷死了。
2. She smothered him with kisses. 她劈头盖脑给他一通狂吻。
3. The voices of the opposition were effectively smothered. 反对党的声音被有效地压制了下去。

cloister
['klɔɪstər]

n. 1. 回廊，禁地；2. 修道院（生活）；*v.* 隔绝

记 clois (=close) + ter → 禁闭的地方 → 回廊，修道院

例 1. The thirteenth-century cloisters are amongst the most beautiful in central Italy. 这些 13 世纪的回廊是意大利中部最美的建筑。

2. The sisters leave the cloister only for emergencies, such as medical appointments. 修女们只在有紧急事务时才离开修道院，比如去看医生。

3. Ten years ago, the inhabitants of a cloistered community in Tennessee vanished without a trace. 十年前，住在田纳西州的一处与世隔绝的社区中的居民们都不见了踪影。

inscription
[ɪn'skrɪpʃn]

n. 题辞，铭文

例 There are no inscriptions or markings to identify the tombs. 没有铭文之类的东西可以识别出各个坟墓。

scarlet
['skɑːrlət]

adj. 猩红的，鲜红的；*n.* 红色的衣服，红色

例 1. She went scarlet with embarrassment. 她窘得满脸通红。

2. The right-hand side of the stands, which was a solid block of scarlet, roared its approval. 右手边的一队全部穿着红色的衣服，他们发出赞同的声音。

obloquy
['ɑːbləkwi]

n. 1. 辱骂；2. 耻辱，不名誉

记 ob (=against) + loqui (=speak) → 说不好的话 → 辱骂

例 1. How can any of these men now contemplate endorsing the object of their obloquy? 这些人怎么会考虑支持这个他们辱骂的人呢？

2. For years they endured the obloquy that follows scandal. 他们数年来都忍受着丑闻带来的耻辱。

List 16

azure
['æʒər]

adj. 天蓝色的；*n.* 天蓝色

例 1. The sky was azure over plains of green, and a distant bird soared above snow-flecked mountains. 绿色的平原之上天空蔚蓝，远处有只鸟飞翔在白雪覆盖的山顶之上。
2. But as we bid farewell to July, it's unlikely that our natural satellite will actually shimmer in shades of azure. 但当我们告别七月之时，我们的天然卫星不太可能在蓝天之下闪烁。

epistle
[ɪ'pɪsl]

n. 1. 使徒书信；2. 书信

例 1. Lambeth Palace Library in London has a partial draft of the *New Testament* epistles. 伦敦的兰贝斯宫图书馆里有一部分《新约》使徒书信的残稿。
2. When rapid-fire emails have replaced lengthy imploring epistles, who needs charm? 当迅如火势般的电子邮件代替了冗长的动人的书信，谁还需要什么魅力呢？

cogent
['koʊdʒənt]

adj. 有说服力的，令人信服的

例 She put forward some cogent reasons for abandoning the plan. 她为放弃这个计划提出了一些具有说服力的理由。

扩 cogency *n.* 说服力

unsocial
[ˌʌn'soʊʃl]

adj. 非正常工作时间的

记 原指让人无法参加社交活动的时间安排

例 I work long and unsocial hours. 我工作时间长，且在非正常时间上班。

wherefore
['werfɔːr]

adv. 为何；*n.* 原因

例 1. Wherefore in this slumbering city should the curse be laid on me alone? 在这座沉睡的城市里，为什么诅咒只落在我一个人身上？
2. I still don't know all the whys and wherefores. 我仍然不知道所有的原因。

plague
[pleɪg]

n. 1. 瘟疫，鼠疫；2. 灾害；*v.* 困扰，折磨

例 1. I avoid my weird neighbor like the plague. 我像躲避瘟疫一样躲避我的邻居。
2. The country was hit by a plague of natural disasters that year. 该国那年遇到了自然灾害。
3. Financial problems are plaguing the company. 财政问题使这家公司焦头烂额。

辨 plaque *n.* 牙菌斑；牌匾

consign
[kən'saɪn]

v. 1. 把…交付给；2. 打发，发落

记 con (=together) + sign (=mark) → 共同写下 → 委托，交付

例 1. What I didn't want was to see my mother consigned to an old people's home. 我所不愿意的是看到我母亲被送进养老院。

2. A car accident consigned him to a wheelchair for the rest of his life. 一次车祸使他落得在轮椅上度过余生的下场。

beacon
['biːkən]

n. 1. 灯塔；2. 无线电信标台

例 1. This new medicine is a beacon of hope for/to thousands of people. 这种新药是成千上万人的希望之光。

2. The plane was guided in by radio beacon. 这架飞机由无线电信标台导航。

apparition
[ˌæpə'rɪʃn]

n. 鬼魂，幽灵

记 appar (=appear) + ition → 凭空出现的东西 → 鬼魂

例 The patient recognized one of the women as the apparition she had seen. 病人认出其中一个女的是她曾见过的幽灵。

aspire
[ə'spaɪər]

v. 渴望，有志于

记 a (=to) + spire (=spirit, breathe) → 呼吸 → 渴望

例 He aspired to be their next leader. 他渴望成为他们的下一届领导人。

扩 aspiration *n.* 志向，抱负；发音送气

aspirant *n.* 有抱负的人

assiduous
[ə'sɪdʒuəs]

adj. 兢兢业业的

记 as (=to) + sid (=sit) + uous → 能坐得住的 → 兢兢业业的

例 The project required some assiduous planning. 这项工程需要仔细的规划。

扩 assiduously *adv.* 勤奋地

assiduity *n.* 勤奋，专注

chimera
[kaɪ'mɪrə]

n. 1. 吐火怪物；2. 妄想，幻想

例 1. She read about Mount Olympus and creatures like the chimera and the phoenix, and then read the story of Prometheus. 她读了有关奥林匹斯山以及吐火怪和凤凰之类的怪物，后来还读了普罗米修斯的故事。

2. Economic stability in that country is a chimera. 经济稳定在该国是个空想。

strenuous
['strenjuəs]

adj. 1. 费力的，繁重的；2. 劲头十足的，奋力的

例 1. Avoid strenuous exercise immediately after a meal. 刚吃完饭避免剧烈运动。

2. The ship went down although strenuous efforts were made to save it. 尽管人们为营救这条船作了很大的努力，它还是沉了。

扩 strenuously *adv.* 努力地

probity ['proʊbəti]

n. 正直，诚实

记 prob (=prove) + ity → 可证实 → 诚实

例 He asserted his innocence and his financial probity. 他宣称自己是清白的，在钱财上没有弄虚作假。

appellation [ˌæpə'leɪʃn]

n. 名称，称呼

记 appeal (=appeal, call) + lation → 叫的称呼 → 名称

例 He earned the appellation 'rebel priest.' 他赢得了"反叛牧师"的称号。

erudite ['erudaɪt]

adj. 博学的，有学问的

例 He was never dull, always erudite and well informed. 他从来就不愚笨，一直都是博学多才、见多识广的。

扩 erudition *n.* 博学，学问

unbend [ˌʌn'bend]

v. (unbent, unbent) 1. 放松，无拘束；2. 拉直

例 1. He could be fun if he'd unbend a little. 如果他在聚会上不那么紧张，会比较有意思一些。

2. He was bending and unbending his fingers. 他当时不断地在伸屈手指。

barter ['bɑːrtər]

v. 以物易物；*n.* 物物交易

例 1. The local people bartered wheat for tools. 当地人用小麦换取工具。

2. The islanders use a system of barter instead of money. 岛上的居民采用以物易物的交易方式，而不是用货币。

effusion [ɪ'fjuːʒn]

n. 1. 流出（物）；2. 感情流露，迸发

记 ef (=out) + fus (=flow) + ion → 流出来 → 感情流露

例 1. Fluid in the joint space, called an effusion, is a sign of rheumatoid disease activity. 关节处出现液体流出，这是关节炎的症状。

2. I did not embarrass her with my effusions. 我并没有太过热情而让她为难。

aroma [ə'roʊmə]

n. 芳香，香味

例 A delicious aroma was coming from the kitchen. 厨房里飘来饭菜的香味。

potentate ['poʊtnteɪt]

n. 权力大的统治者

记 potent (=power) + ate → 有权力的大佬

例 Political, business and Hollywood potentates, a thousand in all, came to pay their respects. 政界、商界和好莱坞的大佬们共一千多人前来（南希·里根的葬礼）表示敬意。

encomium
[en'koʊmiəm]

n. (*pl.* encomia, encomiums) 颂辞，高度赞扬的话

例 Whether he fully deserved the encomiums showered on him is another matter. 他是否真的值得这样的赞扬是另一回事。

downright
['daʊnraɪt]

adj. 十足的，完全的；*adv.* 完全地

例 1. There was suspicion and even downright hatred between them. 他们之间相互怀疑甚至极度仇恨。
2. She couldn't think of anything to say that wasn't downright rude. 她除了破口大骂之外再也说不出什么。

fraught
[frɔːt]

adj. 1. 充满的；2. 焦虑的，忧虑的

例 1. The earliest operations employing this technique were fraught with dangers. 最早使用这种技术的手术充满了危险。
2. Things are as fraught as ever in the office. 办公室的情况和往常一样令人担心。

扩 fright *n.* 惊吓，恐怖经历

bewitch
[bɪ'wɪtʃ]

v. 1. 迷住，迷惑；2. 施魔法，使中魔

记 be (=to) + witch → 做巫师 → 迷惑，施魔法

例 1. They were bewitched by her beauty. 他们被她的美貌所吸引。
2. People believed the girls had been bewitched. 人们当时以为这些女孩中魔了。

carnage
['kɑːrnɪdʒ]

n. 大屠杀

记 carn (=meat) + age → 提供肉类 → 大屠杀

例 Reporters described the highway accident as a scene of carnage. 记者们报道称公路上的事故如同大屠杀。

clamor
['klæmər]

v. 1. 大声要求；2. 大声喊叫；*n.* 1. 吵闹；2. 民众的要求

例 1. People began to clamor for his resignation. 人们开始大声疾呼要求他辞职。
2. The children clamored around them, singing songs and laughing. 孩子们在他们周围大声喊叫、唱歌、欢笑。
3. A clamor outside woke them in the night. 夜里外面的吵闹声把他们吵醒。
4. The clamor for her resignation grew louder. 民众要求她辞职的呼声越来越高。

扩 clamorous *adj.* 骚动的；吵闹的

glamor
['glæmər]

n. 吸引力，魅力

例 1. Now that she's a flight attendant, foreign travel has lost its glamor for her. 她现在是空中乘务员了，去国外旅行对她已失去魅力。
2. Add a cashmere scarf under your jacket for a touch of glamour. 在夹克衫里面围一条开司米围巾会使你更有魅力。

List 16

dissolute
[ˈdɪsəluːt]

adj. 放纵的，放荡的

记 与 dissolve 同源 → 溶解，散开 → 沉迷，无节制 → 放纵的

例 They converted late, often after dissolute or aimless teenage years when they may have indulged in drugs and petty crime. 他们皈依宗教很晚，通常是度过了放纵无度的青少年时期之后。他们沉迷过毒品，犯过一些小的罪行。

vitiate
[ˈvɪʃieɪt]

v. 使失效，削弱效用

例 The impact of the film was vitiated by poor acting. 拙劣的表演消弱了电影的影响力。

crusade
[kruːˈseɪd]

n. 1. 长期斗争，运动；2. 十字军东征；*v.* 长期奋斗

记 crus (=cross) + ade → 为十字架而斗争 → 十字军东征 → 长期斗争

例 1. I admired Reagan's crusade against drugs and alcohol. 我很欣赏里根总统对毒品和酗酒发起的斗争。
2. The headship of Christendom was in his grasp, and schemes for a new crusade began to take shape. 基督国家的领导权当时都掌握在他的手中，而进行新的十字军东征的计划就要开始了。
3. They are crusading against pollution. 他们在与污染作斗争。

outlive
[ˌaʊtˈlɪv]

v. 1. 比…活得长；2. 继续存在

例 1. He outlived his wife by three years. 他比妻子多活了三年。
2. The machine had outlived its usefulness. 这机器已无用了。

clumsy
[ˈklʌmzi]

adj. (clumsier, clumsier) 1. 笨拙的；2. 不得体的，冒犯的；3. 难用的，不便的

例 1. His clumsy fingers couldn't untie the knot. 他的手很笨拙，无法解开这个结。
2. She made a clumsy attempt to apologize. 她本想道歉，但措词生硬。
3. The complaints procedure is clumsy and time-consuming. 申诉程序复杂耗时。

entangle
[ɪnˈtæŋgl]

v. 1. 使纠缠，套住；2. 使卷入，使陷入

记 en (=in) + tangle → 使成团 → 卷入

例 1. The bird had become entangled in the wire netting. 那只小鸟被铁丝网缠住了。
2. He became entangled in a series of conflicts with the management. 他卷入了与管理层的一系列冲突之中。

扩 tangle *n.* 乱团；混乱

tartar
[ˈtɑːrtər]

n. 1. 牙石；2. 暴君

记 可能与鞑靼人 (Tartar) 有关 → 暴君

例 1. If plaque is allowed to collect over time it will harden into tartar. 如

果牙菌长时间累积，它就会变硬，结成牙石。
2. She can be quite a tartar. 她有时真是个悍妇。

invert
[ɪn'vɜːrt]

v. 使倒转，颠倒
记 in (=on) + vert (=turn) → 转过来 → 颠倒
例 In questions, the subject and verb are often inverted. 在疑问句中，主语和动词通常颠倒位置。
扩 inverse *adj.* 相反的

taper
['teɪpər]

v.（使）逐渐变窄；*n.* 1. 细长的蜡烛；2. 渐减
记 可能源于 paper → 纸（莎草）做的蜡烛芯 → 细长蜡烛；变窄
例 1. "You have to taper off these drugs gradually," Brown says. 布朗说："你得慢慢减少对这些药品的依赖。"
2. Fat candles flicker on the walls, and tall dripping tapers sit on the tables. 墙上的粗蜡烛摇曳着，桌子上的细长蜡烛滴着油。
3. Aroma is a critical component of tasting beer, and a glass with an inward taper helps to trap aromas and deliver them to your nose. 酒香是品啤酒的一个关键因素，而一个内部变细的玻璃杯有助于留住酒香，从而能让鼻子闻得到。

tamper
['tæmpər]

v. 篡改
例 Someone had obviously tampered with the brakes of my car. 显然有人捣鼓过我汽车的刹车。

bewilder
[bɪ'wɪldər]

v. 使迷惑，使糊涂
记 be (=thoroughly) + wilder (=wild, lost) → 完全迷失 → 使迷惑
例 She was totally bewildered by his sudden change of mood. 他的情绪突变，搞得她全然不知所措。

loiter
['lɔɪtər]

v. 闲荡，徘徊
例 Town officials have warned Cubans not to loiter in the streets. 城里的官员们已经警告古巴民众不要在街上逗留。

henceforth
[ˌhens'fɔːrθ]

adv. 此后
例 Friday 31 July 1925 henceforth became known as 'Red Friday'. 1925 年 7 月 31 日的这个星期五从此以后就称为"红色星期五"。

uproar
['ʌprɔːr]

n. 1. 吵闹，喧嚣；2. 骚动，怨愤
记 本与 roar（咆哮）无关，但可作联想记忆
例 1. Her comments provoked (an) uproar from the audience. 她的评论激起了听众的鼓噪。
2. The article caused (an) uproar. 这篇文章引起了轩然大波。

List 16

panegyric
[ˌpænəˈdʒɪrɪk]

n. 颂辞

例 The film is a panegyric to old-fashioned virtues. 这部电影是对老派美德的颂扬。

coarse
[kɔːrs]

adj. 1. 粗糙的；2. 大颗粒的；3. 粗鲁无礼的

例 1. He was wearing a shirt and trousers of coarse cotton jean. 他当时穿着衬衣和粗棉牛仔裤。
2. Coarse sea salt weighs even more, 67 grams. 粗的海盐甚至重达67克。
3. Donald Trump, rude, coarse and profane, just keeps on winning, despite everything that everyone can do. 唐纳德·特朗普虽然粗鲁无礼又下流，还是一直在赢（得选举），不论别人做什么事（来阻止他）。

扩 coarseness *n.* 粗鲁，粗糙

populous
['pɑːpjələs]

adj. 人口众多的

例 Indonesia, with 216 million people, is the fourth most populous country in the world. 有2.16亿人的印度尼西亚是世界第四人口大国。

扩 populousness *n.* 人口众多

tillage
['tɪlɪdʒ]

n. 1. 耕地；2. 耕种用的土地

记 till 作动词也有“耕作”之义

例 1. This surface cultivation is less violent than deep tillage and doesn't bring up weed seeds from below. 这种地表耕种比深耕要温和，无法把野草的种子从地下翻上来。
2. This land has long returned to the pasture and tillage of pre-war years. 这片土地很早就恢复到了战前的牧场和耕地状态。

pillage
['pɪlɪdʒ]

v. 抢劫，掠夺；*n.* 抢劫

例 1. Works of art were pillaged from churches and museums. 教堂和博物馆的艺术品被劫掠一空。
2. They brought back horrific accounts of murder and pillage. 他们带回了残杀掳掠的可怕消息。

crafty
['kræfti]

adj. 巧妙的；诡计多端的

例 These crafty tricks not only encourage customers to buy more, but to consume more. 这些巧妙的设计不仅促使顾客买得更多，而且消费得也更多。

扩 craftiness *n.* 巧妙

stale
[steɪl]

adj. 1.（食物）不新鲜的；2. 难闻的，污浊的；3. 陈腐的，老掉牙的

记 stal (=stall, still) + e → 停滞的 → 不新鲜的

例 1. Their daily diet consisted of a lump of stale bread, a bowl of rice and stale water. 他们的日常饮食包括一块不新鲜的面包、一碗米饭和变味的水。

2. A layer of smoke hung low in the stale air. 一层烟雾低悬在污浊的空气中。
3. Her relationship with Mark has become stale. 她和马克之间已经没有新鲜感了。

scepter
['septər]

n. 权杖

例 Traditionally, Securitas is personified holding a wreath in her right hand and a scepter in her left. 根据传统，塞库里塔斯（罗马保护神）的形象是右手拿着花冠，左手拿着权杖。

boulevard
['bʊləvaːrd]

n. 林荫大道

例 She looked down the boulevard for signs of a bus, none coming. 她沿着林荫大道望过去，没有公交车的迹象。

wrench
[rentʃ]

v. 1. 猛拧；2. 扭伤；3. 使痛苦；*n.* 扳手；痛苦

例 1. The bag was wrenched from her grasp. 那只包从她紧握的手里被夺了出来。
2. She wrenched her knee when she fell. 她跌倒时把膝盖扭伤了。
3. His words wrenched a sob from her. 他的话使得她难过得哭泣起来。

invidious
[ɪn'vɪdiəs]

adj. 招人嫉妒的，易引起反感的

记 invi (=envy) + dious → 招人嫉妒的

例 It would be invidious to single out any person to thank. 单独感谢任何一个人都易引起反感。

token
['toʊkən]

n. 1. 代币；2. 礼券；3. 象征，标志；*adj.* 象征性的

例 1. Each Bitcoin has a token of value and a means to transfer that value. 每一枚比特币都拥有面值，而且能够兑换。
2. From time to time, their caretakers give them tokens, which they can then exchange for food. 他们的监护人不时地给他们一些礼券，这样他们就可以拿去换食物了。
3. Having a gym membership is a token of urban life, like a car and a smartphone. 拥有一张健身会员卡就是城市生活的标志，就好像一辆车或一部智能手机一样。
4. The government agreed to send a small token force to the area. 政府同意派遣一小支象征性的部队到那一地区。

voracious
[və'reɪʃəs]

adj. 1. 饭量大的，贪吃的；2. 渴求的，求知欲强的

例 1. Bones, bread, bottles, and bowls lay scattered everywhere, as if voracious giants had gathered to dine. 骨头、面包、瓶子和碗扔得到处都是，好像贪吃的巨人在此聚会过一样。
2. Newspaper editors evinced a voracious appetite for news of the latest breakthroughs. 新闻编辑们培养出了一种渴求最新突破的胃口。

辨 veracious *adj.* 诚实的，准确的

List 16

relent [rɪˈlent]

v. 1. 终于答应；2. 变缓和，减弱

例 1. They had refused to pay and relented only after being threatened with a lawsuit. 他们曾拒绝付款，直到受到诉讼威胁后才终于答应。

2. The police will not relent in their fight against crime. 警方将继续严厉打击犯罪活动。

扩 relentless *adj.* 不停的，无情的

quandary [ˈkwɑːndəri]

n. 困惑，困窘

记 谐音“框的里”→ 困惑

例 George was in a quandary—should he go or shouldn't he? 乔治犹豫不定，拿不准该去还是不该去。

culprit [ˈkʌlprɪt]

n. 1. 罪犯；2. 肇事者

记 culp (=blame) + rit → 应受谴责的人 → 肇事者

例 1. The police quickly identified the real culprits. 警方很快查出了真正的罪犯。

2. The main culprit in the current crisis seems to be modern farming techniques. 当前这场危机的罪魁祸首好像是现代农业技术。

hearty [ˈhɑːrti]

adj. 1. 亲切的，友好的；2. 强烈的；3. 丰盛的

例 1. He gave Harry a hearty wink and strode off. 他朝哈利（·波特）亲切地眨了眨眼，然后大步离去。

2. Our plan won their hearty approval. 我们的计划获得了他们强烈的赞同。

3. Winter is the perfect time for a hearty homemade soup. 冬天正是时候喝一碗丰盛的居家热汤。

concourse [ˈkɑːŋkɔːrs]

n. 1. 大厅，广场；2. 一大群人

记 con (=together) + course (=flow) → 人员流动在一起 → 广场

例 1. Your flight leaves from concourse B. 您的航班从 B 厅登机出发。

2. The great concourse of people seemed to have been similarly impressed. 这一大群人似乎也留下了同样深刻的印象。

liberal [ˈlɪbərəl]

adj. 1. 宽宏大量的；2. 自由的，开明的；3. 慷慨的；4. 通识（教育）的

例 1. Parents must learn to take the larger and more liberal view of the future of their children. 家长们必须学会用更开阔、更开明的眼光来看待自己子女的未来。

2. Some politicians want more liberal trade relations with Europe. 有些政治家想与欧洲大陆建立更加自由的贸易关系。

3. He poured a liberal amount of cream into his coffee, stirred it with his finger, and drank. 他倒了很多奶油进咖啡里，然后用手指搅了搅，喝掉了。

4. Then, of course, a classical education really was the liberal education, the higher education, the ideal education, for it was the sole education. 当然了，经典教育是真正的通识教育，是高等教育，是理想的教育，因为它是唯一的教育方式。

扩 liberality *n.* 尊重，宽容；大方

solecism
[ˈsɑːlɪsɪzəm]

n. 1. 语病；2. 失礼

记 雅典人认为西西里岛的 Soloi 民族说话不讲语法，引申出“语病”之义

例 1. His prose mixes mockney solecisms with highly accomplished standard English. 他文章中高水平的标准英语中不时夹杂着仿伦敦东区口音的语病。

2. There's no more awful social solecism than accusing someone of being dead when they aren't. 最糟糕的失礼行为不外乎宣称某个活着的人已经去世了。

fecund
[ˈfiːkənd, ˈfe-]

adj. 1. 多产的；2. 有新颖想法的

记 谐音“肥垦的”→多产的

例 1. The pampas are still among the most fecund lands in the world. 南美大草原仍然是世界上最肥沃的土地之一。

2. It has now become clear how extraordinarily fecund a decade was the 1890s. 现在已经很清楚 19 世纪 90 年代是多么超乎寻常、成就斐然的 10 年了。

扩 fecundity *n.* 创造力

fidelity
[fɪˈdeləti]

n. 1. 忠诚；2. 准确性

记 高保真（HiFi）音响设备的全称是 high fidelity

例 1. She began to doubt her husband's fidelity. 她开始怀疑丈夫的忠诚度。

2. The movie's director insisted on total fidelity to the book. 电影导演坚持完全忠实于原著。

扩 infidelity *n.* 不忠行为，通奸

grossly
[ˈgroʊsli]

adv. 极度地，非常

例 The freezing seawater rushed in and the flooded, grossly overcrowded boat began to sink. 随着冰冷的海水开始涌入积涝，严重超载的船开始下沉。

poignant
[ˈpɔɪnjənt]

adj. 令人沉痛的，悲惨的

例 1. Her face was a poignant reminder of the passing of time. 她的容颜让人不禁感伤时光的流逝。

2. The decaying factory was a poignant symbol of how far the once mighty textile industry in Kano has fallen. 衰败的工厂成了令人心痛的象征，提醒人们嘉农曾经强大的纺织业已经衰落许久了。

engross
[ɪnˈgroʊs]

v. 使全神贯注

记 en (=in) + gross (=all) → 全部的 → 使全神贯注

例 She gets completely engrossed in her work. 她完全沉浸在自己的工作中。

扩 engrossing *adj.* 引人关注的

fragrant
['freɪgrənt]

adj. 芳香的

记 frag (=branch, smell) + rant → 好闻的 → 芳香的

例 The air was fragrant with scents from the sea and the hills. 空气中弥漫着山和海的芬芳气息。

辨 flagrant *adj.* 骇人听闻的，公然的

扩 fragrance *n.* 香水，香气

virility
[və'rɪləti]

n. 1. 生殖力；2. 力量，活力

例 1. Manipuris believe that by praying at this temple, they can be blessed with prosperity, good health and virility. 曼尼普尔人相信，在这座庙祈祷，就能带来繁荣、健康和多子多孙。
2. Air shows can sometimes look like corporate virility symbols, a chance to outdo rivals. 航空展有时可以看作公司活力的象征，一个使对手黯然失色的机会。

扩 virile *adj.* 强壮的，精力充沛的

atrocious
[ə'troʊʃəs]

adj. 1. 糟透的；2. 残暴的

例 1. She speaks French with an atrocious accent. 她讲的法语带有很难听的口音。
2. "Uber has a zero-tolerance policy for violent behavior, and our thoughts are with the victim of this atrocious crime," Uber said in a statement. 优步公司在一份声明中说："优步对暴力行为零容忍，我们的心跟这些残暴罪行的受害人在一起。"

扩 atrocity *n.* 残暴行为

unmask
[ˌʌn'mæsk]

v. 暴露，揭露

例 Mr. Burkett has unmasked several hundred impostors. 伯克特先生已经揭穿了数百个冒名顶替者。

flit
[flɪt]

v. (flitted, flitted; flitting) 1. 掠过；2. 迁移，迁居

例 1. Butterflies flitted from flower to flower. 蝴蝶在花丛中飞来飞去。
2. I had to change schools every time my parents flitted. 我父母每次迁居，我都得换学校。

gothic
['gɑːθɪk]

adj. 1. 哥特人的；2. 哥特式的，哥特派的；3.（小说）恐怖惊悚的

例 1. Gothic warriors invaded Rome. 哥特人入侵了罗马。
2. The images were Gothic or Byzantine rather than classical. 这些形象属哥特式或者拜占庭式而非古典式。
3. The gothic horror initially had a first print run of just 300 copies. 这部恐怖小说最初只印了 300 本。

sarcastic
[sɑːr'kæstɪk]

adj. 讽刺的，挖苦的

例 During oral arguments, the voluble Scalia often aimed sarcastic verbal barbs at lawyers. 在进行口头陈述时，快言快语的斯嘉丽经常朝律师说一些讽刺的话。

扩 sarcasm *n.* 讽刺，挖苦

decease
[dɪ'siːs]

n. 死亡

记 de (=away) + cease (=cede, go) → 走远，消失 → 死亡

例 The identities of the deceased and circumstances of their deaths were not known. 死者的身份和死亡的环境都无从知晓。

扩 deceased *adj.* 亡故的

malady
['mælədi]

n. 1. 严重问题，痼疾；2. 疾病

例 1. Violent crime is only one of the maladies afflicting modern society. 暴力犯罪仅仅是困扰现代社会的严重问题之一。

2. The patient was suffering from a mysterious malady that the doctors were unable to identify. 病人正遭受着不知名的疾病的困扰，而医生无力诊断。

pugnacious
[pʌg'neɪʃəs]

adj. 爱滋事的，好斗的

记 pugn (=fight) + acious → 打斗的 → 好斗的

例 There's one pugnacious member on the committee who won't agree to anything. 委员会有个爱滋事的人，所有事情一概反对。

扩 pugnacity *n.* 好斗，好战

pertinacious
[ˌpɜːrtɪ'neɪʃəs]

adj. 坚定不移的，义无反顾的

例 Like most successful politicians, she is pertinacious and single-minded in the pursuit of her goals. 跟多数成功的政治家一样，她义无反顾，一心一意地追求自己的目标。

扩 pertinacity *n.* 坚定

paucity
['pɔːsəti]

n. 少量，贫乏

例 Warner Bros., owned by media giant Time Warner Inc., was hit particularly hard in that report for a paucity of female directors. 媒体巨头时代华纳旗下的华纳兄弟影业公司在该报告中尤其受到批评，理由是它缺乏女性导演。

thereupon
[ˌðerə'pɑːn]

adv. 1. 立即，随即；2. 在其上

例 1. The audience thereupon rose cheering to their feet. 观众随即起立欢呼。

2. The jurors discussed the evidence and made their decision thereupon. 陪审员们讨论了证据，并在此基础上作出了裁决。

List 17

revamp
[ˈriːvæmp] *n.*
[ˌriːˈvæmp] *v.*

n./v. 翻新，改进外观

例 1. This switch is the headline move in the first big revamp of America's currency since 1929. 这一转变是 1929 年以来美国货币政策首次巨大转变的标志性举动。
2. The company has revamped the design of its best-selling car. 该公司改观了其最畅销的车型。

balm
[bɑːm]

n. 1. 护肤膏，镇痛软膏；2. 令人安慰或镇定的事物

例 1. A class action lawsuit has been filed against EOS, claiming its lip balm causes skin to crack, bleed and blister. 一起针对 EOS 的集体诉讼声称它的润唇膏造成皮肤龟裂、流血及起泡。
2. Shakespeare wrote in his tragic play *Macbeth* that slumber is a "Balm of hurt minds" and "Chief nourisher in life's feast." 莎士比亚在其悲剧《麦克白》中曾说，睡眠是对"受伤心灵的慰藉"和"生命的滋养"。

扩 balmy *adj.* 温暖惬意的

intestine
[ɪnˈtestɪn]

n. 肠

例 This vitamin is absorbed through the walls of the small intestine. 这种维生素通过小肠壁被吸收。

扩 intestinal *adj.* 肠的

versed
[vɜːrst]

adj. 精通的，熟练的

记 vers (=turn) + ed → 转变迅速的 → 熟练的

例 He was well versed in employment law. 他精通劳动法。

辨 verse *n.* 诗歌；韵文

groundwork
[ˈgraʊndwɜːrk]

n. 基础工作，准备工作

例 Officials are laying the groundwork for a summit conference of world leaders. 官员们正在为世界首脑峰会做准备工作。

fellowship
[ˈfeloʊʃɪp]

n. 1. 伙伴关系；2. 团体，协会；3. 研究生奖学金

例 1. People came to the community dinner to share good food and good fellowship. 人们来参加社区宴会是为了分享美食，享受友谊。
2. At Merlin's instigation, Arthur founds the Fellowship of the Round Table. 在梅林的建议下，亚瑟王创建了圆桌骑士团。
3. He came to the university on a teaching fellowship. 他上大学拿的是教育奖学金。

uppermost [ˈʌpərmoʊst]	*adj.* 1. 最高的，最上面的；2. 最重要，最关键；*adv.* 面向上地 例 1. Water penetrates the uppermost surface of the rock. 水渗透了岩石的表层。 2. These thoughts were uppermost in my mind. 我心里想得最多的就是这些事。 3. Place the material on a flat surface, shiny side uppermost. 把材料放在平面上，有光的一面朝上。
anon [əˈnɑːn]	*adv.* 很快，不久 例 I will answer his letter anon. 我将很快回复他的信件。
bourgeoisie [ˌbʊrʒwɑːˈziː]	*n.* 1. 中产阶级；2. 资产阶级 例 1. By the time of the revolution tea had become part of the aristocratic way of life, and it was beginning to spread to the bourgeoisie. 到革命爆发时，茶叶已经变成了贵族生活方式的一部分，并且当时已经开始向中产阶级蔓延。 2. The saddles, bridles and harnesses he made were prized by the rising bourgeoisie of Louis Phillipe's reign in 19th Century France. 他制作的马鞍、马勒和马具在 19 世纪路易·菲利浦统治的法国很受新兴资产阶级的欢迎。
leaden [ˈledn]	*adj.* 1. 铅灰色的；2. 沉闷的，迟钝的 例 1. Snow fell from the leaden sky. 灰蒙蒙的天开始飘起雪花。 2. The child's eyelids were leaden with sleep. 孩子的眼皮因为困意而沉重。
scuttle [ˈskʌtl]	*v.* 1. 碎步疾走；2. 破坏，阻止；3. 凿沉（船） 例 1. The rain sent everyone scuttling for cover. 下雨让所有人都急着找地方蔽雨。 2. Shareholders successfully scuttled the deal. 股东成功地阻止了这桩交易。 3. He personally had received orders from Commander Lehmann to scuttle the ship. 他个人已收到莱曼司令要求凿沉轮船的命令。
meddle [ˈmedl]	*v.* 1. 干涉，管闲事；2. 瞎搞，乱弄 例 1. He had no right to meddle in her affairs. 他无权干涉她的事情。 2. Somebody had been meddling with her computer. 有人擅自弄过她的电脑。 扩 meddlesome *adj.* 爱干预的
staid [steɪd]	*adj.* 古板的，一本正经的 记 stayed 的变体 → 固定不变的 → 古板的 例 The museum is trying to get rid of its staid image. 博物馆正试图改变其古板的形象。

List 17

aggrieved
[ə'gri:vd]

adj. 1. 愤愤不平的；2. 受害的，受委屈的

例 1. He felt aggrieved by their refusal to meet with him. 他们拒绝见他，这让他愤愤不平。
2. The aggrieved party may cancel the contract. 受害的一方可能会取消合同。

gird
[gɜ:rd]

v. 束，捆上

例 The company is girding its loins for a plunge into the overseas market. 公司正准备打入海外市场。

taboo
[tə'bu:]

n. 1.（文化或宗教）禁忌；2. 避讳；*adj.* 禁忌的

例 1. Death is one of the great taboos in our culture. 在我们的文化中，“死亡”是一个大忌。
2. The subject is still a taboo in our family. 这个话题在我们家里仍然讳莫如深。

3. In this company, dating a coworker is considered taboo. 在该公司，与同事交往是种禁忌。

sufferance
['sʌfərəns]

n. 勉强同意

记 suffer 作动词有表示“迁就笨人、容忍愚蠢者”之义
例 He's only staying here on sufferance. 他是经人勉强同意待在这儿的。

stature
['stætʃər]

n. 1. 声望，名望；2. 身高，个子

例 1. The orchestra has grown in stature. 这支管弦乐队的声望有所提高。
2. He is small in stature. 他个头小。
辨 statute *n.* 法令，条例

primogeniture
[ˌpraɪmoʊ'dʒenɪtʃər]

n. 1. 长嗣身份；2. 长子继承权

记 primo (=prime, first) + geni (=born) + ture → 第一个出生的 → 长嗣身份
例 1. James, by the right of primogeniture that prevails among most families of children, was given the first choice, and picked out the purple one. 詹姆斯拥有当时许多家庭盛行的长嗣之权，因此得以进行首选，他挑了一个紫色的。
2. Under the former rules of male primogeniture, royal sons took precedence over their female siblings, including first-born royal daughters. 根据以前的长子继承权，王室男丁优先于他们的姐妹，包括头胎生的女儿。

proscribe
[proʊ'skraɪb]

v. 宣布禁止

记 pro (=before) + scribe (=write) → 提前写下 → 禁止
例 The principal proscribed the use of cell phones in school. 校长禁止在学校使用手机。
辨 prescribe *v.* 开处方；命令

扩 proscription *n.* 禁止

slavish
['sleɪvɪʃ]

adj. 无独创性的，照搬的

记 slav (=slave) + ish → 费力地、机械地抄袭 → 照搬的

例 He has been criticized for his slavish devotion/adherence to the rules. 人们批评他死守教条。

impudence
['ɪmpjədəns]

n. 粗鲁，不恭

例 No baby boomer ever had the impudence to declare himself the voice of his generation! 婴儿潮时期出生的人没人敢如此粗鲁地宣称自己可以代表这一代人！

辨 imprudence *n.* 鲁莽，不明智

扩 impudent *adj.* 粗鲁的，不恭的

fanatic
[fə'nætɪk]

n. 1. 入迷者；2. 极端分子

记 缩写作 fan，中文音译为"粉丝"

例 1. I became a boating fanatic. 我当时变成了划船迷。
2. I am not a religious fanatic but I am a Christian. 我不是宗教狂热分子，但我是基督徒。

扩 fanatical *adj.* 狂热的

bane
[beɪn]

n. 造成困扰或不快的事物

例 The neighbors' kids are the bane of my life. 街坊邻居的孩子们让我生活得很不安宁。

扩 baneful *adj.* 邪恶的，引起灾祸的

vault
[vɔːlt]

n. 1. 金库；2. 地下墓室；3. 拱顶

例 1. Most of her jewelry is stored in bank vaults. 她的多数首饰都存在银行金库里。
2. She is to be buried in the family vault. 她将被葬进家庭墓室。
3. They gazed up at the vault of the cathedral. 他们看着教堂的穹顶。

conveyance
[kən'veɪəns]

n. 1. 传送，运输；2. 车辆

例 1. Long-distance pipelines were developed in the late 19th century to compete with railroads for the conveyance of crude oil. 19 世纪晚期兴建的远程输油管与铁路争夺原油运输生意。
2. Mahoney had never seen such a conveyance before. 马奥尼以前从来没有见过这样的运输工具。

扩 convey *v.* 表达；运送

restive
['restɪv]

adj. 难驾驭的，不耐烦的

记 rest (=remain) + ive → 保持原样的 → 难驾驭的

例 Greece, with the Balkan countries slamming their gates shut, is becoming a restive holding pen for thousands of frustrated asylum

seekers. 随着巴尔干半岛国家关闭国门，对于成千上万寻求避难的难民而言，希腊成了他们不耐烦地等待听天由命的地方。
扩 restiveness *n.* 桀骜不驯

milksop
['mɪlksɑːp]
n. 懦弱的男子（或男孩）
记 milk + sop → 浸在牛奶中的（面包）→ 懦弱的（男子）
例 Ewan was quiet, and his father thought him a milksop. 伊万很安静，所以他的父亲以为他很懦弱。

redound
[rɪ'daʊnd]
v. 改进，提高
记 与 redundant（多余的）同根 → 去掉（多余的）→ 改进，提高
例 Their defeat redounds to the glory of those whom they attacked. 他们的失败提高了那些受到他们攻击的人的声誉。

errand
['erənd]
n. 差使，差事
例 1. He often runs errands for his grandmother. 他经常给他的祖母跑腿儿。
2. Her boss sent her on an errand into town. 老板派她进城办事去了。
辨 arrant *adj.* 坏透的

envelop
[ɪn'veləp]
v. 包住，裹住
例 1. She was enveloped in a huge white towel. 她裹在一条白色大毛巾里。
2. Clouds enveloped the mountain tops. 云雾笼罩着山顶。
辨 envelope *n.* 信封
扩 envelopment *n.* 包住

ire
['aɪər]
n. 愤怒
记 联想：Ire（爱尔兰）人很 ire（愤怒）
例 He directed his ire at the coworkers who reported the incident. 他把怒火撒向那些报告事故的同事们。
扩 ireful *adj.* 怒气冲冲的

nuptial
['nʌpʃl]
adj. 婚姻的，婚礼的
记 谐音"拿不少"（彩礼）→ 婚礼的
例 I went to the room which he had called the nuptial chamber. 我走进了他称之为洞房的房间。

snug
[snʌg]
adj. 1. 保暖的；2. 贴身的，严密的
例 1. I spent the afternoon snug and warm in bed. 我在床上躺了一下午，又暖和又舒服。
2. The elastic at the waist gives a nice snug fit. 腰间的松紧带使衣服正好紧紧贴在身上。
扩 snugly *adv.* 舒适地；严密地

humbug
['hʌmbʌg]

n. 1. 谎言，欺骗行为；2. 虚伪的人

记 联想：human + bug → 人中之虫 → 虚伪的人

例 1. There was all the usual humbug and obligatory compliments from ministers. 全都是些部长们常说的骗人鬼话和少不了的奉承恭维。

2. What a revolting humbug the man was! 那人真是个令人作呕的伪君子！

proviso
[prə'vaɪzoʊ]

n. 限制条款，附文

记 形似 provision（条款）

例 1. He agreed to their visit with the proviso that they should stay no longer than one week. 他同意他们来做客，但条件是逗留不得超过一周。

2. Their participation is subject to a number of important provisos. 他们的参与受一些重要条款的限制。

patrimony
['pætrɪmoʊni]

n. 1. 遗产；2. 文化遗产，文物

记 patri (=father) + mony → 父亲（留下的）→ 遗产

例 1. I left my parents' house, relinquished my estate and my patrimony. 我离开了父母的家，放弃了我的房产和祖传财产。

2. These historic landmarks are an important part of our cultural patrimony. 这些历史地标都是我们的文化遗产的重要组成部分。

扩 patrimonial *adj.* 遗产的

pantheism
['pænθiɪzəm]

n. 泛神论，泛神崇拜

例 Their creed is the baldest Pantheism: that God is in everything, and therefore everything is God. 他们的信条是赤裸裸的泛神崇拜，即上帝存在于一切之中，因此一切皆为上帝。

scoundrel
['skaʊndrəl]

n. 无赖，恶棍

例 After two years as a scoundrel, he's once again a star in the minds' of many New York Yankees fans. 在当了两年的无赖之后，他重新成为了许多纽约扬基队球迷心目中的明星。

despoil
[dɪ'spɔɪl]

v. 抢劫，掠夺

记 de (=entirely) + spoil (=rob) → 抢夺；spoil 本身有"战利品"之义

例 The landscape has been despoiled by industrial development. 当地的景观已经被工业发展毁坏殆尽。

扩 despoiler *n.* 掠夺者

supple
['sʌpl]

adj. 1.（身体）柔软的，灵活的；2. 易弯曲的

记 sup (=under) + ple (=fold) → 折叠下去，跪下去 → 柔软的

例 1. These exercises will help to keep you supple. 这些锻炼项目有助于你保持身体的柔韧性。

2. Moisturizing cream helps to keep your skin soft and supple. 保湿霜有助于保持皮肤柔软有弹性。

辨 supplemental *adj.* 补充的，附加的

pitiable
['pɪtiəbl]

adj. 1. 可怜的；2. 卑鄙的

记 piti (=pity) + able → 可怜的，卑鄙的

例 1. It is pitiable to see the poor shivering in their thin cotton clothes in such weather. 看到穷人在这样的天气穿着他们的薄棉衣颤抖真是很可怜。

2. This pitiable sight led him to conclude that none of the company could have escaped death. 这些可怕的场景让他相信，这些公司都无法逃脱死亡的命运。

estimable
['estɪməbl]

adj. 1. 值得尊重的，值得敬佩的；2. 可估计的

记 该词是 esteem（尊敬）和 estimate（估计）的形容词

例 1. Both are estimable art films, deserving of a place in almost any festival. 这两部都是值得尊敬的艺术电影，都值得在所有的电影节上拥有一席之地。

2. A pound of man's flesh, taken from a man, is not so estimable, profitable neither, as flesh of muttons, beefs, or goats. 一镑人肉，从人身上割下来，并不是好估量的，也不好卖，不像羊肉和牛肉之类的那样。（——《威尼斯商人》）（见插图）

fable
['feɪbl]

n. 1. 寓言（故事）；2. 谎言

例 1. Each tale has the timeless quality of fable. 每个故事都有其永恒的寓意。

2. The story that he won the battle single-handedly is a mere fable. 他一人赢得了那场斗争，这种说法纯粹是谎言。

indissoluble
[ˌɪndɪ'sɑːljəbl]

adj. 牢不可破的，稳定持久的

记 in (=not) + dissolu (=dissolve) + ble → 不能分散的 → 牢不可破的

例 They are bound together by indissoluble ties. 他们因牢不可破的联系而结合在一起。

morose
[mə'roʊs]

adj. 阴郁的，脾气不好的

例 He became morose and withdrawn and would not talk to anyone. 他变得闷闷不乐，沉默寡言，不愿跟任何人说话。

hereditary
[hə'redɪteri]

adj. 1. 遗传的；2. 世袭的

记 here (=heir) + dit + ary → 遗传的，继承的

例 1. Epilepsy is hereditary in her family. 癫痫是她家的遗传病。

2. British Prime Ministers are traditionally offered hereditary peerages. 英国首相传统上会被授予可世袭

的贵族爵位。
扩 hereditarily *adv.* 遗传地，世代地

betake
[bɪ'teɪk]

v. (betook, betaken) 前往，去（某处）
例 He betook himself to his room. 他进了自己的房间。

discredit
[dɪs'kredɪt]

v. 1. 败坏…的名声；2. 使不相信；*n.* 名誉丧失，丢脸
记 dis (=not) + credit → 使失信 → 败坏名声
例 1. The photos were deliberately taken to discredit the President. 这些蓄意拍摄的照片旨在败坏总统的名声。
2. These theories are now largely discredited among linguists. 这些理论现已大多受到语言学家的质疑。
3. Britain, to its discredit, did not speak out against these atrocities. 英国没有公开反对这些残暴行为，这使其名誉扫地。
扩 discreditable *adj.* 不光彩的，丢脸的

evangelical
[ˌiːvæn'dʒelɪkl]

adj. 1. 基督教福音派的；2. 狂热的，热衷的
例 1. They're evangelical Christians. 他们是福音派基督徒。
2. He delivered his speech with evangelical fervor. 他发表演说时热烈鼓吹自己的思想。

preoccupy
[pri'ɑːkjupaɪ]

v. 使思考，使忧心
记 pre (=before) + occupy → 提前占据（心思）→ 使忧心
例 The question of life after death has preoccupied many philosophers. 人死之后的问题一直使很多哲学家们不能释怀。
扩 preoccupied *adj.* 忧心的，纠结的

contravene
[ˌkɑːntrə'viːn]

v. 违犯（法律等）
记 contra (=against) + vene (=come) → 反向走 → 违犯
例 The company was found guilty of contravening safety regulations. 那家公司被判违反了安全条例。
扩 contravention *n.* 违反

overrun
['oʊvərʌn]

v. (overran, overrun; overrunning) 1. 泛滥，横行；2. 超时
例 1. The house was completely overrun with mice. 这房子简直成了老鼠的天下。
2. Her lectures never overrun. 她讲课从不拖堂。

scribble
['skrɪbl]

v. 1. 匆匆写下；2. 胡写，乱画
记 scrib (=write) + ble → 写下 → 乱写
例 1. She scribbled down her phone number and pushed it into his hand. 她匆匆写下自己的电话号码，塞进他手里。
2. Someone had scribbled all over the table in crayon. 不知谁用蜡笔胡写乱画，桌面上都涂满了。

lukewarm
[ˌluːkˈwɔːrm]

adj. 1. 微温的；2. 无兴趣的，不热情的
例 1. Our food was only lukewarm. 我们的食物只是温乎的。
2. She was lukewarm about the plan. 她对这个计划不大感兴趣。

chastise
[tʃæˈstaɪz]

v. 1. 批评，责备；2. 体罚
记 谐音“掐死太子”→体罚
例 1. He chastised the team for their lack of commitment. 他指责队伍未竭尽全力。
2. Parents are no longer allowed to chastise their children as they did in the past. 父母现在不能像过去一样体罚孩子了。
扩 chastisement *n.* 指责，批评

detriment
[ˈdetrɪmənt]

n. 伤害，造成伤害的事情
例 He was engrossed in his job to the detriment of his health. 他全身心地投入工作，结果损害了他的健康。
扩 detrimental *adj.* 伤害的，有害的

stimulant
[ˈstɪmjələnt]

n. 1. 兴奋剂；2. 有激励作用的事物
记 stimulate 的名词
例 1. Coffee and tea are mild stimulants. 咖啡和茶是轻度兴奋剂。
2. The movie was a stimulant to discussion. 这部电影激起了大家的讨论。

clement
[ˈklemənt]

adj. 1. 温和的，温暖的；2. 仁慈的，宽恕的
例 1. Our challenge is to figure out how this more clement Mars was even possible, and what happened to that wetter Mars. 我们的挑战是弄清为什么火星气候会如此温和，以及更湿润的火星上发生了什么事情。
2. A more clement judge reduced the sentence. 一个较为仁慈的法官减轻了刑罚。

concomitant
[kənˈkɑːmɪtənt]

adj. 同时发生的，相伴的；*n.* 同时发生的事，伴随的事物
记 con (=together) + comit (=come) + ant → 同时来到的 → 相伴的
例 1. The drug's risks increase with the concomitant use of alcohol. 用药时饮酒会增加药品的风险。
2. Political union is an essential concomitant of successful economic union. 成功的经济联盟必然带来政治上的联盟。

filthy
[ˈfɪlθi]

adj. 1. 肮脏的，污秽的；2. 下流的，猥亵的；3. 气愤的
例 1. He never washed, and always wore a filthy old jacket. 他总是穿着一件从来不洗的脏兮兮的旧夹克。
2. Apparently, well known actors were at these filthy parties. 听说有些知名演员也参加了这些下流的聚会。
3. Ann gave him a filthy look. 安气愤地瞧了他一眼。

motto ['mɑːtoʊ]

n. (*pl.* mottoes, mottos) 格言，座右铭

例 "Hope for the best and prepare for the worst" is my motto. 我的座右铭是："抱最好的希望，做最坏的打算。"

ambiguous [æm'bɪgjuəs]

adj. 1. 含混不清的；2. 不明确的

例 1. Her account was deliberately ambiguous. 她的陈述故意含混不清。
2. His role has always been ambiguous. 他的角色一直不明确。

扩 ambiguity *n.* 模糊不清；不明确

precipice ['presəpɪs]

n. 悬崖，峭壁

例 The country was now on the edge of a precipice. 这个国家现在的情势岌岌可危。

扩 precipitous *adj.* 危险的；陡峭的

retrace [rɪ'treɪs]

v. 1. 折回，原路返回；2. 回顾，追溯

记 re (=back) + trace → 向回走 → 折回

例 1. She turned around and began to retrace her steps towards the house. 她转身沿原路向那栋房子走去。
2. Detectives are trying to retrace her movements on the night she disappeared. 侦探试图查出她失踪当晚的行踪。

appall [ə'pɔːl]

v. 使惊骇，使大为震惊

记 ap (=to) + pall (=pale) → 使脸变苍白 → 使惊骇

例 The idea of sharing a room appalled her. 合住一个房间的想法使她惊骇。

扩 appalling *adj.* 使人震惊的

mince [mɪns]

v. 1. 用绞肉机绞（食物）；2. 小步快走

记 min (=mini, small) + ce → 使变小 → 绞碎；小步走

例 1. The recipe says that you should mince the onions. 食谱上说你应该把洋葱绞碎。
2. The comedian minced across the stage. 喜剧演员小步走过舞台。

pittance ['pɪtns]

n. 微薄的工资，极少的报酬

记 与 pity 同根 → 少得可怜的报酬

例 She could barely survive on the pittance she received as a pension. 她拿的养老金很难糊口。

sully ['sʌli]

v. 1. 败坏，有损于；2. 弄脏，玷污

例 1. By cheating they have sullied the good name of their country. 他们的欺骗行为玷污了祖国的声誉。
2. She wondered if she dared risk sullying the gleaming sink. 她怀疑自己是否敢冒险弄脏光闪闪的水槽。

List 17

borough
[ˈbɜːroʊ]

n. 自治镇，行政区

例 The Bronx is one of the five boroughs of New York. 布朗克斯是纽约市的五个行政区之一。

predominate
[prɪˈdɑːmɪneɪt]

v. 1. 数量上占优势，以…为主；2. 占主导地位，有重要影响

例 1. Women predominated in the audience. 观众以妇女为主。
2. Private interest was not allowed to predominate over the public good. 私人利益不得凌驾公众利益。

扩 predominance *n.*（数量上的）优势；支配地位

flog
[flɑːg]

v. (flogged, flogged; flogging) 1. 鞭笞，棒打；2. 出售

例 1. He was publicly flogged for breaking the country's alcohol laws. 他因违犯国家的酒法而被当众处以鞭刑。
2. We buy them cheaply and then flog them off at a profit. 我们低价买下这些，然后卖出获利。

piquant
[ˈpiːkənt]

adj. 1. 辛辣的，开胃的；2. 刺激的，令人兴奋的

记 piq (=pike) + uant → 捅的 → 刺激的，开胃的

例 1. He served the fish with a piquant sauce. 他端上鱼肉，伴以开胃酱。
2. There may well have been a piquant novelty about her books when they came out. 她的书问世时可能的确有引人入胜的新颖之处。

扩 piquancy *n.* 刺激，兴奋

radiant
[ˈreɪdiənt]

adj. 1. 喜气洋洋的；2. 灿烂的；3. 辐射的，放射的

记 radia (=radio, root) + nt → 像根一样（辐射）的 → 灿烂的，放射的

例 1. She was radiant with health. 她身体健康，容光焕发。
2. The sun was radiant in a clear blue sky. 湛蓝的天空阳光灿烂。
3. The earth would be a frozen ball if it were not for the radiant heat of the sun. 如果没有太阳辐射的热量，地球将是一个冰封的世界。

suppliant
[ˈsʌplɪkənt]

adj. 恳求的；*n.* 恳求者

记 sup (=under)+ pli (=fold) + ant → 折叠（跪）在下面 → 恳求者

例 1. She was not the woman he had seen at Jones' Hotel long months before, when she had almost knelt suppliant at his feet. 她不再是那个他数月前在琼斯旅馆见过的女人了，当时她几乎跪在他脚下恳求他。
2. One by one the suppliants crawled past, each crying out an appeal or a grievance. 求见的人逐一匍匐而行，每人都在哀求或喊冤。

扩 supplication *n.* 恳求

upbraid
[ʌpˈbreɪd]

v. 申斥，责骂

例 His wife set about upbraiding him for neglecting the children. 他妻子开始指责他不照顾孩子。

meridian
[mə'rɪdiən]

n. 1. 子午线，经线；2. 最高阶段，最高点

例 1. "Prairie dogs are the main reservoir for plague, and they tend to be west of the 100th meridian," he says. 他说："土拨鼠是瘟疫主要的宿主，而这些土拨鼠主要生活在（西经）100 度以西的地区。"

2. Prior to the institutionalization of standard time, clocks were set using local meridians or local mean time, and they varied widely. 在标准时间实行之前，时间是按照当地的（太阳）最高点或当地平均时间来确定的，而且它们之间差异很大。

wean
[wiːn]

v. 使断奶，使戒除（习惯）

例 1. The calves are weaned at an early age. 这些小牛很早就断奶了。

2. The doctor tried to wean her off sleeping pills. 医生设法使她逐渐停止服用安眠药片。

covert
['koʊvɜːrt]

adj. 秘密的，隐蔽的

记 cover + t → 覆盖住的 → 秘密的

例 He stole a covert glance at her across the table. 他朝桌子对面的她偷偷地瞥了一眼。

扩 covertly *adv.* 秘密地

meager
['miːgər]

adj. 少量且劣质的，微薄的

例 She supplements her meager income by cleaning at night. 她靠做夜间清洁工来补贴其微薄的收入。

List 18

List 18

leer [lɪr]

v. 奸笑，淫笑；*n.* 奸笑

例 1. She complained that some disgusting man was leering at her. 她投诉说有个恶心的人不怀好意地看着她。

2. He looked at her with an evil leer. 他用不怀好意的目光看着她。

扩 leery *adj.* 猜疑的，极力躲避的

calumny [ˈkæləmni]

n. 诬蔑，诽谤

例 1. He was the target of calumny for his unpopular beliefs. 他因为信仰非主流而受到诽谤。

2. He accused the press of publishing vicious calumnies. 他指责媒体恶意诽谤。

扩 calumnious *adj.* 诽谤的

violet [ˈvaɪələt]

n. 1. 紫罗兰；2. 蓝紫色；3. 害羞的人

例 1. "Roses are red, violets are blue, you are the president, and I am your glue," Mrs. Obama said. "玫瑰粉红，紫罗兰绽蓝，你是总统，我是你的贴心人，" 奥巴马夫人唱道。

2. Yellow, violet and burgundy were among his favorites, and strawberry embellishments were added for Wimbledon. 黄色、蓝紫色、深红色是他的最爱，而温布尔敦的装饰中还包括草莓样饰品。

3. None of the women he paints, however, could be described as shrinking violets. 然而，他画过的所有女人中没有一个是羞涩腼腆的。

paddock [ˈpædək]

n. 1. 牧马围场；2.（赛车、赛马的）检阅场

记 联想 dock 停船的地方 → paddock 停放赛车的地方

例 1. The family kept horses in the paddock in front of the house. 那户人家把马养在屋前的小围场里。

2. At the season's Abu Dhabi finale, the cars were not allowed into the paddock until payments were forthcoming. 在本季的阿布扎比决赛中，除非缴费，否则车辆不得进入检阅场。

convent [ˈkɑːnvent, -vənt]

n. 1. 女修道院；2. 女修道院学校

记 con (=together) + vent (=come) → 来到一起 → 修道院

例 1. I spent my adult life growing up in the convent. 我成年的大部分时间都在女修道院度过。

2. She was twenty-two, and only a few years out of her convent boarding school. 她当时二十二岁，刚刚从寄宿的女子修道院学校出来没几年时间。

辨 convene *v.* 聚集，集合

扩 conventual *adj.* 女修道院的

vainglorious
[ˌveɪnˈglɔːriəs]

adj. 自负的，自命不凡的

记 vain + glori (=glory) + ous → 自认为光荣的 → 自负的

例 Franny, is a vainglorious manipulator of other people accustomed to getting his way, often by playing God. 弗兰尼自命不凡，以上帝自居，喜欢操纵别人来达到自己的目的。

扩 vainglory *n.* 自命不凡

embroider
[ɪmˈbrɔɪdər]

v. 1. 刺绣；2. 渲染，润饰

记 en (=in) + broid (=braid) + er → 编织进去 → 刺绣

例 1. She embroidered flowers on the cushion covers. 她在这些靠垫套上绣了花。

2. He is known to embroider the truth about his service in the army. 众所周知，他喜欢把他在部队里的事添油加醋地宣传。

扩 embroidery *n.* 绣花，刺绣

pastime
[ˈpæstaɪm]

n. 消遣，休闲活动

记 pas (=pass) + time → 消磨时间的东西 → 休闲活动

例 Baseball has been a national pastime for years. 棒球很多年来都是全国性的娱乐活动。

punctilious
[pʌŋkˈtɪliəs]

adj. 一丝不苟的

记 punct (=punch, point) + ilious → 一点的 → 一丝不苟的

例 He was punctilious about being ready and waiting in the entrance hall exactly on time. 他一丝不苟地作好准备并准时地在门厅等候。

indemnity
[ɪnˈdemnəti]

n. 1. 保障，赔偿；2. 赔款

记 in (=not) + demn (=damage) + ity → 弥补损失 → 赔偿

例 1. They were charged with failing to have professional indemnity cover. 他们被指控未能提供职业保险保障。

2. The government paid the family an indemnity for the missing pictures. 政府因为丢失照片而付给这家人一笔补偿金。

asperity
[æˈsperəti]

n. 粗暴，严厉

例 She pointed out, with some asperity, that it had all been my fault. 她严厉地指责说这都是我的错。

辨 aspiration *n.* 抱负，志向

consanguinity
[ˌkɑːnsæŋˈgwɪnəti]

n. 血缘，血亲关系

记 con (=together) + sanguine (=blood) + ity → 共同血缘 → 血亲

例 Through fandom, he built a life, a family, and a community not around consanguinity, but around the heart. 通过歌迷会，他建立了一种生活，一个家庭，不是基于血缘，而是发自内心。

扩 consanguine *adj.* 同血缘的

courteous ['kɜːrtiəs]

adj. 礼貌的，客气的

记 court + eous → 宫廷的 → 礼貌的，有教养的

例 The hotel staff are friendly and courteous. 旅馆服务人员友好而有礼貌。

扩 courteously *adv.* 礼貌地

cramp [kræmp]

n. 抽筋，痉挛；*v.* 阻碍，阻止

例 1. She started getting stomach cramps this morning. 她今天早上开始胃痉挛。

2. Tighter trade restrictions might cramp economic growth. 较严格的贸易限制会妨碍经济的增长。

deadweight [ˌded 'weɪt]

n. 1. 重物；2. 重负，累赘

记 dead + weight → 无法自由活动的重量 → 累赘

例 1. A large deadweight seemed to fall through Harry's chest into his stomach. 哈利（·波特）感觉有个巨大的重物从胸口落到了肚子里。

2. My head no longer felt like my head but like a deadweight on my torso. 我的头都感觉不像是头了，好像是躯体上的一个累赘。

limelight ['laɪmlaɪt]

n. 公众注意的中心

记 lime + light → 像白石灰一样雪白的灯（照在舞台上的演员身上）

例 When his new book caused an unexpected controversy, he was thrust into the limelight once again. 他的新书激起了意外的争议，这时他又一次成了公众注意的中心。

blight [blaɪt]

v. 损害，妨害；*n.* 1. 枯萎病；2. 不利因素

例 1. His career has been blighted by injuries. 他的事业不断受到伤病的困扰。

2. Many areas have been devastated by blights which destroyed cereal crops and vines. 许多地区都被谷类和葡萄枯萎病摧毁了。

3. His death cast a blight on the whole of that year. 他的死使那一整年都处在阴影之中。

stitch [stɪtʃ]

n. 1. 针脚，缝；2. 岔气；*v.* 缝补

记 sti (=stick) + tch → 棍状物 → 针缝

例 1. Try to keep the stitches small and straight. 针脚要尽量缝得小而直。

2. Can we slow down? I've got a stitch. 我们慢一点好不好？我岔气了。

3. Her initials were stitched on the pillowcase. 枕套上缝着她名字的首字母。

multifarious
[ˌmʌltɪˈferiəs]

adj. 多种的，各种各样的

例 Spain is a composite of multifarious traditions and people. 西班牙是多种传统和多个民族的合成体。

vend
[vend]

v. 售卖

例 They were taking a break in the hall of their office building, buying a snack from a vending machine. 他们在办公楼的大厅里休息，从售卖机里买了一些零食。

辨 vent *n.* 出口，漏孔

扩 vendor *n.* 小贩，摊贩

proficient
[prəˈfɪʃnt]

adj. 熟练的，精通的

记 pro (=forward) + fic (=fact, make) + ient → 做得很好的 → 熟练的

例 Less than 20 percent of students were deemed proficient in reading and math on standardized tests last year. 去年在标准化考试中不到20% 的学生精于阅读和数学。

扩 proficiency *n.* 熟练，精通

ensign
[ˈensən]

n. 1. 舰旗，商船旗；2. 海军少尉

记 en + sign → 船只国籍的标志 → 舰旗；扛旗的士兵 → 海军少尉

例 1. There is also a large White Ensign on the left shoulder. 他的左肩上有一面很大的英国海军旗。

2. Hoping to serve in naval intelligence, he joined the Navy Reserve and was commissioned as an ensign after the attack on Pearl Harbor. 他希望加入海军情报部门，于是加入了海军预备役，在珍珠港遇袭后被任命为少尉。

tinkle
[ˈtɪŋkl]

n. 叮当声；*v.* 发出叮当声

例 1. The slow intake of a diver's respirator, followed by the tinkle of a stream of bubbles, is the only noise in the video. 视频里只有潜水员的吸气声，紧接着是一串气泡声。

2. A bell tinkled as the door opened. 房门一开，铃声丁零响了。

jest
[dʒest]

n. 笑话，俏皮话；*v.* 开玩笑

例 1. The remark was made half in jest. 这话是半开玩笑说出的。

2. Would I jest about such a thing? 这种事我会说着玩吗?

eschew
[ɪsˈtʃuː]

v. （有意）避开，回避

记 与 escape 形似

例 He had eschewed politics in favor of a life practicing law. 他有意避开政治，而选择过上执业法律的生活。

postscript
[ˈpoʊstskrɪpt]

n. 1. 附言；2. 补充，后话

记 常缩写为 P.S.

例 1. In a postscript to her letter, she promised to write again soon. 在她

信件的附言里，她承诺很快再写信来。
2. An interesting postscript to the story is that the two people involved later got married. 故事的后话很有意思，这两个人后来结婚了。

visage [ˈvɪzɪdʒ]

n. **面容，脸**

记 vis (=vision, see) + age → 看（脸）→ 颜值

例 Alive and dead, Bork's bearded visage has haunted American law and American politics for 30 years. 无论活着还是死后，伯克那张蓄胡须的脸一直困扰了美国司法和美国政治 30 年。

corpse [kɔːrps]

n. (*pl.* corpses) **尸体，尸首**

例 Barbour is also charged with tampering with physical evidence and abuse of a corpse. 巴伯还被控毁坏证据和侮辱尸体。

辨 corps *n.* (*pl.* corps) 兵团；陆军特种部队

aptitude [ˈæptɪtuːd]

n. **天资，天赋**

记 SAT 考试过去的全称为 Scholastic Aptitude Test

例 His aptitude for dealing with children got him the job. 他善于和儿童打交道的本事使他得到了这份工作。

扩 inaptitude *n.* 愚笨，无才

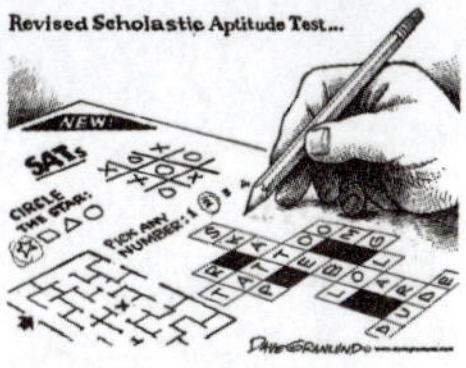

shackle [ˈʃækl]

v. **1. 戴上镣铐；2. 束缚，阻挠；*n.* 桎梏，束缚**

例 1. The prisoners were kept shackled during the trial. 审判期间，犯人戴着镣铐。
2. The people were shackled by poverty. 人民当时受到贫穷的困扰。
3. The country was freed from the shackles of tyranny. 该国从暴君的统治中解放出来。

arraign [əˈreɪn]

v. **控告，提审**

例 Phillips is scheduled to be arraigned March 23 in Providence Superior Court. 菲利浦将于 3 月 23 日在普罗维登斯最高法院受审。

扩 arraignment *n.* 审问，控告

furtive [ˈfɜːrtɪv]

adj. **偷偷摸摸的**

例 1. She cast a furtive glance over her shoulder. 她偷偷往背后瞥了一下。
2. We exchanged furtive smiles across the table. 我们隔着桌子互相偷笑了一下。

扩 furtively *adv.* 鬼鬼祟祟地

disgorge [dɪsˈɡɔːrdʒ]

v. **1.（液体）涌出，倾泻；2.（人）涌出**

记 dis (=out) + gorge (=throat) → 从喉咙吐出 → 涌出

例 1. The pipe disgorges sewage into the sea. 这管道将污水排入大海。

2. The bus disgorged a crowd of noisy children. 公共汽车上涌下来一群叽叽喳喳的孩子。

disseminate
[dɪ'semɪneɪt]

v. 散布，传播
记 dis (=spread) + semin (=seed) + ate → 扩散种子 → 传播（思想）
例 Their findings have been widely disseminated. 他们的研究成果已经广为传播。
扩 dissemination *n.* 传播

ammunition
[ˌæmju'nɪʃn]

n. 1. 弹药；2.（辩论中用来攻击对方的）事实，信息
例 1. The troops were supplied with weapons and ammunition. 部队得到弹药武器的供应。
2. The letter gave her all the ammunition she needed. 这封信给了她所需的一切有力证据。

legion
['liːdʒən]

n. 1.（古罗马）军团；2. 大量，大批；*adj.* 很多的
记 leg (=league) + ion → 一群人 → 军团
例 1. The last of the Roman legions left Britain in AD 410. 罗马军团最后一支部队于公元 410 年离开英国。
2. His delightful sense of humor won him a legion of friends. 他的幽默风趣为他赢得了很多朋友。
3. The medical uses of herbs are legion. 草本植物的医药效用数不胜数。

adjudicate
[ə'dʒuːdɪkeɪt]

v. 1. 裁决；2.（比赛）评判
记 ad (=to) + jud (=judge) + icate → 进行判决 → 裁决
例 1. Their purpose is to adjudicate disputes between employers and employees. 他们的目的是裁决雇主与雇员之间的纠纷。
2. Who is adjudicating at this year's contest? 今年比赛谁当裁判?
扩 adjudication *n.* 评判，裁决

tempest
['tempɪst]

n. 暴风雨
记 temp (=time) + est → 特定的天气时期 → 暴风雨
例 1. A tempest is brewing over the new tax laws. 一场关于新税法的激烈争议即将上演。
2. The whole controversy turned out to be a tempest in a teapot. 整个问题变成了茶壶里的风暴——小题大作。

umbrage
['ʌmbrɪdʒ]

n. 受冒犯，感到不安
记 与 umbrella 同源 → 有阴影的 → 感到受轻视
例 1. I take umbrage at that remark. 对那番说法我感觉受到了冒犯。
2. He takes umbrage against anyone who criticizes him. 不管谁批评

他，他都心生愤懑。

adulation
[ˌædʒəˈleɪʃn]

n. 称赞，吹捧

例 The band enjoys the adulation of their fans wherever they go. 乐队很喜欢所到之处受到的乐迷的吹捧。

扩 adulate *v.* 吹捧

peroration
[ˌperəˈreɪʃn]

n. 1. 结尾，总结；2. 乏味的演说

记 per (=to the end) + ora (=speak) + tion → 最后说的话 → 总结

例 1. That peroration drew one of the night's biggest ovations. 结尾受到了当晚最热烈的喝彩。

2. We sat through a lengthy peroration on the evils of the government's policies. 我们熬过了一场关于政府政策弊端的乏味演说。

扩 perorate *v.* 演说，总结

exult
[ɪɡˈzʌlt]

v. 欢欣鼓舞，兴高采烈

例 Within four years, Hamilton would be dead, but Jefferson did not exult. 四年之后，汉密尔顿死了，但杰斐逊并没有对此感到高兴。

扩 exultation *n.* 兴高采烈

exultant *adj.* 得意的

salvage
[ˈsælvɪdʒ]

n. 1. 抢救；2. 抢救出的财物；*v.* 营救，抢救

记 salv (=save) + age → 抢救

例 1. The ship was beyond salvage. 这艘船无法挽救了。

2. I got the part from an auto salvage place. 我从一个汽车废弃场得到这些零件。

3. The wreck was salvaged by a team from the RAF. 失事船只得到了皇家空军救援小组的救助。

扩 salvation *n.* 抢救，营救

abnegation
[ˌæbnɪˈgeɪʃn]

n. 克制，自制

记 ab (=off) + negat (=deny) + ion → 否认自我 → 克制

例 Free markets are the opposite of oppression; they are the abnegation of authority. 自由市场是没有压制的；它们不允许权威的存在。

ruddy
[ˈrʌdi]

adj. 1. 红润健康的；2. 红色的；3. 讨厌的，可恶的

记 rud (=red) + dy → 红的

例 1. His face is still ruddy and handsome. 他的脸依然红润帅气。

2. Just above Luna is bright Venus, followed by the blue star Spica and faint ruddy Mars. 月亮之上是明亮的金星，接着是蓝色的角宿一以及微红的火星。

3. I can't get the ruddy car to start! 我就是发动不了这破车！

droop
[druːp]

v. 1. 低垂，垂下；2. 沮丧，消沉；*n.* 下垂

例 1. Holding a lunchbox in his hand, he looked worn out and was drooping his head. 他手里拿着便餐盒，看上去累极了，低着头。
2. Our spirits drooped when we heard the news. 听到这消息，我们情绪低落下来。
3. I can tell by the droop of his shoulders, the tremor in his voice, that he said more than he wanted to. 他的肩膀蜷缩着，声音颤抖着，让我知道他有点话不及意。

thorn
[θɔːrn]

n. 1. 刺；2. 带刺的树；3. 肉中刺，眼中钉

例 1. Roses will always have thorns but with care they can be avoided. 玫瑰花上都有刺，不过只要小心就碰不到。
2. A lion gets ready to pounce as it emerges from a thicket of thorns. 一头狮子准备从一丛树棘中发起突袭。
3. The Party was a thorn in the flesh of his coalition. 该党是他所在联盟的眼中钉、肉中刺。

shudder
[ˈʃʌdər]

v. 1. 发抖，打颤；2. 强烈震动，剧烈抖动；*n.* 发抖

例 1. I shuddered at the thought of all the trouble I'd caused. 一想到我闯的祸，我就不寒而栗。
2. The bus shuddered to a halt. 公共汽车剧烈地晃动着停了下来。
3. She gave an involuntary shudder. 她不由自主地抖了一下。

tapestry
[ˈtæpəstri]

n. 1. 壁毯，织锦；2. 复杂丰富的东西

例 1. He sat on a tapestry cushion next to the hearth. 他坐在壁炉边上的一块绣花软垫上。
2. All living things are part of the rich tapestry of life. 所有的活物都是千变万化的自然界的一部分。

prowl
[praʊl]

v. 1.（动物或人）潜行；2. 徘徊，走来走去

例 1. The tiger prowled through the undergrowth. 老虎悄然穿过矮树丛。
2. He prowled the empty rooms of the house at night. 夜里，他在家中的空屋子里踱来踱去。

辨 prow *n.* 船头

disavow
[ˌdɪsəˈvaʊ]

v. 否认，拒绝承担责任

记 dis (=opposite) + avow (=swear) → 坚决说不 → 否认

例 They disavowed claims of a split in the party. 他们否认了党内出现分裂的说法。

扩 disavowal *n.* 否认

chivalry
[ˈʃɪvəlri]

n. 1. 骑士，绅士；2. 骑士制度，骑士风度

例 1. That's a pretty low bar for chivalry, but only Toby jumps it. 这对骑士来说算是很低的栏杆了，但只有托比跳了过去。

2. What the youngsters don't know is that this minimal courtesy is, by older standards, astounding chivalry. 年轻人所不了解的是，这种不起眼的殷勤按传统观点来看就是令人吃惊的骑士风度。

heave [hiːv]

v. (heaved, *or* hove) 1. 举起，拖，拉；2. 起伏；3. 恶心

例 1. I managed to heave the trunk down the stairs. 我用力把箱子弄下楼梯。
2. Her shoulders heaved with laughter. 她笑得双肩抖动。
3. The thought of it makes me heave. 一想到那事我就恶心。

delusive [dɪˈluːsɪv]

adj. 不真实的，虚假的

例 A large redundancy of money in the Treasury, gave a delusive appearance of national wealth. 一些多余的钱放在国库里，带来一种国库充盈的假象。

扩 delusion *n.* 错觉，欺骗

同 delusory

repulsive [rɪˈpʌlsɪv]

adj. 1. 令人厌恶的；2. 引起排斥的

记 re (=back) + puls (=push) + ive → 产生排斥的

例 1. To speak publicly in baby language, even to a baby, is to risk making oneself repulsive. 在公众场合用对待婴儿的方式说话，即使是对婴儿说话，也有可能让自己觉得恶心。
2. The repulsive force within the nucleus is enormous. 核子内部的斥力是巨大的。

psalm [sɑːm]

n. 赞美诗

例 He recited a verse of the twenty-third psalm. 他背诵了《诗篇》第 23 篇中的一节。

moss [mɔːs]

n. 苔藓，地衣

例 Moss disguises the inscriptions engraved on the few headstones still upright. 地衣盖过了仍然直立的几块墓碑上的铭文。

扩 mossy *adj.* 长满苔藓的

vicar [ˈvɪkər]

n. （圣公会的）牧师

例 A vicar of Stratford-upon-Avon describes Shakespeare as "a natural wit without any art at all," and an early critic calls him an "upstart crow." 莎士比亚故乡的一位牧师把他描述成“浑然天成的幽默者”，而一位早期的批评家称他为“自命不凡的公鸡”。

扩 vicarious *adj.* 间接感受到的

plank [plæŋk]

n. 1. 木板，板条；2. 政策准则，核心

记 原指衡量物体的长木条，引申为“(政党的) 准则”

例 1. It was very strong, made of three solid planks of wood. 它由 3 块坚固的木板做成，很结实。

2. The central plank of the bill was rural development. 这一法案的核心是农村发展。

repast [rɪ'pæst]
n. 饭菜
记 re (=again) + past (=graze) → 经常吃 → 饭菜
例 She offered us a light repast before we set out on our trip. 在我们动身出发之前，她请我们吃了一顿便餐。

committal [kə'mɪtl]
n. 收监，拘押
记 commit (=entrust) + tal → 委托给（精神病院、监狱）→ 收押
例 She argued against the committal of the defendant to a mental hospital. 她反对把被告收押进精神病医院。

deduct [dɪ'dʌkt]
v. 扣除，减去
记 de (=down) + duct (=lead) → 使减少
例 The cost of your uniform will be deducted from your wages. 制服费将从你的工资中扣除。
扩 deduction *n.* 演绎；扣除

possessive [pə'zesɪv]
adj. 1. 占有欲强的；2. 不愿分享的
例 1. Some parents are too possessive of their children. 有些父母过分要求子女百依百顺。
2. Jimmy's very possessive about his toys. 吉米的玩具谁也碰不得。
扩 possessiveness *n.* 霸道，独占

plaintiff ['pleɪntɪf]
n. 原告，起诉人
记 plaint (=complaint) + iff → 投诉的人 → 原告
例 All of the plaintiffs' claims are insufficient in numerous ways and should be dismissed. 所有这些原告的诉求在很多方面都不充分，不能成立。

superannuated [ˌsuːpər'ænjueɪtɪd]
adj. 年老的，过时的
记 super (=beyond) + annu (=year) + ated → 年龄很大的
例 It is as if Britain were some superannuated school prefect. 英国好像是学校里某个过气的（维持纪律的）学长。

obtrude [əb'truːd]
v. 强行闯入，搅扰
记 ob (=toward) + trude (=thrust) → 伸出去 → 闯入
例 Music from the next room obtruded upon his thoughts. 隔壁的音乐声打扰了他的思绪。

blot [blɑːt]
n. 1. 门拴；2. 闪电；*v.* 插上
例 1. Once the door closes behind me, I hear a thud like a dead bolt shifting into place. 门在我身后关上后，我听到砰的一声，好像门拴被插上了。

2. The nests are also exposed, which means one stray bolt of lightning could spell disaster. 巢穴是露天的，这意味着一通闪电就可能招致灾祸。
3. The gate bolts on the inside. 大门在里面上闩。

quiver [ˈkwɪvər]

v. 抖动，抽动；*n.* 哆嗦，抖动

记 可能与 quake 有关

例 1. Her lip quivered and then she started to cry. 她嘴唇微微一颤，然后她哭了起来。
2. He felt a quiver of excitement run through him. 他激动得全身一阵哆嗦。

poultry [ˈpoʊltri]

n. 1. 家禽；2. 禽类肉

例 1. Most poultry farmers have to rely on commercially manufactured feeds. 多数饲养家禽的农场主不得不依赖商业化生产的饲料。
2. Eat plenty of fish and poultry. 要多吃鱼和禽肉。

aver [əˈvɜːr]

v. (averred, averred; averring) 断言，确认

记 a (=to) + ver (=very, true) → 说真话 → 确认

例 She averred that she had never seen the man before. 她斩钉截铁地说以前从未见过这个男人。

辨 averse *adj.* 不喜欢的，厌恶的

waver [ˈweɪvər]

v. 1. 减弱，动摇；2. 踌躇；3. 摇曳，闪烁

记 wave + r → 像波浪一样摇摆 → 动摇，摇曳

例 1. She never wavered in her determination to succeed. 她要取得成功的决心从未动摇过。
2. She's wavering between buying a house in the city or moving away. 她举棋不定，不知是在这个城市里买座房子，还是迁居他处。
3. The shadows of the dancers wavered continually. 舞者的身影在轻轻晃动着。

fraternal [frəˈtɜːrnl]

adj. 1. 兄弟般的；2. 兄弟间的

例 1. There was a fraternal feeling among the troops. 士兵中有种兄弟般的情谊。
2. The study involved more than 200,000 twins, both identical and fraternal, who hailed from Denmark, Finland, Norway and Sweden. 研究涵盖了 20 万对双胞胎，包括同卵和异卵，他们来自丹麦、芬兰、挪威和瑞典。

扩 fraternity *n.* 兄弟会；同仁

flimsy [ˈflɪmzi]

adj. 1. 劣质的，不结实的；2. 薄而易坏的；3. 不足信的

记 flim (=film) + sy → 像胶片一样（薄的）→ 不结实的

例 1. The hope is to discourage asylum-seekers from trying to make the

dangerous trip across the Aegean Sea on their own in flimsy boats. 它的目的在于不鼓励寻求庇护者自行乘坐危险船只穿越爱琴海。
2. He marveled at the flimsy fence that separates the two countries at that point. 他对当地的两国隔离栏如此脆弱大为惊骇。
3. The board's report found the program had a flimsy legal foundation and did not lead to significant counterterrorism investigations. 委员会报告指出该计划的法律基础薄弱，不足以支持重要的反恐调查。

intelligentsia [ɪnˌtelɪˈdʒentsiə]
n. 知识界，知识阶层
例 Her new book has been embraced by the intelligentsia. 她的新书获得了知识界的好评。

teem [tiːm]
v. 倾注，倾泻
记 te + em (=empty) → 倒空（瓶子）→ 倾注
例 The streets were teeming with tourists. 大街上游人如鲫。

composed [kəmˈpoʊzd]
adj. 1. 由…组成的；2. 镇静的，平静的
记 compose 作动词有"使镇静"之义
例 1. The committee is composed mainly of lawyers. 委员会主要由律师组成。
2. She seemed outwardly composed. 她表面上好像很镇静。
扩 composedly *adv.* 镇静地

unaffected [ˌʌnəˈfektɪd]
adj. 1. 无动于衷的；2. 真挚的
记 un + affect + ed → 未受影响的；未假装的 → 无动于衷的；真挚的
例 1. Some members of the family may remain unaffected by the disease. 这个家族有些人可能不会受到这种疾病的影响。
2. He has a friendly and unaffected manner. 他非常友好，待人真诚。
扩 unaffectedly *adv.* 无动于衷地；真挚地

welter [ˈweltər]
n. 杂乱的一堆
例 In a welter of litigation, most of the family's assets were sold. 经过一大堆的官司，他们家的财产大都被售卖一空。

benign [bɪˈnaɪn]
adj. 1. 和善的，慈祥的；2.（肿瘤）良性的
记 beni (=bene, good) + gn → 好的；同根词 benefit
例 1. You would never have guessed his intentions from the benign expression on his face. 你永远无法从他脸上和善的表情中猜透他的心思。
2. We were happy to hear that the tumor was benign. 我们听到肿瘤是良性后很高兴。

List 19

truce [truːs]

n. 停战，休战

例 There's been an uneasy truce between her and her parents for the past several months. 过去几个月她跟父母之间的休战持续得非常艰难。

deference [ˈdefərəns]

n. 尊重，听从

例 The flags were lowered out of deference to the bereaved family. 降旗是出于对死者家属的尊重。

辨 defer *v.* 推迟

扩 deferential *adj.* 尊重的

trudge [trʌdʒ]

v. 缓慢地走，费力地走

例 He trudged the last two miles to the town. 他步履艰难地走完最后两英里到了城里。

audacity [ɔːˈdæsəti]

n. 鲁莽，大胆

例 He had the audacity to say I was too fat. 他竟敢说我太胖了。

扩 audacious *adj.* 大胆的，鲁莽的

ferocious [fəˈroʊʃəs]

adj. 1. 凶猛的，残暴的；2. 激烈的

例 1. He had a ferocious look in his eye. 他的眼中有种凶残的目光。

2. The competition among the students was ferocious. 学生们之间的竞争很激烈。

扩 ferocity *n.* 凶残；激烈

hearken [ˈhɑːrkən]

v. 倾听，聆听

记 来源于 hear

例 *Star Wars: The Force Awakens* hearkens back to its origins in George Lucas's original *Star Wars* trilogy.《星球大战：原力觉醒》尊重了原著乔治·卢卡斯的《星球大战》三部曲。

meek [miːk]

adj. 温顺的，谦恭的；*n.* 谦和的人，温顺的人

例 1. They called her Miss Mouse because she was so meek and mild. 他们称她为“鼠小姐”，因为她总是那么温顺谦和。

2. Blessed are the meek: for they shall inherit the earth. 谦卑的人必有福，因为他们必承受地土。(——《圣经》)

扩 meekness *n.* 谦和，温顺

vortex
['vɔːrteks]

n. (*pl.* vortexes, vortices) 1. 低涡，涡旋；2. 感情的漩涡

例 1. The polar vortex is a system of wintertime winds. 极地涡旋是冬季风形成的一个风系。
2. They were caught up in a whirling vortex of emotion. 他们陷入了感情漩涡。

lull
[lʌl]

n. 间歇，平静时期；*v.* 1. 使放松；2. 缓和，减弱

记 可能是源于拟声词 lu-lu，哄孩子睡觉；同根词 lullaby（摇篮曲）

例 1. Just before an attack everything would go quiet, but we knew it was just the lull before the storm. 就在攻击开始前一切都变得沉寂，我们知道这只是风暴前的平静。
2. The vibration of the engine lulled the children to sleep. 发动机的颤动使得孩子们睡着了。
3. His father's arrival lulled the boy's anxiety. 男孩在他父亲来了后便不那么焦躁不安了。

turnpike
['tɜːrnpaɪk]

n. 收费公路

记 turn + pike (=spike, stick) → 移开收费杠 → 收费公路

例 The turnpike commission approved the higher speed limit earlier this month. 收费公路管理处本月同意将限速标准提高。

posse
['pɑːsi]

n. 1. 一群，一伙；2. 地方武装团队

例 1. The movie star and his posse were seen at the new restaurant. 电影明星和他的同伴们现身新餐馆。
2. The sheriff and his posse rode out to look for the bandits. 治安官和武装团队骑马外出寻找土匪。

hackneyed
['hæknid]

adj. 陈腐的

记 源于伦敦附近的地名 Hackney，曾为养马之地，引申为"老马的"→陈腐的

例 That's the old hackneyed phrase, but it's true. 这虽是老生常谈，但却是真理。

somber
['sɑːmbər]

adj. 1. 昏暗的，阴沉的；2. 阴郁的，沮丧的

例 1. It was a beautiful house, but it was dark and somber and dead. 这座房子虽然很漂亮，但是色彩暗淡，死气沉沉。
2. The year ended on a somber note. 那一年在沉闷的气氛中结束了。

predispose
[ˌpriːdɪ'spoʊz]

v. 1. 使倾向于；2. 使易患（病），诱发

例 1. He believes that some people are predisposed to criminal behaviour. 他认为有些人容易犯罪。
2. Stress can predispose people to heart attacks. 压力容易使人心脏病发作。

扩 predisposition *n.* 倾向；体质

broach
[broʊtʃ]

v. 开始谈论，引入

例 She was dreading having to broach the subject of money to her father. 她正在为不得不向父亲提出钱的事犯愁。

eulogy
[ˈjuːlədʒi]

n. 1. 颂辞；2. 悼文

记 eu (=well) + logy (=log, speak) → 说好话 → 颂扬

例 1. The 37-minute speech became part eulogy, part admission of political failure and part constitutional lecture on the Second Amendment. 这个37分钟的演讲（奥巴马的控枪演讲）既有赞美，也有对政治失利的承认，以及对第二修正案的宪法评述。（见插图）

2. In a heartfelt eulogy, the Reagans' daughter, Patti Davis, recalled her mother's struggles after her father died. 里根之女帕蒂·戴维斯在一篇真挚的悼文回忆了母亲在父亲去世后的挣扎。

helm
[helm]

n. 舵柄；*v.* 操纵

例 1. The ship's captain took the helm. 船长控制了舵柄。

2. It was the first time the normally secretive company—helmed by Amazon founder Jeff Bezos—opened its doors to journalists. 这家由亚马逊创始人杰夫·贝佐斯掌控的神秘公司首次向记者打开了大门。

connive
[kəˈnaɪv]

v. 1. 纵容，默许；2. 共谋，狼狈为奸

记 con (=together) + nive (=wink) → 共同眨眼 → 共谋

例 1. She knew that if she said nothing she would be conniving in an injustice. 她明白如果她什么也不说就是在纵容不公正的行为。

2. The government was accused of having connived with the security forces to permit murder. 政府被指与安全部队狼狈为奸允许谋杀。

superstructure
[ˈsuːpərstrʌktʃər]

n. 1.（建筑的）上层结构；2.（社会的）上层建筑

记 super (=above) + structure → 上面的结构 → 上层建筑

例 1. We might try to clear up some of the cabins in the superstructure. 我们可以设法清理出主甲板上面的一些船舱。

2. At the same time the executive superstructure of U.S. Walmart stores has also been trimmed. 与此同时美国沃尔玛的管理高层也被精减了。

trench
[trentʃ]

n. 1. 沟渠；2. 战壕；*v.* 挖沟，建立

记 木 头 上 的 track（ 沟 槽 ）→ trench 沟 渠 → 建立

例 1. Workmen were digging a trench beside the road. 工人们在马路边挖沟。

2. King Edward's letter from 14 June 1916 recounted his experiences in Ypres in Belgium, where soldiers fought in the trenches. 爱德华国王在一封 1916 年 6 月 14 日的信件中记述了他在比利时伊普尔的经历，当时士兵们在一战的战壕里奋战。
3. The rain quickly went from a sprinkle to a downpour, thundering against the leaves and trenching water through the soil. 雨迅速从点滴变成了倾盆大雨，击打着树叶，雨水在地上汇流成河。

medley [ˈmedli]

n. 1. 混成曲；2. 混杂物

例 1. The result is a beautiful, stripped down medley of some of Adele's best songs, which would undoubtedly make the singer proud. 结果成就了一首优美的、精简的阿黛尔最佳歌曲的混合曲，这肯定会令歌手感到自豪。
2. The building was a medley of styles from different periods. 这座建筑混合了不同时期的风格。

subterranean [ˌsʌbtəˈreɪniən]

adj. 地下的

记 sub (=under) + terra (=terrain) + nean → 地下的

例 London has 9 miles of such subterranean passages. 伦敦像这样的地下通道有 9 英里长。

扩 subterraneous *adj.* 地下的

discomfit [dɪsˈkʌmfɪt]

v. 使困惑，使窘迫

例 The governor was clearly discomfited by the question. 政府显然对这个问题感到窘迫。

扩 discomfiture *n.* 窘迫，困惑

imposture [ɪmˈpɑːstʃər]

n. 冒名行骗

记 im (=on) + post (=put) + ure → 用别的东西放上 → 冒名行骗

例 A more recent imposture, which is still having harmful effects, is the vaccine scare that began in 1998. 更近的一次诈骗行为是始于 1998 年的疫苗恐慌事件，它至今还阴魂不散。

辨 impose *v.* 推行，迫使，强加

dingy [ˈdɪndʒi]

adj. 又黑又脏的，昏暗的

记 可能源于 dung（粪便）

例 Moos said manufacturing is no longer associated with a dingy garage: It's inviting, there's a family culture. 穆斯说制造业不再是让人联想起昏暗的车库之类的，如今这里有种融洽的氛围。

fidget [ˈfɪdʒɪt]

v. 坐立不安，烦躁

例 He was fidgeting with his tie before the presentation. 他在做陈述前烦躁地摆弄着他的领带。

complacent [kəm'pleɪsnt]

adj. 自满的，自鸣得意的

记 com (=very) + plac (=please) + ent → 非常高兴的

例 We must not become complacent about progress. 我们决不能因进步变得自满。

扩 complacence *n.* 自满

embolden [ɪm'boʊldən]

v. 使增加勇气，使有信心

记 em (=to) + bold + en → 使壮胆 → 使有信心

例 Supreme Court's ruling last summer to legalize same-sex marriage emboldened civil rights activists to seek greater protections. 最高法院去年夏天关于批准同性婚姻的判决让民权人士信心大增，使他们敢于寻求更大程度的保护。

ebb [eb]

n. 落潮，退潮；*v.* 1. 落潮；2. 衰弱，减退

例 1. She sat in silence enjoying the ebb and flow of conversation. 她默默地坐在那儿，饶有兴致地听着时高时低的谈话声。

2. We decided to leave on the ebb at six o'clock next morning. 我们决定第二天早晨 6 点钟趁退潮时离开。

3. As night fell, our enthusiasm began to ebb away. 我们的热情随着夜晚的降临而渐渐低落下来。

twaddle ['twɑːdl]

n. 胡说八道，蠢话

例 Fortunately, even in a predominantly Catholic country, this kind of insulting twaddle is becoming increasingly less acceptable. 幸运的是，即便在一个以天主教为主的国家里，这种冒犯人的胡话也变得越来越不被接受。

disciple [dɪ'saɪpl]

n. 信徒，门徒

例 Gather with us to commemorate the events that occurred on the night of Jesus's Last Supper with his disciples. 跟我们一起纪念基督与门徒在最后的晚餐时发生的事情。

扩 discipline *n.* 纪律，训导；*v.* 约束

squalid ['skwɑːlɪd]

adj. 1. 肮脏的；2. 丑恶的，卑鄙的

例 1. The migrants have been living in squalid conditions. 移民们的生活条件一直非常差。

2. It was a squalid affair involving prostitutes and drugs. 那是一桩涉及卖淫与毒品的丑事。

remit [rɪ'mɪt]

n. 职权范围，控制范围；*v.* (remitted, remitted; remitting) 1. 汇款，提交；2. 免除，赦免

记 re (=back) + mit (=miss, send) → 送回 → 汇款

例 1. Such decisions are outside the remit of this committee. 这样的决定超出了委员会的职权范围。

2. Payment will be remitted to you in full. 报酬将会全额汇寄给你。
3. The governor remitted the remainder of her life sentence. 总督免除了她的余刑。
扩 remittance *n.* 汇款（金额）

furrow
['fɜːroʊ]

n. 1. 犁沟；2. 皱纹；*v.*（使）皱眉
记 谐音"翻路"→犁沟
例 1. She has had to plough a lone furrow in her pursuit of reform. 她在追求改革时不得不单打独斗。
2. When he frowns a deep furrow forms in his brow. 他皱眉时，眉毛处出现皱纹。
3. Midge's forehead furrowed as she saw that several were drinking. 米奇看到几个人正在喝酒时皱起了眉头。

billow
['bɪloʊ]

v. 1. 鼓起；2. 涌出，大量冒出
记 可能与 belly（肚子）有关
例 1. The curtains billowed in the breeze. 微风吹得窗帘鼓了起来。
2. A great cloud of smoke billowed out of the chimney. 滚滚浓烟从烟囱中喷涌而出。

succor
['sʌkər]

n. 救助，帮助；*v.* 帮助
记 suc (=sub) + cor (=cur, run) → 运行在下面 → 帮助
例 1. We see it as our duty to give succor to those in need. 我们觉得帮助贫困者是我们的职责。
2. Helicopters fly in appalling weather to succour shipwrecked mariners. 直升机在恶劣的天气条件下起飞前去援救遇难的船员。

baffle
['bæfl]

v. 使困惑，难住
例 I'm baffled as to why she hasn't called. 我不明白她为什么没打电话。
扩 baffling *adj.* 令人困惑的

laurel
['lɔːrəl, 'lɑː-]

n. 1. 月桂树；2. 荣誉
记 源于希腊神话中的小仙女，她为躲避太阳神阿波罗的追求，变为月桂树。本词由她的希腊语名字而来。（见插图）
例 1. I remember vividly the moment when the nymph Daphne is transformed into a laurel tree. 我很清楚地记得仙女达芙妮变成月桂树的那一刻。
2. Po's wise master, the red panda Shifu, tells Po to stop resting on his laurels and become a martial arts master. 阿宝的智慧大师红熊猫师父告诉阿宝不要躺在功劳簿上睡大觉，要成为武术高手。

List 19

metaphysical
[ˌmetə'fɪzɪkl]

adj. 形而上学的

例 The book's final section includes larger, metaphysical questions about impermanence and how people relate to the earth and sea. 该书的最后部分包括了一些更大的、形而上的问题，即关于无常，以及人类与地球、海洋的关系。

doleful
['doʊlfl]

adj. 忧郁的，悲伤的

例 You sounded so doleful about your future that night. 你那天晚上说起自己的前途，听起来很悲伤。

辨 dole *n.* 失业救济金

ditto
['dɪtoʊ]

n. 同上，同前；*adv.* 同样

例 The waiters were rude and unhelpful, the manager ditto. 这些服务员态度生硬，服务不周，经理也一样。

bespeak
[bɪ'spiːk]

v. (bespoke, bespoken) 展现，显示

例 His style of dressing bespoke great self-confidence. 他的衣着风格显得十分自信。

enchant
[ɪn'tʃænt]

v. 1. 使着迷，使陶醉；2. 使着魔

记 en (=to) + chant (=cast spell) → 念咒语 → 使着魔，使着迷

例 1. Visitors will be enchanted by the beauty of the place. 游客们将会被此地的美景所陶醉。

2. The story takes place in an enchanted forest. 故事发生在一片被施了魔法的森林里。

扩 enchanting *adj.* 吸引人的

metamorphose
[ˌmetə'mɔːrfoʊz]

v. 使变形，发生质变

记 meta (=change) + morph (=form) + ose → 改变形式

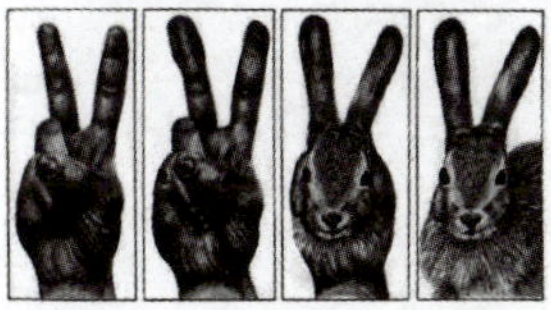

例 1. When the tadpoles metamorphose into frogs, however, mass mortality ensues. 然而，当蝌蚪变成青蛙时，就会发生很高的死亡率。

2. It's as if Hugh Grant were to suddenly metamorphose into Ken Loach. 这就好像休·格兰特（电影演员）突然变成了肯·洛奇（电影导演）。

manor
['mænər]

n. 1. 大宅第；2. 庄园（领地）

例 1. The opening page of Marvel's *Haunted Mansion* explores the theories behind the manor's history. 漫威的《幽灵鬼屋》一开始便探索了这所宅第背后的历史。

2. The Chief Constable deeply resented any intrusions into his manor. 警察局局长对侵入其辖区的行为深恶痛绝。

fastidious
[fæ'stɪdiəs]

adj. 1. 一丝不苟的；2. 讲究整洁的

例 1. He was fastidious in his preparation for the big day. 他认真仔细地准备着这个盛大的日子。
2. She wasn't very fastidious about personal hygiene. 她不过分讲究个人卫生。

扩 fastidiousness *n.* 洁癖

overgrown
[ˌoʊvər'groʊn]

adj. 1. 杂草丛生的；2. 发展过快的

例 1. The garden's completely overgrown with weeds. 花园里长满了杂草。
2. Daphne Farlow, at forty-five, still looked and spoke like an overgrown schoolgirl. 45岁的达芙妮·法洛外貌言谈都还像个稚气未脱的小女生。

vibrate
['vaɪbreɪt, vaɪ'breɪt]

v. （使）振动，摆动

例 Every time a train went past the walls vibrated. 每当火车驶过，这些墙都会震动。

扩 vibration *n.* 振动

sinew
['sɪnjuː]

n. 1. 肌腱；2. 要害处，关键环节

例 1. There was a fearful snapping of bones and tearing of sinews and muscles. 那里有种骨骼断裂和肌腱与肌肉撕裂的声音。(——《贝奥武夫》)
2. The actual title of Churchill's speech was "Sinews of Peace," though most people know it as the "Iron Curtain speech." 丘吉尔演讲的真正标题为"和平的关键"，但多数人都把它称作"铁幕演说"。

brew
[bruː]

v. 1. 酿制；2. 沏茶，煮咖啡；3.（喻）酝酿

例 1. This beer is brewed in the Czech Republic. 这种啤酒产自捷克。
2. She brewed up some coffee while I cooked the bacon and eggs. 当我做培根和鸡蛋时她煮了一些咖啡。
3. Mr. Obama addressed the brewing controversy between the government and Apple, though he declined to comment on the specifics of the case. 尽管奥巴马拒绝评论案件的具体细节，但他还是解决了政府与苹果公司之间产生的争议。

扩 brewer *n.* 啤酒公司

flank
[flæŋk]

n. 侧面，侧翼；*v.* 在侧面伴随

例 1. They attacked the enemy on both flanks. 他们从两翼袭击了敌人。
2. She left the courtroom flanked by armed guards. 她在武装警卫的护送下离开法庭。

strew
[struː]

v. (strewed, strewn) 散布，布满

例 The aftermath was visible Thursday, with rocks and broken glass strewn on the street. 双方战斗的痕迹在周四仍然可见，街上到处都是石头和碎玻璃。

tithe
[taɪð]

n. 什一税，什一捐
记 tenth 的变体
例 We must also ignore the fact that the agricultural tithe only applied to agriculture, which would limit our tax to farmers. 我们必须同时忽略这个事实，即农业十一税只适用于农业，这会限制我们对农民的征税。

ornate
[ɔːrˈneɪt]

adj. 华美的，富丽的
例 This style is a little too ornate for my taste. 这种风格对我的口味来说太华丽了。
扩 ornately *adv.* 华丽地

booty
[ˈbuːti]

n. 1. 财物，战利品；2. 贵重物品
例 1. Troops destroyed the capital and confiscated many works of art as war booty. 军队摧毁了这座都城，并把大量艺术品收缴为战利品。
2. When we got home from our day's shopping, we laid all our booty out on the floor. 我们购物一天回到家里，把搜罗到的好东西都摊开摆在地板上。

interregnum
[ˌɪntəˈregnəm]

n. 政权空白期，权力空白
记 inter (=between) + regnum (=reign) → 两次统治的中间 → 权力空白
例 When Charles II came to the throne he was treated as if he had succeeded in 1649—thus 1649-1660 was called the interregnum. 当查理二世登基时，人们对待他就如同他是从 1649 年继位的一样，因此 1649-1660 年就叫做权力空白期。

eaves
[iːvz]

n. 屋檐
例 You'll need a ladder to inspect the underside of eaves, roof vents and chimneys. 你得需要一架梯子才能检查屋檐的下面、天窗和烟囱。
扩 eavesdrop *v.* 偷听

polyglot
[ˈpɑːliglɑːt]

adj. 通晓多种语言的；*n.* 通晓多种语言的人
记 poly (=many) + glot (=gloss, language) → 会多种语言的
例 1. Self-assured Roman elites had become happily bilingual and biliterate, and in time this helped them rule a widespread and polyglot empire. 自信的罗马精英们幸福地说着两种语言，读着两种文字，这有助于他们统治一个广袤的多语言的帝国。
2. She was a polyglot who was fluent in four languages. 她通晓四门语言。

provost
[ˈproʊvoʊst]

n. 学院院长，教务长
例 Before becoming Cornell's president last year, Garrett was a provost and senior vice president for academic affairs at the University of Southern California. 在去年就任康奈尔校长之前，Garrett 曾在南加州大学做过教务长和主管学术的高级副校长。

shuffle
[ˈʃʌfl]

v. 1. 拖着脚走；2. 坐立不安；3. 洗（牌），打乱顺序

记 本词可表示在播放音乐时“打乱曲目顺序”，苹果公司曾推出过一款叫 shuffle 的 MP3

例 1. He shuffled across the room to the window. 他拖着脚走到房间那头的窗户跟前。
2. Jenny shuffled her feet and blushed with shame. 珍妮来回倒换着脚，羞愧得脸红了。
3. Shuffle the cards and deal out seven to each player. 洗洗牌，然后给每人发七张。

saliva
[səˈlaɪvə]

n. 唾液

例 Plaque is made up of food debris, saliva and bacteria normally present in the mouth. 牙斑是由口腔中的食物残渣、唾液和细菌生成的。

jolly
[ˈdʒɑːli]

adj. 1. 快乐的，高兴的；2. 令人愉快的

例 1. December is a festive month for most cultures around the globe, but yesterday was an especially jolly day on Twitter. 十二月在全球多个国家都是节日之月，但昨天对推特公司来说尤其值得高兴。
2. She had a jolly time at the party. 她在聚会上玩得很高兴。

hoarse
[hɔːrs]

adj. 嘶哑的，沙哑的

记 联想：马 (horse) 的叫声嘶哑 (hoarse)

例 The small British crowd roared themselves hoarse, waving their Union Jacks. 一小群英国人挥舞着国旗，吼得嗓子都沙哑了。

adroit
[əˈdrɔɪt]

adj. 干练的，精明的

例 Powerful arms and long fingers make the gibbons adroit at swinging through trees; they rarely descend to the ground. 有力的臂膀和长手指使得长臂猿爬树时很灵活；它们很少下到地面上来。

辨 android *n.* 安卓，人形机器人

扩 adroitly *adv.* 机敏地
maladroit *adj.* 笨手笨脚的

refectory
[rɪˈfektri]

n. 食堂，餐厅

例 The food in the refectory there was always disgusting, so I cooked my own food. 食堂的饭菜总是很让人恶心，所以我自己做饭。

ambivalent
[æmˈbɪvələnt]

adj. 矛盾情绪的

例 She seems to feel ambivalent about her new job. 她似乎对她的新工作忧喜参半。

diffident
[ˈdɪfɪdənt]

adj. 胆怯的，缺乏自信的

记 dif (=dis, away) + fid (=faith) + ent → 没有信念的 → 胆怯的

例 He was modest and diffident about his own success. 他很谦虚，不愿谈及自己的成功。

扩 diffidence *n.* 缺乏自信，自卑

redolent
['redələnt]

adj. 1. 使人联想起…的；2. 有…气味的

例 1. Why would someone write something so redolent of Nazi propaganda? 为什么有人要写这些让人联想起纳粹宣传的东西呢？
2. The sauce was redolent with the smell of basil. 这种酱有种罗勒的味道。

辨 rodent *n.* 啮齿动物

valiant
['væliənt]

adj. 英勇的，坚定的

例 She made a valiant attempt not to laugh. 她试图强忍住不笑出来。

扩 valiantly *adv.* 英勇地

fealty
['fiːəlti]

n. 效忠宣誓

例 The gun issue also gives Republican politicians a way to attempt to show their fealty to the conservative movement. 枪支问题还给共和党政客们提供了一个机会，让他们表明自己对这场保守运动的忠诚。

chagrin
[ʃə'grɪn]

n. 失望，恼怒

例 She had gained five pounds over the winter, much to her chagrin. 她整个冬天长了 5 磅肉，这让她很失望。

扩 chagrined *adj.* 感到失望的

ingrained
[ɪn'greɪnd]

adj. 根深蒂固的，难改的

例 Many societies have a deeply ingrained belief that female bodies are mysterious and exist primarily to produce children. 许多社会都有种根深蒂固的观念，即女性的身体是神秘的，其首要目的就是生孩子。

pout
[paʊt]

v. 撅嘴；*n.* 撅嘴

例 1. The boy didn't want to leave—he stomped his feet and pouted. 男孩子不想离开，于是他又跺脚又撅嘴。
2. Her lips were set in a pout of annoyance. 她愠恼地撅起了双唇。

stagnate
['stægneɪt]

v. 1. 停滞，不进步；2. 因不流动而污浊

记 stag (=stand) + nate → 站住不动 → 停滞

例 1. I feel I'm stagnating in this job. 我觉得，干这份工作我没有长进。
2. The water in the pond was stagnating. 池塘里的水逐渐变成了死水。

扩 stagnant *adj.* 停滞的；污浊的

bale
[beɪl]

n. 大包，大捆；*v.* 捆成大包

记 ball 的变体

例 1. The fire took about four hours to put out, because firefighters had to pull the bales apart to get to the root of the fire. 火灾用了四个小时才扑灭，因为消防队员们要把大捆东西挪开才能找到火源。
2. The waste paper is baled, then sent for recycling. 废纸被打成大包，

然后送去回收再利用。

morale
[mə'ræl]

*n.*士气

例 Morale amongst the players is very high at the moment. 此刻各选手士气高昂。

辨 moral *adj.* 道德的

扩 mores *n.* 风俗习惯，传统

haze
[heɪz]

*n.*1. 薄雾；2. 迷糊，迷蒙；*v.*1.（使）笼罩在薄雾中；2. 欺负新人

例 1. The sun smouldered through a thin summer haze. 太阳透过夏日的薄雾散发着苍白无力的光。

2. His mind was a haze of fear and confusion. 由于害怕和困惑，他当时处于一种混沌状态。

3. Tribal game officers prefer not to haze the animals and let them travel naturally into the hunting area. 部落中的捕猎官员不喜欢把动物喷晕，而是让它们自己走到狩猎区域。

4. Prosecutors say they have no evidence the coaching staff knew of the team's hazing culture. 检察官说他们并没有证据证明教练团队知晓球队的欺生传统。

folio
['foʊlioʊ]

*n.*对开本

例 The folio is a first edition of the collected works of Shakespeare, published in 1623. 这本对开本是第一版莎士比亚作品集，出版于1623年。

扩 portfolio *n.* 文件夹，公文包

overshadow
[ˌoʊvər'ʃædoʊ]

*v.*1. 使黯然失色；2. 使扫兴；3. 掩盖，遮蔽

例 1. He had always been overshadowed by his elder sister. 他与他大姐相比总是相形见绌。

2. News of the accident overshadowed the day's events. 出事的消息给这一天的活动蒙上了阴影。

3. The garden is overshadowed by tall trees. 花园中大树浓荫密布。

counterbalance
[ˌkaʊntər'bæləns]

*v.*抗衡，抵消；*n.*平衡

例 1. Parents' natural desire to protect their children should be counterbalanced by the child's need for independence. 父母保护孩子的本能愿望应当与孩子获得独立的需求相平衡。

2. The accused's right to silence was a vital counterbalance to the powers of the police. 被告人的沉默权对警方的权力是一种至关重要的抗衡。

List 20

frill
[frɪl]

n. 1. 饰边；2. 不实用的装饰

例 1. The dress had frills around the hem and sleeves. 这件衣服在卷边和袖口处有饰边。
2. He likes plain food without any frills. 他喜欢不加什么佐料的清淡饮食。

sojourn
[ˈsoʊdʒɜːrn]

n. 逗留，暂住；*v.* 暂住

例 1. Our family enjoyed a two-week sojourn in the mountains. 我们家人在山中小住了两周。
2. We sojourned for two weeks at a resort. 我们在度假村住了两周。

prostrate
[ˈprɑːstreɪt]

adj. 1. 俯卧的，趴着的；2. 被压倒的；*v.* 1. 俯卧；2. 使无能为力

记 pro (=forth) + strate (=stretch) → 向前伸展 → 俯卧

例 1. He stumbled over Luke's prostrate body. 他绊倒在卢克俯卧的身躯上。
2. She was prostrate with grief after her son's death. 她因丧子悲痛欲绝。
3. At a temple in his honor, visitors take turns to bow and prostrate themselves before a large statue of Confucius seated on a throne. 在孔庙里，游客们轮流朝座位上的孔子像鞠躬或拜倒。
4. He was expecting to find her prostrated by the tragedy. 他以为这场悲剧会使她一蹶不振。

辨 prostate *n.* 前列腺

扩 prostration *n.* 筋疲力尽；拜倒

curate
[kjʊˈreɪt]

v. 管理（博物馆或画廊）

记 cur (=care) + ate → 照管，管理

例 Sure, Apple curates apps in advance, but very few are ever barred. 当然，苹果公司会预先管理这些应用程序，但这些程序很少被禁止。

扩 curator *n.* 馆长，负责人

respite
[ˈrespɪt]

n. 1. 暂停，暂缓；2. 喘息

例 1. There was no respite from the suffocating heat. 闷热的天气根本没有缓解。
2. His creditors agreed to give him a temporary respite. 他的债权人同意给他一个喘息的机会。

reverie
['revəri]

n. 幻想，白日梦

例 She was jolted out of her reverie as the door opened. 门一开就把她从幻想中惊醒。

interlocutor
[ˌɪntər'lɑːkjətər]

n. 1. 对话者；2. 中间对话者，中间人

记 inter (=between) + locu (=speak) + tor → 站在中间说话的人

例 1. He often challenges his interlocutors with difficult questions. 他经常提出难题为难他的对话者。
2. He is already considered Britain's prime interlocutor with Germany. 他早已被看作代表英国与德国沟通的首席中间人。

ferment
[fər'ment] *v.*
['fɜːrment] *n.*

v.（使）发酵；*n.* 动乱，骚动

例 1. A blend of emotions fermented inside her. 她百感交集，激动不已。
2. Why are some of India's major farming communities in ferment? 为何印度的主要农业地区都在发生动乱呢？

扩 fermentation *n.* 发酵

invocation
[ˌɪnvə'keɪʃn]

n. 1. 求助，祈祷；2. 援引，诉诸

记 in + voc (=voice) + ation → 内心呼唤 → 祈祷，求神 → 诉诸

例 1. The commission also urged the council to "reconsider the inclusion of any religious invocation at public meetings." 该委员会还敦促市议会"重新考虑是否要把公开集会上的宗教祈祷包括在内"。
2. In court, she told Judge Gardephe that the invocation of the rule had "chilled people" from speaking to the defense. 在法庭上，她对法官加迪夫说，援引这一法则已经"让人觉得心寒"，导致他们不愿意与被告说话。

扩 invoke *v.* 援引；祈求神助

sulk
[sʌlk]

v. 生闷气，面有愠色；*n.* 生闷气

例 1. He went off to sulk in his room. 他回到自己的房间，生起闷气来。
2. Jo was in a sulk upstairs. 乔在楼上生闷气。

扩 sulky *adj.* 闷闷不乐的

despondent
[dɪ'spɑːndənt]

adj. 苦恼的，沮丧的

例 Your daughter sounds despondent: it's only the second week of school. 你女儿听上去很沮丧，这才是她上学的第二周。

扩 despondency *n.* 失望，沮丧

instigate
['ɪnstɪgeɪt]

v. 1. 使开始，使发生；2. 煽动，唆使

记 in (=on) + stig (=stick) + ate → 拿东西捅 → 唆使，煽动

例 1. The government has instigated a program of economic reform. 政府已实施了经济改革方案。
2. They were accused of instigating racial violence. 他们被控煽动种族暴力。

扩 instigation *n.* 煽动，怂恿

disaffected
[ˌdɪsəˈfektɪd]

adj. 不满的

例 Saudi Arabia has long had problems managing disaffected royal family members. 沙特阿拉伯早就无法管理那些不满的皇室成员了。

扩 disaffection *n.* 不满，疏远

palate
[ˈpælət]

n. 1. 上腭；2. 味觉，品尝力

例 1. When we put food in our mouths, chemicals slip over taste buds planted into the tongue and palate. 当我们把食物放进嘴里时，化学物质滑过舌头上的味蕾及上腭。
2. She's been working hard on a menu that will please the palates of all her guests. 她一直忙着做一桌尽量让所有客人都爱吃的菜。

辨 palette *n.* 调色板；主色调

扩 palatable *adj.* 可口的；宜人的

reinstate
[ˌriːɪnˈsteɪt]

v. 1. 使恢复原职；2. 使恢复原状，放回原处

例 1. He was reinstated in his post. 他重新回到了自己的岗位。
2. There have been repeated calls to reinstate the death penalty. 不断有人呼吁恢复死刑。

inept
[ɪˈnept]

adj. 缺乏技巧的，无能的

记 in (=not) + ept (=apt) → 无能的

例 They were so inept, defense lawyers argued, that they had used the book *Forensics for Dummies* to help prepare for their crime. 辩方律师说他们很无能，只能用《傻瓜法医学》这样的书来准备他们的罪案。

扩 ineptitude *n.* 笨拙，无能

inviolate
[ɪnˈvaɪələt]

adj. 未受侵犯的，不容破坏的

例 We believed our love was inviolate. 我们相信我们的爱情坚如磐石。

extirpate
[ˈekstərpeɪt]

v. 消灭，根除

例 Such ingrained behavior can never be completely extirpated. 这种根深蒂固的行为很难根除。

扩 extirpation *n.* 根除

turpitude
[ˈtɜːrpətuːd]

n. 堕落，卑鄙

例 The Alabama Constitution dictates that people convicted of felonies involving "moral turpitude" are not able to vote. 阿拉巴马州宪法规定犯有重罪的人不得投票，包括道德堕落的人。

pinnacle
[ˈpɪnəkl]

n. 1. 顶点，顶峰；2. 小尖顶

记 pin (=peak) + nacle → 尖顶

例 1. He spent more than twenty years at the pinnacle of his profession. 他在该行业的顶尖领域从事了二十多年的工作。
2. We could just make out the pinnacles of the cathedral in the distance. 我们从远处仅仅能辨认出大教堂的尖顶。

vegetate
['vedʒəteɪt]

v. 过无聊生活，无所用心

记 本词原指像植物（vegetation）一样生活

例 He spends all his free time at home vegetating in front of the TV. 他一有空闲时间就窝在家里看电视。

扩 vegetation *n.* 植物，植被

dissipate
['dɪsɪpeɪt]

v. 1. 消散，驱散；2. 挥霍，浪费

例 1. Her laughter soon dissipated the tension in the air. 她的笑声很快消除了紧张气氛。

2. He had dissipated his family's fortune in only a few years. 他在短短数年内就败光了家庭的财富。

扩 dissipation *n.* 挥霍；放荡；消散

buckle
['bʌkl]

v. 1. 使搭扣，扣住；2. 压垮，压弯；*n.* 皮带搭扣

例 1. These shoes buckle at the side. 这双鞋从旁边上扣。

2. A weaker man would have buckled under the pressure. 意志薄弱的人在这种压力下可能就垮了。

3. He wore a belt with a large brass buckle. 他系的皮带有一个大的铜搭扣。

jilt
[dʒɪlt]

v. 抛弃，遗弃

例 1. He was jilted by his fiancée. 他被未婚妻抛弃了。

2. It is hardly surprising Turkey behaves like a once spurned and jilted lover.（在应对叙利亚难民一事上）土耳其表现得像个被（欧盟）拒绝被抛弃的恋人，这一点也不出奇。

interrogate
[ɪn'terəgeɪt]

v. 审问，盘问

记 inter (=between) + rog (=ask) + ate → 审问

例 He was interrogated by the police for over 12 hours. 他被警察审问了 12 个多小时。

扩 interrogation *n.* 审问
interrogatory *adj.* 审问的

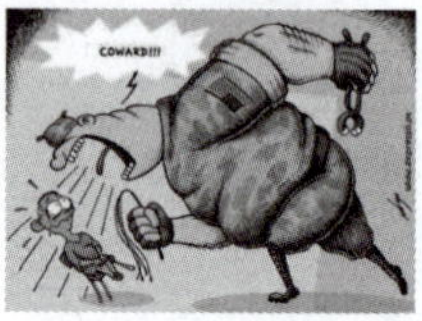

cripple
['krɪpl]

v. 1. 使跛，使残废；2. 严重损坏

记 源于 creep

例 1. He was crippled by polio as a child. 他幼年患过小儿麻痹症，结果腿就瘸了。

2. The pilot tried to land his crippled plane. 飞行员操纵着这架严重受损的飞机试图着陆。

disqualify
[dɪs'kwɑːlɪfaɪ]

v. 使不合格，取消（某人的）资格

例 He was disqualified from the competition for using drugs. 他因使用违禁药被取消比赛资格。

扩 disqualification *n.* 失去资格，取消资格

List 20

acrimony
['ækrɪmoʊni]

n. 尖刻，讥讽
记 acrim (=acrid) + ony → 尖刻
例 The dispute was settled without acrimony. 没有唇枪舌剑，这场纠纷就解决了。
扩 acrimonious *adj.* 尖刻的，激烈的

probation
[proʊ'beɪʃn]

n. 1. 缓刑制，缓刑；2.（新人）试用期；3. 留职察看，留校察看
记 prob (=prove) + ation → 观察以证实（可用）→ 试用期
例 1. The prisoner was put on probation. 犯人已获缓刑。
2. As a new employee, I will be on probation for three months. 作为新人，我有三个月的试用期。
3. The student was placed on probation for copying test answers. 该生因考试抄袭而被留校察看。
扩 probationary *adj.* 试用的，见习的

confiscate
['kɑːnfɪskeɪt]

v. 充公，没收
记 con (=together) + fisc (=public money) + ate → 充公
例 Their land was confiscated after the war. 他们的土地在战后被没收。
扩 confiscation *n.* 没收，充公

mediate
['miːdieɪt]

v. 1. 调停，斡旋；2. 促成解决
记 medi (=middle) + ate → 居中（做）→ 调停
例 1. An independent body was brought in to mediate between staff and management. 由一个独立机构介入，在劳资之间进行调解。
2. They mediated a settlement. 他们找到了一个解决方案。
扩 mediation *n.* 调停，介入

bash
[bæʃ]

v. 1. 猛击，猛撞；2. 严厉批评；*n.* 猛击
例 1. I braked too late and bashed into the car in front. 我刹车太晚，撞上了前面的车。
2. Bashing politicians is normal practice in the press. 严厉批判政治人物乃是新闻界常事。
3. He gave Mike a bash on the nose. 他冲着迈克的鼻子狠狠地打了一下。
辨 bashful *adj.* 羞怯的，忸怩的

regal
['riːgl]

adj. 帝王的，豪华的
记 reg (=king) + al → 帝王的
例 She dismissed him with a regal gesture. 她以尊贵的动作示意他离开。

vociferous
[voʊ'sɪfərəs]

adj. 激昂的，大声疾呼的
记 voci (=voice) + fer (=carry) + ous → 大声的
例 He was vociferous in his support of the proposal. 他大声疾呼，呼吁支持这项提案。
扩 vociferation *n.* 大声叫嚷

bestir
[bɪ'stɜːr]

v. 发奋，振作起来
例 He needs to bestir himself and start looking for a job. 他需要振作起来，找份工作。

smirk
[smɜːrk]

v. 傻笑，自鸣得意地笑；*n.* 傻笑
记 源于 smile
例 1. He smirked unpleasantly when we told him the bad news. 我们把坏消息告诉他时，他脸上现出一丝奸笑。
2. She had a self-satisfied smirk on her face. 她满脸扬扬得意的样子。

sash
[sæʃ]

n. 1. 腰带，肩带；2.（镶嵌玻璃的）窗扇
例 1. She arrived to receive the sash of office from the outgoing president. 她走上前从离任总统手中接过了就职腰带。
2. It is a stucco building with aluminum frame sash. 这是一幢灰泥建筑，带有铝制窗扇。

convocation
[ˌkɑːnvə'keɪʃn]

n. 1. 大型正式会议；2. 召集会议
记 con (=together) + voc (=voice) + ation → 叫到一起 → 召集
例 1. In March, Senator Ted Cruz of Texas used the convocation to announce his run for presidency. 三月，来自德克萨斯州的参议员泰德·克鲁兹利用大会的机会宣布其参选总统。
2. They called for the immediate convocation of the council. 他们要求市议会立即召集开会。

acclaim
[ə'kleɪm]

n. 称誉，高度评价；*v.* 公开称赞
记 ac (=to) + claim (=call, cry out) → 大声叫 → 公开称赞
例 1. Her performance in the ballet earned her critical acclaim. 她的芭蕾舞表演赢得了评论家的赞誉。
2. The work was acclaimed as a masterpiece. 该作品被誉为杰作。
扩 acclamation *n.* 喝彩；赞成

capitation
[ˌkæpɪ'teɪʃn]

n. 人头税，按人摊派的费用
记 capit (=head) + ation → 按人头的 → 人头税
例 The chief source of revenue is the customs, while the capitation tax contributes most to the local budget. 财政的主要来源是关税，但个税对地方的预算贡献最大。

obsolete
[ˌɑːbsəˈliːt]

adj. 过时的，淘汰的

例 With technological changes many traditional skills have become obsolete. 随着技术的革新，许多传统技艺已被淘汰。

扩 obsolescence *n.* 过时，陈旧

travesty
[ˈtrævəsti]

n. 嘲弄，歪曲

记 tra (=trans, over) + vest (=clothe) + y → 过分穿着 →（招来）嘲弄

例 It is a travesty and a tragedy that so many people would be denied the right to vote. 这么多人无权投票，这真是一种讽刺和悲剧。

oblique
[əˈbliːk]

adj. 1. 间接的，不直截了当的；2. 斜的；3. 斜（角）

例 1. His reference to the Cuban Missile Crisis was oblique but unmistakable. 他对古巴导弹危机的提及是隐晦的，但是确定无疑的。
2. The leg came down at an oblique angle and snapped. 腿斜着落地，因此绷断了。

扩 obliquely *adv.* 间接地；斜地

rabble
[ˈræbl]

n. 1. 乌合之众；2. 下等人，贱民

记 可能源于人群聚集时发出的嘈杂声

例 1. He is not accused of actually killing the policeman himself, only being the rabble rouser that led to it. 他并未被指控自己杀死警察，而是挑唆暴民们做了这件事。
2. Their betters keep telling the rabble that survival depends on everyone staying in their "preordained, particular positions." 他们当中的佼佼者们不断告诉这些下层人说，生存取决于每个人呆在自己"命中注定的、特定的位置上"。

calamity
[kəˈlæməti]

n. 灾难，灾祸

例 The Gulf Coast has suffered a series of calamities in recent years. 海湾地区近年来遭受了许多灾难。

扩 calamitous *adj.* 灾难的

glimmer
[ˈglɪmər]

n. 1. 微弱的闪光；2. 一线，一丝；*v.* 闪烁

例 1. We could see a glimmer of light on the far shore. 我们可以看到对岸远处微微闪烁的灯光。
2. I caught the glimmer of a smile in his eyes. 我看到他眼里闪现出一丝笑意。
3. Amusement glimmered in his eyes. 他眼里隐约露出愉悦的神情。

titular
[ˈtɪtʃələr]

adj. 1. 有名无实的；2. 标题的

记 title 的形容词

例 1. Although retired, he remains the titular chairman of the company. 虽然他已经退休了，但仍然是该公司名义上的主席。
2. He played the titular role in *Hamlet*. 他扮演《哈姆雷特》中的主角（哈姆雷特）。

penance
['penəns]

n. 1. 补赎；2. 苦差事

例 1. He did charitable work as a penance. 他做过一些慈善工作来赎罪。
2. She regards living in New York as a penance; she hates big cities. 她把住在纽约视为苦差事，她讨厌大都市。

crook
[krʊk]

n. 1. 骗子；2. 臂弯，弯曲；*v.* 使弯曲

例 1. He thinks politicians are just a bunch of crooks. 他认为政客们都是一群骗子。
2. He was carrying a gun in the crook of his arm. 他臂弯里夹着一杆枪。
3. He crooked his finger at us and led us to the table. 他勾着手指引导我们去往餐桌。

leaven
['levn]

v. 使人愉快；*n.* 发酵剂

记 leav (=lift, raise) + en → 使人（情绪）高涨 → 使人愉快

例 1. Her speech was leavened with a touch of humour. 几分幽默使她的讲话更为有趣。
2. A few jokes add leaven to a boring speech. 几句笑话可以给枯燥无味的演讲增添活跃的气氛。

craven
['kreɪvn]

adj. 胆小的，怯懦的

例 They condemned the deal as a craven surrender. 他们谴责这笔交易为毫无志气的投降行为。

brood
[bruːd]

v. 1. 焦虑，忧思；2. 孵（蛋）；*n.* 一窝鸟；一大家孩子

记 与 brew（酿造）同源 → 加热使产生 → 孵（蛋）

例 1. You're not still brooding over what he said, are you? 你不是还在为他的话闷闷不乐吧？
2. Both birds will be brooding over the eaglets, keeping them warm, hunting for their food and defending the nest against potential predators. 两只大鸟（父母）都会孵化小鹰们，为它们保暖，为它们捕食，保护巢穴，预防天敌。
3. Mrs. Smith took her brood to church every Sunday. 史密斯太太每周日都带一大家孩子们去教堂。

pestilent
['pestɪlənt]

adj. 1. 致命的；2. 有害社会的

记 pest (=disease) + ilent → 致命的

例 1. Any possible pestilent threat to the harvest needs to be eradicated, which often means pesticides. 任何危害收获的致命威胁都需要消除，这就意味着要使用杀虫剂。
2. It is a pestilent heresy to declare that a Christian ought to walk through life like a man with a hidden sickness. 有人宣称基督徒应该一直生活在罪恶之中，这真是有害社会的异端邪说。

扩 pestilential *adj.* 极讨厌的；引起瘟疫的

List 20

congeal
[kən'dʒiːl]

v. 变稠，凝结

记 con (=together) + geal (=freeze) → 冻在一起 → 变稠

例 1. The cold remains of supper had congealed on the plate. 晚餐剩下的冷饭菜已经凝结在盘子上了。
2. The bitterness and tears had congealed into hatred. 苦难与眼泪凝结成了仇恨。

anticoagulant
[ˌæntikoʊ'ægjələnt]

n. 抗凝血剂

例 Scientists also think the venom works like an anticoagulant, preventing the wound from healing and causing it to fester. 科学家们还认为，毒液的作用类似抗凝血剂，能够防止伤口愈合，进而导致其化脓。

扩 coagulant *n.* 凝血剂

atone
[ə'toʊn]

v. 赎罪，弥补

例 He says that he volunteers at the homeless shelter as a way to atone for the sins of his youth. 他说他在流浪者收容所做志愿者以弥补自己年轻时的罪过。

扩 atonement *n.* 赎罪

disburse
[dɪs'bɜːrs]

v. 支付，支出

记 dis (=away) + burse (=purse) → 从钱包取出 → 支付

例 The government has disbursed millions of dollars in foreign aid. 政府已经在外援中花费了数百万美元。

扩 disbursement *n.* 支出，花费

predetermine
[ˌpriːdɪ'tɜːrmɪn]

v. 预先决定，事先安排

例 The sex of the embryo is predetermined at fertilization. 胚胎的性别早在受精时就决定了。

扩 predetermination *n.* 预案，安排

disdain
[dɪs'deɪn]

v. 1. 鄙视；2. 不屑做；*n.* 鄙视

例 1. She disdained his offer of help. 他提出要帮助，遭到她的鄙弃。
2. He disdained to turn to his son for advice. 他不屑向自己的儿子请教。
3. I have a healthy disdain for companies that mistreat their workers. 我很鄙视虐待工人的公司。

辨 detain *v.* 拘留

扩 disdainful *adj.* 充满鄙视的，倨傲的

perspicuous
[pɜːr'spɪkeɪəs]

adj. 明白易懂的

记 per (=through) + spic (=spec, see) + uous → 看得透彻 → 明白的

例 His writings are generally perspicuous and full of light, and often they discover the sardonic and sharp smile of Voltaire. 他的作品通常通俗易懂，非常明了，人们经常能从中发现伏尔泰那种轻蔑的嘲笑。

扩 perspicuity *n.* 清晰易懂

memorandum [ˌmeməˈrændəm]

n. (*pl.* memoranda) 1. 备忘录；2. 建议书，报告

记 memor (=memory) + andum → 提供记忆的东西 → 备忘录

例 1. The company president sent a memorandum to each employee. 公司总裁向每位员工发送了一份备忘录。

2. Obama is issuing a presidential memorandum and action plan that sets forth a series of goals for the federal government. 奥巴马总统发出了一份总统建议与行动计划书，设立了一系列联邦政府的目标。

laity [ˈleɪəti]

n. 平信徒，俗家信徒

记 lay 作形容词有"俗家的"之义

例 The laity have played an important role in the history of the church. 普通信徒在教会的发展过程中发挥了重要作用。

扩 layman *n.* 门外汉；平信徒

surly [ˈsɜːrli]

adj. 脾气坏的

记 sur (=sir) + ly → 主人般的 → 脾气坏的

例 He became surly and rude towards me. 他变得对我粗暴无礼。

opprobrium [əˈproʊbriəm]

n.（众人的）谴责，抨击

例 The administration did not deserve the opprobrium heaped on it by the national press. 全国媒体对行政当局的众多指责并不合理。

扩 opprobrious *adj.* 批评的

emporium [emˈpɔːriəm]

n. (*pl.* emporia, *or* emporiums) 1. 大型商场；2. 专门店

例 1. In 2015, they opened 30 and are planning to entirely revamp the Fifth Avenue flagship, as well as relocate their London emporium. 2015 年他们又开了 30 家店，除了对伦敦的大商场进行搬迁外，还计划对第五大道上的旗舰店进行翻新。

2. It is an emporium of Middle Eastern antiquity tucked away in Gaza. 这是偏隅于加沙的一处中东文物专营店。

lance [læns]

n. 长矛；*v.* 1. 用刀切开；2. 突然迅速传开

例 1. In 1524, Henry was dazed when a lance penetrated his helmet during a jousting tournament. 1524 年亨利（八世）在一次骑马比武中被长矛刺穿了头盔而神志不清。

2. Baron said the result of the referendum would be close and "lance the boil" in the party for good. 巴伦说公投的结果将会很接近，而这相当于在该党中"切开脓肿"治病救人。

3. Pain lanced through his body. 疼痛传到他的全身。

pounce [paʊns]

v. 猛扑，突袭；*n.* 猛扑

记 与 punch 同源

例 1. When a jaguar pounces, sometimes one bite is all it takes to get a meal. 在美洲豹突袭时，有时只要一口就能捕获食物。

2. When prey is close enough, they attack with a fatal pounce. 当猎物足够近的时候，它们将以致命的猛扑袭击猎物。

List 20

parlance
[ˈpɑːrləns]

n. 说法，术语

记 parl (=speak) + ance → 说法

例 A Munro, in climbing parlance, is a Scottish mountain exceeding 3,000 feet. "芒罗"在登山术语里是指高度超过3000英尺的苏格兰山峰。

cringe
[krɪndʒ]

v. 1. 畏缩；2. 尴尬不安

例 1. I cringe every time I walk across the Michigan Ave. bridge. 我每次走过密歇根大道桥时都会感到畏缩。
2. I cringe when I think of the poems I wrote then. 每当我想起我那时写的诗歌就感到很难堪。

collateral
[kəˈlætərəl]

n. 抵押物；*adj.* 附加的

记 col (=together) + later (=side) + al → 一对一的 → 抵押物

例 1. She put up her house as collateral for the loan. 她拿房子作抵押进行贷款。
2. The government denied that there had been any collateral damage during the bombing raid. 政府否认空袭期间有任何附带性的破坏。

扩 collaterally *adv.* 附带地

deliverance
[dɪˈlɪvərəns]

n. 解救，解脱

记 动词 deliver 有"解救"之义

例 She prayed for deliverance as the famine got worse. 随着饥荒加深，她祈求得到解脱。

heathen
[ˈhiːðn]

n. 1. 异教徒；2. 不文明的人，未开化者

记 heath (=waste land) + en → 住在荒野之人 → 异教徒；未开化者

例 1. He preached the *Gospel* to the heathen locals from this spot. 他曾在这里向不信教的当地人宣讲《福音书》。
2. She called us all heathens and hypocrites. 她把我们称为野蛮者和伪君子。

glisten
[ˈɡlɪsn]

v. 闪光，闪亮

记 glist (=glass, shine) + en → 使光亮 → 闪光

例 The road glistened wet after the rain. 雨后的道路润泽闪亮。

illiterate
[ɪˈlɪtərət]

adj. 1. 不识字的；2. 外行的；*n.* 文盲；外行

例 1. He saw black students pushed through the education system so superficially that they came to college illiterate. 他看到黑人学生在教育体系中的进步是如此流于表面，以致于他们上大学时还是文盲。
2. She is politically illiterate and has never voted in an election. 她对政治是外行，从来没投过票。
3. Women, men, young, old, rich, poor, television fanatics and television illiterates—most everyone loved *Downton*. 无论男女、长幼和贫富，也无论电视迷们还是非电视迷们，人人都喜爱《唐顿庄园》。

ennui [ɑːnˈwiː]

n. 无聊，倦怠

记 与 annoy 形似而同源 → 无聊

例 Yet now, after a few go-go years, there is a sense of ennui in the world of tech conferences. 然而，经过了几年的兴隆时期，科技大会上有种倦怠的气氛。

venue [ˈvenjuː]

n. 活动场地

记 ven (=come) + ue → 来到之处 → 活动场地

例 The band will be playing at 20 different venues on their UK tour. 这个乐队在英国巡回演出期间将在 20 个不同的地点演出。

effrontery [ɪˈfrʌntəri]

n. 厚颜无耻（的行为）

例 He had the effrontery to deny doing something that we saw him do. 他真是厚颜无耻，他做的事情我们亲眼目睹过，他也敢否认。

pallid [ˈpælɪd]

adj. 1. 苍白的；2. 暗淡的，乏味的

记 pal (=pale) + lid → 苍白的

例 1. At age 56, he appeared a decade older, his face creased and pallid, his heavy-lidded eyes a tired blue. 56 岁的他好像老了十岁，满脸皱纹而又苍白，眼皮下垂发蓝。

2. Sluggish, disappointing and rather pallid: three ways of describing Scotland's latest retail figures. 只能用三个词来形容苏格兰最近的零售数字：迟缓、无望、以及乏力。

reticent [ˈretɪsnt]

adj. 寡言少语的

例 He was extremely reticent about his personal life. 他对自己的私人生活讳莫如深。

扩 reticence *n.* 沉默寡言

exuberant [ɪgˈzuːbərənt]

adj. 1. 精力充沛的；2. 茂盛的

例 1. Yet the city's exuberant environment did not affect his aesthetics. 然而城市喧嚣的环境并没有影响他的审美。

2. Some researchers now believe the human family tree bore exuberant branches early on. 有些研究人员现在认为，人类家族早些时候可能拥有更加繁茂的枝叶。

扩 exuberance *n.* 茂盛

savvy [ˈsævi]

n. 实际知识，了解；*adj.* 有见识的

例 1. He is known for his political savvy and strong management skills. 他以睿智的政治头脑和强势的管理手腕闻名。

2. Apple is known for savvy supply chain management. 苹果公司出色的供应链管理众所周知。

03

FU LU

附录 1 —— 附录 4

附录

附录 1 美国历史与政治词汇

Government 政府

federal government	联邦政府
American Revolution	美国独立战争
the Declaration of Independence	《独立宣言》
Independence Day	美国独立日
federalism	*n.* 联邦政治，联邦制度
feudalism	*n.* 封建制度
monarchy	*n.* 君主政体，君主政治
imperialism	*n.* 帝国主义，帝制
colonization	*n.* 殖民地化，殖民
Capitol	*n.* 国会大厦，州议会大厦
Representative	*n.* 众议院议员
House (of Representatives)	众议院
the Senate	参议院
Senator	*n.* 参议员
Department of State (State Department)	国务院
Secretary of State	国务卿
Department of Justice	司法部
Attorney General	司法部长
Federal Bureau of Investigation (FBI)	联邦调查局
Central Intelligence Agency (CIA)	中央情报局
Department of Homeland Security (DHS)	国土安全部
Federal Reserve (the Fed)	美联储
framer	*n.*（美国的）建国者，国父
Democratic	*n.* 民主党
Republican	*n.* 共和党
GOP (Grand Old Party)	老大党（共和党）
Ku Klux Klan (KKK)	三 K 党

Law 法律

the Bill of Rights	《权利法案》
provision	*n.* 规定，条款
convention	*n.* 条约，协议，契约
privilege	*n.* 特权，特别待遇；基本公民权利
women's suffrage	妇女投票权
Supreme Court	最高法院
Chief Justice	首席大法官
circuit court	巡回法庭
patent	*n.* 专利，专利权
Prohibition	禁酒令
bootlegging	*n.* 非法制造、运送、销售（酒类等）
unconstitutional	*adj.* 违反宪法的
ratify	*v.* 批准，认可
consolidate	*v.* 统一，合并
promulgate	*v.* 发布，公布

History 历史

Emancipation Proclamation	《解放黑人奴隶宣言》
the Union	联邦
the Confederacy	（美国内战时的）南部邦联
thrall	*n.* 奴隶，束缚
slavery	*n.* 奴隶身份，奴隶制度
persecute	*v.* 迫害
suppression	*n.* 镇压
segregation	*n.* 种族隔离
racial discrimination	种族歧视
integration	*n.* 种族融合
armed conflicts	武装冲突
class warfare	阶级斗争
carnage	*n.*（尤指在战场上的）残杀，大屠杀
massacre	*n.* 残杀，大屠杀
casualty	*n.* 伤亡，伤亡人员
captive	*n.* 俘虏
armistice	*n.* 停战，休战
cavalry	*n.* 骑兵
artillery	*n.* 炮，炮兵

rifle	*n.* 来复枪，步枪
musket	*n.* 步枪
sweeping	*adj.* 扫荡的
tactic	*n.* 策略，战略
disarmament	*n.* 裁军，裁减军备
dismemberment	*n.* 分割，瓜分（国土等）
Pilgrim Fathers	清教徒前辈移民
Puritan	*n.* 清教徒
Quaker	*n.* 教友派成员，贵格会教徒
early settlers	早期定居者
covered wagon	有篷大马车；篷车
wagon train	马车队
migrate	*v.* 移动，移往
blaze a trail	开辟道路，作先导
famine	*n.* 饥荒
hardship	*n.* 困苦，艰难
pasture	*n.* 草原，牧场
plantation	*n.* 种植园，大农场
public domain	（美国政府的）公有土地
agrarian	*adj.* 有关土地的，耕地的
arid	*adj.* 干旱的，贫瘠的（土地等）
Sutter's Mill	苏特矿场
bonanza	*n.* 富矿带
locomotive	*n.* 机车，火车头
Roaring Twenties	兴旺的 20 年代
Great Depression	（1929-1933 年的）大萧条
regrate	*v.* 囤积（粮食，商品等），倒卖
flowering	*adj.* 开花的；*n.* 成熟
（the）Dust Bowl	风沙侵蚀区
greenback	*n.* 美钞
hierarchy	*n.* 等级制度
peer	*n.* 贵族（指公、侯、伯、子、男中的任一爵位）
baron	*n.* 男爵（英国世袭的最低级的贵族爵位）
commoner	*n.* 平民，无爵位的人
redemptioner	*n.* 出卖劳力来抵偿船资之移民
itinerant preacher	巡回牧师，巡回传教士
upheaval	*n.* 动乱，剧变
uprising	*n.* 起义
Indian reservation	印第安人保留地

minority	*n.* 少数，少数民族
philanthropist	*n.* 慈善家
benefactor	*n.* 捐助者，赠送者
Pulitzer Prize	普利策奖
steel magnate	钢铁大亨
muckraker	*n.* “扒粪者”（搜集并揭发丑事的记者）
anomaly	*n.* 不规则，异常的人或物
doctrine	*n.* 教条，学说
trial and error	*n.* 反复试验，摸索

附录 2 SAT 数学词汇

Number & Operations 数与运算

natural number	自然数（不包括 0）
whole number	非负整数
integer	整数
consecutive integers	连续的整数
real number	实数
positive	正数
negative	负数
nonnegative	非负数
rational number	有理数
irrational number	无理数
plus	加
minus	减
subtract	减
multiply	乘
divide	除
sum	和
difference	差
product	乘积
quotient	商
odd	奇数
even	偶数
interest	利息
interest rate	利率
simple interest	单利
complex interest	复利
compound	支付、收取（复利）
dime	10 美分
quarter	25 美分
nickel	5 美分

double	两个
dozen	十二
score	二十
error	误差
number line	数轴
tick mark	数轴上的刻度
square	平方
square root	平方根
fraction	分数
proper fraction	真分数
improper fraction	假分数
mixed number	带分数
simple fraction	简分数
complex/compound fraction	繁分数
numerator	分子
denominator	分母
quarter	1/4
inverse/reciprocal	倒数
decimal	小数
decimal scale	十进制
decimal fraction	分数
infinite decimal	无限小数
recurring decimal	无限循环小数
round off	四舍五入
place value	数位上的值
digit	（从 0 到 9 的任何一个）数字，数位
unit	个位；单位
tenths unit/digit	十分位
ones unit/digit	个位
factor	因数，约数
multiple	倍数
common multiple	公倍数
common factor/divisor	公约数
greatest common factor	最大公约数
least common multiple	最小公倍数
divisible	能整除的
remainder	余数
prime number	质数
composite number	合数

ratio	比率
common ratio	公比
proportion	比例
percent	百分数
imaginary number	虚数 (*i*)
complex number	复数

Algebra & functions 代数与函数

like terms/similar terms	同类项
exponent	指数
index	指数 (*pl.* indices)
base	根，底数
root	根
radical sign	根号
cube root	立方根
absolute value	绝对值
velocity	速度
solution	未知数的值
inequality	不等式
directly proportional to	成正比
inversely proportional to	成反比
quadrant	象限
domain	定义域
range	值域
linear function	线性函数，一次函数
collinear	位于同一条直线上的
slope	斜率
intercept	截距
quadratic function	二次函数
coordinate	坐标
x-coordinate	横坐标
y-coordinate	纵坐标
parabola	抛物线
asymptote	渐近线
trigonometry	三角学，三角函数
radian	弧度

Geometry & measurement 几何与量度

point	点
midpoint	中点
line	直线
(line) segment	线段
angle	角
ray	射线
measure	角度，长度
length	长度
vertex	角的顶点，抛物线顶点 (*pl.* vertices)
acute angle	锐角
obtuse angle	钝角
right angle	直角
round angle	周角
straight angle	平角
supplementary angle	补角
complementary angle	余角
vertical angle	对顶角
adjacent angle	邻角
alternate angle	内错角
corresponding angle	同位角
perpendicular line	垂线
triangle	三角形
equilateral triangle	等边三角形
isosceles triangle	等腰三角形
right triangle	直角三角形
hypotenuse	直角三角形的斜边
arm	直角三角形的短直角边
leg	直角三角形的长直角边
base	底边
height	高
interior angle	内角
exterior angle	外角
congruent	全等的，相等的
similar triangle	相似三角形
quadrilateral	四边形
parallelogram	平行四边形
rectangle	长方形，矩形

square	正方形
area	面积
perimeter	周长
trapezoid	梯形
polygon	多边形
pentagon	五边形
hexagon	六边形
diagonal	对角线
circle	圆
diameter	直径
radius	半径 (*pl.* radii)
arc	弧
sector	扇形
chord	弦
tangent to	相切
inscribe in	内接，内接
circumference	圆的周长
central angle	圆心角
solid	立体
rectangular solid	长方体
cube	立方体
prism	棱柱
right prism	直棱柱
cylinder	圆柱
sphere	球
cone	圆锥
pyramid	棱锥
altitude	高
surface area	表面积
volume/capacity	容积，体积
clockwise	顺时针的
counterclockwise	逆时针的
plane	平面
origin	原点
rectangular coordinate	直角坐标系
coordinate geometry	解析几何
slope	斜率
parallel	平行
transformation	变形

rotate	旋转
reflect	反射，镜面对称
symmetry	对称
point of symmetry	对称点

Data analysis, statistic and probability 数据分析、统计与概率

arithmetic mean/average	(算术)平均数
geometric mean	几何平均数
mode	众数
median	中数，中位数
weighted average	加权平均数
range	极差
standard deviation	标准方差

附录 3 College Board 推荐阅读书目

作者	书名
-	*Beowulf*
Achebe, Chinua	*Things Fall Apart*
Agee, James	*A Death in the Family*
Austen, Jane	*Pride and Prejudice*
Baldwin, James	*Go Tell It on the Mountain*
Beckett, Samuel	*Waiting for Godot*
Bellow, Saul	*The Adventures of Augie March*
Brontë, Charlotte	*Jane Eyre*
Brontë, Emily	*Wuthering Heights*
Camus, Albert	*The Stranger*
Cather, Willa	*Death Comes for the Archbishop*
Chaucer, Geoffrey	*The Canterbury Tales*
Chekhov, Anton	*The Cherry Orchard*
Chopin, Kate	*The Awakening*
Conrad, Joseph	*Heart of Darkness*
Cooper, James Fenimore	*The Last of the Mohicans*
Crane, Stephen	*The Red Badge of Courage*
Dante	*Inferno*
de Cervantes, Miguel	*Don Quixote*
Defoe, Daniel	*Robinson Crusoe*
Dickens, Charles	*A Tale of Two Cities*
Dostoyevsky, Fyodor	*Crime and Punishment*
Douglass, Frederick	*Narrative of the Life of Frederick Douglass*
Dreiser, Theodore	*An American Tragedy*
Dumas, Alexandre	*The Three Musketeers*

Eliot, George	*The Mill on the Floss*
Ellison, Ralph	*Invisible Man*
Emerson, Ralph Waldo	*Selected Essays*
Faulkner, William	*As I Lay Dying*
Faulkner, William	*The Sound and the Fury*
Fielding, Henry	*Tom Jones*
Fitzgerald, F. Scott	*The Great Gatsby*
Flaubert, Gustave	*Madame Bovary*
Ford, Ford Madox	*The Good Soldier*
Goethe, Johann Wolfgang von	*Faust*
Golding, William	*Lord of the Flies*
Hardy, Thomas	*Tess of the d'Urbervilles*
Hawthorne, Nathaniel	*The Scarlet Letter*
Heller, Joseph	*Catch 22*
Hemingway, Ernest	*A Farewell to Arms*
Homer	*The Iliad*
Homer	*The Odyssey*
Hugo, Victor	*The Hunchback of Notre Dame*
Hurston, Zora Neale	*Their Eyes Were Watching God*
Huxley, Aldous	*Brave New World*
Ibsen, Henrik	*A Doll's House*
James, Henry	*The Portrait of a Lady*
James, Henry	*The Turn of the Screw*
Joyce, James	*A Portrait of the Artist as a Young Man*
Kafka, Franz	*The Metamorphosis*
Kingston, Maxine Hong	*The Woman Warrior*
Lee, Harper	*To Kill a Mockingbird*
Lewis, Sinclair	*Babbitt*
London, Jack	*The Call of the Wild*
Mann, Thomas	*The Magic Mountain*
Marquez, Gabriel García	*One Hundred Years of Solitude*
Melville, Herman	*Bartleby the Scrivener*
Melville, Herman	*Moby Dick*
Miller, Arthur	*The Crucible*
Morrison, Toni	*Beloved*

O'Connor, Flannery	*A Good Man is Hard to Find*
O'Neill, Eugene	*Long Day's Journey into Night*
Orwell, George	*Animal Farm*
Pasternak, Boris	*Doctor Zhivago*
Plath, Sylvia	*The Bell Jar*
Poe, Edgar Allan	*Selected Tales*
Proust, Marcel	*Swann's Way*
Pynchon, Thomas	*The Crying of Lot 49*
Remarque, Erich Maria	*All Quiet on the Western Front*
Rostand, Edmond	*Cyrano de Bergerac*
Roth, Henry	*Call It Sleep*
Salinger, J.D.	*The Catcher in the Rye*
Shakespeare, William	*Hamlet*
Shakespeare, William	*Macbeth*
Shakespeare, William	*A Midsummer Night's Dream*
Shakespeare, William	*Romeo and Juliet*
Shaw, George Bernard	*Pygmalion*
Shelley, Mary	*Frankenstein*
Silko, Leslie Marmon	*Ceremony*
Solzhenitsyn, Alexander	*One Day in the Life of Ivan Denisovich*
Sophocles	*Antigone*
Sophocles	*Oedipus Rex*
Steinbeck, John	*The Grapes of Wrath*
Stevenson, Robert Louis	*Treasure Island*
Stowe, Harriet Beecher	*Uncle Tom's Cabin*
Swift, Jonathan	*Gulliver's Travels*
Thackeray, William	*Vanity Fair*
Thoreau, Henry David	*Walden*
Tolstoy, Leo	*War and Peace*
Turgenev, Ivan	*Fathers and Sons*
Twain, Mark	*The Adventures of Huckleberry Finn*
Voltaire	*Candide*
Vonnegut, Kurt Jr.	*Slaughterhouse-Five*
Walker, Alice	*The Color Purple*

Wharton, Edith	*The House of Mirth*
Welty, Eudora	*Collected Stories*
Whitman, Walt	*Leaves of Grass*
Wilde, Oscar	*The Picture of Dorian Gray*
Williams, Tennessee	*The Glass Menagerie*
Woolf, Virginia	*To the Lighthouse*
Wright, Richard	*Native Son*

附录 4 词汇索引

P

Q

R

附录 4

S